THE PLIGHT OF FEELING

THE PLIGHT OF FEELING

Sympathy and Dissent in the

Early American Novel

JULIA A. STERN

The University of Chicago Press | Chicago and London

Julia A. Stern is assistant professor of English at Northwestern University.

The University of Chicago Press, Chicago 60637
The University of Chicago Press, Ltd., London
© 1997 by The University of Chicago
All rights reserved. Published 1997
Printed in the United States of America
06 05 04 03 02 01 00 99 98 97   1 2 3 4 5
ISBN: 0-226-77310-8 (cloth)
ISBN: 0-226-77311-6 (paper)

An earlier version of chapter 2, "Working through the Frame: *Charlotte Temple* and the Poetics of Maternal Melancholia," appeared in the *Arizona Quarterly* 49, no. 4 (Winter 1993): 1–32, © 1993 by The Arizona Board of Regents.

Library of Congress Cataloging-in-Publication Data

Stern, Julia A.
    The plight of feeling : sympathy and dissent in the early American novel / Julia A. Stern.
        p.   cm.
    Includes bibliographical references and index.
    ISBN 0-226-77310-8 (acid-free paper). — ISBN 0-226-77311-6 (pbk. : acid-free paper)
    1. American fiction—18th century—History and criticism.
    2. Politics and literature—United States—History—18th century.
    3. Psychological fiction, American—History and criticism.
    4. Rowson, Mrs., 1762–1824. Charlotte Temple.   5. Foster, Hannah Webster, 1759–1840. Coquette.   6. Brown, Charles Brockden, 1771–1810. Ormond.   7. Emotions in literature.   8. Sympathy in literature.   I. Title.
    PS375.S74   1997
    813'.309—dc21   97-14419
                                                                      CIP

For Michael, with love abounding

Contents

FOUR

Acknowledgments

This book, which explores vicissitudes of fellow feeling in American novels of the post-Revolutionary era, was nourished by sympathetic communion with teachers, colleagues, friends, and family members over the course of many years. At Wellesley College, Terry Tyler, Timothy Peltason, and the late Arthur R. Gold taught me the art of close reading and shared with me their zeal for literary analysis. At Columbia University, where I wrote a dissertation on Brown and Poe—the seed from which this project grew—Ann Douglas provided luminous inspiration with her inestimable scholarship, masterful teaching, and brilliant colloquy. She taught me in equal measures about American theology and narrative, Freudian and French theory, and the power of elegant prose; her intellectual generosity remains a lasting legacy. Jonathan Arac afforded an unparalleled model of scholarly rigor and capaciousness. He pointed my way through eighteenth-century political philosophy and the romantic novel, counseled me about the profession, and extended his kindness without stint; his devoted friendship has been sustaining. Robert A. Ferguson, whom I came to know very late in my graduate career, embraced my project and my prospects as if our association were long-standing. He shared his expert knowledge of the early national period, sharpened my thinking about political dialogism, illuminated my confusion with a draft of his (then unpublished) study of American Enlightenment, and read the entire manuscript tirelessly, some chapters more than once; my gratitude to him is immeasurable. Andrew Delbanco offered valuable support as I navigated the passage from graduate student to assistant professor. Eric Foner and Elizabeth Blackmar read the dissertation with care and acuity; their trenchant suggestions about the contradictory cultural impulses at work in the Federalist era opened up a world of historical scholarship that I might have overlooked.

Friends and classmates at Columbia made those long years less wearying and contributed to the development of my work in important ways. My thanks go to Linda Ainsworth, Christopher Castiglia, Susan Katz, Priscilla Wald, and Liza Wieland. Clare Rossini deserves special mention: she taught me about the rhythms of mourning, both literary and lived, counseled me in fortitude, and hosted me in St. Paul in the happy aftermath of my readers' reports, embracing my pleasure as if it were her own; a model of Smithian sympathy, she is a treasured friend.

Northwestern University has afforded fertile ground for the cultivation of this study. As English Department chair in the early 1990s, Christopher Herbert brought me to Evanston, supported my scholarly and pedagogical efforts, and encouraged my ardor for things gothic. Martin Mueller shared his knowledge of Antigone, Hegel, and the eighteenth-century reception of *Romeo and Juliet;* fostered my work on mourning and sentimentality; and sent me articles about *The Federalist Papers.* Barbara Newman gallantly championed my efforts to balance writing and parenting; her ongoing concern for my intellectual and spiritual well-being helped me weather unpredicted storms. Carl Smith was as generous as he was forthcoming, reading my work with trademark care and skepticism, ruminating philosophically and strategically about surviving the rigors of colic, and making me feel valued as a colleague, teacher, and scholar. Thanks go as well to Susan Manning for enduring friendship and wisdom, professional and personal; to Terry Mulcaire, for generously sharing his own work on Adam Smith and the early American novel, and for camaraderie as well as collegiality; to Sharon Achinstein, for advice about eighteenth-century funereal ritual; to Betsy Erkkila, for help in formulating connections between eighteenth-century ideology and literature; and to Regina Schwartz, for an important conversation about the politics and poetics of mourning.

I am grateful to the Humanities Center at Northwestern University for providing me with a fellowship year in 1995, during which I wrote a major portion of this book; particular thanks go to T. H. Breen, former director of the center, for allowing me to assume the fellowship in calendar 1995, as well as for his ongoing cross-disciplinary conversation about the American eighteenth century; his interest, goading, encouragement, and support have enlivened and enhanced my intellectual ventures. Thanks, too, go to Whitney Davis and Michal Ginsburg for their continuing exchange and particularly for shrewd questions about visual tableau and narrative repetition, which helped hone my conclusions about the relation of genre and form.

Linda Kerber read the *Ormond* chapter in its earliest incarnation; her intuition that the heart of my matter lay in the *post*-Revolutionary aspect of Federalist culture proved crucial to the framing of my larger project. Madelon Sprengnether provided invaluable commentary on an embryonic version of what much later became my chapter on *Charlotte Temple*. In his former capacity as codirector of the American Studies workshop at the University of Chicago, Christopher Looby invited me to present material from the *Ormond* chapter; there, he, Bill Brown, and Laura Rigal raised penetrating questions that enriched my revisions. Dennis Moore provided another such opportunity; Carol Kay's important work on Edmund Burke clarified my understanding of *Reflections* for the final chapter; and Claudia Johnson's inspiring and influential study of politics and affect in the English 1790s gave me a much needed vocabulary for expressing what had been inchoate ruminations about post-Revolutionary America. I am grateful to them all.

Three friends were so central to the creation of this book that without them I might have thrown it over. Michael Meranze convinced me that writing the affective history of literary genre "counted" as valuable scholarly endeavor. He shared with me his own work on Lawrence Sterne and the politics of sympathy, asked hard questions at all the right junctures, and pointed me to sources abstruse and wonderful. Susan Mizruchi read much of the manuscript, training her expansive intelligence on reams of raw material; it was her suspicion that epistolarity was central to my argument. She also generously sent me chapters from her book on sociology and American literature, which helped crystallize my understanding of contagion, sympathy, and democracy. Helen Deutsch shared her unique and deeply felt imaginative relation to eighteenth-century literature, contemporary theory, and popular culture; her brilliant and incisive insights about the body of the manuscript proved crucial to its development; and her friendship and abiding presence—even across the continent—have taught me volumes about the nature of sympathy.

I could not have been more fortunate in having Mitchell R. Breitwieser and Christopher Looby as my readers for the University of Chicago Press. Breitwieser's studies of Puritanism and mourning and eighteenth-century "representative personality" have been vital to my own thinking, and Looby's work on Franklin and Brown has forever changed the way I understand early national narrative. These readers offered searching responses to the manuscript—remarkable intuitions about what I really meant—which made it possible for me to excavate the heart and soul of the book and recast it accordingly. Their intellectual and collegial fellow feeling proved redemptive recompense for my writerly isolation. My debt to both cannot be repaid. At the University of Chicago Press, Alan Thomas's exquisite editorial care and steadfast thoughtfulness afforded a welcome oasis from the traumas of publication; I will always value his graceful blend of professionalism, humanity, and friendship. Joe Parsons was an exemplary copy editor; with a keen ear and a delicate touch, he gave indispensable aid in the final stages of production. Laura Braunstein provided superb research assistance; her passion for archival work enabled mine for exegesis. Finally, without the readerly insight and writerly talent of Jana Argersinger, the endless revisions would have been unendurable, if not actually impossible. Her genius for detecting intellectual connections and gift for sustained sympathetic communion remain a marvel. My thanks and gratitude go to all.

I come at last to the most personal debts, those hardest to express and most deeply felt. My mother, Janet Boshes Stern, and my father, Charles Stern, gave me their love of stories and taught me about the plight of feeling. My siblings, Richard Stern and Patricia Stern, were cotravelers in that journey, and their own academic lives have been equally marked by my parents' example. The love, faith, and generosity of all four have been vital to me. Deborah Boxerman helped me to translate the life of feeling into the life of thought and back again, without which I could not have written this book. Louise Boyd cared devotedly for my son Nicholas Joseph Stern Myers, whose beginnings were coterminous with this book's. Her unstinting love for him made my intellectual labor possible, and my gratitude goes beyond words. Nicholas began to talk as the book was finally taking shape, and by the time it was finished he was fluent. His presence has added indescribable dimension and richness to my life and work, transforming both completely. But my greatest, most abiding, and enduring debt is to Michael Myers. For over sixteen years, he has taught me about love, sympathy, and the importance of dissent. To him, I dedicate this book with love and gratitude.

Engraved frontispiece from the first edition of William Hill Brown's 1789 The Power of Sympathy. *(Courtesy the American Antiquarian Society)*

CHAPTER ONE

The Plight of Feeling

The famous injunction that the story of the 1790s in America should be told as an "*emotional* history" reveals little awareness that the sentimental, melodramatic, and gothic novels of the period in fact constitute the very affective chronicle remaining to be written.[1] Indeed, the explicit omission of fiction from what scholars of the early republic consider the legitimate historical archive is utterly unremarkable. Through the mid-1970s, students of eighteenth-century American politics, as well as critics charting the rise of an indigenous literary tradition, find little of value or interest in the novels of the post-Revolutionary era; rather than read such works on their own peculiar and fascinating terms, they dismiss the nation's first imaginative productions as derivative, bloodless, and maudlin, the effusions of a minor cohort of ersatz new-world Richardsonians. Yet, far more graphically than either public documents or private correspondence, the early American novel brilliantly animates the notion that the Federalist epoch is "an age of passion," dominated by hate, anger, fear, and, most hauntingly, grief.[2]

Attempting to understand the tumultuous era following independence and ratification of the Constitution by reexamining the cultural affect that infuses it, *The Plight of Feeling* charts the tides in American attitudes toward heightened emotion in the years 1789–99. I argue that those eighteenth-century novels best remembered for impassioned excess elaborate, in fictive

1

form, a collective mourning over the violence of the Revolution and the preemption of liberty in the wake of the post-Revolutionary settlement. Such works, I propose, contemplate the possibility that the power of genuine sympathy could revivify a broadly inclusive vision of democracy.

Until very recently, scholars have noted with general disapproval the elevated feeling suffusing the early American novel, maintaining that dramatic effects are a poor substitute for ideas. In fact, sensationalism and self-conscious theatricality mark such works as essentially political, enacting important disruptive notions about the formation of individual and national identity in the decade following the establishment of Federalism. These tales envision and give voice to the otherwise imperceptible underside of republican culture in the age of reason, offering their newly constituted American audience a gothic and feminized set of counternarratives to read against the male-authored manifest accounts of national legitimation.

Translating restrictive conceptions of political enfranchisement into the intimate grammar of domestic life, deploying courtship and marriage and seduction and abandonment as figures for lawful establishment and unrighteous usurpation, early American fiction registers the elaborate cost of the Framers' vision. Such literature suggests that the foundation of the republic is in fact a crypt, that the nation's noncitizens—women, the poor, Native Americans, African Americans, and aliens—lie socially dead and inadequately buried, the casualties of post-Revolutionary political foreclosure. These invisible Americans, prematurely interred beneath the great national edifice whose erection they actually enable, provide an unquiet platform for the construction of republican privilege, disturbing the Federalist monolith in powerful ways.[3] Their gothic story, mournfully retold in the sensational fiction of the period, exposes the decidedly less rational face of post-Revolutionary "Enlightenment."

My intention is to complicate some of the large generalizations scholars have been making about the subversive potency of the novel in late-eighteenth-century America. Elaborating Cathy N. Davidson's claims that such fiction gives voice to, "represents," those numerous figures on the margins of republican culture who do not "count" as citizens, *The Plight of Feeling* carries her assertion to another level of analysis by demonstrating that the eighteenth-century novel acts out a more intricate drama of those invisible Americans. Beginning with the readings offered by Davidson in her groundbreaking literary history, *Revolution and the Word* (1986), and by Jay Fliegelman, in *Declaring Independence* (1992), and then turning to the sometimes eccentric poetics and politics of form that organize early national fiction, I hope to reveal an unappreciated level of novelistic creativity—one that expresses a dialectic of inclusion against exclusion, thereby enacting and to various degrees discomposing the way an elitist culture contains the dissent at its margins. The constitutive power and simultaneous unraveling of sympathy as an operative cultural fantasy become the abiding metaphors through which eighteenth-century American fiction figures problems of social and political cohesion.

Focusing in depth on a given decade and genre, I inaugurate this study with a brief discussion of William Hill Brown's *The Power of Sympathy* (1789) and Charles Brockden Brown's *Wieland* (1798), two American literary "firsts" that almost exactly bracket the Federalist period.[4] These texts function as prefatory touchstones for detailed analyses of three less-studied novels: Susanna Rowson's *Charlotte Temple* (1791/94), extraordinarily popular in the eighteenth century and beyond; Hannah Webster Foster's moderately successful work *The Coquette* (1797); and Charles Brockden Brown's neglected *Ormond* (1799). In their own era, *The Power of Sympathy, Charlotte Temple, The Coquette, Wieland,* and *Ormond* possess reputations inversely proportional to the status accorded them by most twentieth-century academics. Thus, in reading the work of the two Browns against that of Rowson and Foster, and in acknowledging the seriousness of the female writers' emphasis on feeling as a literary subject, I reverse prevailing scholarly procedure, which particularly privileges the "complex" art of C. B. Brown over the critically debased works of his "sensational" and "popular" female cohort (when it treats these women writers at all). Certainly, to suggest that American novelists working in the 1790s are even remotely confederated on intellectual, artistic, or affective grounds, much less to propose the unlikely existence of a fiction-making community in which Brown figures as (feminized) inheritor rather than as (masculine) progenitor, is to counter the intuitions of the tradition's finest recent critics.

Nevertheless, *The Plight of Feeling* champions this assertion, placing it in historical context by drawing from a variety of eighteenth-century English and Continental literary and nonliterary sources, examples from political and moral philosophy and aesthetic and dramatic theory that meditate on the relation of emotion and the public good, written by Jean-Jacques Rousseau, Adam Smith, Mary Wollstonecraft, and Edmund Burke. Such contextualizing works are meant to support rather than supplant my abidingly exegetical intention: to restore to critical view the full formal complexity and cultural resonance of early American fiction. Accordingly, my readings are also influenced by contemporary scholarship in gender and cultural studies and genre and narrative theory, works by Eve Sedgwick, Lynn Hunt, Claudia Johnson, and Peter Brooks. In addition, my project is informed by a historicized metapsychological vocabulary. Excavating the way the novels of the period turn around cultural dynamics like mourning and melancholia, fetishism and disavowal, and the operations of the uncanny, I argue that such language and mechanisms of defense inevitably permeate public discourse when unresolved grief lies at the heart of political society.

Revolution in the 1790s: From Burke to Jefferson

My "affective" reading of the novels of the early republic draws force from the fact that they are written, published, and read between two highly charged moments in an already turbulent period, the years 1789–99. On the one end lies the French Revolution and the convulsive horrors that ensue in its wake; on the other, in 1799, is the contended and acrimonious election of Thomas Jefferson in the so-called Revolution of 1800. Edmund Burke's *Reflections on the Revolution in France* (1790), which menaces its international audience by predicting with uncanny accuracy the Reign of Terror (1793), is avidly read on both sides of the Atlantic during the 1790s. The haunting gothicism that pervades Burke's book provides both a political subtext and a generic template for the tragic narratives that emerge. Indeed, by judging that Burke's treatise gives "at least as much back to sentimental literature as it initially took from it,"[5] Claudia Johnson astutely identifies the dangerous social power inherent in fictional forms—an attribution that applies to the Irish conservative's own imaginative ruminations deployed as theatrical tableaux within *Reflections* as well as to the sensational Anglo-American novels of the 1790s that his book can be said to engender.[6] Johnson's suggestive observation implicitly clarifies why *Reflections* does little to ease the fears of the American ruling elite: Burke's anti-Revolutionary tract provides potent ammunition for those Federalists preoccupied with detecting and combating a native threat of Jacobinism, their manichean code for the ominous murmur of Jeffersonian dissent. Furnishing the ruling class with a frightening vision of the opposition as a fanatical mob caught up in radical energies unleashed by the French, *Reflections* tacitly warns American conservatives: suppress these unruly adversaries, or be overwhelmed by them.

The election of Thomas Jefferson in 1799 sweeps the Federalists from power and changes forever the nature and course of the Revolutionary legacy. Replacing a conservative domination by the virtuous few with a greater empowerment of the many, the Revolution of 1800 moves the once-republican nation in the direction of a nascent liberal capitalism but also keeps African Americans enslaved, Native Americans subject to military "removal," and women of all colors disenfranchised and denied public forms of political expression.[7] "We have called by different names brethren of the same principle. We are all Republicans, we are all Federalists," Jefferson exhorts in his first inaugural address,[8] suggesting that the strident cacophony for which public discussion has become notorious in the 1790s no longer threatens the very future of the nation. This study explores the ways in which the open articulation of cultural conflict is not strictly an effect of the Jeffersonian settlement. Rather, the fiction written, published, and read during the height of the Federalist hegemony (1789–97) envisions post-Revolutionary America in all its multivocality and thus rehearses the range of expressive possibilities to which the third president, in his sanguine (and politically conciliatory) remarks, alludes with such profound expectation. Eleven years prior to Jefferson's Revolution of 1800, early national fiction begins its protean imagination of the nation's encrypted others, making articulation of their stifled voices its unforeseen, if nevertheless defining, cultural work. But rather than simply echo the idealistic federalizing sentiment of 1787[9]—the consensual aspiration that "we the people" could come to speak in one voice—this literature gestures toward a less coherent and more democratic vision of sympathetic communion. The republican novel fancies that, however fleetingly, Americans might imaginatively contemplate if not actually assume one another's political perspectives.[10]

At the same time this fiction anticipates with eerie prescience what will soon unfold as the dark side of Jefferson's dream. As I hope to show in the following chapters, the early American novel gives expression to enunciatory dilemmas with far-reaching political implications. It conjoins the efforts of individuals blending their voices *with* each other—whose experiences of identification become a form of democratic fellow feeling *(Charlotte Temple, Wieland)*—with the practices of those who would speak *for* each other— whose acts of representation degenerate into tyrannical usurpation *(The Power of Sympathy, The Coquette, Wieland, Ormond)*. The era's imaginative narratives thus reenact, as well as critique, the factional dynamics at work in early national politics, rehearsing the confluence and collapse of vocal modes on whose distinction depends the recognition of freedom over against coercion.

Emerging at the twilight of Anglo-European literature's great era of "sensibility," republican fiction is marked by the inhabitation and unsettling of its sentimentality by gothic narrative forms. *The Plight of Feeling* takes such textual disturbances as a central subject of inquiry, positing that, in the face of the overwhelming hate, anger, fear, and grief that grip the nation in the 1790s, the sensational novelistic practices of the era constitute a form of psychic realism.[11] In its tumultuous and even violent representation of opposing voices and incongruent visions, this feminized literature of feeling provides a powerful and prophetic glimpse of what by the mid-nineteenth century will become a tragically fractured national landscape. Offering a theater of emotional excess staged in the incestuous family romances and images of mourning that obsessively constitute the heart of its matter, the novel of the 1790s prognosticates a union sundered by conflicting claims. It represents brothers and sisters who long to commingle bodies despite the separation enjoined by custom and law—but whose voices remain divided, incapable of speaking in unison. Such representations proleptically envision a national quarrel that will find resolution only through the very manichean, melodramatic, and ultimately fratricidal means that republican fiction rehearses in uncanny anticipation of history.

Sympathetic Seeing

The Plight of Feeling also proposes that the eighteenth-century American novel is born out of neither the realm of virtuous republican "disinterest," a space of purported detachment from individual aspiration or relation, nor the neutral territory of imagination, to use Hawthorne's later, wishful (if nevertheless disingenuous) conceit for what he considers the apolitical origins of (his) fiction.[12] Instead, the novels of the 1790s give expression to the latent, reprobated social and political impulses of those Americans who do not "count" in the language of the Founding but whose violent interdiction from the circle of citizenship facilitates the "natural" rights of the nation's elites.[13] Such literature emanates from a feminized zone of imagination highly critical of republican "disinterest," that avowedly transcendent category of judgment actually predicated on privilege and exclusion; far from neutral in its allegiances, the early American novel reveals that virtue unmoored from fellow feeling and contingent on erasure or submersion of social and political difference is a culturally bankrupt ideal.

Pursuing their alternative vision of democratic community, the novels of the 1790s link problems of sympathy with obstacles to perception, characteristically dramatizing crises of fellow feeling in the language of sensory failure.[14] To transform disembodied affect into palpable gesture, to endow emotion with dramatic visibility, early American fiction puts into practice the predominantly visual vocabulary of eighteenth-century aesthetic, political, and moral philosophy. American writers and readers of the post-Revolutionary period absorb Rousseau's primitivist yet protodemocratic longings for unobstructed social relations; they imbibe Adam Smith's liberal idea that sympathy involves a dedicated imagination of the plight of the other, an act of fancy that allows both identification and compassionate transport; and they immerse themselves in Edmund Burke's conservative notions of an organic social order bound—paradoxically—by decidedly theatrical and hierarchical relations. Shared feeling in the work of these thinkers, to name only three influences on Brown, Rowson, Foster, and Brown, is figured through optical metaphors: human sympathy unfolds as Rousseau's transparency, an open window between fellows; as Smith's reflection, a mirror that discloses the interiority of others; or finally as Burke's opacity, a dramatic illusion in which sensational appearance produces reality, a painted scrim to be viewed from a distance.[15]

The connection between vision and emotion, spectacle and sympathy, in early American fiction originates in the profoundly melodramatic *Charlotte Temple*, Susanna Rowson's moving memorial to fellow feeling as a figure for national unity in the decades following American independence. In *Charlotte Temple*, Rowson, a professional actress turned sentimental author, evokes Rousseau's ambivalent attitude toward theatricality in order to imagine a pure and reconstituted post-Revolutionary social order. Rowson's novel is largely composed of dramatic tableaux in which heightened emotion is the rule, but it is also suffused with the narrator's profound—if impossibly melancholic—longing for a pretheatrical, Rousseauvian world of unmediated human relations; there, no emotional distance would separate Rowson's storyteller from her reader, for she has imaginatively—and imperiously—incorporated the audience into her narrative frame.

In that respect, the work replays the paradoxical conclusion of Rousseau's treatise against "spectacles," the paean to the public festival, which he identifies as a protodemocratic forum precisely because it does away with the need for representation. Harvest celebrations allow members of the social body to come together in face-to-face encounters that defeat the theatricality of ordinary human relations, making it possible for individuals to both observe and participate in their own collective merrymaking. He writes, "[L]et the spectators become an entertainment to themselves; make them actors themselves; do it so that each sees and loves himself in the other so that all will be better united" (126). Such *transparent* moments of communion enable individuals to transcend the experience of alienation that obtains in ordinary social exchange. This view of public festivals points phantasmagorically backward to Rousseau's state of nature, concocted in a moment of profoundly reactionary nostalgia in his *Social Contract*.

In *Charlotte Temple*, Rowson darkens the affective palette of the philosopher's tableau by staging collective mourning rather than public celebration as *the* rite that forges fellow feeling, but the politics of her fantasy remain as curiously double-valenced as those of Rousseau's desire for a communal celebration that obviates the self-consciousness of individuals performing in public. Indeed, by setting the novel on the eve of the Revolution, Rowson makes the paradox even more palpable: independence can be survived only if rituals of commemoration, extended mourning for the violence of the Revolution itself and for post-Revolutionary disorder and social exclusion, become the emotional basis for a regenerated polity. Rowson's sorrowful poetics of narrative provide *The Plight of Feeling* with a powerful demonstration of the cultural work that the fiction of this period more generally performs: *Charlotte Temple* not only makes spectacular the notion that the Founding of the republic is a melancholic formation;[16] it actually transforms the experience of grief into an affective ground that might allow Americans to imagine the nation as an egalitarian space.

Despite a will to believe in this operative fantasy of sympathy, Rowson significantly undercuts her own tentative solution to the dilemma of post-Revolutionary fragmentation by creating a narrator whose excessive grief actually obstructs the full achievement of a transparent community of compassion. Thus, while *Charlotte Temple* serves as the affective point of departure for American novels of the 1790s,[17] its own sentimental formulations are always already disturbed by the gothic underpinnings that grow increasingly pronounced as the decade unfolds.[18] The melodramatic luxuriation in heightened states of feeling and expression that characterizes sentimental narrative often veils a brutal—if reprobated—form of violence and rage. Herein lies the connection between sentimental and gothic modes in the

late-eighteenth-century American novel: the two exist in hierarchical relation, like geological strata, the gothic bedrock masked by a sentimental top-
soil. In this respect, sentimentalism is vitally related to fetishistic practices
of disavowal and substitution, enabling the presence of violence to be disclaimed and covered over by an outpouring of feeling that carries only positive valence.

The novelists who write in the wake of *Charlotte Temple* are even less
optimistic than Rowson about the reparative benefits of working through
collective trauma. The fiction of Hannah Foster and Charles Brockden
Brown—and also of William Hill Brown, who anticipates Rowson's concerns—suggests something still darker about the relation between loss and
death and the establishment of the new republic. Implying more insistently
than *Charlotte Temple* that the infant nation is erected on or engendered out
of a figurative grave, they explore the idea that the state depends on the bodies of its legally unacknowledged others—African and Native Americans,
women, and aliens, all of whom are in varying degrees socially dead—to
enable the future of its citizens, who hygienically maintain their privileged
identities through the *cordon sanitaire* of difference. While in its narrative
melancholia and latent gothicism *Charlotte Temple* contains inklings of this
vision, it is in *The Coquette, Wieland,* and *Ormond* that the grim underside of
Rowson's tale becomes fully perceptible. These later works propose that the
new republic is built on a faulty foundation, a metaphorical crypt peopled
by those Americans whose futures have been foreclosed by the incomplete
promises of the Founding.

Primal Scenes

With passionate dedication, the tragic fictions of the early republic, with the
exception of *Charlotte Temple*, explore the dynamic relation between Revolutionary violence and post-Revolutionary morbidity and ossification by
taking the death and burial of a father as their narrative primal scene: they
feature the brutal demise *(Wieland)* or unseemly and furtive interment *(Ormond)* of a powerful patriarch, or they commence in the wake of his funeral
(The Power of Sympathy and *The Coquette).* Only in *Charlotte Temple* is the
spectacle of entombment followed by a hysterical exhibition of grief that involves the death of a teenaged mother. While Jean Laplanche and J.-P. Pontalis have argued that primal scenes obsessively return to and meditate on

disturbingly erotic fantasies of origin,[19] in the early American novel, characters witness the deaths of fathers rather than the passion of their parents. This phantasmagoric displacement in the family romance of republican fiction, the shift from love to death, suggests that Brown, Rowson, Foster, and Brown see the Founding not as a celebration of the birth of the nation but as a funereal rite.

Although in *The Power of Sympathy* the passing of Mr. Holmes antedates the events of the novel, his death casts a decided pall on the rural idyll of Belleview that will soon be shattered by the traumas of seduction, incest, and suicide. The explosive demise of Wieland senior by a mysterious form of spontaneous combustion not only inaugurates Brown's narrative but haunts its later tableau of a family massacred by one of its own in an eruption of psychotic violence. *The Coquette* begins with the death of a reverend patriarch, the heroine's fiance and the gothic doppelgänger of her late minister father, then proceeds to repeat this narrative equation in a series of uncanny reenactments until the heroine herself finally goes the way of the clerical dead. And in *Ormond,* the startling tableau of a woman in a nightdress burying her "father" according to military procedure during a deadly epidemic sets off a chain of bizarre repetitions of gender inversion, bodily contamination, and mysterious death.

In comparison, the trauma of loss comes belatedly in Rowson's tale, providing a terminus rather than a beginning—an important difference in plotting that distinguishes the work from the others in this study. Far more significant, however, is the way in which *Charlotte Temple* itself functions as the primal scene for the early American novel tradition writ large (at least in its tragic and feminized incarnation), acting as the traumatic *ur*text that will be replayed in the fictions of the 1790s. Indeed, Rowson's book engenders an entire subgenre—the gothicized sentimental tale of seduction and abandonment—which *The Plight of Feeling* takes up as its subject.

In its rehearsals of loss and grief, *Charlotte Temple* bequeaths at least one distinctive mechanism to early American fiction, placing fetishism at its center. Various scholars have explored the ways in which the fictional Charlotte and the novel itself become idolatrous objects;[20] taken together, character and book set into motion a form of collective worship previously unseen in America. "Charlotte," a pure phantasm, is "buried" in Trinity Church at the heart of New York City's Wall Street, the center of American commerce, with a headstone that marks no underlying tomb. Her "grave" becomes the object of obsessive devotion in the nineteenth century; mourners moved by

Rowson's story of sorrow make pilgrimages to this bizarre memorial to no-body,[21] bearing witness to the notion that a democratic community can be forged through the power of sympathy.

Beyond serving as the primal scene for the early national novel itself, the tradition's own spectacular "fantasy of origin," the book functions as a relic for the sentimental faithful among its readers. In addition to its own status as a cult object, *Charlotte Temple* actively dramatizes the way fetishism functions in a republic that has disavowed its former king, the figure through whom patriarchal power traditionally displays itself. Lacking a monarch, Americans seek symbolic substitutes who represent a wide range of potential points of identification, from glorious and venerable to pitiful and abject;[22] they exalt the heroic masculinity of the virtuous George Washington and lament the degraded femininity of the once pure Charlotte Temple. In the wake of collective disavowal of post-Revolutionary grief, such paragons absorb a residue of excessive emotion, affording early Americans an imaginary respite from the reality of political mourning. In that regard, the cult of Washington functions very much like *Charlotte Temple*. Channeling both political and sentimental affect, the first president-*cum*-historical icon and Rowson's novel alike powerfully demonstrate that fetishism is itself an encrypted narrative formation, "designed to divert attention from a whole story to a detail."[23]

The republican novel identifies this impulse to disavow lack or absence through a process of material substitution, the overemphasis on an isolated part that can stand for the missing whole, as one of the most powerfully pathological dynamics at work in early national culture. In *Charlotte Temple, Wieland,* and *Ormond,* miniature portraits serve as fetish objects endowed with great affective significance that are either lost and found, created from living models, or alienated and recovered. In *The Coquette,* such artifacts take textual rather than painterly form: the heroine's penitent poetic effusions, found after her death, become the fetish objects that enable the chorus to "veil" her faults and "compose" her epitaph as a sentimental miniature. Each likeness stands in for a more embodied form of intercourse that either has become impossible or has been lost through separation or death; functioning as microcosms, these fateful relics tell emblematic tales about the disruption of fellow feeling suffered at the level of both individual and social experience in the decade following the Founding.

In a tragic gesture of collective denial and abjuration, the tumultuous origins of the republic—the fact that the nation is founded in the "familial" violence of a fratricidal war for independence and then constituted on the graves of the disenfranchised—are erased from the vision of the future the Founders imagine and represent for posterity in the *Federalist* and the Constitution. The emotional aftermath of such momentous disorder proves lingering and socially destructive, but the painful effects of the Revolution— particularly its legacy of guilt—cannot be acknowledged, much less affectively discharged, in the public sphere of the early nation, a distinctly rational space. Instead, they are displaced and replayed, buried and resurrected in the brutal political factionalism and partisan fantasies of conspiracy that mark the Federalist period, where violence becomes a function of disembodied words rather than of murderous deeds. It is in this heated atmosphere that the early American novel, a gothic formation devoted to channeling the voices of the socially dead, explodes into spectacular and dangerous public visibility.

Gendering the Early American Novel

As it takes up the question of who shall speak in the early nation, the late-eighteenth-century American novel transforms political problems into literary dynamics. Adopting the vocal accents of one of the groups occluded and silenced by the Founding, republican fiction manifests the feminization of American culture Ann Douglas describes in her groundbreaking study. According to Douglas, the phenomena originates near the end of the eighteenth century as a shift within mainstream American Protestantism: in this transformation, the rigorous Calvinism that dominated seventeenth- and early to mid-eighteenth-century New England begins to give way to a feminized theology of Christian sensibility, a genteel and compassionate maternal understanding of divinity that supplants the Puritans' notion of an angry and exacting paternal God.[24] This emphasis on sensitivity and fellow feeling inflects the early American novel at the level of gendered narrative dynamics: each of the works in the small and culturally resonant subset that *The Plight of Feeling* takes as a case study is enunciated through the voice of a woman, whether as the product of the (represented) gender of the narrator in Susanna Rowson's *Charlotte Temple,* the result of feminized epistolarity in William Hill Brown's *The Power of Sympathy* and Hannah Webster Foster's *The Coquette,* or the effect of narratorial "cross-dressing," the author's deployment of a persona of the opposite sex, in Charles Brockden Brown's *Wieland* and *Ormond.*

Beyond sharing an arresting feminization of narrative voice, the five novels of seduction explored in the following pages are written in a range of epistolary styles that give rise to a striking homosocial atmosphere. Each book features or problematizes the relation between representations of gender—ascribed to authors, narrators, and characters—and voice—a discursive formulation with embodied effects that emanates from multiple narrative sites: framing apparatus, embedded letters, extended digressions, and the speech of characters, particularly dialogized discourse, words and phrases that conjure the language of others.

In *The Power of Sympathy*, epistolary language is overwrought and artificial, ventriloquized from English and Continental eighteenth-century fiction depicting the "man of feeling." The highly feminized discourses of Lawrence Sterne's *A Sentimental Journey through France and Italy* (1768) and Johann Wolfgang Von Goethe's *The Sorrows of Young Werther* (1774) are not simply sources for William Hill Brown's derivative book; without these progenitors, *The Power of Sympathy* would be deprived of both narrative skeleton and imaginative heart. Indeed, Goethe's novel of self-torment and unrequited love is found flanking the body of the protagonist Harrington; in *The Power of Sympathy*, *Werther* functions as a virtual "how-to" manual for the prospective romantic suicide.

Both *The Power of Sympathy* and its German precursor are told in letters, although in *Werther* correspondence is an entirely one way affair, an appropriate analogue for a narrating consciousness that puts solipsism on the literary map. *Werther*'s pretended epistolarity merely cloaks a form of storytelling that comes closer to the diary or the memoir. If the exchange of letters operates as a metaphor for sympathetic communion with an other, the homosocial undercurrent of these novels is as much a function of the narcissism that marks both Werther and his early American doppelgänger Harrington as it is an effect of gendered patterns of epistolarity.[25] It is no accident that Harrington writes between two and five letters for every one penned by his confidante Worthy: the youth's ultimate erotic object is neither a female sweetheart nor a male beloved but a textual version of himself—reflected in the act of writing.[26]

Lack of "correspondence" in *The Power of Sympathy* also registers at the level of narrative, where a graceless deployment of literary quotation takes the place of heartfelt communication: the protagonist writes an extended series of letters threatening suicide in unmistakably Wertheresque terms before the emotionally disabled Worthy, a "vulgar, uncongenial" soul in a "clay cold carcass," is moved to respond at last.[27] Worthy knows Sterne—he cants pretentiously about *A Sentimental Journey* in the novel's early pages—but somehow he has overlooked Goethe, an interesting lapse in his literary education, with fatal consequences. Like Yorick, Worthy is an eager witness to suffering that unfolds at a sanitary distance, but the immediate duress of his closest companion remains beyond his emotional ken. And, as Brown's signature character in *The Power of Sympathy*, Worthy experiences lapses of articulation that point to a breakdown between affect and eloquence at the level of both plot and narrative. Thus, a book that ostensibly heralds the importance of feeling actually suffers from a nearly fatal form of emotional and expressive anesthesia. Indeed, *The Power of Sympathy* elevates failures of communication to the level of theme by foregrounding the contrast between the desire for a language of the heart and the reality of paralyzed expression. Brown suggests here, even if by omission, that what is called for in the new republic is a fiction that can meet the very demand for novelistic eloquence and feminized readerly sympathy that his own work raises as an ideal standard—yet on which it ultimately founders.

In Charles Brockden Brown's *Wieland*, which, like *Ormond*, is told in the voice of a woman, a different but equally problematic ventriloquism inflects the form of the tale. Clara Wieland dramatically interrupts her own first-person epistolary account—the novel itself—with three male stories, also told in the first person: Henry Pleyel's rationalization for rejecting Clara; Theodore Wieland's confession of guilt in the murder of his family; and Francis Carwin's revelation that he is a "biloquist," the eighteenth-century term for ventriloquist. Thus, the narrator's defiantly feminist reclamation of the tragic history of the Wieland family is severely undermined in an act of narrative abdication to male authority and voice: the Wollstonecraftian heroine of virtue becomes a channel through which Brown circulates the expressive effusions of a cohort of men whose ideological differences are irreconcilable. In a novel that discredits paternal authority as tyrannical, corrupt, and even insane, Clara's decentered, antipatriarchal storytelling fronts for and mystifies a reprobated form of "fraternal" desire. At the same time, *Wieland* recycles and ultimately preserves such brotherly longings in its peculiar fictive form.

The narrative indirection that marks both *The Power of Sympathy* and *Wieland* also figures in the central novels explored in *The Plight of Feeling*. In *Charlotte Temple*, *The Coquette*, and *Ormond*, the language of dissent emanates from a curious space *between* concentric narrative frames and storytelling personae; accordingly, formal complexities—particularly struggles for narrative authority—echo factional conflicts in political culture. All three books are inflected by a parodic discourse that unsettles eighteenth-century expectations about women's speech. In addition, each one of these texts foregrounds the connection between a plaintive female voice and an insistent female body, where the precarious integrity of that body represents the unarticulated limits placed on the exploration of liberty in the new republic.

The great affective power of *Charlotte Temple* lies in the plangent tones of Rowson's narrator; this maternal figure anticipates Wollstonecraft in her commitment to exposing the realities of seduction and economic adversity that await credulous girls in a world run by men. Deconstructing both the norms of the eighteenth-century conduct book and the plots of the period's sensational fiction, the compassionate narrator of *Charlotte Temple* unveils the danger inherent in reading romantic novels as paradigms for life. However, her apparent liberality, based on an expansive vision of fellow feeling, is not without qualification. In fact, Rowson's speaker would banish beyond the pale of sympathy any dissenting reader who might resist her capacious vision or enveloping embrace: such is the despotic underside of inclusively democratic "fraternity."

In *The Coquette,* social tyranny emanates collectively from the voice of the largely female patriarchal chorus, which is dedicated to crushing one woman's resistance from within. By characterizing this majority as "the whole fraternity," the novel's libertine ominously underscores the pervasive and ultimately misogynistic feminization of middle-class culture in late-eighteenth-century America.[28] In *Ormond,* the female narrator and romantic friend of protagonist Constantia Dudley strategically shrouds her identity as an actor in the drama for the greater part of the novel. Choosing to transmit the most compelling details of the plot through digressions and interpolated tales related by other women, Sophia Westyn Courtland averts linear paradigms of storytelling associated with male writers of the period and disenfranchises the masculine voice from expression in *Ormond,* thereby turning the traditional seduction plot completely on its head. *Wieland*'s fraternity can "speak," though only from the safe, sanitary, retrospective distance of Clara's ventriloquistic narrative. But in *Ormond,* Brown extends the implications of *Wieland*'s paradoxically antipatriarchal and homosocial logic by foregrounding same-sex relations between women. Jettisoning *Wieland*'s thwarted male communion, as well as its conventionally heterosexual romantic resolution, Brown closes *Ormond* with an image of brotherhood defeated, displaced by an alternate vision of storytelling sorority.

— —

Epistolary Voice and Vision

Despite the marked relations between affect, gender, and genre at work in the early American novel—its pervasive connection of sexuality and textuality—this literature has remained largely immune to contemporary developments in psychoanalysis, the history of sexuality, and narrative theory, to name only three relevant fields of inquiry. Instead, the finest recent work on republican fiction is actively engaged in the ongoing poststructuralist debate about the primacy of writing over speech.[29] Particularly indebted to such studies, *The Plight of Feeling* posits epistolarity as a formal category that bridges the apparent divide between these expressive modes, arguing in addition that gender in the early American novel inflects both the poetics and the politics of fictive form. Told largely in letters,[30] the republican novel not only foregrounds the bodies and words of women; it actually makes female physicality and literary production—affective embodiment and expressive effusion—into abiding narrative problems. Featuring predominately one-sided, homosocial patterns of correspondence, the novels explored in *The Plight of Feeling* reflect the troubled nature of social and political exchange in post-Revolutionary culture.

Recent scholarship on early American fiction has advanced vocality and textuality as its central categories of analysis, displacing Davidson's important revisionist emphasis on gender in *Revolution and the Word*. In *Declaring Independence* (1992) and *Voicing America* (1996), Jay Fliegelman and Christopher Looby, respectively, challenge Michael Warner's claim in *The Letters of the Republic* (1990) that the disembodied culture of print in eighteenth-century Anglo-America constitutes a "public sphere . . . apart from, and thus . . . capable of being critical of the sphere of the state."[31] Both argue that the political discourse and the literature of the Founding—from philosophies of government to imaginative fictions—are inflected by a profound form of vocal embodiment, what Looby calls "the grain of *voice.*"[32] Early American texts, he maintains, are *imprinted* with sonorous traces of the corporeal body, what Fliegelman would identify as textuality's affective residue. According to both scholars, the embodied voice that speaks through print in the early national period relays a charismatic authority, a cultural force equal to if not actually inseparable from the power Warner finds in the "impersonality" of writing.[33]

The Plight of Feeling locates in the epistolary mode a powerful conjunction of the performative, vocal, and textual dynamics championed separately by Fliegelman, Looby, Warner, Larzer Ziff, and Grantland S. Rice as the dominant feature of early national narrative. Rather than claim that either orality or print is the most expressive or determining cultural medium, this study recasts the discussion by suggesting that both vocal performance and textual inscription come to vivid and powerful life in the two faces of epistolarity. The letter form bridges the acoustic and the textual, creating a dialectic of voice against vision that infuses the novels of the Federalist period with a uniquely affective charge.

On the one hand, epistolarity opens onto history and the public world: letters play a crucial role in the careers of figures like Franklin, the most famous printer of the American eighteenth century, as well as in the fate of the pre-Revolutionary and Revolutionary Committees of Correspondence and in the lives of the Founders. From the period leading up to independence through the mid-1820s, Adams, Jefferson, and Madison, among others, engage in a rich and extended correspondence that, taken in total, constitutes the first unofficial history of the new nation—a chronicle told in letters.[34] In these disparate incarnations, epistolarity functions as a narrative mode that is both outwardly directed and disembodied in the very ways that Warner contends are necessary prerequisites for the establishment of a public sphere capable of criticizing the state.

On the other hand, written correspondence constitutes a fascinating limit case of the workings of private relations: through a unique form of theatricality, both self and other are forged in an act of imaginative projection and inscription. Conveying the vicissitudes of solitary individuals, epistolarity puts a premium on the affective component of such exchange; in that regard, it becomes a dedicated channel for the reflection of fellow feeling, an apt forum for the sort of sympathy Adam Smith describes in his *Theory of Moral Sentiments*. In its physical solidity as an artifact, the letter bears the imprint or "grain of *voice*": its script materializes visible traces of emotion and also the interiority they signify, creating a lingering reminder that the sound of the text emanates from impressions of the pen produced by a living body.[35] Correspondence in the early American novel simultaneously functions as a window onto the outer world of collective affairs and a mirror illuminating the inner states of solitary selves. Letters enable the charismatic authority of voice to circulate in the impersonal world of print, occupying a potent middle ground of quasi-embodied expression and providing a vital bridge between a developing public sphere and a newly emerging private realm, coded masculine and feminine.[36]

As a potentially multivalent narrative form, epistolarity can promote genuine fellow feeling, or, in the case of pseudoepistolarity, it can masquerade as a channel for communion while really overpowering the voice of the other. The letter form functions either as a conduit for equal and open exchange or a guise for vocal tyranny. In that regard, it is useful to contrast the feminized and often protofeminist quality of epistolarity in early American novels written by women, which feature exchanges between actual (fictive) others, with the pseudoepistolarity that marks the work of male novelists such as William Hill Brown and Charles Brockden Brown, where the letter form functions as a disguised mode of communion with self.[37]

The rhetorical power of pseudoepistolarity is clear in Rousseau's "Letter to M. D'Alembert On the Theatre" (1758), where the fiction of correspondence enables forceful framing of political polemic. *The Plight of Feeling* explores the way Anglo-American writers of the 1790s deploy this literary strategy; pseudoepistolarity encodes into the fabric of narrative the implicit representation of an interested constituency eager to witness and affirm the author's enterprise. Accordingly, the narrator of *Charlotte Temple* directly addresses specific readers in a series of emotional interjections that function as pseudoepistolary miniatures; breaking the frame of her tale, she attempts to interpolate a diversely figured audience in order to secure its consent. Publishing *Reflections* one year before Rowson produces *Charlotte Temple*, Burke creates what is arguably the most influential Anglo-American political treatise of the period, a pseudoepistolary production that undoubtedly moves the young Charles Brockden Brown. The Irish conservative's very title telegraphs the way in which the letter form functions as a kind of textual mirror. Just as the French Revolution, according to Burke, holds a haunted glass before the divided English political body, so the form of his *Reflections* both prefigures and legislates its own desired reception.

To chart such repercussions of voice as they echo across the genres of polemic and novel alike, however, is to account for only part of the story *The Plight of Feeling* attempts to chronicle: the tale of post-Revolutionary sympathy and its tragic undoing. In early American fiction, the fate of vision is equally significant. The works under consideration here stage social and political conflict through a formal dialectic that pits the acoustic dimension of narrative against its spectacular aspect in order to suggest a profound incongruence between what is audible and what is visible in post-Revolutionary culture. These two fictive registers grow increasingly dissonant as the 1790s draw to a close. While in *Charlotte Temple* narrative voice offers itself—and fails—as a source of emotional plenitude, professing to envelop understanding readers in its sonorous but ultimately melancholic embrace, *The Coquette*, *Wieland*, and *Ormond* dramatize an even more emphatic collapse in the correspondence between language and vision—a breakdown that points to a crisis of fellow feeling in the new republic.

The disjunction accelerates in *The Coquette*, where an outspoken and dissenting woman, overwhelmed by the roar of consensus, is reduced to a silent and suffering spectacle, and it culminates in the fiction of Charles Brockden Brown, in which narrative voice ultimately becomes unhinged from visual tableau. The story of one woman's spectacular descent from independent outspokenness to submission, silence, and monumentality, *The Coquette* records within itself the shift from voice to vision. Throughout much of Foster's novel, sympathy is figured in auditory terms as vocal harmony, the consonance of the chorus of female friends. Eventually, however, metaphors of ocular perception, the ability or failure to see beyond the self, become more significant and finally eclipse those of voice. Fellow feeling takes two distinct and incompatible forms here. In its republican incarnation, sympathy is a collective practice actively engaged in by a community whose members are united in their "disinterest." If, in theory, this attitude takes the form of transcendent discernment, in practice it translates into fetishistic disavowal, the refusal to "see"—much less to contemplate—any deviation from the norm. In its protoliberal manifestation, such compassion unfolds between avid individuals and is often experienced through the visionary workings of imagination. Once a hallmark of the heroine's correspondence, protoliberal sympathy comes to haunt Eliza's consciousness as a possibility foreclosed, remaining pointedly absent from Foster's representation.

Like most of the letters that together constitute the epistolary structure of Foster's book, the final missive of *The Coquette* is steeped in an outpouring of republican sympathy and culminates in the effusive account of the chorus's efforts to memorialize their seduced, abandoned, and lifeless companion through the text they inscribe on her tomb. Dictated by Eliza's "dispassionate" friends, the epitaph condenses the moralizing discourse of the novel into a sentimental miniature. Reviewing the complexity of the heroine's life and reducing it to the clarity of an emblem,[38] these closing words reflect more about the vision of sympathy that galvanizes the community than they do about the nature or feelings of the deceased. In ending *The Coquette* on a note of failed correspondence that is immediately recuperated and mystified with the language of excessive feeling, Foster exposes how two modes of imagining social relation can be fatally incompatible, and, more, she dramatizes the way in which republican sentiment is actually homicidal.

The dynamic incongruence between voice and vision becomes an abiding theme in *Wieland*, when Charles Brockden Brown elevates ventriloquism to the level of a central device of both story and discourse. Francis Carwin, the mysterious character who disrupts the Wieland family idyll and inadvertently shatters their Jeffersonian harmony, is himself a biloquist who can imitate and throw the voices of others. In addition, Clara Wieland, the novel's first-person narrator, projects a series of other voices that interrupt her own: in the words of her brother Theodore, a religious fanatic turned maniac and murderer, in the speech of Pleyel, her unrequited lover and a devotee of Locke, and in the language of Carwin, a brooding figure for the protoromantic artist and post-Revolutionary "new man"; all three punctuate and disrupt the transmission of her tale. Brown also throws his own voice when he deputizes Clara as his fictive mouthpiece.

The bizarre acoustic phenomena that reverberate throughout the imaginary world of *Wieland* are consistently at odds with its gothic mise-èn-scènes. Clara heeds the frightening and faceless admonitions against prying into the origins of the novel's mysterious voices, but obedience affords her no protection from the violence she is compelled to behold: the brutally strangled body of Catherine Pleyel Wieland, displayed in Clara's own bed, or the virtually unrecognizable corpse of Louisa Conway, whose facial lineaments are rendered illegible by Theodore's homicidal rage. In his deconstructive reading of *Wieland*, Mark Seltzer argues that "saying makes it so" in Brown's nightmarish world: acts of utterance in the novel literally produce its fictive events. Ironically, the voices that lead to murder are not Carwin's ventriloquized tones, emanations from without, but Theodore's psychotic ideations, eruptions from within. Thus, "saying" and "hearing" are not necessarily congruent functions in the universe of *Wieland*, where evidence based on sensory perception—on auditory phenomena, in particular—is almost always mistaken. But if "saying" does indeed make things "so," seeing—and bearing witness—proves the ultimate horror.[39]

At the heart of this grim fable lies an epistemological crisis over the reliability and, indeed, the validity of the conflicting voices and incongruent views of eighteenth-century American culture: religious enthusiasm, enlightened rationality, and proto-Byronic imagination. By attempting and failing to orchestrate these cacophonous utterances and discordant spectacles and, ultimately, by judging them irreconcilable, *Wieland* first interrogates and finally explodes the proposition that the people can speak in unison or share a synoptic view of the future. In the absence of these congruences, the legitimacy of the post-Revolutionary social order becomes increasingly precarious.[40]

In *Ormond*, narrative voice disconnects from visual tableau at the inaugural moment of storytelling; disavowing her central role in the drama she also relates, Sophia makes an emblematic gesture of evasion in a novel that takes failed correspondence and treacherous exchange as its central metaphors for sociality. While republican sympathy is repeatedly discredited in Brown's works, protoliberal fellow feeling offers little alternative; as "the father of the American novel" imagines the coming of the nineteenth century, confidence games, masquerade, forgery, and fraud become dominant modes of fraternal association for privileged white (male) citizens of the new nation. Only in the margins and at the end of his book does Brown remotely suggest an alternative form of social relation: it is in the affectionate bonds between women—ties of loyalty beyond race, class, and even epidemic illness, transmitted largely through narrative—that Brown identifies a remnant of the national body potentially capable of propelling the republic into the future.

Literary Inhabitation

Bracketing the ten-year period with which this study is concerned are the works of two male authors who, though unrelated, are eerily unified in name. Connoting nothing more than strange coincidence, this accidental appearance of identity nevertheless arouses speculations about the nature and problem of sympathetic identification—both homosocial and heterosocial—in the post-Revolutionary novel. Other uncanny conjunctions prove more resonant: by assuming a female narrative voice in *Wieland* and *Ormond*, Charles Brockden Brown tacitly declares his allegiance to a native literary tradition in which women figure as important precursors. While his skepticism over the prospect of feeling as a unifying social force marks Brown's departure from Rowson and Foster, he remains—for better or worse—deeply schooled in their affective worlds, an occupant of their psychic spaces and fictive paradigms.[41] How are we to understand this uneasy affiliation? Is it one of emotional embrace or ominous inhabitation, a testament to the power and significance of female cultural work or a cooptation and burial of women's voices—a reenactment of the Founding's exclusionary drama? Rather than offer a reductive answer to this crucial question, *The Plight of Feeling* hopes to show the ways Brown's complex, qualifiedly antipatriarchal relation to the literary past is also imaginatively enabling: empowering him to transform his suspicious vision of Anglo-American sentimental values into a trenchant gothic critique of early national culture.

The Inversion of Fellow Feeling

Two emotionally charged tableaux—depictions of slavery and incest—from *The Power of Sympathy* and *Wieland* constitute provocative touchstones for *The Plight of Feeling*'s exploration of sympathy as the operative fantasy in the novels of the 1790s. A narrative interpolation devoted to exposing the evils of slavery from William Hill Brown's *The Power of Sympathy*, the "first" American novel,[42] underscores the connection between personal sympathy and social imperative with which I am more generally concerned. The passage reveals the paradoxical emotional logic underwriting humanitarian opposition to African American bondage; according to this form of reasoning, altruism is predicated on and simultaneously fortified by the ongoing suffering of another, the object of benevolence whose affective and experiential difference from its subject is almost absolute. In the scene, a dramatic incident of class conflict provokes Brown's privileged young protagonist into ruminating on the horrors of slavery. Distressed over witnessing his fiancée Harriot, the genteelly bred though orphaned and penniless companion of an upper-class matron, suffer the insults of this haughty woman, Harrington writes: "This Mrs. Francis had the insolence to reprimand Harriot in my presence. I was mortified—I walked to the window—my heart was on fire—my blood boiled in my veins. It is impossible to form an idea of the disorder of my nerves; Harriot's were equally agitated" (85). The episode is meant to convey the protagonist's indignation over the unjust exercise of class domination. Yet one is impressed both by the profoundly theatrical relations that structure the scene and by their political valence, which turns on the question of social visibility. Would Harrington be enraged were Mrs. Francis to have censured Harriot privately, in the absence of a spectator of the matron's own class who remains far from "disinterested" in the exchange? Indeed, would Harriet experience the same mortification and shame were her aristocratic suitor nowhere in sight?

As if seeking to disavow the reality of a scene that underscores how utterly both a woman of privilege and her subordinate depend on hierarchy for self-definition, Harrington escapes to the window for an alternate view. Gazing outward, he is reminded of another spectacle, which turns on the brutally literal and devastating inscription of servitude on the body of a woman. The earlier episode involves the youth's visit to South Carolina, the state which until the Civil War adheres to the strongest proslavery stance in the union (a fact that surely is not lost on William Hill Brown as he plots his tale). There Harrington observes and comes to converse with an eloquent slave mother whose noble carriage intrigues him. He explains:

> I had often remarked a female slave pass by my window to a spring to fetch water. She had something in her air superior to those in her situation—a fire that the damps of slavery had not extinguished.
>
> As I was one day walking behind her, the wind blew her tattered handkerchief from her neck and exposed it to my sight—I asked her the cause of the scar on her shoulder. She answered composedly, and with an earnestness that proved she was not ashamed to declare it. "It is the mark of the whip," said she, and went on with the history of it, without my desiring her to proceed. "My boy of about ten years old was unlucky enough to break a glass tumbler—this crime was immediately inquired into. I did not deny the charge and was tied up. My former good character availed nothing. Under every affliction, we may receive consolation; and during the smart of the whip, I rejoiced—because I shielded with my body the lash from my child; and I rendered thanks to the best of beings that I was allowed to suffer for him." "Heroically spoken!" said I, "may He whom you call the best of beings continue you in the same sentiments. May thy soul be ever disposed to sympathize with thy children, and with thy brethren and sisters in calamity. Then shalt thou feel every circumstance of thy life afford thee satisfaction; repining and melancholy shall fly from thy bosom. All thy labors will become easy—all thy burdens light, and the yoke of slavery will never gall thy neck."
>
> I was sensibly relieved as I pronounced these words, and I felt my heart glow with feelings of exquisite delight as I anticipated the happy time when the sighs of the slave shall no longer expire in the air of freedom. What delightful sensations are those in which the heart is *interested*! In which it stoops to enter into the little concerns of the most-

remote ramification of Nature! Let the vain, giddy, and the proud pass without deigning to notice them; let them cheat themselves of happiness. These are circumstances which are important only to a sentimental traveler.

Hail Sensibility! (85 – 86, my emphasis)

As in the section of Lawrence Sterne's *A Sentimental Journey* entitled "The Captive," on which this scene is based, the protagonist's digressive tableau is inaugurated in a seemingly benevolent act of voyeurism.[43] Sterne's narrator and Harrington, one glimpsing a phantasmagorical male inmate through the portal of a prison door he constructs in imagination and the other gazing at a living woman through the aperture of his plantation room, respectively, conjure the window, an operative late-eighteenth-century metaphor for the theater of compassion.

Because Harrington is a houseguest on a South Carolina plantation, one can only assume that the window through which he gazes is located in a private space designated for visitors' use, either a sitting room or, more suggestively, personal sleeping quarters. In that respect, there is something slightly lurid about his viewing the slave mother from the privileged seat of (borrowed) privacy. Compassion, so-called, begins in an act of surveillance and is followed up in a moment of literal pursuit: it is only because Harrington follows the woman *from behind* (and thus is able to observe the exposure of her scarred flesh) that their conversation and his ensuing exhortation to sensibility become possible. Sexual prurience, or what psychoanalysis would characterize as Harrington's ocular domination of the woman—the voyeuristic variant on sadism, per se, actually enables the sympathy he later claims to feel.

Despite the fact that in both scenes windows would seem to function symbolically, such moments of purported transparency are more accurately understood as experiences of reflection. As such, they deceptively evoke Adam Smith's notion that compassion is constituted through reciprocal ocular exchange. Smith writes in *The Theory of Moral Sentiments* that the ordeal of suffering before another ideally creates a dialectic of sympathy in which the object of compassion and the viewing subject exchange interiorities. By attempting to imagine the predicament of the other, the compassionate subject circulates fellow feeling back to the suffering object, who then reflects it back to the subject again. Smith argues that this mirror of sympathy lessons the pain of both sufferer and witness by making each realize that such experiences do not necessitate emotional and intellectual isolation,[44] but, in Harrington's tableau, the appearance of reflective compassion merely fronts for the dynamics of disavowal. The slave woman (who in her blackness and femaleness is doubly other) literally does not figure in an act of exchange; indeed, while her narrative initiates the youth's ruminations on the injustice of bondage, what it really sets into motion is a process of *speculation* that for private and personal purposes exploits rather than sympathizes with her experience. Thus, far from allowing for the circulation of emotion and affective intercourse between two profoundly different subjectivities, the theatricality of the episode permits Harrington to indulge in an explosion of self-congratulation, launched with his patronizing affirmation of the woman's heroic sacrifice. According to such an emotional logic, slavery is simply a state of mind.

It is unlikely that Brown himself intended this Rousseauvian, antitheatrical reading of Harrington's digression on the evils of slavery; indeed, the manifest narrative of *The Power of Sympathy* censures inequities of many sorts, and particularly those involving class and race. Yet the tableau featuring the slave woman corresponds closely to Rousseau's portrayal of the theater as a forum that teaches people how *not to act compassionately;* in Harrington's case, this would mean a license to declaim against the horrors of slavery rather than actively fight for its abolition. As Rousseau argues in the "Letter to M. D'Alembert on the Theatre":

> In giving our tears to these fictions, we have satisfied all the rights of humanity without having to give anything more of ourselves; whereas unfortunate people in person would require attention from us, relief, consolation, and work, which would involve us in their pains and would require at least the sacrifice of our indolence, from all of which we are quite content to be exempt. It could be said that our heart closes itself for fear of being touched at our expense. (25) [45]

Harrington's extraordinary ejaculation of relief at the end of the scene, the delight he takes in describing the pleasure afforded by his own internal sensations, completely erases the palpable suffering of the African American bondwoman.

This so-called cathartic revelation about the powers of the sympathetic imagination, the whimsical notion that the slave mother can transcend her degraded station through mental exercise, lightens the burdens of Harrington's heart. Meanwhile, the object of his "compassion" remains sunk in exactly the situation in which she began. As such, the scene borrows from the perverse economies of sympathy that structure Sterne's meditation on "The Captive," an episode that has equally little to do with the real suffering of abject others and everything to do with shoring up the narrator's emotional self-satisfaction and self-congratulation. Such moments offer not disinterested windows into the plight of embodied others but mirrors into the narcissistic absorption of disembodied selves.[46] The story of the protagonist's "enlightening" encounter with the African American bondwoman in South Carolina thus dramatizes the way in which white male citizens ostensibly opposed to the practice of slavery in fact depend on it for their own (paradoxical) self-definition as members of a morally democratic elite. Putative hostility to the enslavement of the nation's Africans permits advantaged Americans to partake of "disinterested" forms of fellow feeling that bind them in an exclusive fraternal collective; simultaneously, such sentiments indemnify these men from having to attend to the ongoing suffering of actual black bodies.[47] The political power of sympathy is touted here as a liberating force; but rehearsing the Founding scene of interment, such promise is foreclosed when compassion degenerates into privileged self-affirmation, achieved at the expense of the (ongoing) social death and live burial of the oppressed African American "sister" who is supposed to be uplifted.

Filial relations and their connection to the operative fantasy of fellow feeling take on an altogether different character when they manifest themselves as incestuous longings in the novels of the period; a cultural taboo of nearly universal application, unlicensed sexuality within the family occurs in this literature with obsessive regularity. In *The Power of Sympathy*, a marriage across the lines of class is threatened and then abruptly averted by the revelation that the parties involved are siblings. The privileged younger Harrington is a central figure in the Federalist circle whose social constitution—the nature and limits of its polity—becomes a microcosm for questions of national identity formation. He betroths himself to a placeless woman of unknown parentage, the lovely Harriot, whose very name curiously echoes his own and thus suggests what a self-enclosed world the novel's characters inhabit. In determining to propose marriage rather than to seduce and ruin this socially marginal woman, Harrington signals his own political conversion, the happy emergence of a nascent egalitarian sensibility. Earlier, he had remarked, "I am not so much of a republican as formally to wed any person of this class. How laughable would my conduct appear were I to trace over the same ground marked out by the immaculate footsteps, to be heard openly acknowledging for my bosom companion any daughter of the democratic empire of virtue!" (33). Within the space of twenty pages, having realized that the object of his desire is also worthy of his esteem, he proclaims, "I like a democratic government better than any other kind of government; and, were I Lycurgus, no distinction of rank should be found in my common-wealth" (57).

But, far from becoming a giver of laws, a type of Founding Father, Harrington remains an impotent son, the tragic victim of a parent whose own transgressive foray across the boundaries of rank constitutes an act of imperious domination rather than of capacious social imagination. The product of this decidedly inegalitarian act of seduction is, of course, no other than Harriot. Endorsing the attitude that it is better to waste the bodies of lower class women than to offer them (limited) civic enfranchisement as republican wives, Harrington senior practices a form of sexual imperialism that proves profoundly conservative in its political effects; young Harrington's romantic tendencies—coded as "democratic" by Brown—are overwhelmed by the social horror of a potentially incestuous union with Harriot; indeed, the realization of her parentage propels the youth to suicide. That the senior Harrington's tyrannical exploits go unpunished, while his son's more socially expansive instincts—and with them his future—are crushed peremptorily and buried at inception, is the decidedly reactionary subtext of *The Power of Sympathy*'s ostensibly progressive manifest narrative.[48]

Incest also haunts the self-enclosed familial world of Charles Brockden Brown's *Wieland*, though here it takes a (slightly) more subtle narrative form. Both before and after the intrafamilial murders that mark the climax of *Wieland*, narrator Clara and her brother Theodore, a religious fanatic who believes that the voice of God has ordered him to sacrifice his wife and children, enjoy a degree of attachment that is suffused with illicit desire.[49] Clara describes a nightmare about this unhallowed devotion. In her tableau, she dangles precariously over a gaping pit; through its extraordinary poetics of space, the scene articulates the danger inherent in her relations: "In my dream, he that tempted me to my destruction, was my brother . . . . Who was it whose suffocating grasp I was to feel, should I dare to enter it? What monstrous conception is this? My brother! . . . [N]ow it was my brother whom I was irresistibly persuaded to regard as the contriver of . . . ill."[50] There is an odd and fascinating conflation here between plunging into the gulf and being grasped by an embrace that could crush all breath; strangely and pointedly, Clara's dreaming self locates Theodore not in the pit but across it on the other side. While the fear of falling into an abyss and being smothered to death is certainly terrifying, what are we to make of the fact that Clara characterizes such "destruction" as temptation, an alluring and tantalizing energy that cannot be withstood? This kind of misdirection or subversive topography surfaces again and again in Brown's fiction and emblematizes the lack of boundaries—the instability and fluidity of identity—that his characters repeatedly suffer.

For a brother and sister, what grasp is more "suffocating" than an incestuous one? What embrace demands that participants "dare" to enter it, other than a physical connection that is utterly tabooed? Theodore actually tells Clara outright that he feels for her as he does for no other woman in the world: there is "no human being," he vows, "whom I love with more tenderness" (109). And his fervor does not go unacknowledged. Of their relationship, Clara writes that to Theodore she is a "sister whom he was wont to love with a passion more than fraternal" (185). Without even knowing that Theodore is responsible for the abuse and murder of his wife Catherine *in Clara's bed*, his sister senses that some hideous and massive displacement of forbidden desires has occurred; she notes: "I was the object of [the murderer's] treason; but by some tremendous mistake, his fury was misplaced" (151).

The eruption of such interdicted desire in novels exploring questions of identity and legitimation in the post-Revolutionary period points to the epistemological contradictions that underlie the grounding of selfhood and nationhood in a dialectic of exclusion. In a republic whose first political task is to define itself against the Old World through decidedly manichean means,[51] incest disrupts and deconstructs the taxonomical efforts that further enable citizens to "dis-cover" their selfhood differentially,[52] over and against the bodies of those nonmale, nonwhite, nonnative-born individuals who inhabit America in the 1790s. In *The Power of Sympathy*, an ostensibly exogamous relation is revealed to be one of endogamy: otherness becomes identity. This collapse of difference exposes the fact that elite status is less an effect of blood—of what in the subtitle to *The Power of Sympathy* Brown calls "the truth of nature"—than it is of language, the arbitrariness of naming. Dwelling within the other is a version of the self, a disenfranchised and excluded doppelgänger who reflects back onto the body of the early national citizen the entirely artificial and linguistically constructed character of republican privilege.

Like the *The Power of Sympathy*, *Wieland* uses incestuous logic to literalize what it means to *feel* for a fraternal fellow in the early national period.

The socially inverted world of the novel is one that interdicts sympathetic relations with actual others who are *figured* as brothers or sisters. In this universe, forms of "fraternal" exchange may constitute the theoretical ground of social cohesion, as they do in *Charlotte Temple*'s operative fantasy of sympathy. In practice, however, such intercourse exists far beyond Charles Brockden Brown's imaginative view. Thus, the family becomes the exclusive and ultimately the fatal arena for exchange, which is directed solely inside its perimeters, a destructive and infinitely regressive form of reflection in which the self collapses into its mirror image.[53] There, any semblance of the exterior life or public world, much less of the nation, ceases to exist. Raising grave doubts about early America's future, *Wieland* questions whether the republic's diverse citizens, aliens, Natives, Africans, and others can live together as potential brothers and sisters. Through its deployment of treacherous as well as psychotic voices, the novel dramatizes the violent overwhelming of public dialogue, the collapse and disintegration of collective forms of relation, and the utter perversion of sociality itself. *Wieland*'s extraordinary conjunction of incestuous desire with spousal murder and infanticide point to its author's deep misgivings about a post-Revolutionary vision of communal order based on "fraternal sympathy,"[54] Susanna Rowson's potential solution, to which I will turn in the following chapter.

Despite these concerns, Charles Brockden Brown's critical investment in the operative fantasy of fellow feeling—which his four major novels systematically conjure and vigorously interrogate—is itself utterly dependent on the very sentiment it scorns. In that regard, his work constitutes a compelling terminus for *The Plight of Feeling*, which attempts to reorchestrate the voices and restore the visibility of those Americans silenced and submerged by the promises of the Founding. Brown's gothic redeployment of sentimental structures suggests that the putative father of the early American novel is also a dependent literary son whose creativity is nourished by the unacknowledged efforts of powerful foremothers. The problematic balance he strikes between cohabiting, inhabiting, and coopting their imaginative achievements thus provides a fruitful metaphor for thinking through the gendered divisions of political and literary culture in the post-Revolutionary era and for understanding why republican fiction's rhetoric of feeling achieves most powerful expression through gothic form.

"Charlotte Temple's grave" in Trinity Churchyard, New York. (Courtesy the Newberry Library)

CHAPTER TWO

Working through the Frame: The Dream of Transparency in <u>Charlotte Temple</u>

What is the significance of seduction and abandonment in the charged political atmosphere of the 1790s? What emotional ethos does such a phrase evoke? Literary genres speak to specific historical moments with their attendant cultural and psychological needs. In the American eighteenth century, the novel of virtue in distress—maidenhood imperiled, ruined, and ultimately forsaken—exercises enormous appeal. Like the popular captivity narrative that provides the Puritans with a myth of acculturation into the new world wilderness and assuages their guilt over emigration,[1] the sentimental, melodramatic, and gothic novel of seduction and abandonment also features a female victim and performs an important kind of cultural labor. The task of this literature is to address and work through the unprecedented sense of loss Americans experience in the wake of a Revolution that inscribes with fraternal blood the immutability of rupture from the mother country.

The sentimental *ur*text of this emerging American tradition is Susanna Rowson's *Charlotte Temple*—a work whose melancholic narrative unconscious will inscribe the most important novels of the period and against whose purported, if unrealized, affective politics *The Coquette, Wieland,* and *Ormond* will offer an increasingly gothic dissent. Rowson's novel languishes from neglect after it is published in England in 1791. Three years later, the book makes a spectacular literary "crossing" when it is reprinted and distributed by Matthew Carey in Philadelphia (1794). Thus transported, *Charlotte Temple* becomes a vital touchstone for Anglo-American cultural disjunction in the Federalist period, attempting, if ultimately failing, to afford its readers a transparent vision of social relations that would radically extend the boundaries of the national body imagined in master narratives of the Founding.

Set on the eve of the War of Independence, a phantasmagorical moment of political origin, *Charlotte Temple* articulates conflicting notions of social contract at work in the post-Revolutionary polity. The novel's strategy of retrospection evokes Rousseau's writings on the state of nature: like "The Discourse on Inequality," the "Letter To M. D'Alembert on the Theatre," and *The Social Contract* itself, *Charlotte Temple* is both backward looking— foregrounding the green world of the Temple's rural cottage in its nostalgic representation of the English past—and radically democratic—envisioning through its heterogeneous community of imagined and actual readers an American future that departs in startling ways from this protorepublican pastoral idyll.

In addition, *Charlotte Temple* represents, interrogates, and ultimately condemns the theatrical relations that continental aesthetic philosophers identify as distinguishing social intercourse in late-eighteenth-century culture. Against the background of Diderot and Rousseau's meditations on theatricality as a public problem with disturbing moral implications, Rowson's novel gains important cultural resonance. For Diderot, the danger of the drama lies in its propensity to make spectators forget the reality of authentic feelings, to mistake the world for the stage. For Rousseau, the social world is always already contaminated by theatrical relations: artifice and duplicity mark normative human exchange. Thus, the stage itself becomes a perverse mirror of the corruption of society, making doubly unnatural people's interactions in public.[2] Despite Rousseau's unease about the theater, he is not unequivocally hostile; he actually declares in a footnote embedded at the end of his "Letter To M. D'Alembert" that "I love the drama passionately," adding that he has "never willingly missed a performance of Molière." This ostensible endorsement comes nearly one hundred pages after an important earlier statement on the morality of the drama, strategically highlighted at the beginning of section four of the *Letter*: "But who can deny also that the theatre of this same Molière . . . is a school of vices and bad morals [manners] even more dangerous than the very books which profess to teach them?"[3]

Susanna Rowson's own career on the stage and as a playwright makes especially paradoxical—and Rousseauvian—the ambivalent deployment of dramatic spectacle in *Charlotte Temple*—particularly its equivocal incorporation of melodrama, a theatrical form less reliant on words than are its high-culture precursors, seventeenth-century tragedy and eighteenth-century comedy and farce. But in contrast to Rousseau's polemical rejection of contemporary society's corruption by artifice—duplicity that begins outside the playhouse and that is further amplified and perverted within it—Rowson's anxiety concerns the way theatrical relations displace compassionate exchange and thus enable a form of social dissimulation that victimizes the innocent. In that regard, her apprehensions echo Diderot's misgivings about dramatic representations: the notion that theatricality makes people incapable of deciphering authentic exhibitions of feeling rendered in a nondramatic mode; or the fear that theatrical expressions compel spectators to doubt the legitimacy of heightened displays of genuine emotion, causing them to misread real suffering as artful performance.[4]

Rowson shares some of Rousseau's more striking antitheatrical attitudes, which emerge when one compares the material practices of her career with the ideas she explores in *Charlotte Temple*. Between the years 1786, when she appears on the English stage, and 1797, four years after her permanent relocation to America when she joins Thomas Wignell's theatrical company in Philadelphia, the author of *Charlotte Temple* works as an actress and composes plays, patriotic songs, and odes celebrating the commercial vigor of the new republic and the emblematic lives of George Washington and John Adams, among other Federalist luminaries.[5]

Despite—or perhaps because of—her early professional life in the theater, Rowson's indictment of the way dramatic conventions structure and contaminate the most basic human associations evokes Rousseau's repudiation of the spectacular dynamics that underlie the social order. In contrast to such theatrical relations, *Charlotte Temple* offers an alternative form of communion through which the witnesses to the heroine's plight—characters within the novel and readers outside of it—come together and function as a unified corporate body. Rowson's plot shifts from the villainous La Rue's melodramatic rejection of the supplicating Charlotte, who appears on her treacherous French teacher's doorstep teetering on the verge of death, to a legendary account of the community's sorrow, an oral tradition about the suffering and death of the heroine that springs up within the novel world.

Thus, the narrative swerves abruptly from a moment of heightened theatricality, in which a designated audience refuses to be moved, to an extended account of genuine emotion, in which the power of Charlotte's story to touch those who hear it creates a common emotional ground around the experience of loss. Based on a fantasy of unobstructed relations of sympathy—figured as the indivisible bond between an omnipotent maternal narrator and an audience whose constitution is infinitely expandable, unlimited by the distinctions of race, class, or gender that exclude the republic's "others" from the promises of the Founding—*Charlotte Temple* imagines, creates, and attempts to enfranchise a post-Revolutionary community linked by claims of universal compassion.

As the inaugural work in the fictive genealogy explored in *The Plight of Feeling, Charlotte Temple* stands at the end of a British sentimental legacy originating in Samuel Richardson's *Clarissa* (1747–48). Both English and American literary history make claims for Rowson's novel: this dispute over the native origins of *Charlotte Temple* eloquently attests to an incestuous intermingling of English and American cultures that begins after the events of the Revolution have become eclipsed by the struggle for national legitimation and that extends into the late-twentieth century.[6] Viewed in the context of the American narrative tradition it historically instates, *Charlotte Temple* plays the role of the favored eldest adopted child in a family of biological siblings *(The Coquette, Wieland,* and *Ormond),* all of which remain haunted by the legacy of their powerful Richardsonian progenitor.

In that epic novel of virtue assaulted and ultimately triumphant, representations of fractured familial relations become figures for the problem of female dissent from patriarchal authority.[7] Jay Fliegelman takes up *Clarissa* in order to read the early American novel's own recurring images of domestic strife as a mode of social allegory in which the family stands for the state.[8] Richardson's Clarissa, who functions as the fictional prototype for heroines of early American novels of the 1790s, emblematizes righteous filial rebellion against a brutally authoritarian patriarchy; Fliegelman points out that "the first American editions of *Clarissa* . . . virtually 'rewrite' the novel in such a way as to render it an unadulterated polemic against parental severity." He goes on to note that in the eighteenth-century American revisions and abridgements of Richardson's greatest work, "Clarissa is purely a victim caught between two tyrannies. Her rebellious spirit is not censured in these volumes."[9]

In contrast, literary critics studying *Charlotte Temple* identify Susanna

Rowson's heroine as either child-victim or daughter-object of a paternal practice that is, perhaps, *too* liberal and egalitarian compared with that figured in *Clarissa*. In the Anglo-American version of the myth of seduced and abandoned maidenhood,[10] benevolent and virtuous parental authority is righteous power that should command filial respect and obedience. Clarissa rejects unjust parental power and proves her father wrong, but children like Charlotte, unwittingly in conflict with rational benevolence, cannot be deemed rightful revolutionaries.[11]

Such scholars emphasize the novel's patriarchal and paternal plots, focusing on the framed narrative and its story of father, daughter, and seducer in the course of exploring *Charlotte Temple* for its political subtext.[12] Omitted from any extended discussion of the parental politics operative in *Charlotte Temple* is the symbolic figure of the absent mother who occupies and directs the narrative frame.[13] She is not to be confused with Charlotte's biological mother, Mrs. Lucy Temple, who receives critical attention for her role as forgiving parent, potential surrogate for Charlotte's orphaned infant. Mrs. Temple may be crucial to the "*felix culpa*" denouement of the novel, but her role in the narrative symbolic of *Charlotte Temple* is minimal.[14]

Instead, it is the unnamed and overly present narrator who functions as the novel's absent emblem of maternal power and who does *Charlotte Temple*'s most important cultural work.[15] This symbolic mother stands in analogous relation to the "patriarchal authority" that Fliegelman identifies as central to these early American fictions of the family in distress. Fated to remain a disembodied figure, Rowson's narrator never achieves representational status as a dramatic character, but her parental prerogative needs no visual augmentation. In fact, such noncorporeality enhances the narrator's position in the novel's semiotic regime.[16]

Perhaps the most fascinating, and certainly the most critically unexplored locus of *Charlotte Temple*, the narrator disrupts the unfolding story of Charlotte's decline and fall in important and unrecognized ways. If we are to recover the full narrative complexity and the cultural significance of *Charlotte Temple*, both in its own epoch and as the first American best-seller, which remains in print after nearly two hundred years, we must attend to the centrality of this symbolic absent mother and, specifically, to the narrative form in which and through which she does her work. At stake is a reading of *Charlotte Temple* that extends beyond a reductive decoding of Rowson's politics as patriarchal and conservative, as antirevolutionary.[17]

Paradoxically, *Charlotte Temple*'s more utopian and egalitarian impulses are expressed through the autocratic eruptions of Rowson's maternal story-teller. At crucial moments the narrator breaks the frame of her account in order to regale the reader about the dangers of separation and independence and to argue that naive young women are easily lured by promises of economic, social, and romantic freedom. (In conventional readings of the novel such female innocents allegorize the fate of the new nation itself.) She exclaims, "Oh my dear girls—for to such only am I writing—listen not to the voice of love, unless sanctioned by paternal approbation: be assured, *it is now past the days of romance: no woman can be run away with contrary to her own inclination.*"[18] Insisting that females are particularly vulnerable to the artful wiles and manipulations of social predators, the narrator brings to vivid life Rousseau's antitheatrical prejudice and anticipates Wollstonecraft's brief for women's rationality one year before the publication of *Vindication of the Rights of Woman* (1792): she legislates for Enlightenment on sympathetic, rather than exclusionary, grounds. Had Charlotte been able to decode the dramatic performance underlying the concern the falsely maternal La Rue exhibited in conversations about her future; had the ingenuous virgin exercised reason and forethought instead of succumbing to her mentor's beguiling claims; and had she maintained her elective affinities for mother, father, and grandfather, her woeful seduction, piteous abandonment, and sorry death would have been unimaginable.

In fact, while Charlotte's imprudent rending of family ties—the breach that precipitates her suffering and demise—constitutes the novel's enabling political precondition, the devastating cost of self-government becomes its abiding subject. That such primal separation (what, according to the allegorical reading, we might characterize as the heroine's break with her "English family") cannot be undone is a crucial element in Rowson's radically democratic program. Such fracture allows the maternal narrator—whose own imperious temperament sometimes savors of a despotic will to power[19]—to transvaluate the operations of "independence" and extend the implications of "affiliation" in decidedly unconservative ways.

To argue that the traumas of "revolutionary" separation are remedied when Mr. Temple removes Charlotte's infant daughter from the American scene and restores the babe to the loving embrace of his grieving wife Lucy is to ignore the unique narrative form of *Charlotte Temple*. According to this conservative and plot-driven reading, Lucy Temple the elder (Charlotte's daughter is also, significantly, named Lucy) represents the English motherland mourning its erring colonial child who, though forever lost, has produced offspring worthy of redemption. While the ending of *Charlotte Temple* certainly supports such an interpretation, it stops short of explaining the political significance of the narrator's peculiar intrusive tendencies, which dominate and overtake the novel's form, ultimately obscuring the clarity of its ideological intentions.

If we focus instead on Rowson's maternal figuration of her narrator and explore the filial relationship this absent presence constructs with the audience, the democratic face of the novel comes into sharper focus. Charlotte cannot be restored, but the sorrow that her death provokes—in both narrator and reader alike—allows for the cohesion of an "imagined community" around the wound to the social body that her passing represents.[20] Thus, the fabric of narrative, rent by the death of Charlotte and rewoven by the audience's compassionate response both inside the novel and outside in the world of history becomes Rowson's abiding utopian figure for the new nation itself. Rather than viewing the trauma of post-Revolutionary separation as a condition from which to retreat in some kind of reactionary return-to-the-womb of mother country, Rowson crusades against the pain exacted by independence by transforming sorrow into an ostensibly enabling—because democratic—precondition for the future. The sacrifices exacted by the Revolution—symbolized by Charlotte Temple—and the work of mourning they inspire thus allow for the reimagining of the American polity as a body that is both more cohesive and more inclusive than its pre-Revolutionary avatar precisely because it is grounded in the sympathetic affective relations of its members.

Rowson's vision of collectivity conjures the paradoxical politics of Rousseau's social theory, his writings on culture and the arts, which continue to be understood as uniquely idiosyncratic articulations of both reactionary and radical impulses. The philosopher's antitheatrical works provide a distinctive background against which to situate *Charlotte Temple* in the Anglo-European debate about liberty and civil right unfolding among Enlightenment thinkers in the second half of the eighteenth century. The present reading aligns Rowson with Rousseau but extends the implications of his elegiac fantasy of transparent social communion—epitomized in the harvest festival of his childhood memory depicted in the "Letter To M. D'Alembert" as well as in the winemaking jubilee in *La Nouvelle Heloise* (book V, letter VII).[21] Rousseau argues that such moments of collective transparency tran-

scend the theatricality of everyday social relations by allowing every participant to be both actor in and spectator of the community's labor and pleasure.

However compelling, these episodes of public communion provide only
an ephemeral vision of social equality that cannot translate into historical
terms, as Jean Starobinski argues:

> In the general jubilation it seems that primitive equality has somehow
> been recaptured. . . . In fact, the supposed equality is quite illusory. It
> appears with the holiday rapture and will disappear with it as well. It is a
> mere epiphenomenon of communal happiness.[22]

Starobinski goes on to assert that

> the juridical assumptions of the *Social Contract* are realized—in an emo-
> tional sense—for one brief moment, but the joy of equality, of a society
> free of *corps intermediaires,* will not outlive the holiday. This brief tri-
> umph of fraternity in no way threatens the customary order or economy
> of the estate [at Clarens in *La Nouvelle Heloise*], which is based on the
> domination of masters and the obedience of servants. The egalitarian
> exuberance cannot endure; it contains no promise of continuity. . . . We
> are shown equality in a concentrated moment of great intensity, but it is
> temporary intensity, which lacks the power to perpetuate itself in insti-
> tutional form. . . . It may be that Rousseau sees the ephemeral rapture of
> the festival as an emotional substitute for real equality, for which he is
> not prepared to fight.[23]

Rowson transforms Rousseau's transcendent and collective joy—his vision of
pleasure that is ultimately fleeting—into a far darker, and paradoxically enabling, communal affect: the melancholy that extends via sympathetic contagion from the narrator to the reader. An affliction of soul and spirit that
defies the healing powers of time, such unrelieved sorrow proves the emotional foundation for the egalitarian face of Rowson's imaginative project,
when it does not actually overwhelm the political agenda of the novel. In
Charlotte Temple, the experience of melancholic fraternity endures beyond
the moment, extending into the social practice of a readership that has remained unflagging for over two hundred years.

Without its complex narratology, *Charlotte Temple* would remain a
simple story of seduction and abandonment, indistinguishable from the work
of other eighteenth-century sentimental writers. At best, it might retain

some historical significance as the inaugural women's narrative of this American tradition. What sets *Charlotte Temple* apart from the conventions that would seem to define it is the novel's unique mode of performing loss; its distinctive narrative form makes *Charlotte Temple* an extraordinary artifact, possessed of a specifically gendered mode of cultural power. Vested in the symbolic maternal voice that permeates the narrative of *Charlotte Temple*, this disembodied authority emanates from the point of textual origin, attempting to avail its post-Revolutionary audience of the presence, plenitude, and transparent social relations that echo Rousseau's nostalgic ruminations on the state of nature.[24]

To reconstruct *Charlotte Temple*'s cultural force, and particularly its utopian, Rousseauvian dimensions, we must consider not only the framed tale of seduction but the significance of the frame, not simply the narrative matter of *Charlotte Temple* but also its manner, expressed in disruptions and discontents. As we unpack the complexity of *Charlotte Temple*'s concentric narratives and explore the ways in which the outer story permeates the inner, we will come to a better understanding of Rowson's contribution to a subtle and important cultural conversation concerning gender and loss that was taking place in the post-Revolutionary context of the early American novel.[25] The key to much that remains unexplained about both *Charlotte Temple* in particular and late-eighteenth-century American fiction in general is contained within the dynamics of narrative itself. Reading for the poetics of form will clarify both how and why *Charlotte Temple*, a novel predicated on the healing presence and plenitude of the female voice and underwritten by the attendant fantasy of women's *authorial* power, occupies a central place in the cultural and representational history of an affect: the feminization of loss that pervades late-eighteenth- and nineteenth-century American sentimental fiction.

At the heart of *Charlotte Temple*'s performance of such loss lies the narrator, a figure who rings a change on conventional eighteenth-century Anglo-American fictive depictions of women; Rowson creates a maternal voice notable for its extraordinary *rationality*, a pragmatic worldliness that stands in stark contrast to the tableau of female hysteria it frames. Speaking within the highly artificial context of a novelistic discourse, the narrator is fully aware that young female readers of fiction need to be grounded in the hard realities of the world in which they live. Her goal is to preempt what later would come to be termed "Bovaryism," girlish longings for "the days of romance" (26). In the social code of the eighteenth century, a zealous enthusiasm for sensational novels was thought to debase the faculties of reason;[26] ever mindful of her culture's stereotype of female sensibility, in which all women bear a latent propensity for hysterical dissolution, Rowson's narrator will not dignify such identifications for her community of readers.

But the narrator's rationality, which is crucial to rendering a persuasive case against seduction, represents only one level of her affective experience in *Charlotte Temple;* at the moment in which she confidently registers her soundest judgments, she also inadvertently gives voice to a melancholic grief.[27] Perhaps even more interesting than the narrator's insistence that young women readers not be gulled by fantasies of romantic rescue is her emphasis on proper and improper ways in which to listen to the voice of love. Rowson's speaker ostensibly promulgates "paternal approbation" as the value of choice, offering an endogamous daughter-father dyad in the place of unrighteous—if exogamous—heterosexual attachment, an arrangement that leaves traditional, patriarchal structures of authority firmly in place. But, against this explicit injunction, the narrator sets up an alternative, maternal economy of feeling that substitutes reader and storyteller for female child and male parent; displacing the law of the father with the voice of the mother, *Charlotte Temple* reimagines the gendering of power in decidedly antipatriarchal ways.

This female prerogative does not entirely escape the structures of domination that inform patriarchal practice. Indeed, while the commitment the narrator offers to her audience is total, it is also virtually autocratic: she is willing to lavish an unstinting flow of love, support, and advice on the "young ladies" she identifies as her readers, but this outpouring of generosity and concern is marked by a disturbing emotional extravagance. The narrator's insistence on her readers' approving response suggests that her investment goes beyond that of the civic-minded woman who wishes to educate young girls in the meaning of true virtue; the intensity of the affect betrays the depth of the need. What she attempts to redress through her relationship with the reader is nothing less than a sense of loss that is so overwhelming that it blights every other idea in *Charlotte Temple.*

By asserting that the affective significance of *Charlotte Temple* inheres in the practices of Rowson's narrator, a figure who has at best been known for her intrusive preachiness, I am attempting to shift the ground of contemporary criticism of the early American novel to a cultural analysis of form.

Scholars writing as recently as Susan K. Harris, who take the female narrator's frequent moralistic interruptions at face value, continue to identify the novel as a didactic fable warning against the dangers of seduction and advocating greater social tolerance for wayward girls.[28] Resting comfortably at the level of prescription, such critics accept that *Charlotte Temple* is a novel about ethics, but this line of inquiry stops short of questioning whether the narrator's didacticism may itself be symptomatic of an entirely other set of concerns, pertaining not to action but to feeling and its social implications. The didactic reading reduces to monologue the significantly more complicated and pluralized maneuvers of a narrator for whom female chastity is not, in fact, the last word.

To unravel the multiple voices that together constitute the text that is *Charlotte Temple* is to discover a feminist anatomy-*manqué* of eighteenth-century patriarchal culture. Punctuating the central tale of the virgin seduced and abandoned exists a less visible but perhaps even more powerful story: the tale of a narrator so haunted by the threat of loss that she generates the tightly controlled narrative universe to which we have alluded, a fictive world that encodes its own readership and modes of response in order to perform a preemptive and potentially reparative ritual of maternal mourning.[29]

This powerful wish for control and restitution is acted out not only at the level of narratorial interruption but also through an obsessive retelling of Charlotte's story in the epistolary discourse,[30] melodramatic spectacle, and oral tradition that are deployed *within* the novel's mimetic world.[31] Rowson's narrative economy functions according to a law of superlegibility: the more often the tale can be retold, the better. This strategy for storytelling insures that the affective core of the novel—its horror over loss—will reach nearly transparent representation. If, as Freud argues in "Mourning and Melancholia," mourning is a process of recuperating the ego's investment of libido in the lost object through a *ritual of commemoration and farewell,*[32] the generic multiplicity at work within *Charlotte Temple* would seem to attest to the mournful nature of the narrator's psychopolitical enterprise.

And yet the narrator's framing discourse does not, ultimately, contain the grief unleashed by Charlotte's story. The moralistic interruptions, highly rational exhortations deployed to appeal to the mind as well as merely to the feelings of the reader, take us back to the scene of loss and replay it without allowing us to move on. The narrator's sorrow is unrequited by the end of the tale, her working-through incomplete, verging on the very sort of impasse that marks melancholia.[33] The frame does not close. Written during a period of renewed Anglo-American discussion about the place of women in republican culture,[34] *Charlotte Temple*, with its multinational genealogy and its discourse of maternal loss and a mourning that remains unresolved, speaks to the unfinished business of post-Revolutionary American society. Understood in these terms, we can begin to recover the ongoing appeal of *Charlotte Temple*, which inheres in the staging of maternal grief as a kind of cultural work in progress.[35]

Working through the Frame

The notion of "working through the frame" found in the title of this chapter is meant to be evocative on multiple levels: "working-through" implies both a mode of narrative operations and an affective process, suggesting that the story's frame is the place where the speaker does her most important fictive work. In creating this structure around her tale, and by constantly disrupting its formal boundaries with obsessive and obnoxious interjections, the narrator of *Charlotte Temple* is engaged in a psychological labor that bears political and cultural meaning. The second use of the phrase "working-through" refers to the process of therapeutic healing defined by Freud and glossed by Laplanche and Pontalis as the

> process by means of which analysis implants an interpretation and overcomes the resistances to which it has given rise. Working-through is to be taken as a sort of psychical work which allows the subject to accept certain repressed elements and to free himself from the grip of mechanisms of repetition. It is a constant factor in treatment, but it operates more especially during certain phases where progress seems to have come to a halt and where a resistance persists despite its having been interpreted.[36]

In his essay on "Remembering, Repeating, and Working-Through" (1914), Freud coins the last term to describe the outcome of the process of recollection, repetition, and illumination that is psychoanalysis. Working-through is also the dynamic that marks the operation of mourning: over time, and with much pain, the survivor reviews the "archive of the dead," conjuring memories of lost love, images that can be multiple and contradictory.[37] The task of mourning involves the attempt to reweave the rent in life's fabric that death has exacted; it is the effort to resolve—to iterate and reiterate—multiple images of what has been lost into a single portrait with which the survivor can live. Storytelling and representation lie at the heart of both Freud's theory of mourning and the operations of narratorial working-through in *Charlotte Temple*. The psychoanalytic patient continually revises the tale of her life; repeating elements in the narrative, she places different emphases on them, constantly amending her interpretation to suit the working hypothesis she creates in collaboration with the analyst—a hypothesis that is, itself, always undergoing revision.[38]

In *Charlotte Temple*, the narrator's storytelling follows two dialectically opposed trajectories that, taken together, constitute an attempt at "doing and undoing" or working-through. Within the framed tale, the narrator relates the seduction and abandonment of Charlotte, a fifteen-year-old girl whose emotional development remains at the level of a young child.[39] Charlotte is unable to tolerate parental and, in particular, maternal separation, and, in keeping with this characterological disorder, she projects the identity of mother onto any available female object. The inability to separate from her mother and the propensity to misjudge all potential maternal figures as benevolent both mark Charlotte's infantilization and prevent her from functioning as an adult female in a brutally patriarchal world.

To the mind of the narrator, such a scenario as Charlotte's, featuring as it does the prospect of both abandonment and death, is guaranteed to inspire agony in any reader of feeling. Overcome by the compulsion to assuage readerly anguish *in advance of its experience,* the narrator of *Charlotte Temple,* who is linked with maternity by her empathy, her mode of address, and her connection with all the mother figures in the novel, violates the boundaries of her mimetic world with a series of increasingly maddening interruptions and digressions.

So obsessed is this narrator with achieving transparency—controlling the potential distance between authorial intention and reader response—that she inaugurates her preemptive, intratextual interpretive practices in the preface to her book. The narrator says,

[C]onscious that I wrote with a mind *anxious* for the happiness of that sex whose morals and conduct have so powerful an influence on mankind in general; and convinced that I have not wrote one line that conveys a wrong idea to the head or a corrupt wish to the heart, I shall *rest satisfied* in the purity of my own intentions, and if I merit not applause, I feel that I dread not censure. (L, my emphasis)

Although she claims to be fully content with the righteousness of her endeavor, what is really at stake for the narrator is the persistence of her anxiety; the assertion that she has banished concern at this very early moment is betrayed by the fact that she cannot "rest satisfied" in the belief that readers will keep faith with the program. Refusing to entertain the possibility that she will have to cut her readerly losses (the very willingness to "let go" that is required, psychologically, before one can complete the work of mourning), the narrator is determined to avoid abandonment by any one segment of her audience. Hence, she imagines a panoply of potential readers: the "sober matron" (25), "dear girls" (26), "dear young readers" (56), "dear madam" (67–68), "young, volatile reader," "dear, cheerful, innocent girl" (108), "fair querist," "young friends" (109), and "penetrating gentleman, dear sir" (116–17) are all addressed in turn. The narrator's determination to control the response to her story is the mark of a chronic unease that will fuel the repetitive barrage of didactic interjections that punctuate the entire narrative of *Charlotte Temple*.

Undergirding such obsessive, presumptuously intrusive behavior is the narrator's Rousseauvian longing for a face-to-face relation, the wish to bridge the distance between a female or feminized readership (symbolic daughters and sons of feeling) and a maternal voice determined to undo loss. In fact, the term "bridge" is far too measured to describe what Rowson's narrator would really seem to require: a virtual fusion with her audience. This longing for a transparent union with the reader manifests itself most pointedly in a remarkable digression very early in the novel. Such incursions into Charlotte's story function as formal cues that we are entering the psychological and political heart of Rowson's matter—the following example is paradigmatic:

> I confess I have rambled strangely from my story: but what of that? if I have been so lucky as to find the road to happiness, why should I be such a niggard as to omit so good an opportunity of pointing out the way to others. The very basis of true peace of mind is a benevolent wish to see all the world as happy as one's self; . . . For my own part, I can safely declare, there is not a human being in the universe, whose prosperity I should not rejoice in, and to whose happiness I would not contribute to

the utmost limit of my power: and may my offenses be no more remembered in the day of general retribution, than as from my soul I forgive every offence or injury received from a fellow creature. Merciful heaven! who would exchange the rapture of such a reflexion [sic] for all the gaudy tinsel which the world calls pleasure! (33–34)

Rowson's speaker seeks to surround her reader with a blanket of comfort constructed in words; her language of care attempts to approximate what, in a different context, Kaja Silverman has called "the maternal envelope." In her work on the female voice in psychoanalysis and cinema, Silverman uses this vocal and spatial metaphor to describe "the sonorous plenitude of the mother's voice" as experienced by the infant, arguing that "the maternal voice would seem to be the prototype of the disembodied voice-over in cinema."[40]

In relation to such an omnipotent female voice, the auditor or reader would occupy the subject position of the infant who perceives this parent as all powerful, Godlike. In this passage, Rowson's narrator herself longs to embody such maternal prerogative, which she personifies in the figure of the goddess "Content," who functions as her deitific double:

[H]er name is *Content;* she holds in her hand the cup of true felicity, and when once you have formed an intimate acquaintance with these her attendants. . . . then, whatever may be your situation in life, the meek eyed Virgin will immediately take up her abode with you. (32–33)

Omnipotence, standing in for the narrator in her more egalitarian and expansive mode, takes up residence with the reader in this tableau. At the end of a long list of potential roles Content could play in the lives of audience members occupying disparate ranks on the great chain of being—it is important to note that Content is a true democrat—the narrator concludes:

She will pass with you through life, smoothing the rough paths and treading to earth those thorns which every one must meet with as they journey onward to the appointed goal. She will *soften the pains of sickness, continue with you even in the cold gloomy hour of death,* and chearing you with the smiles of her heaven-born sister, Hope, lead you triumphant to a blissful eternity. (33)

Through her medical ministrations and her capacity to surround the sufferer with a blanket of care that bridges distance in the passage between life and eternity (a kind of midwifing of the dying), Content stands in for the narrator as the maternal envelope; what the goddess achieves in a digressive moment in the mimesis, the narrator echoes at the level of voice.

Even within the narratorial fantasy, however, such blissful moments of fusion exert a powerful violence, hinting at the gothicism that underlies *Charlotte Temple*'s sentimental story and unsettles its idealized vision of democratic fraternity. With an almost Calvinist fervor that contradicts her characteristically democratic impulses and reveals her imperious side, the narrator winnows her readership into wheat and chaff; bestowing on chapter 33 a title that resonates with judgment—"Which People Void of Feeling Need Not Read" (124)—she defiantly admonishes the insensible among her audience, those out of tune with the narratorial project of counterabandonment, that they will be banished to the outer darkness. There is only one representation of a male reader encoded within the text of *Charlotte Temple*, and he figures among the unfeeling, rearing his disgruntled head toward the end of the novel, when the narrator conjures him up to object to the lack of realism at work in the episode of Charlotte's impoverished flight to New York City. It is no accident that this masculine reader takes exception to Charlotte's ignorance of money and economics; he angrily charges the narrator with concocting an unbelievable scenario when she has Charlotte elope from England without first availing herself of material resources, even keepsakes that could be pawned for cash. The narrator responds to this protest with irritation, explaining that the heroine was *unthinking* in her flight; indeed, Charlotte, symbolically no more developed than an infant, personifies unthinkingness.

Here, Rowson's narrator practices an uncharacteristic ethic of exclusion in conjuring the male reader only to discredit him: by revealing that his fixation on petty detail has caused him to miss the heart of Charlotte's matter, Rowson's narrator dispatches the masculine principle from her audience. Controlling the gender identities, as well as the responses of her readers, constitutes another way in which the narrator seeks to recreate a maternal relation through her storytelling. More precisely, only feminized men of feeling—figures such as Mr. Elderidge and Mr. Temple, Charlotte's maternal grandfather and motherly father, and the surgeon who observes her suffering as he delivers her daughter and attends her demise—*count* as worthy witnesses to Charlotte's plight. Accordingly, only male characters possessed of sensibility can double for that masculine sector of the audience capable of extending compassion through acts of imaginative identification.

Through such sporadic but striking maneuvers, the narrator dismisses the dissenting members of the audience and cannibalizes the remainder. Holding her unresisting readers hostage, she subjects them to a powerful and repetitive emotional barrage whose surface message concerns female education and sexual self-control. The subtext, however, has little to do with proper behavior, involving instead the horrors of filial separation and loss. The narrator attempts to ward off the pain of Charlotte's experience by creating a counterexperience at the level of the frame, one that would obviate such sorrow. Thus, the moralizing functions as a defense, and the didacticism operates as a smokescreen for the narrator's real project: the working-through of unresolved maternal mourning.

In her obsessive exhortation of the reader to fuse with her perspective, in her insistence that audience members swerve away from making filial choices that would break a mother's heart, the narrator is protesting too much. Despite the power of her desire for merging, she is unable to diminish any potential gap between herself and her auditors; such a distance makes the narrator so profoundly uneasy that it motivates her obsessive attempt at working through loss *in advance* of its experience, but these efforts to seize control repeat rather than exact revenge on the reality of grief, and the narrator only succeeds in reinscribing the breach between herself and the readerly other. Mourning becomes melancholia, darkening the dream of democratic transparency in *Charlotte Temple*.

Chapter 14, entitled "Maternal Sorrow" (in which Mr. Temple reveals to his wife that Charlotte has eloped), renders its melodramatic tableau of losses in a language of excess virtually unmatched by any other moment in the story and constitutes a microcosm of the novel's larger psychology of female grief; most significant is the way in which the subject positions of daughter and mother—power relations whose hierarchical fixity has been clear, until this point—become fluid, interchangeable. It is here that Rowson's portrait of maternal loss becomes almost luridly visceral. The narrator exclaims, "A mother's anguish, when disappointed in her tenderest hopes, none but a mother can conceive" (55).

As the narrator catalogs a virtual compendium of maternal devotions erased from the minds of the ungrateful daughters who have broken their mothers' hearts, one senses a double vision at work: we are made to see through both maternal and filial eyes *simultaneously*. The general exhortation on the subject of potential daughterly ingratitude would seem to have been provoked by Charlotte's disloyalty to Mrs. Temple within the framed narrative. Thus, the roster of highlights in the history of motherly care would be a flashback, related from the perspective of a mother just like Mrs. Temple.

Yet, at the level of feeling, the narrator communicates an additional sense of longing and loss, an emotion that is not quite congruent with memory, per se. Instead, the tender representation of mother-child communion reads as a kind of projected wish fulfillment, an imaginative enactment of devotions not experienced, but perhaps only longed for, originating from the perspective of a daughter deprived of such care. As we watch the narrator conjure and rehearse the scenes of maternal attention as nostalgia for a state of connection that is now lost, something oddly filial also emerges at the level of represented affect. The maternal tableau unfolded in this episode renders such loss a reflexive female experience,[41] and the polymorphous female subject positions the passage inscribes—positions that are simultaneously occupied by narrator *and* reader—may account for the uncanny appeal *Charlotte Temple* has had for women readers across two centuries.

Maternal connection becomes the space of female salvation in the world of *Charlotte Temple* precisely because, as Rowson will reveal throughout her story, late-eighteenth-century patriarchy takes a fatal toll on disorderly female bodies.[42] And yet, in keeping with a persistent homosociality operating within the narrative unconscious of *Charlotte Temple*, the most virulent misogynists in this novel are women; one could go so far as to argue that male identity is itself an afterthought in Rowson's fictional universe. The most villainous seducer of young womanhood in *Charlotte Temple* is a female, the artful and designing Mlle La Rue, as is the heartless landlord who evicts the pregnant and penniless Charlotte from her only refuge. What Lacan has termed "the law of the father," male control of the symbolic order, in other words, is in the hands of phallic women acting as men. It is only the sound of the speaking mother, the maternally figured narrative overvoice interrupting the story in the ways that have been mentioned, who interrogates the psychological and political efficacy of that law, and it is only this female storyteller who would posit a more nurturing counternarrative of her own, one that seeks to obviate maternal loss by an act of preemptive—if unsuccessful, because pathological—mourning. If novels are structured by a certain degree of wish fulfillment, we must take seriously Susanna Rowson's political imperative: to make men without feeling extraneous and to heed the maternal voice.[43] *Charlotte Temple* embodies such forms of desire.

Although it is the creation of a female author, *Charlotte Temple* does not escape inflection by the late-eighteenth-century Anglo-American climate in which it was written, and, in this milieu, women are figured as property. But the novel does provide two different attitudes toward the female chattel. The scene in which Montraville, Charlotte's disaffected paramour, recovers the jewel box of his soon-to-be-beloved Julia Franklin affords a wonderful occasion for exploring the sexual politics of the novel, which turn around the fetishization of maternal representations. In seducing the virtuous Charlotte—or, rather, after the girl's teacher La Rue has enticed her into eloping from school—and in relieving her of her virginity, Montraville can be said to have "stolen" Charlotte's "jewels." Consumed by a sexual passion that cannot be controlled, the young soldier essentially "spends" Charlotte's "treasure" until it is used up; parental injunction has forbidden him from even considering marriage to a dowerless woman such as Charlotte. Montraville takes possession of that which, for the eighteenth-century female, constitutes her wealth, integrity, and honor, appropriating what does not belong to him, and squandering it. Charlotte herself employs the jewel metaphor to describe her transformation into shame: "I was conscious of having forfeited the only gem that could render me respectable in the eyes of the world" (84).

In contrast, Montraville restores to the wealthy and well-born Julia Franklin a box of jewels that an old man has apparently rescued from Julia's burning domicile and turned over to the handsome soldier. In the face of a literal fire that rages out of control, patriarchy—in the form of the old man—comes in to save the treasure representing Julia's purity and hands it off to the figure most fit to assure its future security, Montraville. Montraville is the preserver of Julia's jewels, in which he determines to invest his future.

In the elaborate scene of exchange that follows Montraville's temporary receipt of this prize, Julia remarks that a treasured miniature is missing from the jewel box. Having thought the likeness was a portrait of his new object of desire, Montraville had planned to maintain furtive possession of the image; the impulse to steal what is not his and to cashier it away would parallel, symbolically, his treatment of Charlotte. But Julia indicates that the portrait is a likeness of *her mother,* the loss of whom, Montraville quickly realizes, on descrying her black arm-band, Julia is mourning; touched by her filial sorrow, he immediately returns the image to the grieving daughter. Montraville is willing to (figuratively) rip Charlotte from her live, though distant, maternal connection, because the virgin's lowly place on the ladder of class and rank renders her of little value, but the maternal-filial bonds of the daughter of privilege must be respected. Moreover, the fact of a dead mother opens up affective space in the life of that young heiress, who must now seek a proper surrogate: Montraville has perfect entrée. As Belcour, the depraved libertine who professes false friendship to Montraville, cynically advises, the latter should "seize the gifts of fortune while they are within [his] reach" (88).

The real tragedy of seduction, argues the narrator, is that it puts young girls in the structural position of orphans:

> [S]he has no redress, no friendly, soothing companion to pour into her wounded mind the balm of consolation, no benevolent hand to lead her back to the path of rectitude; she has *disgraced her friends,* forfeited the good opinion of the world, and undone herself; she feels herself a *poor solitary being in the midst of surrounding multitudes;* shame bows her to earth, remorse tears her distracted mind, and guilt, poverty, and disease close the dreadful scene: she sinks *unnoticed* to oblivion. (69, my emphasis)

It is the poor "friendless" woman's tragic destiny to find that her sexual identity has become an issue of private property, subject only to (black) market conditions, and unregulated by the law. This sad fact forms a striking contrast to the reality of Montraville's sanctified affection for Julia, which belongs to the public sphere. Belcour will break Charlotte's heart, when he sadistically informs the pregnant girl that Montraville: "addresses her [Julia Franklin] publicly [sic]" (106).

Who is Montraville to play such a crucial role in Charlotte's affective life, particularly if, as we have seen, Charlotte is an emotional infant? How can romantic yearning emanate from a child? Charlotte's attachment, though technically a sexual one and therefore a function of the Lacanian symbolic, actually operates in the realm of the imaginary; it is a tie that evokes the pre-oedipal relation to a maternal object. Montraville simply constitutes the last link in a chain of mothers-by-proxy to whom Charlotte has clung throughout the tale. These surrogates include the headmistress of her school, Mme Du Pont, whose name suggests her symbolic function of providing a *bridge* between home and world, and Mlle La Rue, whose evocative appellation conjures associations to the public sphere: to the street, to sexuality and revolutionary danger (the red one), and to regret (as in "I rue the day . . ."). Charlotte's education at the hands of Mme Du Pont has been woefully incomplete, in part because the size of her school prevents this able mistress from exercising personal control over every aspect of its functioning (23). The political critique at work in the description of the headmistress's failed government is distinctly Rousseauvian: Mme Du Pont's delegation of authority constitutes a miniature version of the indirect representation, the nontransparent social relations, that Rousseau rails against in the "Letter to M. D'Alembert" (60–62). The "bridge" has failed to do its duty.

Given the principle of repetition compulsion at work in both the frame and the framed tales, it is hardly propitious that Charlotte has gone to Mme Du Pont's to take up the interrupted education of her mother, Lucy Eldridge Temple, another female seized with the inability to endure parental separation. When faced with the trauma of her mother's and brother's deaths and her father's imprisonment for debt, Lucy fantasizes a tableau of merging into the grave with her remaining parent, "'Oh, my father!' cried Miss Eldridge, tenderly taking his hand, 'be not anxious on that account; for daily are my prayers offered to heaven that *our lives may terminate at the same instant,* and one grave receive us both; for why should I live when deprived of my only friend'" (9, my emphasis). The narrator represents the misfortune experienced by members of the Eldridge-Temple clan in explicitly gothic terms: she figures conflict and malevolence as the violent ripping and brutal separation of bodies once happily bound in a familial embrace. She depicts kinship as a maternal relation, while she casts anyone divided from the family in the structural role of orphaned babe. Mr. Eldridge describes in metaphors of rending the experience of being arrested for debt: "an officer entered, and *tore me from the embraces of my family*"; he depicts the episode as a castration in which "the horrors of that night *unman*" him, and concludes: "what a mere infant I am!" (11, my emphases).

Prey to the manipulations of the falsely maternal La Rue, Charlotte is goaded into behavior of which her real mother would never approve. In fact, the French teacher places humiliating emphasis on the virgin's vulnerability and dependence, sadistically taunting the uncertain Charlotte with the charges that she is infantile: "[H]ave you a mind to be in leading strings all your life time" (28). In a counterscene that rings of the uncanny, Mrs. Temple plans to bring Charlotte home from school in order to celebrate her daughter's birthday, the only festival in the Anglo-American cultural tradition, prior to the advent of Mother's Day at the beginning of the twentieth century,[44] commemorating the mother-child bond. Charlotte never attends her own celebration in the garden of the Temple's rural cottage, Rowson's approximation of Rousseau's state of nature. Instead, it is against the background of the ruined birthday idyll that she elopes from school with La Rue into the arms of Montraville. With this setting for seduction, the maternal bond is violated at its symbolic heart. It is no accident that the episode sets off an extended round of narratorial moralizing par excellence (32); in her function as maternal representative for all of the betrayed mothers in her reading audience, the narrator absorbs the blast detonated by Charlotte's infidelity.

It is also no accident that Charlotte literally must be unconscious (she has "fainted," 48) to effect the elopement. More accurately, as an emotional infant, the heroine is not an agent in her own life, and she cannot be said to have enacted anything; in the getaway scene, Charlotte is rendered passive at the crucial moment, since to assent to such brutal divorce from her family would be unthinkable. Even prior to sailing, the errant girl does not want to separate from her parents: she writes to them that "her only hope of future comfort consisted in the (perhaps delusive) idea she indulged, of being once more folded in their protecting arms, and hearing the words of peace and pardon from their lips" (57).

The fantasy underwriting Charlotte's letter is the notion that mothers possess the authority to heal and forgive, a sentiment that echoes Rowson's view of maternity as a form of affective and political power. But there is little chance for compassion to do its beneficent work when epistolary communication between children and parents is violently interrupted, as it is when Montraville prevents Charlotte's penitent letter from reaching its destination. Lacking such correspondence, Mrs. Temple peremptorily identifies illness rather than unregulated sexuality as the cause of her daughter's failure to return for the birthday celebration. She will fancy that the child lies afflicted before contemplating that Charlotte may have eloped. Determining to rescue the girl from her imaginary malady, Lucy reveals precisely what is at stake in her relationship with Charlotte: "Then she is very ill, else why did she not come [home to the birthday celebration]? But I will go to her: the chaise is still at the door: let me go instantly to the dear girl. If I was ill, she would fly to attend me, to alleviate my sufferings, and chear [sic] me with her love" (54). The blurring of identity within this maternal fantasy typifies the attitudes of the "overindulgent mother," a parental figure whose excessive involvement with her child constitutes the underside of the phallic maternity represented by a character like La Rue. E. Ann Kaplan explains that "the mother-as-constructed-in-patriarchy attempts to get something for herself in a situation where that is not supposed to happen," remarking that "fusional mothers, the one identifying with the child to the extent of vicariously mothering herself, the second getting gratification through exercising control over the child, can be found in many . . . melodramas."[45]

Linking the overindulgent or fusional mother with her phallic counterpart helps to make theoretical sense of an otherwise baffling moment at the climax of the novel. At this point, the pregnant and consumptive Charlotte, on the very verge of death, journeys to New York City in a raging snowstorm. Her mission is to supplicate and obtain relief from the now well-married and socially powerful La Rue, whom in her infantile blindness she still believes to be a loyal mother-figure. In this, the most melodramatic scene of the novel, Charlotte cries out to La Rue with the pain of filial imprecation. On being rebuffed by her former mentor, the ruined young woman begins to speak in psychologically resonant non sequiturs: "[B]ut *I will not leave you;* they shall not *tear me from you,*" she cries to the brutal woman who refuses to be moved (119, my emphasis). The delusion of La Rue as good mother utterly overtakes the reality of the situation, which is, in fact, a scene of abject repudiation.

Such rejection at the level of plot provokes in the narrator the equal and opposite compulsion to possess a maternal power so strong that it could circumvent and even annul the sorrow of a mother like Mrs. Temple; this is the wish that the narrator attempts to fulfill by means of her intrusive storytelling. Though the framed tale of Charlotte's undoing would seem to focus on the child, the voice working through the frame knows better: this is a mother's story. The narrator's very first exclamation says it all:

> While the tear of compassion still trembled in my eye for the fate of the unhappy Charlotte, *I* may have children of my own, said I to whom this recital may be of use, and if to your own children, said Benevolence, why not to the daughters of Misfortune who, deprived of *natural friends,* or spoilt by mistaken education, are thrown on an unfeeling world without the least power to defend themselves from the snares not only of the other sex, but from the *more dangerous arts of the profligate of their own.* (xlix–l, my emphasis)

The initial narratorial interruption, to "my dear sober matron" (25) and to "my dear girls" (26), is filled with maternal fury and a protofeminism: "it is now past the days of romance; no woman can be run away with" (26). As I have noted earlier, the argument here calls for female rationality; in making this case for women's ability to use reason—*pace* Wollstonecraft—the narrator deploys in advance an ironic critique of what will be Charlotte's fate and thus attempts to circumvent it.

Maternal identity proliferates throughout the novel world. When Mrs.

Temple learns that Charlotte has eloped, her first plea to God is to "make her not a mother" (55). The narrator, symbolically fused with Mrs. Temple in her maternal affect, continues where Lucy Temple left off:

> A mother's anguish, when disappointed in her tenderest hopes, none but a mother can conceive. Yet, my dear young readers, I would have you read this scene with attention, and reflect that you may yourselves one day be mothers. Oh my friends, as you value your eternal happiness, wound not, by thoughtless ingratitude, the peace of the mother who bore you: remember the tenderness, the care, the unremitting anxiety with which she has attended to all your wants and wishes from earliest infancy to the present day; behold the mild ray of affectionate applause that beams from her eye on the performance of your duty: listen to her reproofs with silent attention; they proceed from a heart anxious for your future felicity: you must love her; nature, all-powerful nature, has planted the seeds of filial affection in your bosoms. (55–56)

In an earlier glimpse of this passage, I focused on the way in which the sacramental vision of a maternal care no longer valued spoke to the longing of a daughter who had not known such attention. Like the primary processes of infants who hallucinate visual representations of an object world that has disappeared, the fictive orphaned daughter conjures images of the absent mother of her desire, but the narrator's complete identification with the imaginary mother of this passage is also striking. In what must be described as nothing less than a rhapsodic lamentation for the forgotten parent whose devoted solicitude has been erased from filial memory, she attempts to restore the mother to readerly presence by making a virtual fetish out of her nurture.

Even La Rue understands the powerful force of maternity. When she determines to trick Col. Crayton into an immediate—mercenary—marriage, she expedites her plan by passing herself off as an old school chum of the late Mrs. Crayton, who, like La Rue, was also French, and who died after giving birth to her daughter Emily, now Mrs. Beauchamp (61). By invoking the maternal connection, La Rue enters the marriage market with uncanny stealth; the purported tie to the dead mother is strong enough to negate the force of La Rue's degraded status as a seduced and abandoned woman.

In the novel's most significant acting out of an expressly maternal dynamic, there is, tellingly, no breaking of the frame with a narratorial interruption. On disembarking, Mrs. Beauchamp sees the forlorn figure of Charlotte and exclaims, "What a pity" (66). Charlotte catches Mrs. Beauchamp's words and, for the first time, interrogates herself about the way she has jeopardized her future. In the next chapter, which follows this scene immediately and which is appropriately titled "Reflections" (67), Charlotte again subjects herself to a brief but soul-searching process of self-examination. The motif of mirroring functions at the level of form and at the level of content: the two facing pages literally echo each other. Charlotte will repeat her own ruminations: "Charlotte caught the word pity. 'And am I already fallen so low,' said she" (66). "'And am I indeed fallen so low,' said Charlotte, 'as to be only pitied'" (67). Mrs. Beauchamp precipitates Charlotte into the awareness of her own (mournful) separateness; she becomes the maternal mirror who reflects Charlotte's abjection rather than the figure who echoes the (illusory) integrity Lacan postulates babies perceive as they are held before the mirror.

Here I have blurred the Lacanian account of the mirror stage with D. W. Winnicott's theory of object relations, to make a literary point. For Lacan, the maternal presence in the mirror scene is tertiary; what is significant is the baby's (illusory) sense of integrity. For Winnicott, the mother *is* the mirror for the baby; it is by introjecting the mother's beneficent image and affect (or, conversely, by incorporating her rage, disapproval, or sorrow) that the infant develops his or her sense of self. In this reweaving of psychoanalytic theory, Mrs. Beauchamp occupies the structural position of the mother in Winnicott's account, but she is the *sorrowful* mother. Until this mirror scene, Charlotte, metaphorically an infant, has had no real understanding of the abysmal separation she has inaugurated by eloping.

In order to make full sense of Charlotte's melancholic grief over the loss of Montraville, it is necessary to remember that the soldier is less a figure of adult desire than the maternal object of an emotionally arrested young girl. In the face of Montraville's neglect, Charlotte's affect is "plaintive," and "mourn[ful]" (68)—she even plays a kind of *fort-da* game to cope with his absence:

> [S]he would sit at a window which looked toward a field he used to cross, counting the minutes and straining her eyes to catch the first glimpse of his person, till blinded with tears of disappointment, she would lean her head on her hands, and give free vent to her sorrows: then catching at some new hope, she would again renew her watchful position, till the shades of evening enveloped every object in a dusky cloud . . . (68).

Unlike Freud's grandson, who attempted to master maternal separation by creating a game in which a spool on a string was made to appear and disappear, Charlotte knows no such working-through, for the object of her long-ing is inconstant. Once she has willfully and violently separated from her biological parent in an act of supreme infidelity, Charlotte is psychically des-tined to be failed by all of the surrogate mothers she has conjured; the com-pulsion to repeat her own flight *from* independence can lead only to the ulti-mate state of regression and merger—death.[46]

In her sympathy for the heroine, Mrs. Beauchamp becomes a surrogate for the narrator (77). The thought that finally enables Mrs. Beauchamp to reach out to Charlotte is the notion that the latter is someone's *child:* "who knows but she has left some kind, affectionate parents . . ." (78). The dying Charlotte wishes only to see her mother (82). She writes to Mrs. Temple, "Even [when I eloped] *I loved you most*" (84, my emphasis). She continues, "It seemed like a separation of body and soul" (84). Charlotte, as a mother-to-be, has begun to understand the privilege and the torment that is maternal grief (85).

And it is a mother's sorrow that motivates the narrator's final sustained intrusion into the novelistic world; in an outburst that anticipates violent readerly resistance, the narrator imperiously encodes the reader's empathy, to the point that fusion is required. In the penultimate moments of her story-telling, she attempts to seize absolute control of her reader as if, by a law of narrative physics, the anguish provoked by the drama itself requires an equal and opposite narratorial reaction that will quell all pain. Thus, the narrator goes on for two pages, assaulting her audience, challenging its disbelief; em-ploying reverse psychology to ensure closure, she dares the reader to throw down the book and thus makes the prospect of finishing the novel a matter of pride:

> "Bless my heart," cries my young volatile reader, "I shall never have pa-tience to get through these volumes, there are so many ahs! and ohs! so much fainting, tears, and distress, I am sick to death of the subject." My dear, chearful, [sic] innocent girl, for innocent I will suppose you to be, or you would acutely feel the woes of Charlotte, did conscience say, thus it might have been with me, had Providence not interposed to snatch me from destruction: therefore my lively, innocent girl, I must request your patience; I am writing a tale of truth, *I mean to write it to the heart:* but if perchance the heart is rendered impenetrable by unbounded pros-perity, or a continuance in vice, I expect not my tale to please, nay, *I even expect it will be thrown by with disgust.* (108, my emphasis)

It is here, at the moment of hemorrhage, that narrative working-through attempts its ostensibly democratic—if latently tyrannical—task of "undoing" loss: by undertaking to incorporate the reader, to fuse the vision of the audience with her own view of Charlotte's story, Rowson's narrator would undo the distance that marks separation and that she finds psychically intolerable.

But the very melancholic impulses driving the narrative unconscious of *Charlotte Temple* will not allow separation to be bridged; even literal mothers and daughters who coexist in the same physical space cannot experience union. In the final pages of the novel, Charlotte disassociates from her newborn child and does not recognize the baby as her own; nor does she begin to fathom the fact that she is a mother. Charlotte's only comprehension of the mother-infant dyad involves seeing herself as exclusive inhabitant of the infantile role. Thus, the narrator explains, "[S]he was not conscious of being a mother, nor took the least notice of her child except to ask *whose it was, and why it was not carried to its parents*" (122, my emphasis). In perhaps her most revealing speech, Charlotte exclaims:

> Why will you keep that child here: I am sure you would not if you knew how hard it was for a mother to be parted from her infant: it is like tearing the cords of life asunder. Oh could you see the horrid sight I now behold—there—there stands my dear mother, her poor bosom bleeding at every vein, her gentle, affectionate heart torn in a thousand pieces, and all for the loss of a ruined, ungrateful child. Save me—save me—from her frown. *I* dare not—indeed I dare not speak to her. (122)

The fantasy of maternal separation is figured as a gothic apocalypse worked out on the mother's body: the cords of life are ripped; the bosom, locus of maternal nurture, is awash in blood, while life pours out at every other vessel; and the heart itself is shredded by the force of filial disobedience. In an utter inversion of the mother's power to bestow life, the child becomes the vehicle for the cataclysmic destruction of the woman who bore her.

Charlotte's vision of violence directed against a maternal figure would seem to be the tragic side effect of a daughterly will to be separate and not a calculated assault conceived in rage. Yet this graphic representation of brutal destruction of the maternal body is so excessive, so ferocious, that it gives pause, requires further commentary. What might this image of maternal mutilation have to tell us about the connection between female mourning and melancholia, between the sentimental—women's grief—and the gothic—women's rage?

The tableau of apocalyptic ferocity against maternity that Charlotte conjures in the course of her psychotic postpartum ravings can be seen as both a masochistic and sadistic fantasy. Separated perhaps too early from the loving blanket of maternal care, betrayed by a false surrogate mother figure, and seduced and forsaken by an indifferent male object, Charlotte is undone by the grief of these successive abandonments. The image of maternal dismemberment she summons expresses her rage over being cast off; onto the safe, because externalized, ground of another female body, she projects fury against a series of inadequate mother figures that now includes herself.

In this waking nightmare, Rowson reveals the way in which pathological grief may itself be only an intermediate step en route to affective bedrock, another form of defense against an even more painful and culturally prohibited emotion—woman's fury. Moving from framed to framing tale, shifting from the level of the visual spectacle of suffering to that of the narrator's expressive attempt to master the dynamic of loss, Charlotte's masochistic fantasy can be reread as a veiled and inverted acting out of female wrath. If, beneath the narrator's rational and beneficent insight about women's condition in patriarchal culture lies an all-consuming and unresolvable sorrow over female object loss (the price patriarchy exacts for cultural adulthood for women), that sorrow is an emotion in which women may indulge. Thus, Rowson's narrative strategy conforms with eighteenth-century norms of female decorum.

And yet, as we have seen, the mourning process inaugurated by the narrative frame is incomplete, unsuccessful, pathological, disturbed. Working-through has broken down, become fixed at the level of obsession; melancholia expresses an internalized rage against women's place in patriarchy. Only once does Rowson's narrator give direct voice to what we might call her maternal fury: tellingly, this outburst erupts in the same passage in which she angrily insists that women know that it is now past the days of romance and that they cannot be swept away by delusions of love. Immediately prior to that statement, the narrator writes, "My bosom glows with honest indignation, and I wish for the power to extirpate those monsters of seduction from the earth" (26, my emphasis).

As a vision of revenge against male villainy, such retribution is inflected by maternity: the organ of motherly nurture is the specific bodily site of burning ferocity; and even the desire to exterminate seducers is expressed in a metaphor of twisted organic reproduction; in this feminist revisioning of the state of nature, the narrator figures herself as an all-powerful cultivator of the soil, who brutally destroys the noxious weeds—predatory libertines—who menace and defile her beloved garden. The motif of retaliation through organic blight reaches its apotheosis in La Rue's final fate: in a move that literalizes the earlier, figurative wish to plague those figures guilty of seducing and destroying innocence, Rowson will strike La Rue with smallpox, inscribing on her body a living emblem of the disease that festers within.

The signature of the narrator's projected rage is punishment at the level of the framed tale: working-through becomes acting out when the narrator afflicts Montraville, inadequate maternal surrogate, with her own inconsolable grief. Suffused with fury on learning that Belcour has betrayed him in his reports about Charlotte's fidelity, Montraville kills his former friend and dissolves into an incurable melancholia. The narrator writes, "[B]ut to the end of his life [Montraville] was subject to severe fits of melancholy, and while he remained at New York, frequently retired to the church-yard, where he would weep over the grave, and regret the untimely fate of the lovely Charlotte Temple" (130). In the imagined world of Rowson's novel, such is the penalty a maternal surrogate must pay for failing to perform a nurturing object relation—a life sentence with the very affect that proves so undoing to a mother, the grief that will not heal.

The wish fulfillment expressed in *Charlotte Temple* is ultimately conservative, or, more precisely, regressive; Rowson's message to young women would seem to be "if at all possible, do not separate." Yet the reality principle at work in *Charlotte Temple* is much more hard headed: since separation is the likely fate of most young women, and since patriarchal culture is brutally hostile to females, it is crucial to be educated, rational, pragmatic, and aware. Not for nothing does Rowson cast La Rue and the landlady as central antagonists who represent the foreign worlds of sexual and economic politics, figures whose unfeelingness suggests that the "natural" impulse to seek a pervasive maternal nurture can also become a fatal compulsion to repeat.

The Career of Genre

With the compulsion to repeat comes an attendant emotional misfire, the mark of melancholia. The bereaved daughter seeks surrogate objects to reconjure the experience of communion; such is her attempt to deny separation and loss. But, because the absent love exists not in the world but encrypted within the self, substitutions cannot fill the rent left in the life that must go on. Thus, the melancholic's search to reclaim and restore the missing object takes on the character of an obsession, as the healing powers attributed to time fail to do their purported work and the wound remains immune to closure.

The suffering heroine of *Charlotte Temple* is not the only figure in the novel to find psychic separateness an alienating and terrifying state. In her zeal to remain attached, not only to her audience but to the subject of filial loss itself, Rowson's narrator is equally afflicted. She cannot be satisfied by telling Charlotte's story in a finite, linear manner. Rather, the narrator's powerful wish for control and restitution is acted out not only at the level of narratorial interruption but through an obsessive retelling of Charlotte's undoing in the epistolary discourse, the melodramatic spectacle, and the oral tradition that are deployed within the novel's mimetic world.

In the service of a principle of conservation and nonseparation that exists at the level of storytelling, Charlotte's fate becomes a literary career. Having dispatched sub- and parallel plots in the early chapters of the novel, Rowson is free in the remaining pages to recycle the tale of Charlotte's fall into a tour de force of genre. The repetitive redeployment of the story of misfortune through multiple embedded literary modes within the novel form marks a crucial way in which this narrative moves between mourning and melancholia; no single genre is adequate to the task of making fully legible the expressive truth of filial loss or discharging the sorrow it evokes. Nevertheless, compulsive repetition through generic variation serves an important political function: it furthers the narrator's democratic urge for transparent social relations by translating into multiple affective registers—a range of languages, literary, performative, and demotic—the universalizing story of Charlotte's woe.

Rowson's narrative economy privileges excess and repetition over restraint and ingenuity: bombarding the reader with the central message rather than evoking its implications in a subtle fashion, the narrator bespeaks the desperation of her desire and ensures the unobstructed communication of the emotional essence of loss. To replay the tale of woe in three different forms would seem to mark a kind of progress in the journey through grief, but the career of genre in *Charlotte Temple* constitutes less a terminus than a refrain: the dynamic that should be a mournful passage *through* more closely resembles a circling around the abyss of sorrow at the core of the novel.

Using embedded epistolary discourse, Rowson presents an *ur*version of the larger novel, a microcosm of *Charlotte Temple*. Like its larger, polygeneric doppelgänger, the miniature epistolary *Charlotte Temple* takes as its subject the problem of sustaining attachments and suggests more directly than does the greater novel that sexual ties cannot hold a candle to maternal bonds. In *Charlotte Temple*, a link to the figure of a mother, whether biological or symbolic, enjoyed with a woman or with a nurturing man of feeling, is figured as the object relation of ultimate value.

Thus, displacing Montraville's initial seductive letter to Charlotte, which Rowson's narrator censors, is a love letter from mother to daughter, written in anticipation of the girl's birthday, the anniversary of their bond. Scholars have argued that Rowson's narrator suppresses Montraville's dangerous letter from representation in order to protect the female audience from corruption by illicit correspondence, asserting that Rowson's narrator intervenes with her own moralizing discourse to redirect the lesson and thus to educate the audience in the ways of virtue.[47]

While this reading is congruent with the traditional interpretation of the novel as a didactic fable for young women in the new republic, it overlooks the way in which the letters Rowson actually represents in their entirety communicate an important message about proper forms of love. In the epistolary discourse of *Charlotte Temple*, mother-daughter longing stands in for adult heterosexual desire not because sexuality is necessarily incongruent with virtue but, rather, because the reciprocal yearnings of mother and daughter represent desire in its purest state. "Mothers are the *best* lovers in the world,"[48] asserts Jo March in Louisa May Alcott's *Little Women;* a male lover would be hard-pressed to replicate, much less outdo, such "monogamous" devotion on the part of a maternal object. Written eighty years after the publication of *Charlotte Temple*, Alcott's novel aptly reprises the affective atmosphere of Rowson's fictional universe and speaks to a recurring maternal homosocial dynamic at the heart of the American sentimental form.

Unfolded in sequence, the major letters Rowson represents within her fictional universe constitute a précis of the novel's affective core—its mother-daughter love story *manqué*. The four remaining missives that constitute the embedded epistolary discourse of *Charlotte Temple*, letters that Rowson allows to reach their destinations within the novel world and actually includes within the narrative, ring variations on the theme of appropriate and unfortunate attachments, Mrs. Temple's central subject in her first letter. The second epistle, an anonymous note to the headmistress of Charlotte's school announcing the young woman's elopement, can be read as a (purported) filial proclamation of divorce from parental authority; tellingly, the writer attests to the virgin's consent in the matter, but the sentiment is ventriloquized—the message bears no signature. At this unlikely moment, the bonds of surrogate maternity are conjured: Charlotte is declared to be in the "safe" company of Mlle La Rue. Male instruments come second in the great chain of culpability when females with perverse notions of nurture act as agents of corruption and set their sights on ingenuous young women.

Subsequent letters reiterate a distinctly nonsexual thematic: Montraville, having met a more socially suitable and virtuous woman in New York City, rejects Charlotte in a letter that codes his infatuation with her as a fatigue that she mistook for the fever that is passion. As a maternal proxy, the inconstant Montraville proves treacherous substitute. In the next embedded epistle, which follows almost immediately on the heels of Montraville's repudiation, Charlotte pens a love letter of farewell to her mother. We can infer from the association of these two letters that for Charlotte, Montraville's presence and significance in her life have had less to do with his sexual allure than with his ability to play—however briefly—the role of maternal stand-in. Charlotte's final communication mirrors in abject form Mrs. Temple's initial letter to her daughter; in what must be seen as her oath of filial fidelity to the maternal bond, Charlotte asserts of her elopement "even then I loved you most" (83).

The final embedded letter of the novel, written by an utterly wretched Charlotte who, sick, hungry, and pregnant, turns to the now well-married La Rue for charity, bespeaks the depth of daughterly desire for maternal comfort. Charlotte alludes to their former life in England as if they shared a "native land," eliding La Rue's French origin to emphasize a natal bond that exists only at the level of wish fulfillment. In this plaintive missive, the ruined woman begs La Rue not to allow her to remain succorless, or, in psychological terms, to be fatally separate: she writes that she has "no where . . . wherewith to supply the wants of nature" (115–16).

Charlotte's epistolary imprecation to La Rue, which is met by the latter's utter disavowal of any previous connection, sets the scene for a necessary generic leap; if the medium of the letter—formal, distanced, disembodied—fails to achieve full presence in communicating the message of filial agony, then a different and more transparent expressive mode is required.[49] The privatized realm of epistolary exchange must be supplanted by a more public, visceral communicative mode—the spectacular acting out that Peter Brooks has identified as melodrama.[50]

Enacted in the final portion of the novel, the heroine's histrionic supplication of her evil antagonist marks only the most sensational staging of theatrical expression in Rowson's book. One could argue, in fact, that melodramatic formations—of character, of action, of villainy, of closure—haunt the discourse of realism that ostensibly organizes *Charlotte Temple*. Spectacular drama surfaces most obviously in the embedded story of Charlotte's maternal grandparents: the Eldridge family's involvement with an evil libertine who, enraged over his failure to seduce daughter Lucy, singlehandedly bankrupts the father, sending him to debtor's prison, and engages the son in a fatal duel. This catastrophe precipitates the unexpected demise of Mrs. Eldridge, who suffers a fatal collapse into grief over the loss of her son and the arrest and removal of her husband.

Derived directly from the conventional plots of eighteenth-century melodrama, the heart-wrenching history of the Eldridges is not only fit for, but no doubt was inspired by, productions from the very stage on which Rowson herself performed. It is no wonder that, in resisting Montraville's initial advances, Charlotte regales him with a spectacular image of the wholesale destruction of her loved ones; to indulge her sexual desire would be to inaugurate nothing less than a familial apocalypse. Conceiving of experience in exclusively melodramatic terms, Charlotte oscillates between the wish to act out the prescriptions of a conduct manual for virtuous behavior and the fear that any deviation from such comportment will involve her in the depravity of a lurid dramatic tableau. In the latter scenario, her gratification of sensual pleasure spells doom for the family that cherished her; piled in a gothic heap of bodies on the stage of her adolescent imagination, the Temples must atone for Charlotte's guilty career.

Far more interesting than the histrionic fantasies of this fifteen-year-old protagonist are the ways in which La Rue manipulates the very cultural script of the seduced and abandoned woman within which Rowson herself is working and from which *Charlotte Temple* marks a subtle dissent. Both Charlotte and La Rue's prospective husband, Col. Crayton, make up the credulous audience for La Rue's manipulations of melodramatic self-presentation. The cunning French teacher has staged her own life story as a potential drama of ruined womanhood to evoke the compliance of Charlotte before their mutual elopement and to provoke Col. Crayton's proposal of marriage. In the latter episode, La Rue fabricates a narrative of sexual ruin at the hands of Belcour, who she claims had seduced her from her friends with a promise of marriage and afterward betrayed her. La Rue has effectively recycled her own autobiography in the service of her ambition;[51] with a protean gift for dissimulation worthy of a professional actress, she recreates herself in the role of virtuous heroine wavering precariously on the precipice of imminent ruin.

In Charlotte's penultimate scene of distress, with the now richly married La Rue as her audience, the dying girl uncannily enacts the abject fate of the seduced and abandoned woman that La Rue had conjured in her own, earlier histrionic self-portrait; the heroine *incarnates* in transparent and primitive form what was for La Rue a merely fantastic narrative of true womanhood become wretched. Though utterly heartfelt in its sincerity and unexaggerated in its form, Charlotte's staging of anguish before La Rue remains absolutely spectacular: rushing past a host of servants ordered to bar her entry, clasping her hands, on bended knee, accompanied by floods of tears, the ruined girl entreats her evil mentor to have motherly mercy on her and then falls senseless onto the floor. So affecting to all but her former teacher is Charlotte's supplication of the hardened heart that even La Rue's self-interested young paramour is moved to sympathize with Charlotte; in this young soldier, Rowson encodes a figure for the most resisting male reader, who cannot help responding with sympathy in the face of Charlotte's plight.

Devoid of the "natural compassion" Rousseau identifies as the basic quality of human beings in the state of nature, where people live as equals and communicate face to face, La Rue animates the notion that social exchange is an artful performance rather than a transparent channel for the transmission of authentic feeling.[52] Her apparent insensibility to Charlotte's suffering underscores the irony of Rousseau's distinction between the pity of savages and the unfeelingness of civilized beings,[53] the idea that compassion is "so natural, that the very brutes themselves sometimes give evident proofs of it. Not to mention the tenderness of mothers for their offspring, and the perils they encounter to save them from danger, it is well known that horses show a reluctance to trample on living bodies."[54] Rousseau goes on to relate the parable from Mandeville's *The Fable of the Bees*, which scholars of sentimentalism in American literature take as a proof-text for the workings of the genre,[55] Mandeville's

> pathetic description of a man who, from a place of confinement, is compelled to behold a wild beast tear a child from the arms of its mother, grinding its tender limbs with its murderous teeth, and tearing its palpitating entrails with its claws. What horrid agitation must not the eye-

witness of such a scene experience, although he would not be personally concerned! What anguish would he not suffer at not being able to give any assistance to the fainting mother and the dying infant.[56]

This tableau of visual identification and corporeal powerlessness, borrowed from Mandeville in what is itself a fascinating rehearsal of writerly sympathy, constitutes a haunting recapitulation of the melodramatic scene from *Charlotte Temple* in which the heroine simultaneously plays the role of prisoner, mother, and infant to La Rue's devouring beast.[57]

The villainess also resembles the spectator from Diderot's *Le Paradoxe sur le comedien* who has, in the words of Marshall, "forgotten theater"—lost the ability to believe that representations of sensibility bear any relation to genuine emotional states.[58] The depraved Frenchwoman gives life to Rousseau's idea that professional actresses prostitute themselves by trafficking in dissimulation; claiming that they seduce the public for money, he argues that women on stage are themselves inured against experiencing real compassion.[59] The philosopher could be proposing the etiology of La Rue's particular corruption when, in his earlier description of the inherent theatricality of the world beyond the state of nature, he writes:

> It now became the interest of men to appear what they really were not. To be and to seem became two totally different things; and from this distinction sprang insolent pomp and cheating trickery.[60]

He goes on to contend that man

> must be sly and artful in his behaviour to some, and imperious and cruel to others; being under a kind of necessity to ill-use all the persons of whom he stood in need, when he could not frighten them into compliance, and did not judge it his interest to be useful to them. Insatiable ambition, the thirst of raising their respective fortunes, not so much from real want as from the desire to surpass others, inspired all men with a vile propensity to injure one another, and with a secret jealousy, which is the more dangerous, as it puts on the mask of benevolence, to carry its point with greater security.[61]

As a figure of sheer art—partaking of no *human* nature—La Rue is the most "social" creature in *Charlotte Temple,* incarnating what is for both Rousseau and for Rowson the gothic product of late-eighteenth-century "civilization." Driven by overweening ambition and insatiable greed, Rowson's Frenchwoman could have been lifted from the pages of the "Discourse on the Origins of Inequality": her history reflects Rousseau's assertion that "the destruction of equality was attended by the most terrible disorders. Usurpations by the rich, robbery by the poor, and the unbridled passions of both, suppressed the cries of natural compassion and the still feeble voice of justice" (87).

If the plaint of genuine sympathy and the tones of righteousness make an appearance in *Charlotte Temple,* they are not to be found in the accents of the implacable La Rue but, rather, in the narrator's vocal effusions, which in the imaginative world of Rowson's novel serve as the phantasmagoric source of potential plenitude. By identifying fictive voice as *Charlotte Temple*'s point of emotional origin, we can better understand why the heroine's epistolary and melodramatic efforts within the story miscarry so disastrously and thus require supplementation by more transparent forms of communication. Both the distance of the heroine's letter *and* the relative proximity of her embodied performance of suffering fail to move La Rue because, as an utterly theatrical being, she is unwilling to believe in the interiority—the genuine affective reality—of others.

In shifting from epistolary to dramatic display—from written to corporeal representation—Rowson expands the range of her imaginative address; when the stony La Rue refuses to function as a receptive audience for Charlotte's plight, the narrator opens her story to the more compassionate community of American colonists dwelling within the fictive frame, who come to stand for Rowson's readership itself. In doing so, she brings her mimesis closer to the plenitude of voice. In *Charlotte Temple*'s final generic leap from melodrama to the oral tradition—in which the heroine herself becomes a maternal fetish, the obsessive object of collective discussion and desire— characters who functioned as failed surrogate mothers for the heroine take on the role of intratextual stand ins for the greater audience. Both Mrs. Beauchamp (Charlotte's only New World friend, whose necessary absence from the neighborhood has left the girl abandoned in extremis) and Montraville himself (returned from his honeymoon just in time to witness inadvertently the conclusion of Charlotte's interment) become auditors of the oral legend of Charlotte that has sprung up during her final illness and following her death. Reappearing too late to save the dying penitent (Mrs. Beauchamp merely succeeds in easing the material circumstances of her demise), they can only give ear to the story of her noble spirit and, by so doing, be moved.

Shifting from the highly literary mode of epistolarity through the more embodied and visceral form of melodrama to the most primitive version of storytelling, the legend that is transmitted by word of mouth, Rowson raises the account of Charlotte's fall to the level of myth *within the very imaginary world of her story.* Transmitted by medical professionals, soldiers, servants, and the working poor to their social superiors in the novel, the internal legend of Charlotte Temple is powerful enough to cross the boundaries of class and to affect a heterogeneous early American audience.

In the most forceful example of the workings of *Charlotte Temple's* internal oral tradition, a surgeon brought to the hovel where Charlotte lies dying divines the symbolic significance of the suffering he has witnessed. "Determined to make her situation known to some of the officers' ladies," [the surgeon] "told his *little pathetic* tale" [to Mrs. Beauchamp] (123, my emphasis). Neither doctor nor neighbor has any clue as to the identity of the suffering young woman. Yet the surgeon's little tale of pathos is of such a dimension that it inspires the following response: "'[W]here is she, Sir? we will go to her immediately. Heaven forbid that I should be deaf to the calls of humanity. Come, we will go this instant.' Then seizing the doctor's arm, they sought the habitation that contained the dying Charlotte" (123). It is as if Charlotte has become so emblematically potent, so excessively compelling in her need for nurture, that only the physical structure in which she lies expiring can keep her contained at a distance from saving care. Rowson has created a figure utterly innocent in her abjection and universally desirable to the sensible heart; thus, the heroine need not be recognized, known, or even seen to inspire compassion in those who hear her story, both inside the novel world and in the reading audience. The circulation of Charlotte's legend within the fictive universe of *Charlotte Temple* bears powerful witness to the way in which separation is the real villain of Rowson's piece.

In her act of framing the tale, Rowson's narrator attempts to contain her grief, to make it into a picture. Despite her herculean efforts to maintain control, that image will neither resolve into a final stasis nor move beyond its own all encompassing sorrow, an unresolved mourning that hints at a deeper rage. The career of genre in *Charlotte Temple* proves that movement itself constitutes no guarantee of closure in the work of grief; the stasis that is melancholia can be most treacherous and recalcitrant when disguised in dynamic form. *Charlotte Temple* is a story that oscillates between mourning and melancholia: written as a ritual of commemoration, it is a novel that cannot say farewell.

Working through and ultimately breaking the frame of her narrative,

Rowson's storyteller reaches out to her reader in order to defeat the theatrical relations that ordinarily obtain between a narrator and her audience; in so doing, she attempts to make real the Rousseauvian dream of transparency—a democratic relation between storyteller and reader that exists face to face. But the kind of failure to contain grief I have attempted to identify as existing between the framed and the framing narratives of *Charlotte Temple*—its affective leakage—suggests the extraordinary difficulty underlying imaginative realization of this egalitarian impulse.

It is, oddly enough, in the world of history that *Charlotte Temple*'s most utopian effects take material form. Davidson, Douglas, and Eva Cherniavsky have discussed the way in which actual Americans in the Victorian era reach, as it were, back through the frame of the novel in their fetishistic desire to commune with Charlotte Temple, thereby reproducing in reverse the narrator's impulses to bring the reader into the fiction.[62] These scholars argue that late into the nineteenth century, devoted readers of *Charlotte Temple* made pilgrimages to a gravestone in Trinity Churchyard in New York City to tend the burial site of a woman they believed to be the actual Charlotte Temple. Historians have maintained that no such real-life Charlotte lies buried there (the marker is a monument covering no actual grave) and that the hagiography and reliquy surrounding *this* Charlotte testify only to the novel's power to arouse the grief and sympathy of a loving audience decades beyond its initial publication. In this regard, the narrator's desire to incarnate filial sympathy is utterly successful, for we can read these pilgrimages as part of the mourning process, a working-through *beyond* the frame, at the level of real life, of a grief that was originally only imaginative.

But, perhaps, being unwilling or unable to let go is just the point. Registering the limitations of fictive wish fulfillment as a space for reparative working-through, the complex narratology of *Charlotte Temple* also attests to what we might term the *psychic realism* of the sentimental form. It is in Hannah Foster's *The Coquette* that the gothic underbelly of this novel of feeling, the subtext that *Charlotte Temple* adumbrates in its fleeting vision of maternal gore and narratorial rage, will reach full representation; written in the wake of Rowson's book, the latter novel offers a definitive dissent from *Charlotte Temple*'s idealized—if clouded—vision of a democratic community of compassion. Without the mediation of an intrusive narrator, *The Coquette* stands in paradoxical relation to *Charlotte Temple*'s fantasy of vocal plentitude and the dream of sympathy it conjures; predicated on the quasi-embodied texture of writing rather than the phantasmagoric embrace of pure voice—a vision that points to modernity rather than to a past that is tragically lost—*The Coquette* offers bitter insights about the limits of female agency that in *Charlotte Temple* remain relatively sub-rosa. In that regard, when it comes to the representation of female losses, a narrator's inconsolable sorrow may be all that stands between an author's rage and her audience. The history of reader response to *Charlotte Temple* would suggest that female devotees of the novel, far from being overwhelmed by the grief it exhibits or repulsed by the rage and maternal violence that it cannot quite contain, are deeply attuned to and identified with both.

Engraving of the famed late eighteenth-century horse "Cornplanter" from Ricketts' Circus. (Courtesy the Newberry Library)

CHAPTER THREE

Beyond "A Play about Words": Tyrannies of Voice in *The Coquette*

In *Charlotte Temple,* Susanna Rowson attempts to extend the franchise of fellow feeling to every member of her audience endowed with an understanding heart. Those who dwell outside the circle of literacy may be excluded from direct access to her story, but, like the fictive auditors who hear the legend of Charlotte's demise inside Rowson's narrative, the illiterate members of the public can receive its healing benefits as the tale passes orally from reader to listener well into the nineteenth century. This image of an audience whose numbers are infinitely expandable provides a compelling fantasy of cultural cohesion, the dream of a protodemocratic model for the nation as a capacious and ultimately compassionate body. The power of transparent sympathy, eighteenth-century American fiction's abiding subject, reaches its idealized apogee in Rowson's book, despite the darkening effects of the narrator's melancholia. Indeed, its peculiar Anglo-American genealogy and extraordinary history of reception constitute a fitting analogue for the work of cultural translation and accommodation that the early novel performs in the new republic. But fellow feeling in *Charlotte Temple* comes at great emotional cost, adumbrated in those currents of violence and rage simmering under the story, as well as in the heroine's psychotic delusions, which actually boil through the surface. In the works that follow *Charlotte Temple,* sympathy suffers an even more overtly gothic fate. We need only attend to a subsequent story of seduction and abandonment, Hannah Webster Foster's 1797 epistolary novel *The Coquette*,[1] to trace the continued unraveling of fellow feeling in the final years of the century.

Foster encapsulates *The Coquette's* most pertinent cultural themes in two evocative spectacles of leisure enjoyed by the privileged cohort of genteel republicans who constitute her dramatis personae; these emblematic tableaux refract in miniature the tragic double vision with which the author imagines the paradoxical nature and limits of liberty in post-Revolutionary America. The first scene involves a heated drawing-room debate in which members of both sexes argue the merits of female interest in the public sphere; in the course of this passage, one woman expropriates the voice of her ordinarily outspoken female companion in order to draw conclusions about the circumscribed prospects for women's political agency in the new nation. This episode, much commented on by recent scholars of the novel, pits dramatic against civic discourse but at the same time reveals that, from the moment of the Founding and into the Federalist period and beyond, politics function as America's primary form of national theater.

Unaccountably ignored by Foster's critics, the second tableau exposes the political underpinnings of theatrical expression itself. In this later episode, the female spokesperson of the republican chorus—the cohort of patriarchal women and men of feeling who constitute the heroine's community—unleashes a tirade against several types of public entertainment found in Boston in the mid-1790s. The objects of Lucy Freeman Sumner's moral indignation include a performance of Shakespearian tragedy and the self-display of female equestrians in the early national circus; in vivid contrast, Bowen's Museum, which exhibits wax effigies of prominent public figures of the late-eighteenth-century Anglo- and Franco-American world, receives her heartfelt endorsement.

Each of these tableaux foregrounds theatricality as a forum in which rival notions of fellow feeling vie for ascendancy in the new republic. Such clashing discourses of sympathy reflect the political divisions plaguing early national culture in the 1790s, as well as the attendant notions of sociality such competing visions suggest. The dominant mode of compassion the novel represents is connected to republican ideology and its constitutive components: the centrality of the community rather than of the individual, the idea of a material self-sufficiency that enables the transcendence of personal "interest," and a belief in collective sacrifice for the sake of the greater good. An exclusively public principle, such sympathy works along the lines René Girard elaborates in *Violence and the Sacred:* the cohesion of the republican community is predicated on the reality—indeed, the necessity—of a certain form of violence. Any individual who threatens the integrity of the group must be expelled in order to guarantee the hygienic purity and virtue of the collective.[2] We can identify this version of compassion with the practices of the feminized patriarchal chorus led by Lucy Freeman Sumner, the moral majority that controls the workings of the social milieu Foster's novel explores in detail.

The other form of sympathy *The Coquette* reveals to its readers commands far less influence among the fictive population and is related to then-emerging liberal modes of thought and their central tenets: a focus on the autonomous individual, the dedicated pursuit of economic advantage, and an understanding of the commonweal predicated on the well-being of solitary citizens. Such compassion is entirely a private matter; in this protoliberal version of fellow feeling, mutual understanding unfolds between independent persons who experience the social world largely as free agents rather than as members bound in collective relation. Following the schema outlined by Adam Smith in his *Theory of Moral Sentiments,* such sympathy arises only when one is able to envision taking another's place in order to feel his or her part.[3] Such imaginative extension of humanity involves the exercise of the mind as well as the heart and requires that individuals function as mirrors of compassion for their suffering fellows. That Foster's fiercely independent heroine Eliza Wharton is the only character in the novel who exercises this version of sympathy is precisely the fact that spells her doom: in the absence of an empathic respondent to reflect much-needed compassion, this female practitioner of protoliberal fellowship remains ideologically isolated, socially invisible, and emotionally erased.[4]

While both republican and protoliberal notions of sympathy provide important touchstones for describing the cultural conflicts that underwrite Foster's book, it is crucial to emphasize that the politics of her novel do not unfold in dualistic fashion but, instead, are intricately knotted. By employing manichean methods of historical analysis in their readings, recent critics who attempt to secure the political meaning of *The Coquette* reduce the richness of its narrative. Scholars have located the significance of the novel as an artifact of the early national period in a manner that reprises the rigidly factional

language and thought of the 1790s. One camp attempts to assert the congruence of Foster's book with the republican tradition of civic humanism that
persists through the last decade of the eighteenth century. Historians and
literary critics alike have entered these debates. Arguing that the novel
upholds the conservative values of republicanism, scholars read Eliza's seduction as a parable of liberty losing her virtue in the face of aristocratic
temptation. Linda Kerber, for example, sees Foster imparting a warning
(ironically, in the form of a novel) against women's novel reading. Claire C.
Pettengill interprets Eliza's fall in terms of her failure to practice the values
of "sisterhood in a separate sphere"; she identifies in this network of female
friendship an ideological contradiction: sisterhood serves a conservative
social purpose by limiting women to the roles of "republican wives" (Jan
Lewis's term) and "republican mothers" (Linda Kerber's), and it simultaneously performs a more progressive, perhaps even protofeminist function by
placing ultimate value on women's experience.

The other group seeks to demonstrate the novel's affinities with an
emerging liberalism that will come to characterize the early nineteenth century. Davidson links Eliza's quest for freedom with Wollstonecraftian notions of female equality, and Smith-Rosenberg sees in Eliza's dilemma the
individualism that struggles in the late eighteenth century to break free of
conservative republican notions of virtue, which reprobates self-interested
economic activities and relentlessly promotes the public good. This bifurcated debate about the political identity of Foster's book recapitulates on literary grounds the very dualism that divides the historians who write about
the early national period.[5] Indeed, the interpretive controversies provoked by
both the fiction and the politics of the Federalist era themselves point to and
replay the decade's most decided dynamic: its inability to tolerate conflict,
opposition, difference of any kind and its tendency to reprobate any such
impulses as factional, Federalist code for what is unspeakable about the nature of the political process itself.[6]

This dominant impulse to demonstrate that *The Coquette* embodies either republican or liberal tenets actually forecloses our understanding of the
cultural import of the book. Instead, we might consider the ways in which
Foster's imagination is entangled in a form of political double vision, reen-
acting the very paradoxes such ideological conflict invariably generates.[7]
Within the boundaries of Foster's imaginative world, an increasingly ossified and inward-turning Federalist elite struggles to maintain its hegemony
against the incursion of a rising oppositional force, personified in two eco-

nomically ambitious individuals who do not conform to the conventions or fully embrace the values that have kept the republican circle both potent and closed. But, far from functioning as a piece of ideological propaganda in the factional wars of the 1790s, *The Coquette* refuses to choose sides; instead, it localizes the losses that such divisions produce in its depiction of the spectacular disappearance of a transgressive female voice. In doing so, the novel stages the struggle between what Raymond Williams has called a "dominant" (republican political) and an "emerging" (liberal economic) culture[8]—not only revealing the tangled relations that obtain between republicanism and protoliberalism but also complicating, if not collapsing, the false dualism of such accounts.

Eliza Wharton's protoliberal impulses are ultimately stillborn and her rebellious nature recontained because she cannot imagine a life beyond the very republican cohort that would stifle and bury alive her powerful desire for freedom. Foster's narrative form—the novel's dialectical expression and erasure of the female voice—reflects and replays this fact. The heroine's tragedy finally involves her failure to function as the sympathetic spectator of her own plight. When Eliza can no longer provide the mirror of compassion *for herself*, once she loses the capacity to see her dissent from the majority's tyranny as a valid desire, her interpellation into the ideology of republican fellow feeling becomes complete. Eliza moves from serving as the object of collective scrutiny to playing the victim in a public sacrifice; in the final ironic twist of her unhappy fate, the heroine orchestrates her own violent expulsion from the community. This act of self-immolation enables the female chorus to reconsolidate its hegemony over her recently buried corpse in gothically literal fashion. Indeed, as Eva Cherniavsky remarks, Eliza's "fall reintegrates [this] disembodied body as a body of mourners, which forms again around the locus of an absence, (re)assembles around a grave."[9] Having incorporated the majority's values as her valedictory act, the heroine offers her life in exchange for a sympathy that can exist for her only in theory precisely because it is predicated on her expedient demise. Eliza's death thus takes on a redemptive, if not a transformative, power for the feminized chorus. Renewed and reconstituted by the tragedy, the community must continue to disavow the transgressive reality of the pleasure, possibility, and imaginative freedom afforded them by Eliza Wharton's life and letters. In the ultimate transaction of republican sympathy, neatly mystified in the chorus's exorbitant exhibition of grief, the heroine proves more valuable to her peers as a fetishized corpse than she has as an animated and exuberant friend.

Faction and Tyrannical Majority

In a scene that foregrounds the preoccupation in the early republic with who shall possess political voice, Foster pits the world of theater against the realm of politics:

> The general topic of conversation . . . was politics. Mrs. Richman and Miss Wharton judiciously, yet modestly, bore a part; while the other ladies amused themselves with Major Sanford, who was making his sage remarks on the play, which he held in his hand. General Richman at length observed that we had formed into parties. Major Sanford, upon this, laid aside his book. Miss Laurence simpered; and looked as if she was well pleased with being in a party with so fine a man; while her mother replied, that she never meddled with politics; she thought they did not belong to ladies. Miss Wharton and I, said Mrs. Richman, must beg leave to differ from you, madam. We think ourselves interested in the welfare and prosperity of our country; and consequently, claim the right of inquiring into those affairs, which may conduce to, or interfere with the common weal. We shall not be called to the senate or the field to assert its privileges, and defend its rights, but we shall feel for the honor and safety of our friends and connections, who are thus employed. If the community flourish and enjoy health and freedom, shall we not share in the happy effects? If it be oppressed and disturbed, shall we not endure our proportion of the evil? Why then should the love of our country be a masculine passion only? Why should government, which involves the peace and order of the society, of which we are a part, be wholly excluded from our observation?[10]

In this incident, the characteristically vocal heroine of *The Coquette* is curiously silent. Stifled at the center of this scene is Eliza Wharton, who is given body in Selby's epistolary tableau but deprived of the voice we have come to identify as the most eloquent and imaginative force in Foster's novel. More precisely, during a conversation about the proper relationship between American women and the political realm, an exchange in which she is alleged to bear "a part," Eliza Wharton does not speak for herself but instead is spoken for. Women's speech emanates from the centrally embedded narrative core of this letter, but it is framed and recast at multiple removes.

Mr. Selby omits whatever Eliza might have expressed about politics in his missive reconstructing the tableau for Boyer; he effectively reports that she has "judiciously, yet modestly," borne a part in this conversation and then censors her contribution in an act of nonrepresentation. What he chooses to depict is the point at which another woman determines to *vocalize for Eliza,* the moment when Mrs. Richman takes it on herself to *speak representatively* for a fellow member of the female sex. The enunciatory complexity of the episode comes full circle as Mr. Selby relays Mrs. Richman's speech in his written account of the incident, thus inscribing an act of ventriloquism by turning oral expression into epistolarity. Significantly, it is a male voice (in the letter form, a male signature) that unfolds this scene of vocal cooptation within the female community through a transvestite mode of narrative. Foster, the female author, cloaks herself in the persona of Selby, a male correspondent who does surveillance by proxy for the Reverend Mr. Boyer, Eliza's straightlaced suitor. In his epistolary report to Boyer, Selby relays the dialogue of General Richman, Mrs. Laurence, and Mrs. Richman with a narrative ease that masks the intricate expressive dynamics that have given rise to his writing.

The episode brings into focus issues central to the political debates unfolding in the decade after the Founding: the dilemma of which voices shall be enfranchised and questions about the nature of representation itself. Translated into the fictive terms of *The Coquette,* such concerns become an inquiry into the workings of narrative transmission: Why does Foster choose to dramatize this charged discussion of female political agency in the words of a masculine correspondent? Why does she deputize a male persona to filter the exchange through reported speech, a stylistic maneuver that deprives Mrs. Richman of immediate expression? Why is it that, within the mimesis, Mrs. Richman does not utter her opinions on her own but elects to appropriate the words of her ordinarily outspoken friend in order to enter into the conversation at all? And, finally, why is Eliza Wharton rendered silent in a scene that foregrounds women's articulation as a form of political action?

Such instances of the dislocation and suppression of women's political voices haunt *The Coquette,* extending from Eliza's mysterious silence and Mrs. Richman's vocal appropriation within the fictive world to Mr. Selby's epistolary repetition of her gesture and Foster's own transvestism at the level of narrative. The dynamics of this scene anticipate and rehearse the way in which the novel's patriarchal majority, figures who regardless of gender employ a characteristic feminized discourse, annex women's language in order to promote civic values—at the same time foreclosing on any possibility for emerging liberal sympathy. This emblematic appropriation and erasure of female speech at the moment of enunciation, what Eve Sedgwick would call the "live burial" of the female voice,[11] functions not only as the defining principle of *The Coquette*'s narrative form. In fact, the gothicization of women's expression is Foster's very subject.

This inaugural moment of expressive displacement in which one female opinion and the subjectivity for which it stands is rendered unspeakable by the force of another woman's words is symbolic of *The Coquette*'s deepest concerns, all of which reflect issues that trouble the Federalist era: a preoccupation with the dangers of factions, depicted in Foster's narrative as the threat that dissenting (female) voices could take on coherent form; a fascination with spectacle, played out in the novel's collapsing of politics and theatricality; the insistent fetishization of powerful figures, enacted here through an insidious process of substitution by which characters displace and ultimately replace each other; and the abjuration of the violence from which the virtuous republican community is born, dramatized within *The Coquette* by an utter disavowal of the brutality that underwrites the novel's own feminized performance of republican sympathy.

Linking these claims about the gothicization of women's expression to such Federalist concerns is the potent force of patriarchal repression, which makes alternative modes of knowledge or being unspeakable. If faction is a dynamic that identifies dissension at the very moment of attempting to oppose it in the social body, then to be hostile to faction is to attempt to deny the fact that such conflict always already exists. Theatricality, as Rousseau observes, substitutes artifice for sincerity in social exchange, obscuring the transparent relations that mark protodemocratic culture. Fetishism puts into practice the impulse to disavow the reality of human and particularly male insufficiency. By projecting the perception of absence onto those female or feminized bodies that exist in contiguous relation to masculine lack, fetishists seek to ward off their own experiences of painful deficiency by attributing such incompletion to those persons they construct as "other."

In that regard, fetishism is not unrelated to the republican vision of fellow feeling elaborated in *The Coquette*. Such sympathy itself simultaneously depends on and must bury its constitutive relationship to violence—the way in which intense, often destructive actions or forces make possible an affinity between people that inclines them to think and feel alike. Although this characterization of republican compassion would seem to evoke exactly the dynamic that *Charlotte Temple*'s narrator exploits in her problematic but profoundly democratic zeal to forge transparent relations with the audience, there is a vital difference between Rowson's vision of collective fellow feeling and the spurious sympathetic impulses at work in *The Coquette*. As I shall show in the following discussion, the narrow-minded Federalist community is the unacknowledged agent of the violence that Eliza Wharton ultimately internalizes in *The Coquette*. Far from enabling the social inclusion of those outside the majority's purview, the sacrifice of Eliza empowers the community to reaffirm its elitist values. The fear of faction, the compulsion to fetishize, and the repression of the link between violence and sympathy all inflect the narrative manner of Foster's book, contributing to its intricate, underexplored poetics and politics of form.

While the language of *The Coquette*'s outspoken heroine is met with a reception that images live burial, the voices of the novel's dead father figures—both of them ministers—refuse to remain interred. Instead, the moral vocabulary of these patriarchs uncannily rematerializes, channeling itself through two different forums: the predictable conduit of men of rank and authority (the Reverend Mr. Boyer and General Richman) and the unlikely avenue of the novel's female chorus, a far less obvious medium (Mrs. Richman, Lucy Freeman Sumner, Mrs. Wharton, and Julia Granby). This collaboration between a decorous minister and a cohort of articulate, middle-class, female epistolarians constitutes a veritable proof text of the alliance Ann Douglas charts in *The Feminization of American Culture* between a "disestablished" clergy and the genteel women of letters who come to public prominence in early nineteenth-century America.[12] Together, the voices deployed by men of feeling and women possessed of patriarchal values make up the feminized moral majority that dominates Foster's epistolary world.

The coercive aspect of that majority begins to show itself in an episode whose dynamics will recur compulsively as a kind of thematic and narrative template: this important passage, unfolding in the third letter Eliza pens to Lucy Freeman, in which she describes her resurrection from the world of the dead father, functions as the novel's primal scene of factional conflict. Eliza is brought back to social "life" during a visit to the Richmans' one month after the death of her fiancé, the minister Haly. Throwing "aside the habiliments of mourning" (8), she attends a festive assembly and at one point wanders from a group that is walking in the garden:

> An enthusiastic admirer of scenes like these, I had rambled away from some of the company, when I was followed by Mrs. Laiton to offer her condolence on the supposed loss, which I had sustained, in the death of

Mr. Haly. My heart rose against the woman, so ignorant of human nature, as to think such conversation acceptable at such a time. I made her little reply, and waved the subject, though I could not immediately dispel the gloom which it excited.

The absurdity of a custom, authorizing people at a first interview to revive the idea of griefs, which time has lulled, perhaps obliterated, is intolerable. To have our enjoyments arrested by the empty compliments of unthinking persons, for no other reason, than a compliance with fashion is to be treated in a manner, which the laws of humanity forbid.

We were soon joined by the gentlemen, who each selected his partner, and the walked was prolonged.

Mr. Boyer offered me his arm, which I gladly accepted; happy to be relieved from the impertinence of my female companion. (9)

Crucial aspects of this episode suggest that what might seem a trivial social exchange in fact portends with remarkable accuracy the heroine's larger struggle against the social values of her culture, particularly as they are brought to bear on unmarried women.

Eliza's description of being overtaken with enthusiasm indicates that she exists anachronistically in an uncongenial cultural landscape: rather than blending decorously into the Augustan scenery of post-Revolutionary Connecticut, she is more at home in the realm of heightened emotion, familiar with the sort of fervor that marks the Great Awakening—the repercussions of which are felt in the Connecticut River valley for decades after its initial eruption. That Eliza cannot require herself to remain with her cohort but instead "ramble[s] away from . . . the company" foreshadows her rejection of the conventional route prescribed for women; indeed, waywardness and eccentricity ultimately become her characteristic spatial patterns. But the social geometry that organizes this scene in fact suggests that Eliza's initial achievement of physical freedom, beginning with her escape from a marriage to Haly, may itself be an illusion, for no sooner does the heroine initiate her ramble than she is pursued and overtaken by Mrs. Laiton, self-deputized representative of surveillance and discipline, a one-woman panopticon, empowered by the patriarchal community to wield its scrutiny. While Frank Shuffelton argues that Foster's fictive community fails to keep up the brotherly watch, a seventeenth-century Puritan system in which moral guardianship takes the form of an interested supervision, his notion of the gaze and of the community is decidedly less Foucauldian—and thus, less ominous—than my own is here.[13]

Having appropriated the authority to invoke what (according to the conventions of polite eighteenth-century America) would be considered an indelicate subject, Mrs. Laiton makes a "supposition" about Eliza's loss of Mr. Haly that cuts two ways, each inflicting its own measure of brutality. According to Richard L. Bushman, "delicacy . . . meant the capacity for fine discriminations[,] . . . . required a sensitivity to human feelings, an exact discernment of the emotional effects of a word or an action, and a desire to protect people from every hurt. Delicacy forbade an individual to assert superiority or to degrade another."[14] Mrs. Laiton's indecorous locution could indicate that she believes in, imagines, or understands the probable certainty of Eliza's misfortune or, conversely, that she regards the heroine's grief as mistaken or only pretended. What maddens Eliza is the fact that this gesture of compassion masks the violence of the woman's real intentions, which are to reprove her for an inappropriately brief exhibition of mourning. That Mrs. Laiton should feel entitled to return Eliza to the inner scene of sorrow when the heroine has telegraphed through the semiotics of fashion (having thrown "aside the habiliments of mourning") that her grief has run its course is only slightly less offensive than the implication that Eliza has never lamented Haly's death at all.

In the indignant rebuttal she addresses to Lucy Freeman, the confidante who by the end of the novel will come to sound like Mrs. Laiton's proxy, Eliza reveals the umbrage she takes at Mrs. Laiton's unseemly overfamiliarity on first acquaintance. Particularly ironic is Eliza's counter reproach that the woman's remarks are empty and motivated by "no other reason, than a compliance with fashion"; indeed, supposed violations of social forms are precisely what move Mrs. Laiton to criticize Eliza. The older woman's observations may in fact be accurate, but the depth of Eliza's resentment suggests that more is at stake here than the sting of an impertinent if potentially incisive rebuke by a stranger. What makes this instance of female intrusiveness particularly disturbing to the heroine is its naggingly familiar quality. At issue is Eliza's disgusted aversion to functioning as public property, to being made "town talk" (99), a spectacle open to collective scrutiny rather than a voice whose opinions the community values.

Eliza's initial capacity to recognize the cadences of patriarchal social censure, the feminized voice of the majority, as it emanates from this individual and seemingly unfamiliar female body oddly fails to alert her to a more insidious reality: the possibility that collective opposition to her social "waywardness" might be channeled through the letters of women friends, figures who allege to feel compassion—to take Eliza's part—but who can neither understand nor in any way identify with her transgressive point of view. In that regard, the episode evokes the novel's central insight about the way in which social cohesion in this republican cohort depends on sacrifice. The ostensibly liberal claims of sympathy voiced by the chorus become the decorous veil under which collective pressure to make individuals conform does its violent work. In the social economy of the novel, Eliza's unwillingness to "pay" for small transactions such as the one with Mrs. Laiton does not go unaccounted for; instead, she begins to accrue another and more dangerous kind of debt at the larger level of communal exchange where being in arrears can spell certain disaster.

In the final movements of the scene, as in the closing pages of the novel itself, Eliza is rendered silent by a judgmental matron; soon after this, Mr. Boyer "relieve[s her] from the impertinence of [her] female companion." That Eliza could mistake the minister's act for deliverance from a disapproving woman peer becomes both her inaugural and her abiding mistake. Seeking to escape from the tyranny of social forms, she unwittingly rushes headlong into the arms of the novel's most ardent and brutal spokesman for propriety. This fantasy of rescue will devolve into the horror of recapitulation when, by the midpoint of the narrative, Mr. Boyer reveals his true identity as a facsimile of Mrs. Laiton, who is in turn a patriarchal conduit.

Boyer does not simply stand in for all the women who keep the voices of dead male authorities alive and circulating in *The Coquette*. He also reprises the novel's law of incestuous repetition, a principle inaugurated by Eliza's deceased fiancé, the minister Haly.[15] With a name that evokes astronomical recurrence, Haly himself reenacts the fate of the Reverend Mr. Wharton, Eliza's father, who had invited the ailing younger cleric to convalesce in his home before dying unexpectedly himself. Already a doppelgänger figure, Haly is not fated to be the last minister to appear on Eliza's romantic horizon and burn a path across her "volatile" emotional life. That is Boyer's role. Painfully conscious of the uncanny parallel between these men, Eliza writes to Lucy that Boyer's "conversation, so similar to what [she] had often heard from a similar character, brought a deceased friend to mind, and rendered [her] somewhat pensive" (12). The heroine's uncharacteristically thoughtful attitude here reveals more than a simple replaying of grief for the dead minister; it silently signals her fear of and resistance to the prospect of romantically venturing into the realm of (symbolic) death. Yet the fact of Boyer's familiarity is precisely what makes him a perfect candidate for the heroine's affections in the eyes of the community. In the fictive world of *The Coquette*, where the desire for social movement signifies a form of class betrayal, to stagnate in a "situation in life . . . as elevated" as that of a clergyman's wife is "perhaps" as much as Eliza has "a right to claim" (27).

Embodying in her "lively," "various," "wayward" self a principle at odds with what seems to be a male monopoly on morbidity and ossification, Eliza Wharton struggles to avert a marriage in which all appropriate prospects are clones of her deceased father. Such a union would guarantee self-immolation. Foster's plot, reduced to its most primitive form, turns around Eliza's attempt to bypass marriage to a living corpse so as to avoid becoming Mrs. Wharton. The link between such incestuous social impulses and the reproduction of mothering is the great unspoken subject of both *Charlotte Temple* and *The Coquette*. Charlotte goes wrong at precisely the moment she takes up Lucy Eldridge's own interrupted education; while the seduced and abandoned girl does not become *her own mother*, Rowson's heroine nevertheless becomes *a* mother, if only for a brief time. Charlotte's particular tragedy would seem to lie in her failure to assume Lucy Temple's mantle, but the narrator's figuration as a maternal voice that not only incorporates the audience but that is also incorporated by it[16] suggests something far more radical: that the most fruitful post-Revolutionary family relations—and the political structures they evoke—are inclusive and democratic.

Through epistolary humor—what her friend Lucy has demeaned as a "play about words" (31)—Eliza fancifully entertains the impulse to resist the incestuous pressures of the Federalist patriarchy in which she circulates, writing to Mrs. Richman, "My mamma is excessively partial to [Mr. Boyer]; though I am not yet jealous that she means to rival me. I am not certain, however, but it might be happy for him if she should. For I suspect, notwithstanding the disparity of her age, that she is better calculated to make him a good wife than I am or ever shall be" (68). Life with a clergyman threatens to replicate for Eliza her parents' narrow dependence on, and subtle subordination to, their parishioners in the Federalist gentry, and it imperils any prospect of her social transformation, which in the post-Revolutionary period hinges on economic mobility.[17]

The right to say no to a virtuous proposal of marriage, the prerogative of asserting a longing to remain romantically un-"connected" (13) while preserving social attachments, is the ultimate aim of the struggle for authentic female expression in *The Coquette*, a battle that the heroine eventually loses. At stake is the notion that claims for women's freedom are socially legitimate and not simply a "play about words" (31). Taken together, these issues speak to the problem—to the limits—of liberty in the Federalist era. Translated into the political language of the 1790s, Eliza's fate at the hands of the feminized majority becomes a potent metaphor for the tyranny of the many as they seek to annex or to crush the opposition of the few.[18]

The Coquette's recurring trope for conflict—a figure that explicitly links the internal dynamics of the novel with the workings of the larger Federalist world outside—is "parties" (7). Indeed, the narrative itself is constructed from letters that largely report on a round of visits, balls, and leisure-time occupations undertaken by a small group of privileged women and their male counterparts in post-Revolutionary New England. The action of Foster's book is predicated on an insistent sociability. Despite this fact, various correspondents from the feminized majority—particularly General and Mrs. Richman but also Mr. Boyer—imply that those characters wont to join gatherings "avowedly formed for pleasure" (14) are engaged in dangerous and conceivably transgressive activities. That Mrs. Richman invokes this phrase to condemn the association of only two characters in the novel—Eliza and her libertine suitor Major Sanford—is a social indictment freighted with political significance.

Carroll Smith-Rosenberg has eloquently explicated the way in which Eliza, against the reasoning of the novel's feminized chorus, seeks to link pleasure with a desire for independence and liberty; by doing so, Smith-Rosenberg argues, the heroine contradicts the majority's view that "virtue and happiness are tied to prudence and a socially appropriate marriage, that pleasure and fancy will endanger both."[19] In this light, Eliza's seeking to include herself in *parties* for pleasure takes on a figurative resonance; it implies that involvement in potentially decadent forms of social intercourse might itself become an act of political opposition. As a possible faction, the "party for pleasure" could constitute a space from which Eliza might resist the stifling precepts of her peers.

The passage we have chosen to begin our discussion (44) reenacts Foster's primal scene of faction (6) in a larger and more overtly political form and thus becomes a provocative site for thinking about how a "party for pleasure" might oppose the feminized majority in *The Coquette*. During the gathering at the Richmans', an apparent dichotomy opens between one group of female guests assembled around Major Sanford to discuss "the play" and another set of women who cluster beside General Richman to talk about "politics." At the manifest level of narrative, the division in the drawing room would seem to turn on what eighteenth-century theorists of faction identify as differences of interest rather than of principle—of social station rather than speculative precept; according to David Hume, whose work influenced the most important post-Revolutionary American thinkers writing about parties, such divergences are unavoidable in a free state but can be "adjust[ed] through compromise and thereby prevented from growing into irreconcilable divisions of principle."[20]

Major Sanford is aligned with the pleasure of theatricality and the Richmans with the business of politics; such a split follows logically from the social conflict that divides the novel's characters. In his visual composition of the scene, which he translates into epistolary form, Mr. Selby, the good Federalist, emphasizes dichotomy and inflects it with moral judgment: he pits the "judicious . . . modesty" of the women in General Richman's group against what he sarcastically characterizes as the "sage remarks" of Major Sanford, which are made for the purposes of mere "amuse[ment]." Depicted with play in hand, holding forth as if on stage himself, the libertine is captured in a moment of pure performance. According to the values of the feminized chorus, there can be no virtue in such activity. General Richman, whose military rank and social prestige make him Foster's fictional stand-in for George Washington, responds to the spectacle of the rake's theatricality by observing that the company "has formed into parties." He is undoubtedly provoked by the charismatic Sanford who, in his assumption of command over an admiring group of women, threatens to displace the general at the center of sociability. Under the guise of political humor, General Richman expresses an anxiety that is decidedly serious. Selby fails to record the tone in which the general condemns the formation of parties; nevertheless, we might infer from Major Sanford's response that General Richman implicitly has communicated his belief that faction involves differences of principle rather than of interest, that social division is utterly unacceptable. How else are we to understand the extraordinary fact that Major Sanford, who in an earlier letter to a fellow rake has boasted that he is "independent of [the Richmans'] censure or esteem" (35), does an abrupt swerve and, on the general's remark, lays down his book (44)?

What is the significance of Major Sanford's capitulation to the general's tacit demand for consensus? On the face of it, his response would seem simply a matter of good manners: General Richman, a military leader accustomed to dictating the comportment of his company, indicates displeasure over social divisions in his own drawing room, and Sanford, the aristocratic guest highly conscious of decorum, acts to smooth over the schism he has caused. But this account of the social dynamics at work in the scene does not fully explain its charged political atmosphere. What does it mean for theatricality to bow to politics? How does General Richman's objection to Major Sanford's activity obscure the role theatricality plays in his own orchestration and direction of social exchange? Are the arts of performance and of government really unrelated? Might not Major Sanford's gesture, itself a dramatic exhibition of gentility, also be seen as a calculated political maneuver? Indeed, as Sanford seeks to seduce the Richmans' houseguest Eliza, must he not defer to the General's wishes in order to maintain access to his intended victim? In the early stages of a sexual conquest, "theatrical" manners can be seen as a form of "political" strategy. The distinction General Richman seeks to make between the theatrical and the political, between dramatic spectacle and the deployment of power and authority, is one that Foster's novel ultimately will collapse. The Major Sanfords of this world always already exist *within* the confines of genteel culture.

By creating the parallel between Richman and Washington, Foster signals that her novel must be read in the context of its time. Even in 1796, a year before she published *The Coquette*, when James Madison becomes firm in his belief that the Federalist agenda is threatening to destroy the Founding principles of the new republic and thus that the "Republican interest . . . [is] the kind of opposition force that need[s] protecting," factionalism continued to be the dirty word of early national politics. Stanley Elkins and Eric McKitrick note that "in a revolutionary state such [opposition] parties do not emerge without severe resistance . . . and the uncertain future of the new republic, reared as it was upon revolution, was not the only factor that made for powerful inhibitions against the forming of parties. Such inhibitions were also supported by a whole system of political beliefs and doctrine that long antedated the Revolution, reaching well back into early eighteenth-century England, in which party and faction in any form were seen as disruptive, subversive, and wicked." The most outspoken opponent of factionalism in the Federalist period is Washington, who beyond any political leader of the era comes to personify a hatred of parties. According to Elkins and McKitrick, Washington, "the living symbol of nonpartisan politics, was an almost ideal republican embodiment of the Patriot-King," Bolingbroke's "transcendently benign ruler above petty considerations of party who could, without resorting to tyranny, subdue the spirit of party through wise and disinterested statecraft."[21]

Playing the role of exemplary father in the fictive world of *The Coquette*, General Richman resembles the first president, at the level of national fantasy. But if Foster's Richman represents Washington, he is not the man who in his first term of office is able to collapse and transcend all notions of difference and division in the political body. He is instead the Washington of the later 1790s, the Washington of the "Farewell Address," who both incarnates hostility to faction and, however unwittingly, functions as a partisan.[22] By depriving figures like Sanford of "sanctioned channels of expression," General Richman attempts to combat social contention, but, rather than arresting the potential challenge to his hegemony, the general's actions only serve to reroute it; opposition remains a furtive dynamic, simmering unspeakably under the surface of the Federalist period's gothic narrative of faction. When Eliza consummates her sexual relationship with Major Sanford under her mother's own roof, she acts out this gothic dynamic in transgressive form: the heroine's desecration of domesticity proves that "furtive, pent-up and vicious" oppositional energy never simply dies but, rather, always returns with a vengeance.[23]

Though temporarily silenced, Major Sanford is actually the beneficiary of his transaction with the general; for despite the fact that the Richmans already have identified the libertine as an oppositional threat to their genteel society,[24] the couple cannot utterly exclude him from their circle. Foster provides two subsequent accounts of the general's concern over Major Sanford's ability to divide the company into factions and to make Eliza Wharton his partisan. The first comes in a letter Mr. Selby writes to Boyer about the conduct of the woman he admires: "As I handed Miss Wharton in, [General Richman] observed jocosely, that she had changed company. Yes sir, she replied, more than once, as you doubtless observed. I was not aware, said Mrs. Richman, that Major Sanford was to be of your party today. It was quite accidental, madam, said Miss Wharton" (45). Then, in a letter penned shortly after Mr. Selby's deposition-like testimonial to the minister, Eliza recounts the incident herself, noting, "the General and his lady rallied me on my change of company" (51). The general's "jocose" observation about their houseguest's shifting allegiances, which his wife elaborates in more pointed form, telegraphs the pair's anxiety about the disreputable nature of the company she keeps. Yet, in both the reported dialogue and her own characterization of events, Eliza refuses to affirm any determined preference for Sanford—and thus for a commitment to *the* party for pleasure. Her straightforward response—her insistence on neutrality—which goes largely ignored by her interlocutors, indicates an ambition that is decidedly less ideological than partisan sentiment. Eliza's resistance to the general's moral judgment about parties comes in the interest of a freedom that has no specific object; what the heroine underscores is simply her wish for change, per se.

For dissent from the majority to take coherent form, passion and commitment must crystallize around a definitive goal. Such clarity of vision eludes Eliza for the entire course of the novel, marking as "wayward" (108) her ambivalent efforts to navigate the social pressures of her culture. The community, which is capable of comprehending conflict only according to a paradigm in which the evil powers of faction beset a virtuous majority, finds Eliza's unruliness disturbingly illegible. To protect against the threat to social cohesion posed by even the most indeterminate form of dissent, the community consolidates all opposition by identifying its origin in the transgressive body of Sanford; this calculated displacement temporarily protects the female members of the chorus from the prospect of fissures opening within their own ranks.

We can identify this impulse as a form of manichean allegory that seeks to locate conflict in external forces that can be demonized and thus made more manageable. In this very way, the struggles between the Federalists and members of the emerging Republican Party are largely played out in antagonisms over appropriate forms of international allegiance, the battles over whether the United States should embrace universal neutrality or invest in partisanship with either Britain or France during the wars of the French Revolution in the 1790s; Charles Brockden Brown will rehearse this dynamic in *Ormond*'s drama of hostile émigré neighbors. While postcolonial theorists use the vocabulary of manichean allegory to describe practices of domination specific to the late nineteenth and early twentieth centuries and to the European subjection of India and Africa, it remains instructive for thinking through certain problems faced in the early American republic, which has itself only just emerged from the status of colonialized nation. Indeed, since the new nation's enfranchisement of its no-longer-monarchical subjects is limited to the bodies of white males, the paradigm is particularly evocative for thinking about how the dissent of women and Africans—not yet accorded the status of African *Americans*—could be figured by those "postcolonial" men who have simply assumed at the level of politics and law the structural position of their former colonial oppressors.[25] It is thus less the libertine's absolute power that ultimately compels Eliza into his embrace than the community's coercive insistence that all members with remotely opposi- tional views declare their allegiance to party.

Sanford's presence thrusts in the face of General Richman's virtuous co- hort a disturbing reality about the diversity of the post-Revolutionary social landscape; at the same time, the libertine serves as a target on which the community can project its collective indignation over differences of opinion and social practices that menace its coherence. Sanford thus facilitates the majority's compulsion to deny internal dissent no matter how amorphous its form. Dedicated to its own social reproduction, the feminized chorus is in- vested in supervising and disciplining marriageable women like Eliza Whar- ton in its own patterns of association. That such a republican daughter should seek to "change company" suggests a willingness to make unsanc- tioned forays into alien territory where the unlucky succumb to seduction and the more fortuitous, who marry above or below themselves, commit a form of class betrayal. The community's articulation of a fear of parties does not simply mark either an exercise of social vigilance or a display of repressive power; it exposes the majority's sense of collective vulnerability and consti- tutes a tacit acknowledgment that a party for pleasure is a force that always already exists within itself and with which it must begin to contend.

From the beginning of the novel, General Richman insists on identify- ing Eliza with a dissenting faction (14); yet the abiding refrain of the hero- ine's letters is one of resistance to all such classificatory incursions. Eliza em- braces neither the strident tones of a partisan nor the self-righteous moral complacency of the chorus. Instead, she traverses with full fluency—indeed with veritable polylinguality—multiple cultural discourses: her language is marked by both the prescriptive conduct-book tones of the feminized ma- jority and the transgressive wit of the outspoken woman, humor that borrows its figures from the masculine public sphere. Consider the following pas- sage, which typifies the post-Calvinist rhetoric of genteel eighteenth-century American Protestantism and in that regard is steeped in the language of the chorus: "He is gone. His fate is inalterably, and I trust, happily fixed. . . . This event will, I hope, make a suitable and abiding impression upon my mind; teach me the fading of all sublunary enjoyments and the little dependence which is to be placed on earthly felicity" (6). Indeed, removed from its origi- nal context, these lines easily could be mistaken for Mr. Boyer's. More precisely, this lamentation for the minister Haly resurrects from beyond the grave the austere tones of patriarchal benediction; by an extraordinary feat of cultural ventriloquism, it is as if the deceased is speaking for himself. As a representation of personal voice, uninflected by local or idiosyncratic elements, the passage erases any aspect of the individual signatory relation that ordinarily obtains between epistolary speaker and his or her speech act; instead, the statement achieves an authentically generic status. That it is Eliza Wharton who channels these sentiments in her opening letter eloquently reveals the ambivalent nature of her relationship with community. On the one hand, the declaration is an index of her allegiance to the values of her social milieu; on the other, her conscription of the hegemonic patriarchal voice operates in subtle distinction to the feminized majority's own deployment of such language. The chorus of women correspondents, Lucy Freeman (Sumner), Mrs. Richman, and Julia Granby, practices a thoroughgoing ideological ventriloquism as it spouts conventional views of marriage and morality, women's circumscribed place, and the joys of domesticity. Women are patriarchy's finest spokesmen in *The Coquette*. In this regard, Davidson's claim that the "bulk of the novel is woman talk" is not fully accurate.[26] While women sign more than two-thirds of the letters that make up the narrative, their linguistic practices are profoundly imbricated with male modes of address: these women either employ the feminized patriarchal language of the chorus or commandeer the lexicon of the masculine public sphere, a maneuver that underscores the poverty of authentic female modes of expression.

As much as it may seem that Eliza is speaking in the tones of the chorus, whose values and vocabulary of virtue, self-restraint, and antiluxury originate in the overlapping eighteenth-century Anglo-American discourses of the conduct book and republicanism,[27] until the tragic conclusion of the novel, her fluency in dominant linguistic modes does *not* signify her interpellation by the closed Federalist circle. It is the dialogic form rather than the generic content of Eliza's language that distinguishes it from the expression of the community. The chorus utters the virtuous, conventional patter of a feminized clergy with neither self-consciousness, humor, nor irony; its rhetoric is monological, operating at no distance from itself and excluding alternative voices from its authoritative purview. While in her letters the heroine may conjure the familiar tones of the majority, she always frames such passages with decidedly other modes of address, particularly the ironic sallies she constructs from phrases from various professional (i.e., masculine) dialects such as the languages of finance, politics, diplomacy, theater, religion, literature, law, and the military. These disparate locutions never sound like natural expressions but carry the aura of quoted speech, pointing to alternative (male) worlds of discourse and action and yoking them to the incongruous (female) context at hand. Using financial figures, Eliza writes, "I presume on a large stock in the bank of friendship" (9), and "merit always has a large share in that bank" (25). Blending economic with political and diplomatic metaphors she pens, "I do not feel myself greatly interested in the progress of the negociation [*sic*]" (32). Taking up a theatrical vocabulary, she describes her courtship by Boyer as a "farce" (28) and its aftermath as a "tragic comedy" (120). Drawing from the religious lexicon, she asserts, "sometimes I think of becoming a predestinarian and submitting to fate, without any exercise of free will" (24). Alluding to the literature of romance she remarks on her own "bewitching charms" (12) and characterizes Mr. Boyer as her "enamerato" and Major Sanford as the "intruder" (32), while she identifies the unknown suitor Emmons as an "enamoured swain" (61). Invoking the profession of the law, she speaks of Mr. Boyer's "cause" and her friends' "dissertation on his merits" (28). And turning to a military idiom, she discusses her experience of making "conquests" (8) and feeling "besieged" (28).

In her final moments, Eliza does come to internalize the monological message of the chorus and thus to channel its views without irony, but, before that cooptation, her language characteristically operates in multiple registers; in the context of her repressive social milieu, double-voicedness becomes a mechanism for the quiet articulation of opposition, enabling transgressive thoughts to achieve audible, if cryptic, form. Eliza's letters are marked by an insistent dialogism, and in that regard Bakhtin's notions of the polyphonic nature of the novel illuminate the way in which modulations of voice register political meaning in *The Coquette*. Summarizing Bakhtin's argument in *The Dialogic Imagination,* Caryl Emerson and Michael Holquist write, "Everything means, is understood, as part of a greater whole—there is constant interaction between meanings, all of which have the potential of conditioning others. . . . A word, discourse, language or culture undergoes 'dialogization' when it becomes relativized, de-privileged, aware of competing definitions for the same things. Undialogized language is authoritative or absolute."[28] Multivocal expression becomes the space of possibility in Foster's book, the only forum for resistance in the face of the chorus's "authoritative or absolute" communicative practices.

The language of political economy, a world from which women are traditionally debarred, operates jointly with the heroine's other important co-

optations of male speech, but, of all these moments, her allusions to speculation and debt carry the most specifically political freight. In such references
to banking and investment, Eliza Wharton becomes the primary character
in the novel to evoke the policies of Alexander Hamilton, the Anglophilic
Secretary of the Treasury in Washington's first administration, who wagers
the nation's fiscal fortunes in a hazardous program of economic expansion.
Hamilton's policies prove enormously contentious, functioning as the principal political lightening rod of the early 1790s around which conflict within
the Federalist ruling elite galvanizes in explosive ways. Within Washington's
administration, Madison and Jefferson violently oppose Hamilton's designs
for the formation of a national bank and the funding of the federal debt. In
concert with related strife over the nature of international alliances, Hamilton's financial vision largely sets the terms of the schism that finally divides
the Federalist party in 1796.

Such evocations return us to the contentious landscape of factional politics in the early national period, but complicating any facile explication of
Foster's meaning here is Eliza's double-voicedness. Thus, when in her figurative language she points to forms of economic activity that the classical
republicans of the chorus find morally reprehensible—and that are personified in the character of Sanford, the archetypal new man "of paper and
place"[29]—we must not read her remarks as statements of allegiance either to
such practices themselves or to the people who promote them. Instead, Eliza's linguistic appropriations from the masculine public sphere, her forays
across the borders of her culture's gendered discourses, allow her to reclaim
at the level of language aspects of experience from which women are excluded
in practice. This quietly transgressive humor is the only forum through
which the heroine can criticize the politics of courtship that obtain in her
culture. Invoking the notions of having "stock" and "shares" in "the bank of
friendship," Eliza would seem to be asserting the claim that females possess
capital in themselves to invest in the marriage relation, a relatively radical
notion.[30] But, in the realm of late-eighteenth-century American economics,
such speculative practices are both materially risky and socially suspect. Thus,
Eliza communicates through her metaphor a far darker fact, one that will
resonate hauntingly in her own life: women who gamble with themselves
become subject to the unstable conditions of the matrimonial market, which
leaves them dangerously exposed when the bank of friendship fails and renders worthless both their "large stock" (9) and the "merit" (25) to which it is
inextricably connected.

Eliza is the only character in *The Coquette* who would seem to challenge (if in an ephemeral voice) the community's vision of the nature and limits of liberty in the post-Revolutionary period. Mrs. Richman may assert the right of republican wives to supplement the political agency of their husbands, and the libertine engages in predictable incursions against the community's virtue, personified in the body of Eliza, but the "opposition" of both is produced under patriarchal supervision and thus is always already coded as internal to the community. The freedom of dissent is promised to Americans by the Declaration of Independence and the recently ratified Constitution but is withheld from women, who are not identified as independent citizens. In letters yearning for independence, where Eliza significantly emphasizes her own signature—and thus her role as "signer"—the heroine ironically redeploys the language of the Founding, committing linguistic piracy that exposes the gaps underwriting the republic's guarantees of liberty.

Eliza's double-voiced mode of articulation defamiliarizes and makes uncanny the language of the chorus that it also reflects. Mimicry, which is unique to the heroine's letters in *The Coquette,* exposes her ambivalent relationship to both the authoritative discourse and the repressive social practice of her culture. Eliza's ability to move between what we might term the "languages of the center and of the margin" is an index of her unique unwillingness to "confine" herself either inside or outside the monological vocal norms of her culture. She subtly defies the authoritative voices that would restrict her, and, as she fights confinement, a word that rings through her story with an urgent plangency, she confronts all that it would suggest: limitations on movement and freedom, imprisonment, lying-in, and sequestration within the domestic realm. This ability to cross with (apparent) impunity the discursive frontiers of her decorous and repressive Federalist community is the hallmark of Eliza's power at the beginning of *The Coquette.* In her description of an early encounter with Boyer, she relates the way in which her "sentimental and sedate" conversation is "perfectly adapted to the taste of [her] gallant" (12). Such instinctive theatricality, the ability to assess, perform, and thereby embody the desire of the other, wins the heroine scores of admirers; indeed, this is the very innate dramatic predisposition lying at the heart of Adam Smith's vision of fellow feeling.[31] But Eliza is far from celebrated for this gift of sympathetic social understanding; instead, the chorus mistakes such empathic abilities for wily romantic stratagems and brands Foster's protagonist with the reputation of a coquette. The attribution implies a base insincerity at the heart of Eliza's social interactions, and it is no accident that the author, using parallel phrases throughout the novel, identifies Major Sanford as embracing the identical dynamic: both talk about their horror of being shackled, their love of freedom, and their hatred of social censure.[32]

Nevertheless, while these characters share a common lexicon, a certain economic ambition, and even an ostensibly comparable set of notions about "liberty," they do not constitute a like-minded faction. Sanford seeks freedom as a means to an end, exchange as a forerunner to pleasure. Sexual conquest serves a dual function, providing sensual gratification and simultaneously affording an opportunity for social revenge: the elitist community can be given its comeuppance when the seduced and abandoned woman on whom it formerly fixated casts a tragic reflection on its own frailties. In this respect, Sanford's dissent from the values of the chorus would seem to be both coherent and identifiable; but, while his conflict with the community at first appears distinctly oppositional, as the novel unfolds it becomes increasingly clear that Sanford reenacts patriarchal tenets in exaggerated form and thus fails to offer an authentic intervention from outside.

While freedom for Sanford means sexual license, the liberty *to* pursue with impunity a state of intimate connection, it entails for Eliza exemption *from* having to engage in conventional romantic commitments. In the face of a host of unappealing choices, what the heroine wants is latitude, the space from which she can forbear from making a conclusive decision; as the novel progresses, this reluctance to locate her desire in a specific male body becomes code for seeking freedom—absolute liberty to choose her own connections—as an end in itself. Thus, after proclaiming in a letter to Lucy Freeman that she "renounces" Major Sanford "entirely," she avers that, "if [her friends'] predictions are verified, [she] shall be happy in a union with the man of their choice" (59). Structured according to the logic of a tautology, this assertion gestures on the surface toward affirming the majority's point of view; in fact, however, it only declares that the heroine's friends may or may not be correct in their prognostications about Eliza's future. This multivoiced moment becomes emblematic of Eliza's larger dilemmas of affiliation and place: it drives home with full force her uncertainty about where she stands in the context of a female community that requires marriageable women to assume their proper role.

By announcing at the end of the letter that her desire for social exchange remains unaffected, Eliza categorically subverts whatever placating effect the tautological statement might have for her friends, "I am told, that a servant man inquires for me below; the messenger of some enamoured swain, I suppose. I will step down and learn what message he brings.—Nothing extraordinary; it is only a card of compliments from a Mr. Emmons, a respectable merchant of this city, requesting the honor to wait on me to the assembly this evening. A welcome request, which I made no hesitation to grant. If I must resign these favorite amusements, let me enjoy as large a share as possible, till the time arrive" (62). This passage suggests that Major Sanford is far from being either the source of Eliza's predicament or, by extension, the ringleader of a dissenting faction in which she numbers. What the heroine reveals at this moment is not an embodied yearning but a compulsion to circulate without restriction. Motivating such waywardness, to use the heroine's own term, and distinguishing it from the libertinism of a Sanford is the elusive prospect of emerging liberal sympathy, a form of fellow feeling in which affinities of mind are not purchased at the price of denying acknowledged differences, through sacrifice of the individual for the greater good of the collective. Such are the connections she does desire.

Adam Smith views the need for sympathy as a problem produced by people's essential isolation from each other, a challenge that moral beings must surmount. In his *Theory of Moral Sentiments,* Smith elaborates the difficulty of expanding the imagination in order to envision and then feel for the troubles of an-*other.* Smith's notion of compassion is a liberal, indeed a protodemocratic, impulse: it imaginatively leaps toward and embraces the other, domesticating differences under the larger umbrella of a common humanity. The republican version of sympathy, in contrast, pointedly identifies otherness and interdicts it from the affective circle, decidedly rejecting Smith's premise that difference does not compel alienation. Such understanding is what Eliza idealistically believes she has enjoyed with her female companions before their marriages made a "tomb of friendship" (24), but, while the heroine's language would suggest that women are only annexed by the patriarchal republican cohort at marriage, the example of the sparkling Julia Granby—Eliza's unattached doppelgänger—actually implies that interpellation begins far earlier in the female life-cycle, as soon as a young woman becomes eligible to enter the romantic lists. The model Julia plays powerful foil to Eliza, cultural counterexemplum.

Eliza's trenchant characterization of the losses women suffer in the ritual of matrimony emphasizes the link between the feminized chorus and the dead patriarchs whose voices it channels: the metaphor underscores the way in which marriage functions as a mechanism of live burial for the female homosocial cohort. It also underscores the alienation the heroine confronts

in the face of such gothic affiliations; avoiding her own encryptment necessarily distances her from the moribund world of her married friends, whose
emotional absence she keenly feels. Writing to the newly married Lucy Freeman Sumner, Eliza exclaims, "Oh that you were near me as formerly, to share
and alleviate my cares! to have some friend in whom I could repose my confidence, and with whom I could freely converse, and advise, on this occasion,
would be an unspeakable comfort!" (106). The heroine's lamentation operates on multiple levels. Literally, she is mourning over the geographical gap
that now separates the married Lucy from her childhood friend, but the distance is also psychological: Eliza's wish for interchange and dialogue—for
conversation itself—suggests that such sources of empathy have become remote, indeed, have dried up for her, and her use of the term "unspeakable"
to communicate the cathartic relief she dreams of achieving through an un-
inhibited exchange points up the ways in which her feelings have already
been made gothic by the misapprehension of the chorus.

How does the bungled handling of a courtship that, from its beginnings,
is marked by a failure of fellow feeling create such dislocation among close
female companions? How can the crisis of understanding that opens between
Boyer and Eliza become a contagious force infecting the health of the heroine's female relationships? What threat to collective coherence does Eliza's
romantic failure unleash? The answers lie in the cohesion of Foster's fictive
Federalist community, which is predicated on the identifications that obtain
between its members, affinities of political sentiment and social practice.
Among the women, subtle differences of rank or economic privilege are
diminished by the bonds of "republican daughterhood," "wifehood," and
"motherhood"; through these three socially sanctioned roles, patriarchy an-
nexes female political agency for its own purposes and reroutes it inside the
family, enabling middle-class white women in post-Revolutionary America
to take up public identities at no cost to a conservative social agenda.[33] By
resisting republican wifehood, by withstanding what in Foster's fictive world
opens a great divide between ostensibly similar women, Eliza is virtually
alone in her cohort. In numerous letters to friends who are embarking on or
have recently traversed the threshold of this transformation, the heroine's
opposition to her own prospects for marriage, combined with vocal declarations against the wedded state in general, threaten to weaken crucial links of
republican sympathy.

Eliza is accused by both her mother and her friends of nurturing economic ambitions in her thoughts about matrimony, charges that she does not

deny. Indeed, she acknowledges in a letter to Lucy that reflects on her initial attraction to Major Sanford, "his liberal fortune was extremely alluring to me, who, you know, have been hitherto confined to the rigid rules of prudence and economy, not to say necessity in my finances" (60–61). To pursue for just a moment the economic implications of her limited prospects, Eliza is faced with a series of (non)choices: she can go backward in order to maintain social and economic ground—permanent regression with Boyer; she can move laterally into a sphere that is ever narrowing in the face of pressures for women to marry and bear children—temporary stasis with the dwindling female peer group; or she can run around in circles, "waywardly," deluding herself that Major Sanford's offers of "freedom" will somehow translate into the material metamorphosis of an aristocratic marriage. That Sanford never intends to propose is a fact brought painfully home by Lucy Freeman, who observes in a relatively early letter, "I do not find, in all your conversations with him, that one word about marriage drops from his lips. This is mysterious? No, it is characteristic of the man" (57). Not long after Boyer's final rejection of Eliza, Sanford weds an heiress for money, thus removing himself from contention for Eliza's hand, which apparently he could never have "afforded" in the first place. The heroine attempts to convince herself that she truly loved Boyer once he no longer desires her, but close reading of Eliza's letters reveals that she really wants to avoid marriage altogether, to remain romantically un-"connected" (13)—a prospect her feminized community cannot abide.

The heroine's matrimonial prospects among the ministerial population disappoint not only her aspirations for wealth and social advancement—but also, more troublingly, her need for a companion able to understand and sympathize with her unconventional desires. This affective incongruence between Eliza and virtually every figure who crosses her social path—male or female—propels her on a wayward quest for fellow feeling whose dynamics become tragically circular: the more resentful of her friends' romantic choices she grows—"I hope my friends will never again interpose in my concerns of that nature" (13), she writes in an early letter to Lucy—the more intrusive and disapproving the chorus becomes. Their anxiety drives Eliza further and further from the fold, while at the same time exacerbating her yearning for sympathy.

Unlike Eliza, as a white man of rank and reputed fortune, Major Sanford is granted the luxury of remaining aloof from the judgment of the community. Whether we take at face value the rake's vaunting proclamation that he is "independent" of the Richmans' "censure or esteem" (33), it is clear that Sanford can operate in relative autonomy to the chorus; he is fully aware of the way it feels about him—"I know I am not a welcome visitor to the family" (35)—but such negative judgments do little to keep him at a distance. Eliza, on the other hand, an undowered woman who relies on the community's patronage for invitations to visit, attend balls, and meet eligible gentlemen, is utterly dependent on its esteem. While often disagreeing with the voice of the chorus, most particularly on marital matters, she is hardly in a position to transcend its warnings.

It is only in unrestricted social congress that Eliza can pursue her quest for fellow feeling. Intuiting and performing the desire of the other affords the possibility that her own fancies may be heard and understood in kind—whether in direct social intercourse or in letters. Terry Eagleton has characterized as the key to genuine epistolary correspondence "speech-for-another," the mutual construction of both writer and audience in the context of the letter. In *The Rape of Clarissa,* he explains, "[T]he letter can never forget that it is turned outward to another, that its discourse is ineradicably social. Such sociality is not just contingent, a mere matter of its destination; it is the very material condition of its existence. The other to whom the letter is addressed is included within it, an absent recipient present within each phrase. As speech-for-another, the letter must reckon that recipient's likely response to every gesture."[34] "Speech-for-another" represents a kind of limiting condition of sympathetic exchange, in which the identities of self and other are produced in the process of writing or speaking. In that regard, the heroine's epistolarity repeats at the level of narrative the very desire for an affirming reflection that she also seeks in the social universe of Foster's story. Similarly, Eliza's correspondence replays as failures of vision—of reading and interpretation—the misunderstandings with both suitors and female peers that plague her within the represented world. Thus, Eliza's genius for sensing the emotions of her correspondents and interlocutors enacts, though on her side only, Smith's paradigm of sympathy as an exercise of imagination, projection, and transformation.

Eagleton's account of the constitutive power of epistolarity, which enables letter writers to forge identity through the act of discursive exchange, helps to explain both the driving energy underlying Eliza's correspondence with her friends and the uniquely double-voiced character of her speech. The heroine's early missives to members of the chorus reach across a subtle but nevertheless crucial divide in wealth and status that separates Foster's protagonist from her more affluent cohort; through this writing, Eliza attempts to minimize social distance as well as negotiate a space in which her equivocal dissent from the romantic norms of her culture might be found admissible. She seeks a form of sympathy in which efforts of imagination enable the transcendence of economic and ideological differences, the emerging liberal version of fellow feeling Adam Smith describes—and exactly the form of compassion that *Charlotte Temple*'s narrator attempts to extend to her audience.

In an early interchange with Lucy Freeman, we see the way in which the heroine uses irony in an attempt to purchase a mirroring response from her friend; she craves the smallest affirmation that her reluctance to become involved with Mr. Boyer, however incongruent with Lucy's normative expectations, remains comprehensible. Although she is disinclined, in the words of Mrs. Richman, to become "suitably and agreeably connected" in marriage (13), Eliza's notions of freedom in no way entail being cut adrift from all meaningful ties; indeed, a primary reason for writing to Lucy of her resistance to Boyer's suit is to garner her friend's reassurance about the depth and validity of the one relationship the heroine really treasures. After relating her famous pronouncement that "marriage is the tomb of friendship" (24), Eliza describes the numerous ways in which she has attempted to deflect Mr. Boyer's romantic declarations. And she concludes by asserting that she has refrained from making "a single observation on the subject, until [she] knows [Lucy's] opinion" (26).

Eliza's somewhat disingenuous declaration of editorial self-restraint deserves explication in light of the fact that her letter is steeped both in decided ambivalence about the romantic prospect of Mr. Boyer and in downright antipathy to the estate of marriage itself. In fact, her humorous allusion to feeling "besieged" and the darker suggestion that she would prefer to avert entombment give expression to the palpable danger she detects in Boyer's advances. Rather than withholding self-reflective commentary, the heroine in fact has made her feelings figurative, channeling them through the register of wit and humor. This instance of double-voicedness is emblematic of Eliza's repeated attempts to articulate inclinations that the chorus cannot abide. After virtually stating outright that she feels no romantic compulsion for the minister, she feigns deferential interest in Lucy's opinion in order to keep the channels of communication open; her final remark has little to do with either wanting to read of Lucy's disapproval or secretly craving to be convinced of Boyer's worth. The heroine writes because she does not wish to suffer the fate of becoming socially un-"connected"; as a virtuous form of intercourse, letter writing affords its own real emotional pleasures.

Eighteenth-century epistolary fiction obsessively thematizes the erotic satisfactions of written correspondence. One thinks here not only of Richardson's *Clarissa* and Rousseau's *La Nouvelle Heloise,* but particularly of Laclos's pre-Revolutionary French novel *Les Liaisons Dangereux,* in which sexual and epistolary exchange literally merge as the Viscount Valmont writes a letter on the back of his mistress in the midst of their erotic conjunction.[35] As this graphic example suggests, letter writing need not necessarily be a displaced form of sexual pleasure; indeed, epistolary gratification creates its own corpus of bodily effects, including laughter, tears, anxiety, hysteria, and melancholia, to mention just a few of the more obvious affective states produced in *The Coquette.* Such a catalogue suggests that intercourse in letters can prove more moving than its carnal counterpart.

For Eliza Wharton, at least, sexual exchange never lives up to the exquisite joy of being recognized and understood in emotional terms by a female correspondent, although such pleasure is itself less an active dynamic than a nostalgic memory in the female homosocial epistolary discourse of *The Coquette.* It is telling that, in a novel constructed entirely of letters, Foster never includes or mentions a single missive passing from Major Sanford to the heroine; nor does she represent or allude to a solitary letter, much less multiple letters, from Eliza to the libertine. With the exception of an invitation to escort Eliza to a ball, and several notes announcing that he has come to call on her, all of which go unrepresented, Sanford's intercourse with Eliza remains unmediated by the pen. The significant absence of a correspondence between Eliza and Sanford is an index of the emotional limitations of their exchange. In that regard, I agree with Davidson's assessment that Eliza's sexual fall is almost an afterthought in the narrative economy of *The Coquette.* Her forfeiture of virginity simply foreshadows Eliza's final capitulation to the equation of marriage with death, the connection that she had sought so assiduously to uncouple in the first half of the novel.[36]

Lucy's willful misinterpretation of the heroine's message is another story entirely. Her reply to Eliza vividly telegraphs the brutal way in which the chorus processes potentially disruptive proclivities: "And so you wish to have my opinion before you know the result of your own. This is playing a little too much with my patience. But, however, I will gratify you this once, in hopes that my epistle may have good effect. You will ask, perhaps, whether I would influence your judgment? I answer no; provided you will exercise it

yourself: but I am a little apprehensive that your fancy will mislead you" (26).
In an imperious stroke, Lucy rewrites what Eliza has said, collapsing the
heroine's (somewhat calculated) reticence about her situation into the oddly
self-important assertion that Eliza's opinion is somehow produced in the
wake of Lucy's own. Given the heroine's celebrity in the Federalist community for possessing an "accomplished mind" and "polished manners" (10)—
a social charisma effected by a powerful personality and the verbal acuity to
express it—the contention that she has no opinion about the prospect of
marrying Boyer is patently absurd. Reducing the complexity of Eliza's letter
to its most literal level, disavowing whatever dissonance emanates figuratively
from it, her friend assumes full license to elide the heroine's central ambivalence. From this early moment in the novel, the chorus's primary activity becomes the deliberate misapprehension and strategic revision of Eliza
Wharton's words, a process that accelerates in violence as the story moves to
its conclusion and Eliza fades from volubility to erasure. Although this dynamic suggests the latent aggression in *Charlotte Temple*'s narrator—her ve-
hement embrace of a reader on whose consent she depends—the politics of
sacrifice at work in the two novels are opposed: egalitarian and democratic in
Charlotte Temple and elitist and classically republican in *The Coquette.*

Lucy's censorious epistle and Eliza's reply reveal what lies at the heart of
their letter-writing energies. Lucy valorizes the content of their correspondence at the expense of understanding the more meaningful and sustaining
nature of its form; approaching the prospect of writing to Eliza as a pedagogical opportunity, Lucy embraces the epistolary analysis of courtship and
its vicissitudes as a forum for the renovation of the heroine's wayward character. In contrast, the heroine celebrates the way in which epistolary composition enables her to come into dialogic relation with an important other;
writing for the pleasure of exchange and connection, she pens letters that
themselves abound in the representation of people speaking: her dispatches
are marked by reports of dialogue, conversation, and verbal repartee. While
the epistles of her friends are largely composed of the kinds of rhetorical
platitudes found in late-eighteenth-century conduct books, language that
has lost its vital connection to spoken interchange and an origin in the physical body, Eliza's initial letters sparkle with energy and the sense of play, a joy
in articulation for the sake of provoking response. Thus, in the letter that
follows Lucy's schoolmarmish warning about playing with her patience, Eliza
writes, "I have received, and read again and again, your friendly epistle. My
reason and judgment entirely coincide with your opinion; but my fancy

claims some share in the decision: and I cannot yet tell which will preponderate" (28). What is there to "read again and again" in Lucy's missive? What does the heroine, the novel's undisputed master of figurative language, hope to find embedded between the lines of an epistle marked by blatant literal-mindedness and a profound sense of limitation, in which Lucy argues that Mr. Boyer's "situation in life is, perhaps, as elevated as [Eliza has] a right to claim" (27)? Eliza is searching for some kind of sympathetic reflection of herself in Lucy's letter, the acknowledgment that "fancy claims some share in the decision" despite the community's ongoing disapproval of her "eccentric" vision.

In the eighteenth-century sensationalist psychology derived from John Locke's *An Essay Concerning Human Understanding* (1690), fancy is linked to imagination.[37] Locke characterizes "fantastical" ideas as a source of error, opposing them to "real" ones, and arguing that "those are fantastical which are made up of such collections of simple ideas as were really never united, never found together in any substance: v.g. a rational creature, consisting of a horse's head, joined to a body of human shape, or such as the *centaurs* are described."[38] But, as Julie Ellison notes, by "the late eighteenth century, fancy was established in aesthetic writing as an inferior but therapeutic faculty," treating "experience as matter that can be manipulated but not transformed."[39]

Translated into the terms of *The Coquette*, fancy enables Eliza's imagination of what, for Locke, would be an "unreal combination"—the coexistence of romantic liberty and sympathetic connectedness within the Federalist circle—but affords no material means for changing her condition. Describing the politics of sensibility in works by women writers who employ fancy as a dominant figure, Ellison could be speaking of Foster's heroine when she writes that "sensibility can become, under certain circumstances, an idiom of female ambition and citizenship, invested in national success, as well as a means of resistance," an "allegory of women's literary ambition." She remarks that "[o]therness elicits representations of distance that invite the adventures of fancy and call forth prospective scenes of warning, hope, and prophecy. These excursions allow the fanciful subject to be mobile and self-pleasing, if only briefly so. Fancy's visionary excursions are pleasurable only until fancy suffers its characteristic crisis of confidence."[40]

The imaginative faculty is uniformly reprobated by eighteenth-century propagandists of female virtue, as Ellison observes at an early point in her discussion: "when women relied on the politics of fancy, criticism of their positions collapsed into attacks on their sex."[41] Indeed, well before her sexual capitulation to the libertine, Eliza herself blames this ungovernable faculty for her infatuation (100). In that regard, scholars have traditionally understood the chorus's moralizing remarks about fancy along the lines of Foster's manifestly didactic narrative intentions: according to such readings, Lucy's final letter, which recovers Eliza's wayward history as an emblematic warning to the "American fair" against the dangers of seduction (168), constitutes a veritable précis of the novel's condemnation of imagination.[42]

Yet in *The Coquette* fancy and imagination are inextricably connected to the quest for a freedom that, while guaranteed to enfranchised citizens of the new republic, becomes an elusive object for Eliza. In inventive but trenchant style, she articulates her desire for independence through language that hauntingly echoes the promises of the Founding. Inaugurating her campaign to remain romantically unconnected by pointedly linking her future liberty to the freedom of the republic, the heroine plays on the rhetoric of the Framers, declaring her own intention to remain independent from the bonds of a less-than-perfect union: "I wish not for a declaration from anyone" (12), she freely proclaims.

By condemning as "fancy" the self-consciously political language in which Eliza exercises her imagination, the chorus *rationalizes* its discomfort over her desire. Ignoring the decidedly serious content of her words, the female community calls on eighteenth-century Anglo-American culture's suspicion of fancy to justify such disapproval of its "wayward" friend. To understand Eliza's dilemma and her fall solely in terms of its value as a negative female paradigm, then, would be to read *The Coquette* through the community's monocular gaze, as a conduct book rather than as an early American novel.

But fancy and imagination need not be dismissed as the degraded products of the heroine's whimsy, invention, and "eccentric" zeal for liberty; they are related to collective cultural forms of play that exist at the margins of Foster's novel and that constitute the heart of its latent and oppositional narrative of female possibility. Thus, rather than taking Mrs. Richman at her moralistic word as she argues against the dangers of Eliza's "lively imagination" (13), we might consider the way in which the fictive workings of female fancy and the historical enterprise of the woman novelist are linked in early republican culture. That is to say, the insistent effacement of the female voice inside the imagined world operates in homologous relation to the author's dilemma as a woman writer in the 1790s; under the rubric of moral fiction,

Foster is inadvertently writing a political book in a post-Revolutionary climate deeply suspicious of female voices, female politics, and the novel itself.[43]

Against such a background, what does it mean for the chorus to try to dismiss the heroine's desire for liberty as an amusing whim, a verbal game? Speaking for the community, Lucy writes to Eliza, "You are indeed very tenacious of your freedom, as you call it; but that is a play about words" (30–31). Her comment is remarkable, in light of the fact that the nation's Founding is constituted in the very transformative acts of language from which Eliza draws her essential vocabulary. Beginning in a "play about words"—in pamphlet wars, broadside campaigns, and newspaper crusades and developing into the Declaration of Independence of the 1770s and *The Federalist Papers* and Constitution of the 1780s [44]—America's talk of freedom is "tenacious" indeed. In this context, the assertion that liberty bears no relation to linguistic performance, that verbal and written utterances have no power to conjure into being realities far from fanciful, signals historical amnesia on the part of the chorus; it is to deny what Bernard Bailyn has termed the "ideological origins of the American revolution," the idea that the colonists' pursuit of freedom both found its source and took its form in self-consciously political language.[45]

In so cavalierly dismissing Eliza's provocative talk of liberty, Lucy Freeman trivializes and attempts to squelch the disruptive impact of her friend's expression, but the vehemence of her censorship implies that the heroine's language has effects that extend threateningly beyond the purview of a verbal game enacted in privacy. The novel's poetics of space suggest that the notion of a private sphere may in fact be anachronistic to the represented world of *The Coquette;* Foster's story unfolds at the very moment in which the absence of a separate domain, the absorption into the public realm of what after the early nineteenth century will be coded as "private" affairs, becomes a gendered crisis. Eva Cherniavsky remarks that, "as an uncovered feminine presence occupying a kind of social nonspace—living under the protection, the coverture, as it were, of women who, being themselves covered, have no protection to extend—Eliza forms a middle-class women's community with neither social nor economic legitimacy, engenders an identity that cuts across the division of public and private." [46] The heroine's fate points to the need for and emergent rise of the domestic as separate space, a female world with its own particular dynamics and ritual practices that might enable the unmarried woman to take up a place in genteel white urban American culture.

In fact, Lucy's criticism tacitly acknowledges that Eliza's double-voiced articulations carve out, at the levels of both oral and written utterance, a multitude of symbolic spaces from which she can operate simultaneously, positions she is denied in the social world of the novel. For Eliza, language becomes what Richard Poirier has called a "world elsewhere,"[47] her own arena of freedom. Poirier argues that "[t]he great works of American literature are alive with the effort to stabilize certain feelings and attitudes that have, as it were, no place in the world, no place at all except where a writer's style can give them one." It is interesting that all the examples about which Poirier writes date from the nineteenth century, beginning with the works of Cooper, and the worlds elsewhere they describe through style unfold as fantasies of escape from history. In contrast, style in an American eighteenth-century epistolary novel such as *The Coquette* is localized as a feature of individual narrative voice, and the "feelings and attitudes" that Eliza Wharton attempts to "stabilize" through her humorous and transgressive language are yearnings, not to transcend the conditions of "economic, political, and social systems" (17) but to be included in the public sphere from which female fancy is debarred. The realm of politics functions as an imaginary space for Eliza precisely because early national culture excludes women from the symbolic domain. The narrator of *Charlotte Temple* proves a fascinating exception to this generalization, and one that influences Foster in *The Coquette*. Figured as a vocal rather than a textual presence, Rowson's storyteller is nevertheless the proxy for her creator; using the narrator to deflect her operations, Rowson functions in the symbolic under the guise of the imaginary. For both Rowson and Foster, language becomes an arena of freedom through which the heroine can express the wish to take up a meaningful existence within the economic, political, and social systems that Poirier's American heroes and heroines seek to surpass and escape.

Although the chorus sees no value in the heroine's "tenacious" wish for freedom (30), fancy is the transgressive space of female possibility to which Foster returns at crucial moments in the novel. Indeed, were the female imagination a faculty of no real significance, incapable of producing material results, *The Coquette* itself would not exist as an enduring literary artifact. As much as Foster, identifying with the chorus at the didactic level of her tale, might seem to be dismissing the effects of imagination as debased forms of play, the link between female fancy and her own literary production is indisputable. The author rejects the historical archive of male-authored newspaper and sermon accounts denouncing the depravity of the actual Elizabeth Whitman in order to rescript her tragic story into a compelling fictional por-

trait of Eliza Wharton; by so doing, Foster privileges her own acts of imagination over the powers of reason.[48] At stake in asserting a crucial connection
between Eliza's fanciful wordplay and Foster's complex fictive practices is a
claim about the power of language as a cultural force to which women have
access in late-eighteenth-century America, one that reverses the usual Lacanian association of language with the (masculine) symbolic rather than the
(feminine) imaginary. Warner's discussion of political agency and the "imaginary" order in the early national period bears directly on the issue:

> [I]maginary participation in the public order is . . . a precondition for
> modern nationalism, though it is anathema to pure republicanism. The
> modern nation does not have citizens in the same way that the republic
> does. You can be a member of the nation, attributing its agency to your-
> self in imaginary identification, without being a freeholder or exercising
> any agency in the public sphere. Nationalism makes no distinction be-
> tween such imaginary participation and the active participation of citi-
> zens. In republicanism that distinction counted for everything. So the
> early phase of post-Revolutionary nationalism is marked by a gradual
> extension of a national imaginary to exactly those social groups that were
> excluded from citizenship—notably women. Women were more and
> more thought of as symbolic members of the nation, especially in their
> capacities as mothers. But this symbolic reclassification changed the na-
> ture of the nation and the imaginary of its extension more than it
> changed the access of women to the public sphere. For the public of
> which women were now said to be members was no longer a public in
> the rigorous sense of republicanism, and membership in it no longer
> connoted civic action.[49]

Eliza Wharton's fanciful identifications with the political thus prefigure
nineteenth-century impulses toward liberal nationalism;[50] her desire for freedom, articulated through the exercise of imagination, is reprobated partly
because it violates culturally bound notions of participation in the state that
republican theory genders as male and locates in the public sphere.

This application of Warner's argument verges perilously on a reading of
the heroine as the protoliberal American citizen who embraces individualism
in anticipation of its emergence as a dominant economic and historical reality
in the early nineteenth century. To resist characterizing Eliza Wharton in
such dualistic terms (according to interpretive practices in fact bequeathed to
contemporary criticism of the novel by the Federalists), it is crucial to em-

phasize that her quest for liberty unfolds *within* the interstices of republican theory itself. Despite her "tenacious" talk, Eliza never imagines her own freedom operating at any distance from the genteel Federalist cohort that constitutes her social world. The heroine has no access to a normative form of liberalism that could pose a challenge to the oppressive limitations of the community. The democratic and individualistic Jeffersonian universe that might embrace her independent sensibility exists far beyond the margins of Foster's representation. And while seeming to offer Eliza the lure of resisting the majority's values, Sanford embodies the ultimate *illusion* of freedom; his libertinism is utterly dependent on the patriarchal structures it mimics. James Turner writes that "libertines may be seen . . . as not simply above the law, but deeply in need of the law to guarantee their privileges and to fuel their emotional rebellion. They confirm in the very act of infraction."[51] Upper-class civility, represented in *The Coquette* by the Richmans and their set, is in some vital sense brought into focus, if not actually constituted by, the incursions of the libertine; his assault against their propriety makes it possible for the gentry to identify precisely where the boundaries of their class and comportment begin. The libertine's position, then, is always already internal to this elite. Eliza has no interest in rejecting her republican allegiances. Paradoxically, the heroine's quest for liberty comes into sharpest focus as a desire to create an expressive space within the Federalist community itself. Rather than capitulating to the pressures of the marriage market, Eliza seeks to preserve communal ties, to sustain the bonds of homosociality in which her virtue *and* her happiness have inhered.

An abiding paradox structures Eliza's desire and takes material form in the novel's epistolarity. While her letters give voice to Eliza's transgressive yearnings, her dream of freedom, they simultaneously express a powerful need for dialogue and exchange, the longing to remain enmeshed in the female collectivity, or with *anyone* who will engage in genuine dialogue, which is Sanford's main attraction. Given the range of narrative strategies available to an Anglo-American author in the 1790s, it is interesting to reflect on the political implications of Foster's formal decision. The epistolary novel enacts on multiple narrative levels Eagleton's notion that a letter implies its own reader.[52] Composed of imaginary missives that themselves construct invented correspondents, the novel in letters is a written artifact whose very legibility is doubly dependent on the existence and attention of literate others: the characters who write and receive missives inside the fictive world and the audience that shares these letters from an outside vantage point.[53] Epistolary fiction represents a vision of community within its very form. At the same time, it affords the illusion of enfranchising individual voices. As such, it offers a powerful narrative analogue for the dilemmas of representation early national political culture faced: the challenge of addressing the needs of the many while also privileging the merits of the few.

The Coquette translates this paradox in fascinating ways. The elasticity of the letter form allows Foster to embody simultaneously the expansive nature of Eliza's social desire and the constricted vision of the chorus with whom she corresponds. The volume of mail that the heroine dispatches to her community is disproportionately large compared to the number of letters they return to her. While Eliza's missives provide a dramatic series of mis-en-scènes meant to open dialogue and elicit the engaged responses of her female intimates, their programmatic replies reflect the inward orientation of the Federalist community and its tendency toward monologic thought. Although the women of this cohort share and circulate Eliza's letters, they rarely write to her of their own hopes, dreams, fears, and concerns. Claire Pettengill has noted that, while the exercise of "sisterhood" in *The Coquette* is marked by "openness" and "receptivity to criticism," it is not a reciprocal practice: only Eliza Wharton is expected to embrace these qualities. Pettengill writes, "As the novel progresses . . . it becomes clear that the criticism, and to a large extent the openness, work in only one direction. Eliza expends great energy in relating numerous details of her private life, and her friends expend similar energy criticizing her behavior. They never go into detail about their own lives (beyond platitudes about their happiness), and she never presumes to criticize their personal decisions or actions."[54] If the eighteenth-century epistolary novel imagines community through the patterns of exchange that organize its narrative form, how are we to read the limited if not impoverished use to which Foster puts the genre in *The Coquette*? In comparison with the polymorphous employment of letters in *Clarissa*, a novel whose characters not only exploit the possibility for interference with the post but actually take such manipulations to their furthest theoretical limits, Foster's characters make minimal use of the mail as an instrument of illicit power. Letters in *The Coquette* neither cross each other nor fail to reach their destination; they are never stolen, forged, or destroyed.

In both Richardson's and Foster's works, letters travel along homosocial lines: same-sex correspondence dominates *Clarissa* and *The Coquette*. Eliza writes only three letters to Boyer, and he pens three to her; otherwise, beyond General Richman's note announcing to the heroine the birth of his daughter, men and women do not exchange letters in the fictive world of *The Coquette*. It is interesting that Charlotte Temple's letters to her mother and her various maternal surrogates—letters that are misdirected, intercepted, or fated to remain unread—point toward the text/absence pole of the continuum on which voice/presence conversely figures. In a fictive universe that values transparency over all else, the distance that marks the letter form is bound to make epistolary exchange seem theatrical and opaque. In contrast, the letters that make up *The Coquette* achieve a kind of transparency, immediacy, and embodiment—at least when they emanate from Eliza. Writing in the metaphorical equivalent of the first-person plural, the chorus remains distant and disembodied.

The sort of "plotting" that motivates Lovelace's epistolarity takes a backseat in *The Coquette* to Eliza's one-sided circulation of feeling and the majority's response to her desire for reciprocation by reprobating imaginative excess. Far more than it records the dramatic exercise of domination across the lines of gender, correspondence in Foster's book registers the yearning for and failure of a specific form of female homosocial exchange. Despite Sanford's ultimate sexual cooptation of the heroine, he remains forever outside the social circuit that epistolarity affords Eliza. We have noted that the libertine rarely writes to his victim, but even more significant is the fact that, although Sanford dispatches eleven epistles to Mr. Deighton, no replies are represented.

If correspondence is a figure, or even a substitute, for erotic exchange, the libertine's writing must be seen as onanistic. This suggests that Sanford's agency to do Eliza harm is, in the end, secondary to the totalizing power of the chorus, with whom she unsuccessfully attempts to share playful words, ambivalent feelings, and, ultimately, despair. Fittingly, the heroine's sexual fall marks only the last acting out of an earlier and more devastating emotional crisis: being misread, misheard, and misunderstood in the letters of the chorus, in the minister's notorious note of rejection, and in her female friends' correspondence throughout the novel. The disruptions of the mail that exist in *The Coquette* must be seen as *internal* to the epistolary process itself, as problems of interpretation rather than of circulation. Letters are disturbed and rerouted not through the interception or forgery of machinating men but, rather, through the misapprehension of the feminized majority, a force whose destructive powers make the physical threat of the libertine decidedly anticlimactic.

Foster's circumscribed exercise of epistolarity becomes even more legible as a specifically American form when it is compared with Charles Brockden Brown's unique and bizarre use of letters to frame his fiction, a distinction taken up in the following chapter. For now it is only necessary to consider that Brown's best novels all open as extended epistles to an absent other who never achieves representation in the fictive world; his tales then proceed to unfold in diarist form, subsuming in the charismatic power of the narrating voice both the illusion of that readerly other and any possibility for exchange between these "correspondents." That Brown's fiction charts the profound failure of collective forms of authority, sociality, and sympathy tells us about the very different use Foster makes of the epistolary mode in her book. In contrast with the narrative dynamics at work in Brown's fiction, letter writing in *The Coquette* seems positively Richardsonian in its emphasis on both the potential for fellow feeling and its inevitable failure.

Most significantly, epistolarity affords Foster's heroine the space to display her fancy as it exercises itself in language. Before her letters move from expansive and playful exuberance to terseness and finally to self-erasure, Foster dispatches thirty such messages from Eliza's pen as opposed to twenty-eight missives that emanate from the hands of the chorus: eight from Lucy, nine from Julia Granby, one each from General and Mrs. Richman and Mrs. Wharton, and eight from Mr. Boyer. It is through verbal play, the ephemeral ground on which intimate epistolary exchange is itself constructed, that Eliza briefly flourishes. An irreverent use of words marks the ultimate space of the heroine's resistance to both matrimony and the greater culture that would "confine" her in the domestic realm (29, 47, 53, 61, 66).

From this perspective, the heroine's whimsical employment of the Hamiltonian language of venture and risky speculation is not merely frivolous, or even potentially provocative; in fact, her social enactment of these principles is absolutely coterminous with what she says. In early republican culture, the form that Eliza's and indeed any undowered lady's investments can take is almost exclusively linguistic: in the face of various romantic propositions a woman can respond with a "yes," "no," or "I am willing to consider." Such is the extent of her "economic" power. And yet Eliza refuses to be restrained within the straits of such linguistic limitation. Even at the moment when she comes closest to accepting Boyer's proposal she hedges her bets with verbal virtuosity, refusing to employ grammatical forms outside the future tense and the subjunctive mode. Thus, Mr. Boyer writes, "she owned that she intended to give me her hand, but when she *should* be ready, she *could* not determine" (76, my emphasis).

Although they would deny the heroine the power to mean what she says when her language invokes such problematic desire as the reluctance to be "shackle[d]" (13), Eliza's friends are nevertheless obsessed with extracting a "declaration" of romantic intent from her lips or her pen. In its typically coercive mode, the chorus remains invested in controlling, legislating, and, most importantly, producing the heroine's speech. It is Mrs. Richman even more than Mr. Boyer who encourages Eliza to "own" herself "somewhat engaged" (30). This oxymoron speaks volumes about female freedom in the new republic: to own—to acknowledge, to know, to recognize—oneself as a woman is to *disown* self-possession. Coverture, the legal absorption of an individual married woman's public self under the guise of her husband's protection, is the formal term for the dynamic being worked out under the surface of Mrs. Richman's ironic expression. To be most self-aware as a woman is to recognize the limits of female self-agency. Freedom for women in the world of *The Coquette* is something to "resign" (30), cede, or surrender, like one's maiden name, one's signature, and one's legal identity.

Thus, Eliza's assertion that she has sacrificed fancy to reason in her initial promise to marry the ailing Haly and the parallel notion that it is her mind and not her imagination (or heart) that leads her to Boyer reveal why the heroine views as a moribund activity the exercise of reason in isolation from imagination. Mary Wollstonecraft's emphasis in *Vindication of the Rights of Woman* on the importance of female rationality (and Rowson's politically prescient anticipation of these arguments in *Charlotte Temple*) provide an evocative comparison here. Foster's point is not that women should proceed according to irrational impulses but rather that exercise of the imagination is equal to reason in its importance for women's achievement of political agency. Witness Foster's own complex and even equivocal expression of such enfranchisement in *The Coquette*. Even Edmund Burke notes that "in natural feelings we learn great lessons; because in events like [the French Revolution] our passions instruct our reason."[55]

Pure rationality in *The Coquette* is associated with the voice of the clerical patriarchy, located in the past and emanating from the grave. Mrs. Richman might warn, "beware the delusions of fancy! Reason must be our guide" (51), but she too will ultimately speak from within the crypt. Through the ideology of republican motherhood, the general's wife would seem to rationalize on patriotic lines the value of female reproductive labor; her speeches on the subject, to which I will return, affirm the doctrine that women make a political investment in the American future through acts of procreation, but Mrs.

Richman's creative efforts become aligned with death when Foster sacrifices her daughter Harriot for the sake of the plot. Reason cannot immunize women from the powerlessness of their subordination.

It is no wonder that, if fancy has provided Eliza with a venue for thinking through the promise of liberty, she will experience the failure of such hopes as a scourging of the imagination, her last resort. She writes Lucy two melancholic accounts of her despair over Boyer's rejection of her own radical proposal of marriage, the "sacrifice of female reserve" (102) she makes to the minister one year after he misconstrues her intimate yet virtuous exchange with Sanford and summarily throws her over. In a worried yet exasperated response to Eliza's despairing second missive, Lucy protests, "it did not afford me with those lively sensations of pleasure, which I usually feel at the perusal of your letters." She goes on to "require" Eliza, in the name of her "own happiness and honor," "to dissipate the cloud that hangs over [her] imagination," assaulting the heroine with a conduct-book lecture on the dangers of succumbing to the darkness of fancy and the importance of "fortitude" in "braving and steering through" the "storms of life" (112).

As we have seen, the chorus identifies Eliza's fancy as a transgressive site, a faculty that provokes anxiety and hostility precisely because it expresses political desire. So it is not surprising that Lucy would conjure Eliza's heretofore virtuous reputation in admonishing the heroine to transcend the emotional climate in which she seems sunk. She cannot affirm that Eliza's melancholia might be a valid response to a serious loss of esteem; instead, the head of the chorus erases the reality of the heroine's pain and attempts to instill the necessity of maintaining a character above reproach, both the idée fixe and emblem of the feminized community itself.

One communal benefit of Eliza's elevated mood would seem to be the production of letters that could entertain and divert her female friends from the "circumscri[ption]" of the "marriage state" (24). Indeed, in the rare moments in which she is not condemning the irreverent nature of such performances, Lucy finds real pleasure, amusement, and even consolation in the heroine's theatrical commentary on courtship as a game to be played with skill. At the end of a particularly disapproving letter about her involvement with Sanford, Lucy reaches out for Eliza's levity, writing that she is "busily engaged" in preparations for her marriage: "The solemn words 'as long as ye both shall live,' render me thoughtful and serious. I hope for your enlivening presence soon; which will prove a seasonable cordial to the spirits of your Lucy Freeman" (59). This passage marks the sole instance in which Lucy either expresses the remotest ambivalence about her own wedding plans or alludes to the link between the patriarchy and a living death; it also is the only time she specifically invokes the heroine's lively fancy, Foster's code for Eliza's expression of resistance to her culture's romantic protocols.

Thus, to argue that Eliza suffers exploitation exclusively at the hands of men who devour her playful wit while they simultaneously condemn her coquetry would be to emphasize only the most obvious feature of her dilemma; it also would be to mystify the fact that the feminized community is equally invested in the charms of the heroine, enjoying with her male admirers the pleasure she offers and simultaneously speculating with them in moralistic fashion on the alarming course of her future. Such distinctions of gender have little explanatory power in *The Coquette* precisely because the clergy and its minions number the female chorus members among their own.

Spectacle

Lucy's programmatic diatribe on the heroine's failure of resolution is followed in the same letter by perhaps the most fascinating and certainly the least explored passage in Foster's novel. Mrs. Sumner proceeds to unfold at Eliza's request an extraordinary disquisition on the moral inadequacy of Boston's "public and private places of resort" (113), the popular amusements at which she has been a spectator. It is here that the forms of play operating at the margins of Foster's representation come into view as cultural analogues to the heroine's "wayward" and "eccentric" female imagination.

The crucial connection between women's fancy and freedom that Lucy reprobates throughout *The Coquette* takes material shape in the forms of late-eighteenth-century mass entertainment she catalogs for the heroine. Sermonizing passionately, Lucy inveighs against the theater's unseemly exhibition of private woes and the circus's indecent exposure of female bodies. This harangue unwittingly evokes singular parallels to Eliza's own experience: not only have her romantic difficulties made her into a local curiosity, but, even more painfully, she has been scrutinized and commodified by the gaze of a community that includes both Lucy herself and her husband-to-be Mr. Sumner.[56] Lucy writes, "My swain interests himself very much in your affairs. You will possibly think him impertinent; but I give his curiosity a softer name" (31). Eliza indeed resents the intrusive gaze of the chorus. "I hope my friends will never again interpose in my concerns of that nature" (13), she declares at the opening of the novel, and she takes offense at the prospect that Boyer's peers will "claim the right of scrutinizing every part of [her] conduct" (29).

Yet Eliza has orchestrated the community's speculation largely to her own advantage, and in that regard she is not entirely without agency, at least for the first half of Foster's book. She characterizes her participation in the drama of courtship as "my part of the farce, for such it might prove after all" (28); and writing to Lucy of the performative quality of her interactions with the minister, she remarks, "I have just received a letter from Mr. Boyer, in the usual style. He expects the superlative happiness of kissing my hand next week. O dear! *I believe I must begin to fix my phiz.* Let me run to the glass and try if I can make up one that will look *madamish*" (61, first emphasis mine). For all their bravado, however, the heroine's witty, theatrical self-characterizations constitute another way in which she articulates her protest against a wearying social dynamic that she cannot ultimately escape. By describing her meetings with Boyer in the humorous terms of satiric comedy, she strives to expose the folly of such a union to the partisan chorus.

Eliza expresses more passion and animation in this letter to Lucy in which she projects the imaginary tableau of making-up before the mirror, performing her femininity as masquerade,[57] than she does in describing any of her encounters with the minister. The heroine's capricious notion of fixing her "phiz" to "look madamish" gives dramatic expression to her awareness that she would have to enact a fiction of genteel submission in order to satisfy Boyer's romantic expectations. To embody such a fantasy would indeed be to *fix* her future, in the sense of hardening, arresting, or canceling her prospects for freedom. In the face of pressure to accept the minister's hand and be done with the business of courtship, such theatrical fancies dispatched to her female correspondents give humorous voice to the gravity of Eliza's dilemma, at the same time enabling her to imagine her own defiance of the tyranny of the marriage market. Scripted exclusively for the eyes of the women who read her letters, such fictive tableaux afford the heroine the liberty to construct, if only in ephemeral fancy, a moment of cathartic opposition. That the spectacle of the heroine's mugging before an imaginary looking glass should be the very scene she translates into an epistolary plea for fellow feeling makes perfect sense, for what Eliza seeks is nothing less than a sympathetic reflection of her decidedly unconventional vision of marriage, the prospect that her beloved friend could mirror her point of view.

Rather than affirm the heroine's ambivalence and partake of her amuse-ment in a romantic scenario that leaves Eliza "strongly tempted . . . to laugh" (66), however, the community actively campaigns for her to accept the min-ister's hand. Despite her whimsical wishes, in expecting the chorus both to take pleasure in her humor and to decode it for the social protest it contains, Eliza sadly miscalculates the allegiances of her friends. I have established that in *The Coquette* fancy is a political category that threatens the values of the republican community. Lucy affirms this conclusion in her description of her own horror over viewing "griefs [that are] imaginary" on the theatrical stage (113). In the same letter, she trivializes the significance of Eliza's melancholy by locating its source in her "imagination" (112), denying the possibility that the heroine's despair might express a cultural problem: the unmarried wom-an's lack of access in republican America to a meaningful venue for the ex-pression of liberty.

Lucy's outrage over a Boston production of *Romeo and Juliet* replays in intriguing ways her disapproval of Eliza's imaginative "indulgence of melan-choly" (112). As the tirade against the performance begins to slip loose from its referent and to point toward other forms of dramatizing and fanciful ex-cess—namely, Eliza's behavior in the face of romantic failure—Foster sug-gests the extent to which theatricality is particularly provocative as a mode of political expression in early national culture.[58] The object of Mrs. Sumner's indignation is the very Shakespearian tragedy that, according to Kenneth Silverman, was "the single most popular play in the colonial theater from 1763–74."[59] Given the historical period in which *The Coquette* is set,[60] a more conventionally mimetic rendering would have Lucy patronizing the best-attended production of the 1790s, American novelist Royall Tyler's comedy of manners, *The Contrast*.[61] In the history of the eighteenth-century American theater, performances of *Romeo and Juliet* are most often associ-ated with the final epoch of English domination of the colonies, although the annals of the Boston stage record that the play continues to be put on there throughout the Federalist period.[62] But the politics of genre prove more significant to Foster's representation than do the poetics of realism.[63] Includ-ing Lucy in the audience of a drama identified with the pre-Revolutionary past links the heroine's most intimate friend with the morbidity and backward-looking orientation of the chorus. The plot of *Romeo and Juliet* also constitutes a Shakespearian analogue for the post-Revolutionary context of Foster's story. Dramatizing what happens when anxiety about parties and socially unsanctioned sexual unions explodes into its most gothic manifestation,[64] the story of *Romeo and Juliet* could also serve as a rough précis for Eliza Wharton's ultimate fate in *The Coquette.*

At some level identifying without in any way acknowledging the singular parallels between (fictive) life and (doubly fictive) art, Lucy writes to Eliza about her disturbing experience as a spectator witnessing the theatrical representation of "imaginary grief":

> Last evening I attended a tragedy; but I will never attend another. I have not yet been able to erase the gloom which it impressed upon my mind. It was Romeo and Juliet. Distressing enough to sensibility this! Are there not real woes (if not in our own families, at least among our own friends, and neighbors) sufficient to exercise our sympathy and pity, without introducing fictitious ones into our very diversions? How can that be a diversion, which racks the soul with grief, even though that grief be imaginary. (112–13)

Lucy's antitheatrical diatribe recapitulates her hostile attitude toward Eliza's "imaginary woes." At the same time, her feverish reaction to the distressing nature of dramatic spectacle suggests some basic recognition, however disclaimed, that "our very diversions," whether humorous epistolary salvos or tragic dramas on the public stage, serve as arenas for articulating collective conflicts, what Jane Tompkins calls the "doing of cultural work."[65]

While the manifest narrative of outrage would suggest otherwise, Lucy's speech in fact affirms by omission Aristotle's argument in the *Poetics* that tragic drama provides the body politic with a forum for catharsis; in refusing to witness the spectacle of tragedy, citizens like Lucy turn away from the exercise of civic virtue at the level of imagination. Even Edmund Burke, whose conservative politics would appeal to a Federalist of Lucy's stripes, argues for the civic value of the theater. He writes that, "indeed, theater is a better school of moral sentiments than churches, where the feelings of humanity are thus outraged."[66] Lucy is utterly unwilling to acknowledge the seriousness of Eliza's emotional extremity, to understand what she terms "the real woes . . . among our friends and neighbors," much less to valorize the essentially political implications of the heroine's situation. In similar fashion, she refuses to take on ever again the "imaginary grief" of Shakespearian tragedy. We must read her outraged letter as a narrative symptom, indicating that the play, rather than thrusting unpleasant but "fictitious" woes squarely into her face, actually reflects Eliza's plight, the reality of which Lucy is invested in denying. To see such familiar distress performed as a diversion suggests that such a subject might be legitimate and worthy of the community's consideration and reprises the unpleasant fact that theater and politics in the new republic are profoundly intertwined.

In her narrative of theatergoing as traumatic assault on sensibility, Lucy's capacity for authentic fellow feeling is exposed as both shallow and narrow; her powers of sympathy extend no further than to those of the chorus able to mirror her irreproachable comportment. The matron's moralistic harangue is particularly interesting, in light of Fliegelman's insight that "American virtue was . . . rooted in the consumer end of theatricality, in a concept related to impersonation, but whose threat to the stability of self had positive rather than destructive moral consequences: the operations of sympathy and identification, the experience of being moved. Those operations that permitted one, in Pope's popular phrase, 'to feel another's Woe,' were routinely described in the eighteenth century with reference to what happens to a spectator in a theater."[67] According to Fliegelman, the late-eighteenth-century American playhouse is an arena in which virtue, classically understood by republican theorists as a specifically *disinterested* quality,[68] becomes increasingly aligned with sympathy. In this description of what we might call "early national affective politics," Fliegelman points to a marked shift away from classical republican notions of dispassionate communality and toward a proto-democratic ethos of collective absorption and shared fellow feeling, the affect toward which *Charlotte Temple* reaches.[69]

Lucy's horror over being forced through fictive operations of identification to experience another's woe is emblematic of the discomfort with the expression of feeling we are tracing here. The matron's disavowal of tragedy is entirely consistent with her role as spokeswoman for a community whose emotional practices are virulently antidemocratic. Displaced into her anti-theatrical tirade, her abiding failure of compassion for Eliza's plight offers an ironic commentary on Rousseau's warning (counter to Aristotelion theory) that the false emotions conjured up in the playhouse actually deaden the spectator's capacity for feeling the real sorrows of a neighbor by "substituting a simulacrum of sympathy for actual human interaction."[70] Lucy gives lip service to the Rousseauvian formulation that "people think they come together in the theater, and it is there that they are isolated . . . they go to forget their friends, neighbors, and relations in order to concern themselves with fables, in order to cry for the misfortunes of the dead, or to laugh at the expense of the living."[71] But her outraged reprobation of dramatic spectacle,

actually expressed in the tones of melodrama, remains thoroughly discon-
nected from any sympathetic impulses of humanity she might in fact practice
in the novel. Indeed, Lucy's histrionic claim that tragic drama proves nothing
less than an indulgent diversion, mere entertainment that mutes one's ability
to feel for one's friends, utterly fails to translate into a heightened sensitivity
toward Eliza's pain. Rousseau's tract against spectacles, which emphasizes
both the dangerous theatricality of everyday relations and the way in which
imaginative drama only magnifies and reflects this crisis of sympathy, eerily
prognosticates the matron's hard-hearted attitude toward Eliza Wharton's
woes, her indictment of the heroine's feelings as the self-dramatizations
of a coquette. Lucy's behavior underscores the very lack of humanity that
Rousseau locates in the relation between the dramatic actor and his or her
audience—the failure of sympathy antitheatricality means to combat—and
points to the dangerous insincerity inherent in republican social relations.[72]

That Lucy's manifesto against tragic drama constitutes a politically inflected discourse on the limits of sympathy comes into sharper focus when
compared with an another repudiation of the theater, found in an earlier
epistolary novel of seduction. In its evocative linguistic detail, the following
passage in all likelihood functioned as the source for Lucy's tirade: "Yet, for
my own part, I loved not tragedies; though she did, for the sake of the in-
struction, the warning, and the example generally given in them. I had too
much *feeling*, I said. There was enough in the world to make our hearts sad
without carrying grief into our diversions, and making the distresses of others
our own."[73] Foster herself provides the cues for making the link to this passage from Richardson's *Clarissa*, which appears in a letter written by Lovelace
to his friend Belford. Traces of her imaginative involvement with Richardson's book are inscribed throughout *The Coquette*. For example, by creating a
scene between the heroine and Mrs. Richman that takes *Clarissa* as a proof
text against the evils of seduction, Foster engages in no less than a metanarrative commentary on her own procedures and formal strategies. In an early
letter to Lucy, Eliza records a conversation with her hostess about the inap-
propriateness of Major Sanford as a suitor. When Mrs. Richman calls Sanford a "seducer," the heroine exclaims,

> I hope, madam, you do not think me an object of seduction! I do not
> think you are seducible; nor was Richardson's Clarissa, till she made her-
> self the victim, by her own indiscretion. Pardon me Eliza, this is a second
> Lovelace. I am alarmed by his artful intrusions. His insinuating attention

to you are [*sic*] characteristic of the man. Come, I presume you are not interested to keep his secrets, if you know them. Will you give me a little sketch of his conversation? Most willingly, said I; and, accordingly, related the whole. When I had concluded, she shook her head, and replied, beware, my friend, of his arts. Your own heart is too sincere to suspect treachery and dissimulation in another; but suffer not your ear to be charmed by the syren voice of flattery; nor your eye to be caught by the phantom of gaiety and pleasure. (38)

Mrs. Richman's elision of the fact that Clarissa is not seduced but raped by Lovelace while she is under the influence of drugs is not inconsistent with moralizing readings of the novel made by Americans in the late eighteenth century, including no less than John Adams himself, who asserts in an 1804 letter that "Democracy is Lovelace and the people are Clarissa."

What is interesting in Mrs. Richman's attitude is the utter lack of compassion for Richardson's virtuous heroine, who more typically had the eighteenth-century audience dissolving into extremities of sympathetic identification. Affected readers include characters who receive letters within the novel—figures like the libertine's confidant Belford, who takes up the heroine's cause against Lovelace, on being so moved by her plight—and extend to the villain himself. Actual members of the reading public go so far as to correspond with Richardson, imploring him to change Clarissa's fate. Set against this background, Mrs. Richman's cruel indictment of Clarissa, her failure of readerly fellow feeling, constitutes a foreboding prolepsis of the chorus's ultimate view of Eliza.[74] In an extraordinary moment, through the correspondence of *The Coquette*'s most vocal proponent of female virtue, Foster ventriloquizes the theories of a libertine whose compulsion to test the limits of his own capacity for compassion leads him to drug and rape the only woman who commands his love—a gesture that surely complicates, if not explodes, the didactic reading of her book. Until the point of the rape, the libertine is repeatedly undone—rendered ineffectual—by the heroine's sentimental displays. It is only when the immobilized Clarissa, having been drugged into unconsciousness, ceases to embody a dramatic tableau that the villain can set aside his sympathy. The libertine becomes transformed into a rapist precisely at the moment in which he disavows all compassion for his victim.[75]

The intertextual echoes between these two passages suggest that it is not Major Sanford (who is afforded minimal vocal representation) but in fact

Lucy Freeman Sumner and her minions in the feminized community who speak the lethal language of seduction in *The Coquette*. Thus, like the narrator of *Charlotte Temple*, the majority also practices a form of verbal seduction on its (internal) audience, exercising tyranny in the name of republican virtue just as the purportedly democratic narrator of Rowson's book reveals her slyly despotic nature.[76] Although Mrs. Richman warns Eliza against the powers of the libertine's eloquence, she misapprehends the fact that the most dangerous wielders of words in the novel are her own female peers. In far more subtle and unwitting form, and to an entirely different political end, the ominous practices of the feminized chorus begin to resemble—in their effects—those of the corrupted La Rue, *Charlotte Temple*'s most destructive seducer. It is Mrs. Richman herself who ultimately convinces Eliza to embark on the action that she had only contemplated and that proves fatal to her equanimity: the writing of a letter to Boyer, in which the heroine invents an eccentric desire, with no real object but freedom, and in which she relocates and reinvests her amorphous longings in the very figure who would withhold such liberty, the minister himself (100).

The chorus projects onto and channels through Eliza social yearnings that are properly their own; without such prodding, it is unlikely that Eliza would have written Boyer the repentant letter seeking a romantic reunion. This is not to minimize her ongoing ambivalence, which registers itself unmistakably in the formal structure of a message penned to Lucy immediately before she addresses the parson. Giving vivid expression to the power of Eliza's mixed feelings, the associative logic of her ruminations records her hesitation and reluctance even in the flush of regret for having let Boyer slip away: after ending a paragraph on the subject of her desire for his esteem, she wonders, "what has become of Major Sanford! Has he too forsaken me? Is it possible for him willfully to neglect me? I will not entertain so injurious a suspicion" (100). To rescript her feelings for the minister is automatically to reassert an investment in Sanford as well, who in the heroine's emotional economy enacts the logic of the supplement to Boyer. These figures, rather than serving as the manichean rivals that the community constructs them to be, actually constitute two sides of a patriarchal coin from which the heroine can find no escape.

In that regard, Eliza's proposal of marriage to Boyer constitutes a fascinating study in double-voicedness. Despite the fact that its contents would seem to have been authorized by the chorus, the form of the heroine's extraordinary offer embodies a subtle but powerful protest against being *dic-*

tated to by the community. The epistle is marked by the disavowal and duality that largely inflect the heroine's earlier locutions: commandeering her lines from a masculine romantic script, Eliza continues to speak in two registers, even while the community would try to vocalize for her. By deploying her own offer of marriage in a remarkable moment of epistolary outspokenness, the heroine usurps what according to the elocutionary conventions of the period should rightly be the minister's demonstration of desire.

Protestations of repentance notwithstanding, Eliza reveals in this gesture a continued unwillingness to forsake her pursuit of the expressive freedom that republican culture affords to men. In that regard, the minister's engagement to another woman at the time of the heroine's proposal must be seen as incidental to his rejection of her; whether or not Boyer is entangled otherwise, he cannot abide a wife who would presume to speak for him. What leaves Eliza bereft is not the loss of the minister, per se, but the forfeiture of the vital link he represents to a female community whose powers of sympathy prove increasingly inelastic in the face of opposition to their collective will. Thus isolated, the heroine plunges into melancholic despair, a form of social death figured by the absence of the lengthy and ebullient letters she characteristically has written to her friends. This collapse, from which she never recovers, precedes by almost a year her sexual capitulation to Sanford and suggests that neither the minister nor the libertine is in fact the agent of her undoing.

Rather, Eliza's tragedy is a homosocial problem; more specifically, the women doing the cultural work of the feminized clergy in *The Coquette* pose the gravest danger to its outspoken heroine. Lucy's most ominous act of patriarchal ventriloquism unfolds in the only supportive letter she writes to Eliza after Boyer's final rejection, dispatched immediately prior to the epistle in which we can locate the heroine's sexual fall. In this missive, Lucy strikes at the heart of her friend's wish for freedom by recalling Mrs. Wharton's Aristotelian notions of an interrelated social order in which knowing one's place also means inhabiting it contentedly. She writes, "Slight not the opinion of the world. We are dependent beings; and while the smallest trace of virtuous sensibility remain, we must feel the force of that dependence, in a greater or lesser degree." Then, in a moment reminiscent of her Lovelacian speech about the theater, Lucy continues, "No female, whose mind is uncorrupted, can be indifferent to reputation. It is an inestimable jewel, the loss of which can never be repaired. While retained, it affords conscious peace to our own minds, and ensures the esteem and respect of all around us" (133).

While articulating the conventional sentiments of eighteenth-century conduct literature, this speech is also organized by metaphors that can be traced to the seventeenth-century English theatrical tradition; one certain source is the language of Iago, the most notorious false friend in the Shakespearian corpus, whose ideas about the importance of preserving female reputation prove the catalyst for Othello's homicidal madness. Iago's speech to Othello on the subject of his reputation is especially pertinent here: "Good name in man and woman, dear my lord, / Is the immediate jewel of their souls. / Who steals my purse steals trash; 'tis something, nothing; / 'Twas mine, 'tis his, and has been slave to thousands; / But he that filches from me my good name / Robs me of that which not enriches him, / And makes me poor indeed."[77] It is particularly ironic that the character in Foster's novel most hostile to tragic drama should borrow the words of a Shakespearian villain to discipline the heroine into conformity.

However reprobated by the spokeswoman of the community, the theater in *The Coquette* is a figurative site that registers decidedly undidactic identifications between the chorus and the libertine. It also functions as a public space in which the heroine's own drama is recast and displayed. But, if the dramatic stage bears a transgressive symbolic weight in the novel, the circus evokes even more powerfully subversive associations to the heroine's quest for freedom. In the second section of her disquisition on popular amusement, Lucy renders another rabid judgment, this time on the indecent spectacle of other women's moving bodies, rather than on the unwelcome experience of being bodily moved: "The circus is a place of fashionable resort of late, but not agreeable to me. I think it inconsistent with the delicacy of a lady, even to witness the indecorums, which are practiced there; especially, when the performers of equestrian feats are of our own sex. To see a woman depart so far from the female character, as to assume the masculine habit and attitudes; and appear entirely indifferent, even to the externals of modesty, is truly disgusting, and ought not to be countenanced by our attendance, much less by our approbation" (113). Lucy's initial claims in this passage are in fact historically accurate: notable figures in the early national community do indeed patronize the circus. Both George Washington and John Adams attend performances in the 1790s; Washington makes at least two recorded appearances at Rickett's Circus, in Philadelphia, in 1793 and 1797, including a visit on April 22, 1793, coincidentally the day on which he declares the Neutrality Act that allows American ships to carry tonnage for either England or France.

Washington's celebration of "neutrality" at this early point in the 1790s is both emblematic and—against the background of the national movement toward a two-party system at the end of the century—ultimately ironic, as well as suggestive for our reading of *The Coquette*. The first President is renowned for remaining impartial; more than any American of the post-Revolutionary period, he embodies the "disinterested" classical republican. But as the growing partisan divide becomes more rancorous, Washington can no longer continue uninvolved. By the end of his second term, when the Federalists have stopped speaking exclusively for the nation—when the opposition has become a de facto party—the President has to declare his allegiance openly. Washington's inability to maintain neutrality in the sphere of international relations has suggestive resonance for Eliza's domestic situation, where she too eventually capitulates to the demands of the majority.[78]

Theatrical entertainments appealing to Americans of different classes offer venues for heterogeneous political expression in the early republic, and the late-eighteenth-century circus proves no exception: the pantomime of Ricketts' program in 1796, for example, is a "dramatic and patriotic entertainment based on Washington's suppression of the Whiskey Rebellion of 1794."[79] This presentation enacts the failure of an unruly cohort of Pennsylvania democrats whose attempts to defy the orders of the federal government are defeated when a military brigade on horseback, led by President Washington himself, rides into Pennsylvania and faces down the insurgents. Of all the episodes of political dissent in the early national period available for spectacular translation to the center ring, the Whiskey Rebellion proves particularly felicitous: it features both the military and the equestrian fanfare that were to become hallmarks of the American circus, which come together in the person of George Washington astride his horse. Given the first President's renown as the foremost rider in the early republic—Thomas Jefferson characterizes his fellow Virginian as "the best horseman of his age, and the most graceful figure that could be seen on horseback"[80]—the pantomime of the Whiskey Rebellion operates as a fictive showcase for the Federalist hegemony, enacted through the virtuosity of Washington's body.[81] As I hope to suggest, equestrianism in *The Coquette* becomes a figure for a certain kind of political command, and in that regard Washington functions symbolically: his masterful horsemanship reflects at the level of metaphor the President's unique ability to balance the nation's complex affairs and internal divisions and instabilities.

If the pantomime of the Whiskey Rebellion marks Rickett's dramatic affirmation of Federalist policies, his employment of female equestrians gives shape to decidedly other ideological valences. As Lucy's outrage over the women riders suggests, female equestrians in late-eighteenth-century America to some extent share the transgressive cultural status of actresses. Faye E. Dudden observes, "All the theatre's [sic] promises were limited by the fact that women's presence in the play or at the playhouse took place under a moral cloud. Ever since their initial appearance on the English-speaking stage in the Restoration, actresses were associated with sexual immorality. The women who made their living performing on the stage worked in uncomfortable proximity to the 'public women'—slang for prostitutes—who crowded the third tier."[82] Circus equestriennes might very well evoke such associations between theatrical women and sexual pollution, but such an assessment of female performers is by no means universal in the early republic.

That only three women in the 1790s are known to have executed feats on horseback in America suggests that, rather than the vulgar commonplace Lucy implies, acrobatic woman riders are in fact a rarity and, as such, must stir Foster's own imagination in powerful ways. Only two of these three, the famous Mrs. Spinacuta of Ricketts's Circus and a Miss Vanice (Venice) of Lailson's Circus, actually appear in Boston.[83] In its August 31, 1796, edition, the *Columbian Centinel* [sic] reviews Lailson's opening performance and remarks that "[t]he horses had been nearly twenty days on their passage from Europe and suffering from the wounds incident to a sea passage their docility would have gained additional credit to a more healthy and disciplined troop. Miss Venice [found] her horse extremely restive from his wounds and insects [and] he started before she had regained her appropriate balance, and she fell but recovered her situation with a grace and spirit which interested every spectator and commanded the most animated applause."[84] Rather than expostulate on the indecent comportment of a female body on graphic display, this newspaper extols Miss Venice for the equanimity she exhibits on recovering from her fall; the reaction of the audience, reported in the review, suggests that it is her performance of poised refinement, rather than any exhibition of sexual titillation, that earns applause.

This sort of spectatorship calls up Adam Smith's most powerful and compelling metaphors for the experience of sympathy. At the opening of *The Theory of Moral Sentiments*, Smith specifically conjures a circus tableau in order to elaborate his thesis about the workings of fellow feeling. He writes, "The mob, when they are gazing at a dancer on the slack rope, naturally writhe and twist and balance their own bodies, as they see him do, and as they feel that they themselves must do if in his situation." Smith's location of the gaze of sympathy at a circus performance is a striking philosophical parallel—and perhaps the source—for Foster's scene, which represents Lucy's reluctance to indulge in the pain of fellow feeling at a similar exhibition: "But setting aside this circumstance, I cannot conceive it to be a pleasure to sit a whole evening, trembling with apprehension, lest the poor wight of a horseman, or juggler, or whatever he is to be called, should break his neck in contributing to our entertainment" (113). Although gender constitutes the crucial category of difference in the two tableaux, it is nevertheless telling that Lucy exhibits a lack of compassion so profound that it shades into outrage at a sight very like the one that moves Smith's theoretical observer into sympathetic identification. Lucy's attitude toward others and their plights perversely parodies the notions of sympathy and compassion that eighteenth-century aesthetic and moral philosophers—particularly Rousseau and Smith—are espousing.[85]

Despite the fact that in *The Coquette* genteel women all ride horseback for exercise and diversion, equestrianism is immediately problematized as a forum for the heroine's waywardness. The author literalizes this quality through representations of Eliza's immoderate physicality, a zeal for riding that is figured as somewhat unnatural. Foster may be the first American woman writer to use equestrianism as a metaphor for female sexuality: Eliza's problematic desire is embodied in her willingness to travel "so far" in excess of Nancy Laurence, who stands as the norm of female decorum in an early scene. In contrast to Miss Laurence, Eliza is "induced . . . to protract the enjoyment of [the ride] abroad" (46). Almost all of her early and innocent encounters with Sanford involve expeditions on horseback. In light of such detail, the woman equestrian at the Boston circus serves as an objective correlative for Eliza in her quest for freedom. In the expropriation of an activity associated with men and the public sphere, the acrobatic horsewoman embodies a complex and resonant expression of female fancy. Like Eliza before her capitulation to Sanford's erotic advances, the woman equestrian is both sexually suspect and technically innocent of public indecency, and she is simultaneously transgressive in her departure "from the female character" and her assumption of "masculine habit[s] and attitudes," enacting through her exuberant physicality what Eliza expresses in her ironic language.

Tellingly, Eliza's last social commentary, a rare moment in which neither humor nor irony figures in her discourse, comes as a rejoinder to Lucy's castigation of female equestrians in phrases one might use to speak of prostitutes. Eliza's response to Lucy's most salient objection, that these women riders become masculinized, marks the only time she articulates her feelings about female freedom in a single voice, turning to the language of rationality rather than fancy: "Your remarks on the public entertainments are amusing, and as far as I am a judge, perfectly just. I think it a pity they have not female managers for the theatre. I believe it would be under much better regulations, than at present" (124).

Read as an extended metaphor for the heroine's analysis of the politics of gender in early national culture, her advice for regulating the theater proves particularly haunting. If social life is a kind of spectacle, a public stage with political implications, is it not telling that Eliza Wharton desires female executive power to better regulate the system? [86] And if women equestrians represent, on one level, the public commodification of female sexuality as spectacle for the male gaze, Eliza's proposition that female managers could better direct and control such displays suggests something further: that women on horseback, like their male equestrian counterparts, may be both as virtuous and as virtuosic as Washington himself if guaranteed the proper liberty. Women's sexuality, *when managed by women*, need not be debased as theater.

In Lucy's assessment of Boston's popular entertainment in the Federalist period, both the tragic drama and the equestrian circus constitute deeply unruly if not actually transgressive cultural forms, but Bowen's Museum, the third and final place of resort mentioned in her letter on amusements, proves a genteel exception to this disturbing pattern: "With Mr. Bowen's museum, I think you were very much pleased. He has made a number of judicious additions to it, since you were here. It is a source of rational and refined amusement. Here the eye is gratified, the imagination charmed, and the understanding improved. It will bear frequent reviews without palling on the taste. It always affords something new; and for one, I am never a weary spectator" (113). According to Lucy's narrative account, the local modes of mass entertainment break down into three important typologies that reflect late-eighteenth-century ideas about perceptual experience: that of sensibility, both head and heart, undone by tragedy; that of the gazing eye, outraged in its vision of the circus; and that of disembodied reason, elevated by the museum. [87] Both the theater and the circus are modes of spectacle that produce their generic effects through the articulation of physical sensation, but, while the drama calls for a visceral response that immediately translates into cerebral activity, the circus would seem to pander to the baser nature of its audience. Waxworks like those exhibited at Bowen's Museum, in contrast, make of embodiment an uncanny thing: existing on the middle ground between theater and painting, wax figures defamiliarize both the animation of dramatic performance and the stasis of the painted portrait. Such likenesses afford their beholders a greater emotional remove than do theatrical representations, because of their striking resemblance to human bodies that have been cosmetically transformed for viewing before burial. Indeed, as Marie-Hélène Huet suggests in the chapter on Mme Tussaud in *Monstrous Imagination,* evocatively titled "Family Undertaking," there exists a fascinating connection between the art of the mortician and that of the sculptor using wax as a medium. In her discussion of Tussaud's wax museum, Huet argues similarly that the wax figures occupy a transitional space between life and death; Tussaud crafts the faces for her chamber of horrors from death masks she casts from famous personages of the French Revolution.[88]

As an art form whose origin lies in mortuary practices, waxworks make particularly evocative objects of admiration in *The Coquette,* given the associations between the patriarchal majority and the clerical dead that Foster draws throughout. I will return to this connection shortly, but before doing so it is important to understand something more about the origins and nature of the cultural forum in which these waxworks are displayed.[89] Daniel Bowen's museum originates as a traveling exhibition that moves up and down the eastern seaboard in the post-Revolutionary period. Its growth and development, though given scant detail, are recorded briefly in histories of both the early American theater and the circus as well as in books on the origins of waxworks in the new nation. Amplifying on contemporary newspaper reviews that enumerate the contents of the collection in the 1790s, Isaac Greenwood provides a late-nineteenth-century account:

> In 1788 and '89, Mr. Bowen had a much more extensive exhibit at No. 74 Water street, opposite Crane Wharf [in New York City], with which he had come up from the Carolinas; it included the Royal Family, several of the prominent clergy of the city, some scriptural and humorous subjects, and the President, with a flying figure overhead crowning him with laurel.[90]

Late-eighteenth-century newspaper advertisements for the museum provide an extensive if hyperbolic catalogue of its curiosities (most likely composed by Daniel Bowen himself). A notice run on December 7, 1795, announces in somewhat less heightened language that

BOWEN's Columbian Museum At the head of the Mall, BOSTON, WAS opened (for the first time) on Thursday last, Containing a large and elegant collection of PAINTINGS, historical, theatrical, and fancy subjects; with portraits of some of the most distinguished characters in the United States; Landscapes, Drawing, &c. Wax figures in a detached room; a perfect representation of a man suffering under the guillotine. The assassination of John P. Marat by Miss Charlotte Carde [*sic*]. Baron Trench loaded with chains in a Dungeon. A great variety of more pleasing Wax Figures placed in the museum hall. *Curiosities*, natural, and artificial, among which, are a Glass Ship; a real Scalp of an Indian Chief, lately taken at the Westward; together with a Collection of Birds, in the highest state of preservation, &c.[91]

These historical facts allow us to make some informed speculations about the symbolic import of the curiosities Bowen displays to the public and to which Lucy makes general reference in *The Coquette*.

In its elaborate totality, the exhibit constitutes a narrative representation of early national identity formation at work. As scholars of Charles Brockden Brown have argued, the American subject—read native or English born, white, male, and middle class—is constructed over against the bodies of the new republic's reprobated alien, African, Native, "savage," female, and indigent others who function as the negative of this picture. The effigy of Charlotte Corday telegraphs in elegantly economical fashion a composite version of the loathed trio of American altierity: the alien (she is French); the savage (like the Native Americans who threaten the frontier, she too is a barbarous murderess); and the female. While Bowen's waxen image of the guillotine reinforces the impact of Mlle Corday's homicidal power and underscores the Federalists' virulent hostility to the events, practices, and material artifacts of the French Revolution, the scalp of the Native American becomes not only an emblem of the vicious ferocity of the republic's aboriginal enemies but also an index of early American colonial prowess; in this fetishistic display of the scalp, early republicans can disavow their own decided affinity for savage acts of violence, behavior that unsettles any claims to moral and cultural superiority attending the establishment of national identity and of individual republican selfhood.[92]

In light of the contents of the exhibition, patriarchal power—incarnated in the figures of George the Third and his family, notable members of the local clergy, and George Washington being crowned with laurel—would

BY PERMISSION.
EXHIBITION of WAX-WORK.

MR. *BOWEN* respectfully in-
forms the publick, that THIS
EVENING, will be exhibited in the
HALL of the *American Coffee-House*, in
State-Street, a large

Collection of WAX-WORK :—
*Among which are the following Principal
Figures*, LARGE AS LIFE :—

THE PRESIDENT of the United States, and his
LADY : With an elegant Reprefentation of the
Union of LIBERTY, JUSTICE, PEACE, and
PLENTY.

Doctor FRANKLIN, in a fuit of black,
Bifhop PROVOST, and the Rev. Dr. ROGERS,
New-York.

The KING and QUEEN, of Great-Britain, and
the PRINCE OF WALES

&Baron TRENCK, who was confined upwards of
on years in a Dungeon, at Magdeburg, in Pruffia.
He is ftanding on his Tomb-Stone, in real chains, of
great weight.

A handfome young Lady, elegantly dreffed, called,
" A PHILADELPHIA BEAUTY."

A NUN at confeffion, kneeling before a ERIAR.
The SLEEPING BEAUTY.

An INDIAN CHIEF, painted and dreffed in his
War-habit, holding a real Scalp—With a variety of
other FIGURES.

☞ This Exhibition has met the approbation of many of the moft refpecta-
ble characters on the continent, and is
univerfally allowed to merit the patronage and attention of the publick.

The Proprietor has been at great ex-
penfe in completing his Exhibition in
that manner, which he hopes will entertain agreeably, all thofe who may ho-
nour him with their company.

*Time of admittance will be from 7 until
9 o'clock, every evening, (Sunday's excepted.)*

☞ Tickets, at 3ſ. each, for Ladies and Gentlemen, and 1/6 for Children,
may be had at the Door, in the evening,
or at any hour of the day.

Tickets, (not transferable) for the Sea-
fon) *One Dollar.*

MINIATURE PAINTING perform-
ed at the fame place, on reafonable terms

*Newpaper advertisement for
Bowen's Museum, from the*
Columbian Centinel *[sic], 1 June
1791. (Courtesy the Newberry
Library)*

seem to be the prevailing theme of Bowen's wax assemblage. This panorama is peopled by an idealized if phantasmagoric gathering of the early republican elite who coexist in odd array with their former political nemesis and his kin. The characters of the two wax Georges, the literal (ex)-monarch of the Anglo-American community and the figurative "father" of the new nation, reflect two visions of authority existing in such close proximity in the Federalist imagination that their boundaries begin to blur;[93] though his wreath is made of laurel rather than gold, the spectacle nevertheless enacts the wish that Washington be crowned.[94] If we read the tableau as a narrative, the separate parts of which exist in syntactical relation to each other, the contiguity of these two Georges becomes significant. Despite the powerful and transformative reality of the American Revolution, these uncanny mirror figures signify that the republic's orientation lies as much in a patriarchal and autocratic past as it does in any rising liberal future.[95] The notable figures of the local clergy only reinforce this reading, and their presence in the display conjures the spectral patriarchs of Foster's book, the ministers Wharton, Haly, and Boyer.

While the tragic and equestrian entertainments recast *The Coquette*'s abiding thematic issues in uncanny form, the museum's curiosities constitute a far more direct if nevertheless exalted reflection of the novel's social world. Crafted in wax, which gives them the unnatural aura of corpses,[96] the figures in Bowen's Museum dramatically display what we might call the "consolidated ego ideal" of the Federalist elite; composing a striking vision of hegemonic political authority en route to ossification, the collection personifies the values of the community for which Lucy Freeman Sumner speaks in *The Coquette*.

Projecting and affirming an idealized image of the world she actually inhabits, the museum is the perfect "place . . . of resort" for Lucy Freeman Sumner (113); it becomes not only a site of recreation or entertainment but also a refuge and a resource. In fact, Foster's word bears both meanings: deriving from the Old French term "to escape, ally," resort is related to the word "resource," which comes from the Latin for resurrection and means a "source of supply or support," "something to which one has recourse in difficulty," a "possibility of relief or recovery."[97] In the second half of the novel, the notions of resort and resource take on vital importance, as the letters that pass between the heroine and her community begin to chart the progressive disappearance of such forms of respite for Eliza in the face of her quest for freedom.

The Female World of Love and Ritual

The nostalgia infusing Eliza's ruminations over cherished moments of female communion suggests that, for the heroine, resort has existed exclusively in the homosocial circle. Lying at the center of Eliza's yearnings, the world of female friendship that had sustained her grows increasingly barren with every rite of passage undertaken by one of its members. It is no accident that Foster populates her novel with a group of women who exist at significantly different points on the developmental continuum of female experience: Mrs. Wharton is a widow; Mrs. Richman becomes a mother and then is bereaved of her child; Lucy Freeman turns into a bride, losing her significant maiden name; Eliza exists in the throes of courtship and failed betrothal; and Julia Granby emerges to usurp the heroine's place as an eligible young lady.[98] Every transformation of status further disturbs the equilibrium that grounded what we might call this idealized *republic* of women—Eliza's fantastic vision of an elite collectivity in which virtue and interdependence are the hallmarks of social relations. But this utopia exists only in fancy, as the example of Julia Granby proves: the girlhood community is always already shaken by tremors emanating from the marriage market, the pressures of which are virtually inescapable.

As its members realign along heterosexual and reproductive lines and the doctrines of republican wife and motherhood bear down on them, annexing their energy and redirecting it inside the family, the center of this collective shifts significantly. Having lived at the hub of the circle, Eliza finds herself gravitating toward its margins, compelled by her "eccentric" and "wayward" impulses to resist confinement by republican ideologies constructed to channel and bind women's nondomestic impulses. In the novel's most important critique of republican marriage, Eliza writes of the Richmans' contentment as a kind of social withdrawal and inversion: "They should consider, said I, that they have no satisfaction to look for beyond each other. There every enjoyment is centered; but I am a poor solitary being, who need some amusement beyond what I can supply myself. The mind, after being confined at home for a while, sends the imagination abroad in quest of new treasures, and the body may as well accompany it, for ought I can see" (14–15). The heroine's analysis of this union, which in its exercise of mutual interest and affection marks the nuptial ideal of the novel, in fact reveals the contradiction lying at the heart of early national domestic ideology; it is not the protoliberal Eliza who seeks to retreat into the recesses of privacy but rather the "disinterested" and civic-minded Richmans who mask their possessive individualism with the rhetoric of late-eighteenth-century American republican marriage.

In the resounding refrain that "marriage is the tomb of friendship" (24), Eliza articulates the judgment that matrimony does more than simply dampen the impulse toward public virtue and sociality; her assertion suggests that wedlock actually destroys such communitarian impulses. The incisiveness of this insight comes hauntingly home during Lucy's wedding. Foster emphasizes the heroine's grief over her friend's transformation by having the outspoken Eliza make her own silence a recurring motif of the letter in which she recounts the nuptials. This episode rings a change on the scene where Mrs. Richman imperiously presumes to speak for the heroine, an act of vocal cooptation unfolded from Mr. Selby's external, dramatic point of view. Finding the voice she had uncharacteristically lost at the wedding, Eliza pens an eloquent missive to Mrs. Richman in which she relates the disquieting experience of being unable to bring herself to utter a word: "Every eye beamed with pleasure on the occasion, and every tongue echoed the wishes of benevolence. Mine only was silent" (70).

Eliza's muteness on the occasion of Lucy's marriage prefigures the silence with which she will respond to her traumatic initiation into adult sexuality; if female homosocial bonds are knit of epistolary fabric, heterosexuality is the force that unravels such ties in Foster's fictive universe. On the eve of Lucy's marriage Eliza reflects, "Though not less interested in the felicity of my friend than the rest, yet the idea of a separation; perhaps, an alienation of affection, by means of her entire devotion to another, cast an involuntary gloom over my mind" (70). That the most outspoken woman in the novel should have nothing to say in the face of Lucy's submission to the rituals of patriarchy suggests that silence itself becomes an expressive venue when there is no audible space for dissent.

Yet the chorus's ability to decode the meaning of the heroine's reticence proves as poor as its grasp of the irony that marks her letters. Thus, to Boyer, Eliza's sorrow over Lucy's wedding becomes an opportunity for advancing his own romantic cause, not an occasion for extending the sympathy and commiseration for which the heroine virtually pleads, "Permit me, Miss Wharton, said he, to lead you to your lovely friend; her happiness must be heightened by your participation of it. Oh no; said I, I am too selfish for that. She has conferred upon another that affection which I wished to engross. My love was too fervent to admit a rival. Retaliate, then, said he, this fancied wrong, by doing likewise. I observed that this was not a proper time to discuss that subject" (70). Eliza's refusal to affirm the felicitous nature of Lucy's metamorphosis marks another moment in which her language, notable here as an eloquent failure of expression, articulates her resistance to romantic norms. The negativity she expresses by withholding her congratulations extends beyond the level of a pointed violation of social forms and into a statement of censure by omission. As the novel's incarnation of convention and propriety, Mr. Boyer responds to Eliza's silence in predictable fashion, endeavoring to script her behavior, produce her appropriate congratulations, and extract her consent to his offer of marriage. Such acquiescence remains unspeakable for Eliza until she finally appropriates the minister's language and extends the offer herself, thereby subverting Mr. Boyer's demand for her compliance and annulling his desire for her hand.

Major Sanford is equally unsuccessful in generating language of consent from the heroine: her sexual capitulation to the libertine takes place outside the representational register, neither discussed in the remaining letters she writes nor depicted in dramatic form by the novel's other correspondents. Like Boyer, Sanford wishes to obtain words of concurrence from Eliza, but the rake is able to value the tragedy of the heroine's silence in ways that the minister is not. Immediately prior to her flight from home, he reports a moment in which speech fails Eliza: "I begged leave to visit her retirement next week, not in continuation of our amour, but as a friend, solicitous to know her situation and welfare. Unable to speak, she only bowed assent" (160). A vital, if ostensibly reprobated, member of a community that would ventriloquize for the heroine, Sanford nevertheless recognizes the way in which Eliza has been confined by the dominant voice of the chorus—whose opinion she ultimately internalizes in an act of capitulation that marks her movement toward death.

The heroine's final fate in the novel suggests that it is not only marriage, per se, but heterosexuality itself that binds women's zeal for liberty and engenders their "confinement." As we have seen, feminist historians studying the early national period note that the ideologies of republican daughterhood, wifehood, and motherhood reenvision the operations of domesticity as outlets for political expression. Foster's story troubles the recuperative thrust of these accounts by exposing the fact that women in the Federalist period are themselves aware of the limits and internal fissures that mark such roles. In that regard, Mrs. Richman's rhapsodies about the civic benefits of republican motherhood ring the sound of early national patriarchal propaganda that the novel itself will disrupt. Her most famous articulation of the formula comes in the statement that "the *little community* which we super-intend is quite as important an object [as former associations like friend-ships]; and certainly renders us more *beneficial to the public*" (25, my empha-sis). As an ostensible form of female agency that in fact operates through mechanisms of displacement, how does republican motherhood give women real power to influence the public sphere? Foster short-circuits any efforts to draw political conclusions when she issues a generic blight on maternity in *The Coquette* by killing off every child born within its pages.[99]

The author identifies Eliza with Mrs. Richman's ill-fated baby Harriot, from the beginning of the story: the heroine visits the Richmans during the pregnancy, playing the role of surrogate child; she is effectively replaced in Mrs. Richman's affections by Harriot's arrival, evidenced by the paucity of postpartum letters from the new mother; and her destiny is portended omi-nously in the little girl's death before her second birthday. It is no accident that the fact of Eliza's fall from sexual innocence—a transformation never narrated from her own point of view—is displaced onto her report of the death of the Richman's babe (134). A double for Eliza, the daughter of Fos-ter's Washington figure incarnates in female form a sense of hope for the new republic and, simultaneously, the precariousness of its survival.

The death of this baby carries complex symbolic resonance: it stands for the fragility of republican motherhood as an efficacious occupation for patri-otic women, and it dramatically enacts the new nation's hostility to both fe-male creativity and a viable female future. Equally emblematic is Foster's gendering of the novel's other newborn babies and her depiction of their fates: Major Sanford's wife, the lovely and unappreciated heiress Nancy, de-livers a dead baby boy. The dissipated aristocracy has reached the end of its line in a legitimate but stillborn male Sanford heir. Meanwhile, Eliza's mis-begotten babe, who dies shortly after birth, is represented without being gen-dered, erased of the basic rudiments of identity and rendered placeless by its illicit genealogy.

Good republican stock, however, survives the trauma of birth and actu-ally flourishes for nearly two years. One cannot help speculating on potential political allegory at work here; as a vision of republican life in the era without Washington, Foster's novel would portend bleak prospects for America in-deed. In that regard, it is significant that the only female baby in the novel is also the only child who weathers the storms of infancy. In this gesture, Foster makes an important connection between young Harriot and Eliza as republican daughters, figures whose status remains tied to their families of origin rather than to their future marriage choices or any children they might produce.[100] Equally suggestive is the developmental detail that the author provides about Harriot: we learn from a letter penned by Mrs. Richman that the little girl, approaching two, has not yet learned to talk. In a moment of joyful expectation, ruminating on the potential pleasure of hearing her daughter speak for the first time, the mother exclaims, "How delightful to trace from day to day the expansion of reason and the dawnings of intelligence! Oh, how I anticipate the time, when these faculties shall be displayed by the organs of speech; when the lisping accent shall heighten our present pleasure" (97). This maternal fantasy, the auditory projection of a baby girl's voice at the dawn of its expressive career, takes us as close to an image of uncorrupted female language as we are to reach in *The Coquette*. Like the theatrical tableaux that appear in Eliza's letters, this too is an epistolary daydream, but one that rings a change on the heroine's dramatic self-inventions, for, despite her linguistic efforts at resistance, the wish to be known as a voice rather than as a phenomenal vision, Eliza remains immersed in the realm of the visible, even in her fancy.

Mrs. Richman's imaginings would seem to uncouple female expression from the specular regime and relocate it in sonorous language. But her fantasy proves as ephemeral as any of Eliza's whimsical flights. Though phantasmagorically Harriot's words remain immune to totalizing forms of patriarchal inscription, what Lacan characterizes as the imprint of the "symbolic register," these infant utterances never reach articulation. The dream of an imaginable female language that in fact will never materialize becomes Foster's most powerful metaphor for the failed promise of women's expression in Federalist America. Rowson's utopian fantasies about a maternal voice so powerful that it could register in the symbolic regime of language and culture form a vivid contrast to Foster's more gothic vision of the possibilities for female expression—the vision of Harriot Richman shut up in the grave. The dead babe is thus a figure for the heroine's blighted possibility, the end of her "youthful" career, and the loss of her womanly innocence and liberty. If to Eliza domesticity has meant constriction, then that equation will be brutally literalized in her final experiences: once she gives up her freedom, symbolized by her virginity, the tragic result is a one way journey of "confinement," pregnancy, labor, delivery, and, finally, death, the ultimate form of restriction, isolation, and alienation.

The letter recounting the demise of baby Harriot can be seen as Foster's pessimistic meditation on the limits of women's creativity, for it also describes Eliza's very changed attitude toward epistolary composition itself: "Writing is an employment, which suits me not at present. It was pleasing to me formerly, and therefore, by recalling the idea of circumstances and events which frequently occupied my pen in happier days, it now gives me pain" (134). As the likelihood of sympathetic understanding and exchange narrows down to near impossibility, the prospect of writing to a hostile audience loses all appeal. Thereafter, the heroine's letters are prompted by the need to transmit pressing social information; thus, she relays the news of Harriot Richman's death, which is followed by a drawn-out, abstract meditation on bereavement over children. Eliza is mourning for Harriot, for herself, and for her own unborn child: none of these figures has the remotest chance of surviving in the world of *The Coquette*. All acts of female invention—writing and childbearing—would seem to lead from a delusive pleasure to silence, loss, and death.

That ideologically inflected maternity guarantees neither women's patriotic occupation nor their happiness in Foster's fictive world is made clear by the loving but distant connection that exists between Eliza and Mrs. Wharton; their relationship, marked by a shared reluctance to engage in intimate exchange, is the only ongoing mother-daughter bond that Foster represents. Although each pays lip service to a mutual devotion, in fact the heroine and her mother correspond only twice until Eliza's final confession and request for absolution in the closing pages of the novel. Punctuating Eliza's letters to the chorus, the reports of their conversations reveal a pointed failure of communication that takes one of two unfortunate forms: each woman suppresses her true thoughts and feelings in full cognizance of the other's opinion; alternatively, Mrs. Wharton indulges in the monitorial censure of the chorus, while Eliza responds with angry defiance. Once she has eloped, Charlotte Temple fares little better than Eliza in her experience of the mother-daughter bond, though in Rowson's novel attempts at connection are thwarted by the forces of villainy rather than by vast temperamental differences between parent and child. Nevertheless, it is worth noting that the most powerful maternal-filial bond in *Charlotte Temple* is disembodied and phantasmagoric, as if even in its utopian heyday the early American novel cannot incarnate this union in material and inner-textual form.

Early in the novel, despite the uneasy reality of actual relations with her mother, Eliza expresses the longing that the maternal embrace could provide a respite from the tyranny of the majority, whose exertions on behalf of Mr.

Boyer's suit have begun to alienate her. She writes to her mother, "The different dispositions of various associates, sometimes perplex the mind, which seeks direction; but in the disinterested affection of the maternal breast, we fear no dissonance of passion, no jarring interests, no disunion of love. In this seat of felicity is every enjoyment which fancy can form, or friendship, with affluence, bestow; but still my mind frequently returns to the happy shades of my nativity. I wish there to impart my pleasures, and share the counsels of my best, my long tried and experienced friend" (39). That Mrs. Wharton has been squarely aligned with the community's strictures is clear from Eliza's inaugural letter, in which she describes how both parents had been instrumental in urging the match with Haly (6). In light of that fact, this laudatory epistle must be read not as a mimetic account of maternal liberality, but instead as the heroine's idealizing wish to escape the oppressive majority for a comfortable and tolerant maternal breast—one that exists primarily in her imagination. In the name of "disinterest," a key term in republican theory and one that both *The Coquette* and the other early American novels explored in this study rigorously interrogate, the heroine enlists her mother to take her side, but her mother's home, an ongoing repository of associations to the patriarchal dead, is the very place from which Eliza had initially sought to flee.

Under the guise of loving concern, Mrs. Wharton's failure to affirm her daughter's desire for succor is utterly in keeping with the values of the community she has always upheld. Eliza writes to Lucy, "My mamma doubtless saw the disorder of my mind, but kindly avoided any inquiry about it. She was affectionately attentive to me but said nothing of my particular concerns. I mentioned not my embarrassments to her. She had declared herself in favor of Mr. Boyer; therefore I had no expectation, that she would advise impartially" (89). Refraining from any entreaty about her daughter's troubles, Mrs. Wharton offers a form of "affectionate attention" that becomes tantamount to emotional tyranny when, in the following passage, she determines to speak for Eliza without her daughter's knowledge. Eliza relates the conversation in which her mother concedes that she has dismissed Major Sanford from their door: "she thought it unnecessary to call me, as she presumed I had no particular business with him" (89).

Beginning with the mutual exchange of speechless gazes telegraphing the reality of all that cannot be said and ending with the mother's imperious usurpation of her daughter's agency, this entire episode enacts a powerful dialectic of specularity and silence that comes to dominate Foster's representation of Eliza in the final portion of the novel. At the end of the scene, the heroine speaks out, castigating her mother for interfering with her romantic affairs. But, in the face of the chorus's efforts to foreclose her expressions of dissent, Eliza later increasingly withdraws into reticence and immobility. The articulate heroine becomes a monumental and voiceless spectacle, transformed into the object of a gaze she can no longer legislate by a chorus that refuses to harken to her transgressive language.

In that regard, silence, which initially functions as a mode of resistance, ultimately marks Eliza's internalization of the community's real desire that she cease and desist from disputing its admonitions. With her death in sight, the heroine claims no expectation of forgiveness from "the general voice" (143), by which she means the feminized chorus under whose censorious judgment and opprobrium she suffers. Eliza asserts that all she desires is the consolation of maternal forgiveness: "From the general voice I expect no clemency. If I can make my peace with my mother, it is all I seek or wish on this side of the grave" (143). What Eliza never fully grasps is the tragic fact that the maternal voice and the general voice are fatally intertwined.

Fetishism and Live Burial

> At the hour appointed, I went tolerably composed and resolute into the garden. I had taken several turns, and retired into the little arbor, where you and I have spent so many happy hours, before Major Sanford entered.
>
> (Eliza Wharton to Lucy Freeman, 91)

As a space of resort, the female world of love and ritual that Eliza nostalgically recalls in this letter haunts Foster's novel in two important ways: within the fiction, a women's sphere exists only in the girlhood of Eliza's past; and outside the book, in the world of history, a sanctioned female homosocial realm does not come into meaningful existence until the first quarter of the nineteenth century.[101] By attempting to identify sisterhood as a redemptive arena for women's action in Foster's book, critics such as Pettengill seek to recuperate the novel from its melancholy ending, but, in the present tense of *The Coquette*'s historical moment, a separate sphere of adult women, living in meaningful relation to each other inside but apart from patriarchal culture, is simply a fantasy. Pettengill is attentive to the contradictions republican ideology presents to American women in the early national period, noting that Eliza is angry at the "inadequacies of both sisterhood and republican motherhood, which have promised so much and delivered so little" (197). But her idealizing argument that homosocial bonds constitute a distinct space of possibility for women ignores the fact that the female community, pointedly called "the whole *fraternity*" by Major Sanford (158, my emphasis), exists at no distance from the dominant culture and in fact has been thoroughly penetrated by the patriarchal values for which it speaks.[102]

The "world of love and ritual" Carroll Smith-Rosenberg identifies in the essay of that name is a very different place from the fictional universe of Foster's book. Smith-Rosenberg writes that this was a domain "in which hostility and criticism of other women were discouraged, and thus a milieu in which women could develop a sense of inner security and self-esteem." She goes on to note that "an intimate mother-daughter relationship lay at the heart of this female world" and that the marriage relation did not foreclose on the intimacy of women's friendships, which were recognized as socially "viable forms of human contact—and as such, acceptable throughout a woman's life."[103] In the imaginary realm of *The Coquette,* the female community expresses hostility to the heroine's quest for freedom from the beginning of the novel; she cannot depend on her mother to provide interested and supportive relief from the romantic pressures that burden her; and marriage diminishes if not destroys the depth and power of her female friendships.[104] A separate sphere constituted by, of, and for women simply does not exist in *The Coquette.* Pointing beyond the margins of Foster's book, Eliza Wharton's tragic quest for freedom eloquently bespeaks the need for such a world.

Under this illumination we can read the nostalgic quotation from Eliza's letter in two different ways. It suggests, on the one hand, that what the heroine really seeks in the arbor is a reprisal of the kind of bond she has shared with Lucy, even if such sympathy emanates from the libertine. Indeed, Eliza understands her capitulation to Sanford solely in terms of his willingness to offer her the conversation, companionship, and understanding that the chorus has failed to provide: "I embraced with avidity the consoling power of friendship, ensnaringly offered by my seducer" (145). On the other hand, a far darker reading is possible. Major Sanford is surely the snake in Eliza's current garden. The odd syntax of the sentence describing the libertine's sudden advent endows him with a peculiar destructive power that collapses the multiple temporalities organizing the heroine's description: it is as if he has come to destroy both the present moment with Boyer as well as the past pleasures of a lost homosocial paradise. The fantasy of a female world of love and ritual is always already shattered by the presence of a destructive force woven into its very fabric, embodied either by a third figure who breaks up its characteristically dyadic bonds or by an internal attribute of the other in the pair who fails to function as a sympathetic mirror. Sanford is able to glide seamlessly into the space that has been inhabited by the spokeswoman of the chorus precisely because the two figures incarnate, in superficially antagonistic form, the same repressive principle. Whether driven into melancholic despair, silence, or illicit sexuality by the intolerance of the chorus or actually consumed and wasted by the voraciousness of the rake, Eliza Wharton is destined to suffer an unrelenting fate, one that in either case involves erasure, invisibility, and, finally, death.

That the impulses of the female community prove as sadistic and destructive to Eliza's equanimity as the physical incursions of the libertine, that, indeed, they are symbolically *linked,* is brought home in the curious behavior of Julia Granby, the confidante Eliza recruits from Boston to take Lucy's place, on the latter's defection to marriage. After a one-year absence and in the company of a new wife, Major Sanford returns to Hartford, news that provokes Eliza to remark that she "has no wish to see him," since "his presence may open the wounds which time is closing" (117). Rather than affirming the heroine's resolve and restraint, Julia's advice to Eliza is perversely monitorial: "I see no harm in conversing with him, said Julia. Perhaps it may remove some disagreeable thoughts, which now oppress and give you pain. And as he is no longer a candidate for your affections, added she, with a smile, it will be less hazardous than formerly. He will not have the insolence to speak, nor you the folly to hear, the language of love" (117). As the community's ultimate spokeswoman, Julia imperiously believes it is her prerogative to determine and script its vocal practices.

The newcomer also wants to retrace the primal scene of Eliza's close encounter with and avoidance of sexual transgression in the arbor. The heroine notes, "Julia and I have been rambling in the garden. She insisted upon my going with her into the arbor, where I was surprised by Major Sanford" (109). Designed to instruct Eliza by provoking her aversion in the form of unhappy memories, this bizarre exhortation is offered under the guise of moral exercise. But Julia's notions of leisure and reflection constitute nothing less than an attempt to execute the punishment of the chorus in all its sadistic self-righteousness. How else are we to understand her compulsion to reenact the drama in which Eliza's disastrous romantic fate is sealed? Symbolically, of course, Julia's gesture rehearses the wish to insert herself into Lucy's structural position, to reprise the role of the heroine's companion at the scene of their youthful female pleasures, but, in "insisting" that Eliza accompany her into the arbor, she also recapitulates the very demand that Major Sanford has made, the exigency that has ruined Eliza's prospects with Boyer. In requiring Eliza to restage that trauma, Julia metaphorically identifies with the libertine. Thus, these two ostensibly divergent readings—one innocently homosocial, the other demoniacally heterosexual—are in fact congruent: Lucy and Sanford and Julia Granby herself all are linked inextricably in Foster's narrative economy.

Despite a moral zeal that puts Julia in the forefront of the chorus, she is tagged as a virtual doppelgänger for the heroine as well, personifying, according to Eliza, "all that I once was; easy, sprightly, debonair" (108). Julia embodies Eliza's finest qualities without her unreasonable desire for freedom; she replicates the heroine's charms while she simultaneously reflects back on the community the level of moral hygiene it requires. Eliza continues her praise of Julia in a remarkably terse letter to Lucy, the last epistle she will ever write to Mrs. Sumner. She opines that Julia is "a valuable friend. Her mind is well cultivated; and she has treasured up a fund of knowledge and information, which renders her company both agreeable and useful in every situation in life" (127). Eliza's withdrawal from what had been her most intimate and meaningful correspondence must be read in the context of Julia's advent in Hartford: knowing that her friend will triumph under the chorus's scrutiny, Eliza cedes her social stakes to Julia, who begins to absorb the glare of collective attention. It is fitting that immediately after Eliza drafts the letter commending Julia as an ideal life companion, she withdraws from the quasi publicity of epistolarity into the private recesses of the female body and gnomic silence. As Eliza bows out of a spectacle in which she can no longer bear to play a starring role, Julia, the perfect understudy, assumes the lead in the patriarchal drama of proper female comportment.

Once Julia becomes the central correspondent in the final quarter of the novel, she also seizes narrative hold of Eliza Wharton's life; by doing so, the newcomer literally usurps the last vestige of control Eliza maintained over her destiny—the power to tell and shape her own story. Julia even attempts to appropriate Eliza's language: she is the only woman in the novel to borrow the heroine's ironic locutions from the public sphere, remarking that "a treaty of peace, and amity (but not of commerce)" has been "ratified" between Eliza and the libertine (120). In her efforts to occupy the heroine's linguistic place, she uncannily repeats the earlier moment in which Mrs. Richman also spoke "for" Eliza. The desire to assume the voice of the dangerously political woman becomes tantamount to rendering her mute: for to occupy another woman's subjectivity in *The Coquette* is to annex and ultimately to efface it.

From the time of her rejection by Mr. Boyer to the point at which she succumbs to Major Sanford's sexual demands, Eliza charts a trajectory of increasing social withdrawal, domestic confinement, physical immobility, and epistolary silence. In her drive to escape relegation to the world of domesticity by asserting her sexual freedom as a last resort, she winds up as confined, homebound, and trammeled as the most docile of republican wives. Eliza's capitulation to Sanford under her mother's roof marks the final enactment of her double-voicedness: an attack on the very heart of domestic ideology, Eliza's defilement of maternal space at the same time reveals that, despite her hostility to home and hearth, she cannot escape their pervasive reach.[105] The immobility that overtakes Eliza operates in direct contrast to her former propensity to remain always in motion. Wayward desire has become paralyzed. In fact, it is not an overstatement to say that Eliza begins to suffer the symptoms of agoraphobia (literally, fear of the marketplace) after having been utterly exploited by market conditions: "I intended, this week, to have journeyed to Boston with Julia Granby; but my resolution fails me. I find it painful even to think of mixing again with the gay multitude. I believe the melancholy reflections, by which I am oppressed, will be more effectually, if not more easily, surmounted, by tarrying where they are rendered familiar, than by going from them awhile, and then returning" (126). Eliza's bad feelings allow her space neither for dissent nor even for escape but render her incapacitated and frozen; in contrast, having assumed Eliza's former life and identity, Julia Granby is able to travel with full mobility.

That we can locate Eliza's sexual fall in the period of Julia's ill-timed visit to Lucy, when the heroine, sunk in the depths of despair, needs the newcomer's companionship more than ever, suggests how unmerciful the majority's adherence to republican ideology can be. Despite the overpresence of the moralizing chorus and its rhetoric of sororial care, the community's investment in "disinterest" becomes code for an inability to tolerate fanciful behaviors like melancholic resignation. Such brutality is not unique to Julia. Both Lucy and Sanford himself turn their backs on Eliza's predicament at the end of the novel, the former in order to travel into the country with her husband and the latter so he can protect his property from confiscation by angry creditors. The matron and the libertine uphold, respectively, two defining attributes of the classical republican citizen: allegiance to republican wifehood and concern for the preservation of financial independence; allowing such ideologically driven considerations to supercede the claims of any possible "interest" in Eliza, both Lucy and Sanford show their dispassionate colors while the heroine is sacrificed in the wake of their insensibility.

Claims for sympathy become compelling to the community only after the threat posed by Eliza's zeal for freedom is neutralized by her death: from outspokenness to silence to immobility and dissolution, the heroine regains her appeal to her women friends as she moves toward the monumentality of an emblem.[106] Indeed, Julia will liken the no-longer-virginal Eliza, reclined on a settee, to a statue, "in a very thoughtful posture," sitting "'Like patience on a monument, smiling at grief.'" (137). Her quotation from *Twelfth Night* (2.4. 110–115) is evocative on multiple levels. Iconographically, it likens the heroine's stasis to the fixity of the patriarchal dead, suggesting that in her stillness, Eliza has herself become tomblike. The allusion to Shakespeare's comedy of cross-dressed women "assuming [the] masculine habit and attitudes" (*Coquette*, 113), also deepens the connection between Eliza's transgressive quest for female freedom and her eventual confinement and death. Finally, Shakespeare's words resonate on the metanarrative level: they are spoken by Viola who, dressed as a boy, concocts the story of a sister—fictional doppelgänger for her transvestite self—who "never told her love" (2.4. 110). The theme of speaking for the silent woman who is herself a product of the fancy of a cross-dressed narrator brings us back to the central political and aesthetic issues of Foster's book, as well as to her unique dilemma as a woman writer in the Federalist period. The majority can align the dead Eliza, as they could not do romantically when she lived, with the clerical patriarchs whose uncanny power she sought so desperately to escape. No longer able to express her dissent through either voice or pen, Eliza is nevertheless more audible after her passing than she was during her final decline: remnants of her writing from the period of her confinement surface and circulate as community property, enabling the chorus to *re-cover* its vision of Eliza by selectively revising the words its members had found so problematic.

In a novel absorbed with a failure of female decorum, it is apt that Foster foregrounds the metaphor of the veil to describe these practices of re-covery and re-vision. "Veiling" is *The Coquette*'s term for the process we have come to call "fetishism," the chorus's magnification of and substitution for the heroine's transgressive qualities in order to occlude or ward off the disturbing sight of her imperfection or lack.[107] Although this mechanism is usually associated with Freudian psychoanalytic theory and as such with a late-nineteenth-century European sensibility, in fact the general dynamic takes significant social and political form in the early culture of the American 1790s—most notably in the national fetishization of Washington.[108] Idealized by the people and their representatives as the living incarnation of republican virtue, the great Washington, less private man than public totem, eclipses any competitor who could appear on the political landscape. Indeed, his gigantic shadow obscures the very sight of those smaller men, Adams, Jefferson, and others, who are diminished simply by living in Washington's wake. This national investment in a primal father enables the illusion that government and politicians themselves are not riddled by interest, venality, and deficiency; the fetish of Washington makes it possible for Americans to disavow the reality of increasing political conflict by facilitating a fantasy of paternal care so powerful that it might ward off social contention forever. The idea of Washington is virtually all that keeps the Jeffersonian democratic-republican cohort, already operating coherently beneath the surface of Federalist politics by the early to mid-1790s, from becoming fully visible at the level of public acknowledgment.

In Foster's novel, which translates national politics into social drama, the practice of fetishism is not unique to the chorus. Indeed, Eliza's doomed engagement to the invalid Haly can be seen as the collective acting out of a fetishistic impulse. By allying herself "romantically" with the ailing minister, Eliza diverts the negative gaze of the community from the sight of her singleness: that the man is dying affords the heroine both the prospective protection of coverture and the promise of future freedom. Reciprocally, by fetishizing the heroine's betrothal to the minister, the chorus can disavow and defend against the reality of Eliza's waywardness, volatility, and zeal for liberty, the incontrovertible fact of her resistance to republican marriage. As a collaborative act of fetishism, the engagement temporarily affords the heroine the tolerance of the chorus, while it appeases the majority's need for Eliza's social compliance. The only figure excluded from this collective conspiracy is the Rev. Haly, who, dying in a state of celestial assurance, remains detached from the profane machinations of his fiancée and her friends.

Such mutuality offsets the violence of a dynamic that in its more characteristic form is decidedly brutal to its living objects. In his letter of denunciation to the heroine, the Rev. Boyer writes of the way in which he had disavowed Eliza's "levity," "extravagance," and self-adornment until the fatal revelation in the garden with Sanford: "Many faults have been visible to me;

over which my affection once drew a veil. That veil is now removed" (84). That the cleric's "resentment of her behavior has much assisted [him] in erasing her image from [his] breast" (82) only completes the veiling process begun earlier; in order to construct of Eliza a woman he could love, Boyer has shrouded to the point of near obliteration the very qualities of wit and whimsicality that most define her politically. In his final communication with the heroine, the minister reveals the lengths to which he has been able to go to deny her most threatening attributes: "Whatever we may have called errors, will, on my part, be forever buried in oblivion; and for your own peace of mind, I entreat you to forget that *any idea* of a connection between us *ever existed*" (104, my emphasis). Boyer's fantasy of encrypting the heroine's faults gives full voice to the community's repressive impulses, its inclination to bury alive potent expressions of resistance to its social convictions.

Eliza's literal death allows the chorus to achieve what for Boyer has only been figurative: the definitive entombment and selective *re-covery* of the heroine's reputation through fetishistic rituals of memorial. Louise Kaplan remarks that, "unlike a fully alive, human female being with dangerous, unpredictable desires . . . fetish objects are relatively safe, easily available, undemanding of reciprocity."[109] Death renders irrelevant Eliza's emphatic need for mutuality; thus, she perfectly fulfills the requirements of a community fetish. In that sense, Eliza functions most successfully after she is dead, for as a memory and a monument she can no longer resist being inscribed by the language of the majority.

Although the heroine's own literary productions take on a perverse half-life postmortem, her personal agency continues to be erased. In that regard, her passing becomes a fact of public record before it is privately known among her family and friends (161). Epistolarity, the representational form through which Eliza has had some (fictive) agency in constructing a self, yields sway before the faceless attention and power of the newspaper report; personal tragedy becomes fodder for endless judgment and speculation when the semiprivate realm of the personal letter is overtaken by the public sphere of print. As an object of the press, the heroine will be penetrated by the gaze of the communal eye and devoured by a popular appetite for scandal. Such commodification proves inescapable for Eliza, who is fated to exist as a form of public property even after death.

The heroine's final words suffer a more ironic and complicated fate. Like pieces of the true cross, her repentant reflections *in writing* become objects of worship for her mourners. Julia notes that Eliza's brother, who namelessly emerges into narrative representation as another doppelgänger for the clerical dead, appearing only as the heroine moves into her final decline, is deputized to retrieve his sister's most important, because *written*, effects from the tavern in which she dies. Writing remains detached from the vocal charisma of the affective body and as such constitutes a more plastic medium for ideological manipulation than does voice:[110] "Mr. Wharton has brought back several scraps of her writing, containing miscellaneous reflections on her situation, the death of her babe, and the absence of her friends. Some of these were written before, some after her confinement. These valuable testimonies of the affecting sense, and calm expectation she entertained of her approaching dissolution, are calculated to sooth and comfort the minds of mourning connections. They greatly alleviate the regret occasioned by her absence, at this awful period" (162–63). Although this passage would seem to imply that Eliza's enigmatic brother has collected the entirety of the heroine's random textual remains, the notion that some of these "several scraps" were "written before, some after her confinement," in fact intimates that a careful culling process may have taken place. If this editorial selection indeed occurred, who would have been its agent? Eliza's brother is certainly the likely candidate, for, in his capacity as Mrs. Wharton's deputy, he works for the community and as such is invested in preserving and disseminating only the most moral and sensible effusions of his sister's pen.

But the fact that pieces of the collection antedate Eliza's removal and lying-in suggests another, more ominous reading: that the heroine's public "silence" may have been coterminous with a burst of private expression in which she internalized and then articulated the chorus's maxims in writings for an audience constellated in imagined anticipation of her death.[111] Like the bromides of the clerical patriarchs whose ossifying influence she has failed to avoid, Eliza's last words are composed according to patriarchal prescription, and, aptly, they issue as if from the grave. Significantly, Foster does not directly represent any of Eliza's pious meditations in extremis: instead, Julia Granby, ever eager to speak for the heroine, provides a general précis. In expressing the essence of what it takes to be the *real*—i.e., the penitent— Eliza, the chorus chooses the paraphrase as its preferred genre, thus repeating once and for all its own abiding and tyrannical impulse to redirect the words of the once outspoken heroine.[112] She writes knowing that, between her weakness from self-starvation (the characteristic affliction of seduced and abandoned heroines in eighteenth-century fiction) and an imminent and dangerous confinement, she cannot possibly endure.[113] Thus, the ruined heroine ultimately collaborates with the fetishizing impulses of the community that would "re-cover" her; she colludes with a majority that has denied her both freedom and expression by offering at last what it wants to hear. As Elkins and McKitrick note, "the tyranny of the majority . . . exerts its coercions not through naked power; it overcomes all but the hardiest resistance by working from within."[114]

The community's posthumous celebration of Eliza's professions is thus perfectly congruent with its earlier disavowal of the gravity of the plaintive epistles she dispatched in her last year of life. Yet the chorus's consolation, the notion that the "regret occasioned by her absence" could really be "greatly alleviated" by her pious scraps of writing, remains a scandal of sympathy, for, while the heroine's earlier letters, faithfully mimetic effusions of her volatile nature, disturbed the propriety and equanimity of her friends, the funereal shards to which the grieving community clings conjure none of the living power of her "play about words." When Lucy mourns for "Not only the life, but what was still dearer, the reputation and virtue of the unfortunate Eliza" (163), we see the fetishizing impulse at work. She notes that the heroine lives "still in the heart of her faithful Lucy; whose experience of her numerous virtues and engaging qualities, has imprinted her image too deeply on the memory to be obliterated" (167). Entirely erased from this hagiographic tableau is any recognition of the positive power of Eliza's fancy, which defined her charm as well as her unhappy fate; in the eyes of the community, the heroine's extravagant zeal for liberty casts her beyond the pale of sympathy,[115] leaving her isolated from decorous republican society. At such a sanitary distance, the chorus can disclaim the way in which her fall casts a shadow on their collective enterprise, tainting the purity of their ideas of independence, disinterest, and virtue itself.

The majority's renunciation of the heroine's totality, its erasure of her fancy and imagination as vital aspects of her being, constitute the ultimate forms of violence against Eliza Wharton. Such fetishism, inscribed on her very tombstone, goes far beyond Sanford's power to harm precisely because it exists in the monumental public sphere.[116] Consider this final act of cooptation:

THIS HUMBLE STONE,

IN MEMORY OF

ELIZA WHARTON,

is *inscribed* by her weeping friends,
to whom she endeared herself by uncommon
tenderness and affection.
endowed with superior acquirements,
she was still more distinguished by
humility and benevolence.
let candor *throw a veil over her frailties,*
for great was her charity to others.
she sustained the last
painful scene, far from every friend;
and exhibited an example
of calm resignation.
her departure was on the 25th day of
july, a.d. -----,
in the 37th year of her age,
and the tears of strangers watered her
grave.

(169, my emphasis)

In *The Coquette,* weeping words etched in granite or marble become the definitive mode of inscription by ossification. Indeed, the genre of the funeral monument stands as a perfect metaphor for the community's zeal to write its signature all over such objects of "affection" as Eliza Wharton.

In marked contrast to the enduring tombstone, the chorus's concluding textual production, Eliza's last autographical act (her final piece of "public" writing) is tragically mutable. In the early pages of the novel, the heroine has made much ado about maintaining her maiden name: writing to Lucy she affirms, "Whatever my fate may be, I shall always continue your ELIZA WHARTON" (9), and soon afterward she confesses to her friend that until she meets the man who unites graces and virtues, she "shall continue to subscribe [her] name Eliza Wharton" (22). But after fleeing her mother's home and finding a haven at Salem,[117] the heroine agrees "to chalk the initials" of Major Sanford's name "over the door, as a signal to [him] of her residence" (157), a gesture that grotesquely parodies the dynamic of coverture. In the abbreviated signature, a mark of legibility heading toward degree zero, the formerly prolix Eliza will inscribe in place of her own name the appellation of the male who has destroyed the purity of hers yet to whom she has no legal tie. That the heroine promises to use chalk as the medium for her communiqué signifies the way she has begun to fade from comprehensible view, first from the universe of textuality and finally from the world of visibility itself. In its insubstantiality, chalk is an apt instrument for inscribing the ephemeral: come the first rain, all traces of presence and identity are washed away.

In keeping with her wish to dissolve from the public picture, Eliza implores Julia in a letter to submerge the reality of her "crimes in the grave" (156). But the "veil" the majority constructs exhibits a part rather than buries the whole of these frailties; Eliza remains marked even in this act of covering. The performative phrase "let candor throw a veil," conjuring Mr. Boyer's wish to cloak Eliza's real nature, constitutes a wonderful example of the simultaneous exhibition and disavowal that mark the fetishistic act. Even in death, Eliza remains the ready object of the voyeur's gaze: she must either be looked at, compulsively, or shrouded. Fetishism is a profoundly divided impulse, fixated on the very thing it also wants to hide.[118]

The text of the gravestone, framed by "weeping friends" and "the tears of strangers," neatly summarizes the distance charted by Eliza's community in its affective relation to her. Abandoned by her so-called friends well before she flees their sight, she is effectively mourned by strangers. More precisely, the two groups have in an important sense exchanged identities: though she is barely alive, Eliza has captured the interest of those alien folk who attend her, while she remains estranged from the companions whose disinterest led her into melancholic despair and, eventually, the arms of Sanford. In this regard, she follows almost exactly the pattern of her literary forerunner, Clarissa Harlowe, who dies in the care of the Smith family, middle-class drapers whom she chances to meet during her final phase of decline. With the important exception of Mr. Belford, the sentimental circle that forms around the dying Clarissa is composed entirely of strangers who lavish more love and attention on the heroine than she has ever known in her natal family, beyond the misguided affections of her grandfather, which set the entire plot in motion. Coming full circle, Eliza is reinscribed in the epitaph by the cohort of women who failed to commune with her in life because, in the face of her dissent, it could countenance no dialogue.

Consecrated to fixing forever the wayward eccentricity that characterized the heroine, the chorus determines to transform her story into an emblematic warning to the "American fair" (168), on the model of the conduct book. According to the politics of genre at work in the early national period, this move effectively neutralizes the social and cultural significance of the heroine's resistance and negates the tragic import of her life. In her final face-to-face exchange with Julia, Eliza had expressed the desire for "pity" (143) rather than "censure and reproach" (142), the wish to be read through the lens of tragedy rather than according to the dictates of the advice manual.[119] Instead, her life in letters moves from active to passive: from the empowered subject writing in the first-person voice to the effaced third-person object of another's sentimental discourse—or, most painfully, the mouthpiece for maudlin effusions when Eliza has internalized the community's language and begins to pen pious reflections on the eve of her death. Thus, the heroine known for her sparkling irony is reduced to a moralistic paradigm, embodying the role of fallen virtue outlined in eighteenth-century manuals of advice or, even more pointedly, in a certain form of didactic fiction not unlike the manifest narrative of *The Coquette*.

Out of a gothic tragedy the community reconstructs a heroine of sentiment and inscribes itself for posterity. While Eliza's transgressive writing diminishes to the point of nonexistence, the chorus writes furiously *about* her.[120] If grammatical forms can be read for symbolic content, it is surely interesting that, in her final epistolary reports to Eliza's grieving mother, Julia Granby dispatches her information about the heroine's last days in the first-person-plural voice (161). Although I have spoken of the feminized majority that dominates the discursive world of *The Coquette*, that term has been less literal than suggestive: in the final pages of Foster's book, however, the most aggressive and self-righteous member of "the whole fraternity" (158) begins to speak as "we," erasing any possible distinctions of perspective within or among the female friends. Thus, the wound to the social fabric created by Eliza's death has a perversely reparative effect on the majority left behind. The coherence and uniformity of the chorus have never been greater than at the moment when Julia proclaims to Mrs. Wharton, in the final letter of the novel, "I hope . . . that you will derive satisfaction from these exertions of friendship" (169).

That such collective forms of relation are not all they purport to be, that communities based on a proudly held "disinterest" may in fact be destructive, is nevertheless the latent suggestion of the novel's penultimate epistle; in it, Lucy Sumner makes an uncanny statement about the impulses of affiliation: "to associate, is to approve; to approve, is to be betrayed" (168). On the surface, her statement alludes to Eliza's efforts to seek avenues of exchange outside conventional venues: Major Sanford is the obvious, though unmentionable, referent of her maxim. Yet it is precisely Eliza's wish to remain independent of associations that jeopardizes her relationship with the community. The price she pays for her reluctance to associate or approve of the feminized majority is nothing short of being betrayed by their indifference. In fact, it could be said conversely that the ultimate associations and betrayals Eliza faces come not at the hands of the libertine but from the heart of the majority of which *he* is a member. In her final moments, Lucy continues to insist that Eliza's troubles can be located outside the safety and security of the Federalist community. But the duality of her own aphorism suggests something far darker: that the sources of destruction lie within the very disinterested impulses of republicanism itself.

The Coquette is less a didactic or even a subversive novel than it is an early American palimpsest. Constructed of an ostensible panoply of voices, it tells the story of an outspoken republican woman who ultimately fails to be heard. The book unfolds as a dialectic of revelation and erasure, which becomes the author's subject and which also dictates her form. Foster's transvestite storytelling embodies at the level of narrative Eliza's impulse to venture into the linguistic terrain of the masculine public sphere, which is figured in the novel by the woman equestrian. Novelist, heroine, and minor character alike traverse this difficult border to make statements about women's freedom that will be audible above the roar of the feminized patriarchal discourse that characterizes post-Revolutionary culture. The significance of Foster's achievement, paradoxically, rests on its constitutive failure: in bypassing the discourse of sentiment for the vocabulary of politics, or more precisely, by speaking the language of liberty but overlaying it with the rhetoric of moral feeling, she reaches for a level of expression foreclosed to republican women at the very moment she buries it alive. Thus, the auditory apparition of Eliza's voice as it takes form in her remarkable epistles resonates beyond the bleakness of *The Coquette*'s ending; raising haunting questions about the success of such efforts of entombment, its tones evoke the enormous cultural power available to women such as Foster when they presume to play about words.

DEBORAH SAMPSON.

Published by H. Mann, 1797.

Engraving of Deborah Sampson, the possible prototype for Ormond's *Martinette de Beauvais, frontispiece of* The Female Review, *Herman Mann's 1797 biography of Sampson. (Courtesy the American Antiquarian Society)*

A Lady Who Sheds No Tears: Liberty, Contagion, and the Demise of Fraternity in _Ormond_

From the melancholic obstruction of sympathy obscuring _Charlotte Temple_'s dream of democratic transparency, to _The Coquette_'s narrowing, darkening vision of republican fellow feeling, we have seen a fraying of the bonds of sociality in the fiction of the Federalist era. With the work of Charles Brockden Brown, muse of the American fin de siècle, the gothicism underlying the early national novel erupts into full visibility. Brown's abiding subject is the unraveling of sympathetic relations, the betrayal of fraternity: strategically assuming the female voice in his telling of _Ormond_, he imagines a polity beset by epidemic disease, where brotherhood, masculinity, and affect itself are perilous liabilities. Against this post-Revolutionary landscape, classical republican notions of liberty and disinterest become fault lines along which Brown exposes the fragile underpinnings of a Founding based on the social death and live burial of those "others" who do not count as citizens. Clamoring from the margins of his four major fictions, the voices of women, blacks, Native Americans, and alien émigrés bear witness to the limits of American Enlightenment, proleptically figuring the nation as it moves toward both liberalism and modernity _and_ fratricidal war.

Featuring virtuous sisters and maniacal brothers more prominently than omnipotent mothers and moribund fathers, _Ormond_ explores the relationship between contagion and sympathy, inverted, multivalent figures for the fate of collective fellow feeling as it strains toward dissolution in the Federalist era. Simultaneously possessed by and acutely suspicious of the vision of sympathy that by 1799 has become a legacy of the early American novel, *Ormond* unmasks this fantasy as a national chimera. For its more resourceful female figures, epidemic illness actually enables compassion, reopening arid channels of sociality, but, at the hands of *Ormond*'s male and male-identified characters, fellow feeling takes increasingly poisonous forms, from naive and self-destructive delusions of sympathy to cunningly theatrical and homicidal performances of "fraternal" understanding. While *Ormond* dramatizes the operations of true and false sympathy, it also offers compassionlessness as an affective paradigm associated with radical notions of liberty. Brown incarnates the principle in a revolutionary "sister" who has assumed male garb to fight for both independence, in 1776, and liberté, égalité, and fraternité, in 1789. In her civilian allegiances, Martinette exhibits no "traces of sympathy," "merely . . . large experience, vigourous faculties and masculine attainments."[1] Disavowing sorrow, refusing to mourn—the very conduct that signals democratic compassion in a work like *Charlotte Temple*—the martial woman personifies Brown's violent reaction against emotion itself, his rejection of the dream that brotherly and sisterly sympathy could ground social bonds in the new republic.

Through the discordant careers of its central characters, *Ormond* ponders the persistent link between liberty and violence that bewilders Americans at the turn of the eighteenth century: the memory of Revolutionary upheaval, the pain of an exclusionary Founding, and the prospect of social fracture. The book also represents unconventional embodiments of gender, interrogating the connection between personal and political identity and the threat of the "alien" in the late 1790s.[2] Foregrounding problems of perception and thwarted vision in its very plotting, *Ormond* deploys transparency, reflection, and opacity as governing tropes; through this visual vocabulary, Brown contemplates and ultimately challenges the operative fantasy of fellow feeling with which the tragic, feminized, epistolary fictions of the 1790s remain consumed. Like the other works examined in this study, *Ormond* fetishizes portraits and letters in its thoroughgoing articulation of American anxiety about identity—apprehension over the validity of national origin and the legitimacy of republican political processes unleashed in the aftermath of the post-Revolutionary settlement.

Ormond also powerfully distinguishes itself from the female-authored tragic fictions of the period in one vital regard: its representations of race relations, which surface fleetingly in a depiction of compassionate affinity across the color line and in Ormond's blackface masquerade as a chimney-sweeping slave. We have seen how in *The Power of Sympathy* so-called fellow feeling for a black bondwoman enables a white male's privilege. Royall Tyler and Hugh Henry Brackenridge also dramatize scenes of African and African American servitude in their picaresque novels *The Algerine Captive* and *Modern Chivalry*, using comic technique to underscore the brutality of institutionalized racism in the new republic. But it is primarily in *Ormond* (as well as in Brown's 1799 *Arthur Mervyn*) that slavery, which remains unspeakable and unspoken in the Constitution itself, reenters the tragic lists of the early American novel as a philosophical subject. Providing a glimpse of a master who exploits the power of color and visibility in profoundly *interested* ways, Brown uncovers the dynamic relation between black social death and political invisibility and white male privilege—crucial variables in the gothic equation that enables the nation's Founding.

Set in the midst of the yellow-fever epidemic of 1793, and written in 1799, one year after a second outbreak that nearly takes its author's life, *Ormond* exposes the uncertain grounding of a post-Revolutionary polity verging on collapse. John Adams in fact opines that the republic would have foundered, but for the yellow-fever epidemic of 1793, such was the violence and the menace of Jacobin interests. In a letter reflecting on "the terrorism of the day [the 1790s]," written to Thomas Jefferson in June of 1813, Adams remarks, "You certainly never felt the Terrorism, excited by Genet, in 1793, when ten thousand People in the Streets of Philadelphia, day after day, threatened to drag Washington out of his House, and effect a Revolution in the Government, or compell [*sic*] it to declare War in favour of the French Revolution, and against England. The coolest and firmest Minds, even among the Quakers in Philadelphia, have given their Opinions to me, that nothing but the Yellow Fever . . . could have saved the United States from a total Revolution of Government."[3] Far from being a cause of the republic's underlying communal plight, the fever holds a mirror to a social body that is already infirm. Werner B. Berthoff notes that the plague is "a medium of trial and revelation, in which whatever is latent—the weakness of an individual constitution, the secret truth about society—is shocked into the open."[4] While the contagious properties of the disease become subject to heated debate during the period,[5] its hideous effects remain indisputable: yellowing of the skin, vomiting of black matter, violent fever, and internal bleeding are the more horrible symptoms of the disorder, the likely consequence of which is agonizing death.[6]

The destructive power of yellow fever acts as a potent cultural metaphor in *Ormond*, giving shape to a novel generally considered Brown's least coherent.[7] Contagion and containment, medical terms describing the course of the disease, function as supple figures for sympathy and liberty in the book—becoming, in fact, analogues for fictive form itself. Marked by startling complexities of transmission, the larger plot of *Ormond* is interrupted by several extended, self-contained digressions in which narrative disavows its own linear impulses, aspiring toward multiple avenues of expression. Far from shattering the coherence of the stories Brown relates (as critics have traditionally argued—thereby disclaiming the obligation to decipher ostensibly unintelligible associations), such tangents and marginalia become the repositories of Brown's deepest meanings. Unfolding as an emblematic series of embedded miniature tableaux, twice- and thrice-told tales deployed by its first-person narrator, *Ormond* echoes with gothic voices whose materiality and history have been utterly displaced. Such stylistic indirection and narrative fracture give haunting expression to the fragility of republican sociality as it loosens to the point of unraveling in the decade following the Founding.

Like the larger story of *Ormond*, a key digression involving male voyeurism reaches representation through this circuitous and pointedly female homosocial path. The nativist tale of English émigré Baxter's mysterious demise from the fever after spying on the Frenchwoman who is his nearest neighbor is conveyed from one female narrator to another across economic lines that stratify the City of Brotherly Love in the post-Revolutionary era; as this oral legend traverses the community, its itinerary reveals the fluid social contours of a polity in crisis. Storytelling functions as a medium of countercontagion in *Ormond*, through which women face loss and attempt to reweave the social fabric their republican brothers have critically weakened. To that end, in the period immediately following her husband's death from a harrowingly protracted case of fever, Baxter's widow relays his story to Constantia Dudley, the heroine of *Ormond*, Brown's almost allegorical representation of republican innocence under duress.[8] During earlier, more affluent days the virtuous maiden employed Sarah Baxter, a washerwoman laboring for Philadelphia's genteel community. Personifying ductile sympathy, Constantia is moved by Baxter's story, which she conveys to Sophia Westywn

Courtland, her beloved confidante and the narrator of *Ormond*—the final mediator (within the textual world) of all its tales. Raised together (Sophia is a wealthy orphan) and educated like males according to Enlightenment models in the manner of Brown's Clara Wieland and Clara Howard, Constantia and Sophia incarnate a level of independent rationality rarely limned in even those Anglo-American novels of the 1790s that feature women as protagonists.[9] Like Rowson, Brown articulates the plea for female education throughout his literary career, despite wavering political allegiances and even after renouncing his radical influences and becoming a merchant and Federalist pamphleteer during the Jeffersonian ascendancy.[10]

As the imaginary embodiment of a *female* narrative voice, Sophia occupies a particularly charged position in *Ormond*. Indeed, it is rare in the early American novel tradition for a male writer working in the first person to cross gender in his creation of a fictive persona.[11] While literary historians occasionally note Brown's employment of this "transvestite" technique, used to somewhat different ends in *Wieland*, and routinely register that both *Wieland* and *Ormond* are told in the personae of women, Jay Fliegelman remains the only scholar to consider the cultural significance of Brown's extraordinary narrative strategy. In his introduction to the Penguin edition of *Wieland*, Fliegelman asserts that "Brown was fascinated with the paradoxes of power and helplessness. . . . Indeed, Brown's use of a female narrator in *Wieland* suggests a perverse coveting of the 'status' of women as social and cultural victims."[12] I shall argue, in addition, that Brown's narrative identifications with women are the formal analogue to his critique of post-Revolutionary fraternity. What remains to be considered is how this artistic strategy inflects the dilemmas of agency and liberty traditionally articulated by male voices in eighteenth-century American fiction. Instantiating a "female" voice at the point of enunciatory origin, Brown uses narrative cross-dressing in *Ormond* to authorize an antipatriarchal interrogation of post-Revolutionary social cohesion.

In so doing, Brown writes in full awareness of the long shadow cast by the master narratives of the Founding—the embodied documents and images, authored and signed by elite white male republicans.[13] According to such accounts, the nation is constituted by circles of white men figured first as brothers in the Revolutionary Sons of Liberty and then as Fathers in the Constitutional era of the late 1780s.[14] These masculine bands deploy words in their exercise of authority, conjuring the new republic into political being as signers of the Declaration of Independence and drafters of the Constitution.[15] No less conscious than the Framers of the legitimating powers of language, Brown writes a series of novels in the last two years of the century, offering complex countervisions to the myth of the Founding—visions deeply indebted to and at the same time challenging the literary mothers, Rowson and Foster, who supplant the fathers as imaginative progenitors.

Composed as extended epistles, Brown's four major works self-consciously highlight their fictive origins in *written* language. Of this quartet, *Ormond* is the imaginative production most uniquely enfranchised to speak in the "republic of letters."[16] More than *Wieland, Edgar Huntly,* or even *Arthur Mervyn,* whose concerns come closest to *Ormond's,* the novel illuminates the dark underside of the Framers' promises, the subtext of the documents establishing and authorizing the United States. If the Declaration and the Constitution unfold according to Enlightenment notions of equality and natural right, the gothicism of *Ormond* exposes the fact that certain Americans must be excluded from political and cultural representation in order to enable the very act of legitimation itself.[17] Foregrounding problems of perception and concealment, *Ormond* brings the fates of these invisible Americans into narrative view. In so doing, the novel excavates the cracks in the foundational story the republican brothers tell about themselves.

An important feature of Brown's critique involves lodging narrative control in the (fictive) hands of a woman who circumvents the allure of fraternity by locating her desire in a republican "sister." In this gesture, the author abruptly inverts the homosociality of the revolutionary brothers. More precisely, female homoeroticism in *Ormond* erupts from its interdicted position as a crucial subtext of the Richardsonian seduction plot. With its powerful discourse of female homosocial desire, the love of Clarissa Harlowe for Anna Howe, Richardson's eponymous novel constitutes the great textual precursor for *Ormond's* depiction of romantic friendship between women.[18] Undergirding and, ultimately, overtaking the story of the libertine's threat is Sophia's feminist and homosocial tale; in this counternarrative, female-female love proves strong enough to foil the machinations of heterosexual violence. Nominally married to the enigmatic Courtland, a cipher who appears in a subordinate clause and shortly thereafter is dispatched beyond *Ormond's* American purview, Sophia expresses passion for Constantia Dudley alone. Cautiously and awkwardly, critics have acknowledged for decades the lesbian dimensions of *Ormond* without unpacking the important political valences such representations of desire necessarily encode.[19] In a novel where characters embrace unconventional gender and sexual affiliations, female homo-erotic longing becomes a pliant medium for Brown's investigation of republican fraternity's failure.

Vision

While phantasmagoric voice—the potential source of presence, plentitude, and transparent exchange—contests theatrical display in *Charlotte Temple*, *The Coquette* imagines community as a patriarchal chorus bound by immutable scripts and dramatic imperatives. Femininity as masquerade, its constitutive social fiction, is a show that must go on, whatever the costs. Bound by domestic formulae that dictate women's roles—opposing republican daughter or wife to licentious coquette—Federalist culture is incapable of registering female resistance from within; only as an exemplary corpse can the outspoken heroine be reincorporated by her "disinterested" community. Between the disembodied maternal tones of Rowson's narrator and the ossified accents of a cohort channeling paternal will from beyond the grave, the novel of the 1790s envisions political authority as familial drama in which voice opposes vision.

Neither political ideologue nor literary adherent to genre or convention,[20] Charles Brockden Brown employs and unsettles the abiding themes of republican fiction in both *Wieland* and *Ormond*. His first novel deconstructs *Charlotte Temple*'s dream of sonorous presence as a tenable source for national legitimation.[21] *Wieland*'s pastoral idyll evokes Rowson's politics of nostalgia, but, far from affirming *Charlotte Temple*'s protodemocratic face, Brown exposes the reactionary undercurrents of the novel. While Rousseau's aesthetic philosophy haunts *Charlotte Temple*, feeling—even in its melancholic form—ultimately triumphs over performance there. In *Wieland*, however, theatricality poses insurmountable problems, for there the villain is also a ventriloquist. Dramatic spectacle figures in two crucial scenes: the reader's introduction to Francis Carwin by discredited Lockean Henry Pleyel, who reports his sighting of the protean dissembler in a Spanish amphitheater disguised as a Catholic peasant; and Theodore's massacre of his wife, children, and Louisa Conway, a tableau of horror that grotesquely rehearses (while it also makes impossible) their planned amateur performance of an imported German tragedy. Brown's plotting here, in which (fictive) life imitates (fictive) art, raises important questions about the morality of spectacles—both imaginative and real—bringing to mind Rousseau's indictment of dramatic artifice and Diderot's concerns about the problem of forgetting theater.

If, in *Wieland*, Brown figures the dilemma of Revolutionary political consensus through unreliable utterances, in *Ormond* he interrogates Enlightenment ideology and its miscarriage of sympathy in a disintegrating post-Revolutionary culture through metaphors of failed vision. *Ormond*'s fascination with acts of perception is evident in virtually every important scene or digression in the novel: Brown makes at least twenty-one references to things ocular in his narrative. These allusions range from such banal statements as Sophia's affirmation that her "eyes almost wept themselves dry over this part of her tale" (27) to Constantia's more significant articulation of humiliation as a "shrinking from exposure to rude eyes" (31) to events of great symbolic import: Mr. Dudley's blindness, which immediately follows his being ruined by the forger Craig; and the illicit voyeuristic practices of Baxter as well as of Ormond himself.

Such overdetermination at the level of language and theme confirms that, far beyond functioning simply as a recurring motif or even as the novel's overarching organizational principle, perception actually informs *Ormond*'s political dimension as well—calling up a network of philosophical, moral, and aesthetic issues in its thrust toward political meaning.[22] The narrative foregrounds visibility and invisibility as crucial categories for resolving who "counts" as American in post-Revolutionary society. Brown's skepticism over whether "illumination" and "universal progress" will prove efficacious for the future of the nation—his philosophical divergence from the Founders—is reflected in the book's subtitle, *Ormond; or, The Secret Witness*. Significantly, the term "witness" derives from the Old English for knowledge; in fact, the notion of a clandestine observer—who has the insight to attest to what he or she sees but chooses to remain concealed—is an oxymoron that carries decidedly subversive implications for American Enlightenment culture.[23]

The idea of a secret witness recalls the author's fascination with William Godwin's *Caleb Williams* (1794), the gothic novel featuring covert surveillance that profoundly influences Brown's fiction.[24] The judicial quality of this term also evokes Brown's aborted career as a student of law.[25] Both Godwin's book and the American writer's fascinated revulsion toward legal thinking provide background for the problem of witnessing in *Ormond*, but the word's theological sources afford particular insight. Western discussion of witnessing originates with the *ur*moment of cultural Founding detailed in the Hebrew Bible: Moses' summoning of the disgruntled Israelites for the reading of the Ten Commandments, his dissemination of sacred Law.

The divine injunction of the ninth commandment, "thou shalt not bear false witness against thy *neighbor*" (Exodus 20 : 16, my emphasis), conversely implies that attesting to the truth of one's social vision is a moral obligation. To withhold such warrant violates the tenants of God's holy covenant. By extension, to observe one's neighbor in secret becomes a kind of false witnessing by omission, disobedience not unrelated to the commandment that forbids coveting one's neighbor's house, wife, servants, and possessions. Secret witnessing perverts basic imperatives by which Judeo-Christian cultures maintain cohesion, obligations that require community members to respect social boundaries between neighbors ("thou shalt not covet") and simultaneously, to uphold a sense of responsibility to the greater group ("thou shalt not bear false witness").

This ethics of perception has an interesting American legacy in the Puritan brotherly watch.[26] By the end of the eighteenth century, in the face of ascendent liberalism's emphasis on the economic fortune of individuals rather than the spiritual fate of the collective, both the notion of social vigilance and the very viability of fraternity begin to break down. Nevertheless, the idea that vision bears a moral valence remains profound in Brown's novel, at the level of narrative as well as plot: there, narrator Sophia justifies her own writerly descent into voyeurism by invoking the necessity of bearing honorable witness against Ormond's explicitly unrighteous forms of observation. I will soon take up the fact that scopophilia constitutes the ultimate unfilial form of a "brotherly" watch in *Ormond;* indeed, the book is obsessed with exposing the way various fraternal figures, including the villain himself, prove incapable of envisioning, much less engaging in, the dynamic exchange that enables fellow feeling and, by extension, communal understanding.

First, however, it is necessary to explore the ontological significance of vision in *Ormond,* a work in which identity as well as sociality itself—independent being and connection to the world of others—come into existence through *specular* relations. Selfhood is a property that is lost, hunted, and sometimes found or recovered in certain forms of looking. In *Ormond,* the existence of the other in all his or her altierity is thus crucial in the construction of the individual psyche and also of the national body. Both personal and corporate, the processes of identification that Brown charts in the novel depend on a peculiar poetics of visibility.

This emphasis on vision, reflection, and the power of appearances extends to *Ormond*'s fictive shape: the seeming incoherence that marks the book—its temporally fractured mode of unfolding—can be traced not only to the structural metaphors of contagion and containment but also to Brown's translation of painterly perception into narrative form. Lamenting the disjointedness typical of his work, scholars draw conclusions about the author's haste and sloppiness; to attempt cataloging the negative critical refrain regarding his careless compositional methods would be to generate, in effect, a comprehensive list of nearly every scholarly article and book written about Brown since the advent of the New Criticism's emphasis on aesthetic unity. These negative judgments are inflected by conventions of literary cohesion themselves derived from canonical works of eighteenth-century fiction: the novels of Richardson, Sterne, and even Jane Austen, who postdates Charles Brockden Brown by almost twenty years. Oddly, such critics ignore the work of the English gothicists who are his exact contemporaries and of the Irish and Scottish gothicists who follow them, writers whose fictions share many of the digressive, convoluted, and fragmentary qualities reproved in Brown's work. I am thinking here, in particular, of figures such as Ann Radcliffe and Charles Maturin, who routinely include interpolated tales within their gothic fictions. Informed by developments in theories of gender and the history of sexuality, current readings attempt to account for the formal aberrations for which these and other novels of the 1790s, 1810s, and 1820s were relegated to the back burner of British literary history (also termed the "Romantic novel in English") until reconsideration of the canon in the wake of poststructuralism, civil rights, feminism, gay studies, etc.[27]

A more useful context for considering the American's idiosyncratic aesthetic, however, is the visual art of the period. Brown draws on three types of late-eighteenth-century Anglo-American painting in *Ormond* as analogues for his narrative procedures; expanding as a series of likenesses in *miniature*, interlarded with more extended biographical *portraits* and dynamic *historical tableaux*, the novel's very form partakes of the genres in which British and American artists are trained at the turn of the eighteenth century.[28] Despite its episodic nature, *Ormond* does not develop in the manner of traditional eighteenth-century picaresque fictions,[29] in which a coherent narrative eye and "I" provide the reader with a panoramic sweep through a succession of adventures, an itinerary mirroring the protagonist's education. Instead, Brown's novel unfurls as a series of isolated glimpses into a fictive gallery of portraits whose individual subjects exist in tenuous, if nevertheless authentic, relation to one another. Fragmentariness of form becomes a kind of eloquence in *Ormond*, expressing brokenly, through abrupt and self-enclosed shifts of narrative focus, the rending of post-Revolutionary social relations. Conjoining metaphors of perception and infection/enclosure at the level of structure, the narrative contours of the novel underscore the profound linkage in Brown's imagination between visual pathways and the contagion of feeling, in its pathogenic, as well as its paradoxically wholesome, strains.

Voyeurism

Brown incarnates these connections between perceptual and emotional infection in *Ormond*'s most underappreciated digressive episode. Set during Philadelphia's 1793 yellow-fever epidemic, the scene spotlights surveillance, contamination, and mysterious death:

> A man, perched on a fence, at midnight, mute and motionless, and gazing at a dark and dreary dwelling, was an object calculated to rouse curiosity. When the muscular form, and rugged visage, scarred and furrowed into something like ferocity, were added; when the nature of the calamity, by which the city was dispeopled, was considered, the motives to plunder, and the insecurity of property, arising from the pressure of new wants on the poor, and the flight or disease of the rich, were attended to, an observer would be apt to admit fearful conjectures. (67)

In this tableau, we watch Martinette, a refugee Frenchwoman, bury a shrouded corpse in military fashion while her neighbor Baxter, an English expatriot, furtively surveys her from behind a fence in an act of voyeurism that ultimately proves fatal. With this grimly mysterious midnight panorama, Brown's second novel, renowned for its wooden exposition of Godwinian philosophy[30] as well as its fragmented incoherence, explodes into interest.

Adding contagious disease to the Founding's dramatic enactment of promise, foreclosure, and burial—its funereal rites—the Baxter digression stages the derailment of sympathetic communion we have traced in *The Power of Sympathy, Charlotte Temple, The Coquette,* and *Wieland*. At the same time, however, this episode of voyeurism subtly undermines the Founding's primal scene by finally defeating the usual dynamics of the gaze and by pointing toward female homosociality as a respite from the structures of patriarchy. Spying on someone who is both French and female, and failing to recognize her in all her redoubled otherness, Baxter dramatizes the operations of exclusionary power as it hinges on distinctions of gender and nationality. At the same time, such patriarchal and national authority is resisted through the very channels of visual exchange deployed in its own practices of domination. Joining forces with the narrating Sophia (Brown's transvestite persona) at the level of plot, the French woman warrior who dresses, fights, and withholds tears like a man advances the author's antipatriarchal campaign by literally facing down received notions of gender as well as national identity. However, the alternative social vision toward which this tableau gestures is less than robust: contagion intrudes, passing through and infecting the avenues of visual exchange by which individuals might be bound into sympathetic community.

Featuring a cast of European émigrés,[31] the drama played out in the embedded tale evokes the wars of the French Revolution by importing the specter of continental conflict onto American soil.[32] In this ostensible digression from the primary plot,[33] the narrator relates the enigmatic demise of the veteran grenadier Baxter, who suspends his loathing for all persons French and his terror of yellow fever in order to inquire into potentially untoward events on the Monrose property directly abutting his own back yard. This French family, publicly known as father and daughter, though in fact sharing no biological bond, occupies a house that Brown has endowed with a richly provocative history. The list of its tenants—from the historical William Penn, to the fictional woman warrior and revolutionary Martinette de Beauvais, alias Miss Monrose, to Constantia Dudley herself—recapitulates notable episodes in the narrative of the European immigration to and settlement of Philadelphia; it highlights the attendant shift from spiritual to political innovation that occupies the city's newcomers from the Quaker migration in the seventeenth century, to the Revolutionary War and establishment of a republican government in the third quarter of the eighteenth century, and finally to the post-Revolutionary climate of the 1790s, when French refugees from the Reign of Terror and the San Domingo Revolution pour into the city in great numbers.[34]

The narrator's account of Baxter, who is "deeply and rancorously prejudiced" against France (64), would suggest that the retired grenadier draws no distinction between the soldiers of the ancien régime, whom he fought in both the War of the Austrian Succession and the Seven Years War,[35] and members of such moderate revolutionary factions as the Girondists (Martinette de Beauvais's party) who flee to America during the Terror: all are French, and thus equally despicable. Indeed, at the outset of the dreadful epidemic, Baxter resists "entering the house" of his potentially afflicted neighbors, who have disappeared from view, much less offering "his aid," since he has "too much regard for his own safety and too little for that of a frog-eating Frenchman, to think seriously of that expedient" (64).

Yet, as the thrice-told tale of Baxter's demise finally reaches Sophia's pen, an odd affective leakage suffuses a report that ostensibly emanates from the Francophobe himself, contradicting his manifest political allegiances. The narrator depicts Baxter's sense of the elder M. Monrose as a figure of "tarnished splendour" (63)—a phrase that reaches for the chivalric masculinity of the ancien régime, echoing the nostalgic longing Edmund Burke plangently expresses in *Reflections on the Revolution in France* (1790).[36] However unlikely, the pathos that permeates this description alerts us to the complexity of Brown's own reading of the French Revolution and the backlight that struggle casts on the author's ideas about the American War for Independence and the subsequent Founding of the republic.

By the decade in which he takes up the writing of novels, Brown is clearly identified as a patriot. Despite this fact, the American Revolution remains for him an ambivalent event: the public convulsion that disrupts his childhood, violates the pacifistic principles of his Quaker upbringing, and deprives his family of a paternal presence during the eight months in which Elijah Brown is interned with other Philadelphia Quakers who will not sign a patriot loyalty oath.[37] Out of this traumatic history, Brown develops a puzzling and contradictory series of political allegiances in early and middle adulthood, inconsistent attitudes of which scholarship has yet to make full sense.[38] Nevertheless, the representations of revolution that recur across his major works—visions of patricidal violence described in bittersweet, melancholic tones—are, if not decidedly reactionary, at least steeped in an ethos Christopher Looby characterizes as "complex[ly] counter-revolutionary."[39]

Against this background, the strange story of Baxter's "nativist panic"[40]— his fatal response to viewing the midnight burial of M. Monrose—takes on an evocative political charge. That Baxter believes the French are "exempt" from yellow fever suggests a congruence in his mind between the individual body's open borders and the nation's collective perimeters. According to this fantastic logic, true citizens of the new republic can only be numbered among the native born or the formerly English who unite in their susceptibility to pestilential affliction. Foreign émigrés, in contrast, distinguished in the era of the Alien and Sedition Acts (1798) by radical differences of language and culture, remain immune to those domestic influences that join (Anglo-) Americans as a suffering corporate body. The salutary value of collective affliction, which Rowson brings to vivid life in *Charlotte Temple*, is an American notion that originates in the seventeenth-century Puritan migration. According to Sacvan Bercovitch, such tribulation constitutes both a sign of God's punishment and his promise to New England—a ritual curse-as-blessing that guarantees the cohesion of the community.[41]

In scripting these associations, Brown plays on a contemporary racialist and nativist medical discourse infusing the writings of doctors and civic leaders confronted with the epidemic. It is striking that figures as diverse as Mathew Carey, an Irish émigré printer and entrepreneur who publishes libelous descriptions of the black community during the plague, and Dr. Benjamin Rush, Philadelphia's leading physician and a known abolitionist and advocate of civil rights, maintain that blacks are immune to the disease. Indeed, as J. H. Powell notes, "the Negroes had no better friend in all America than Benjamin Rush, and Rush certainly thought them immune until the middle of September," six weeks into the pestilence.[42] Along with African Americans, French immigrants—particularly refugees from San Domingo—are also deemed invulnerable. Martin Pernick writes that "some physicians declared that blacks and West Indian immigrants were more immune than respectable white Philadelphians, a costly error."[43] This spurious diagnosis enables public officials to justify the near-conscription of the black population into caring for the sick and removing the dead when one half of Philadelphia's white inhabitants close their houses (sometimes against their own kith and kin) and flee the city, George Washington and Thomas Jefferson among them.[44]

Susan L. Mizruchi's reading of the link between sympathy, contagion, and death in the work of W. E. B. Du Bois (1900) illuminates this earlier moment in American cultural history. Mizruchi locates the overlapping discourses of fellow feeling, infection, and black extinction in the work of America's pioneering nineteenth-century social scientists, scholars such as Nathaniel Shaler, who describes nationalistic sympathy as a beneficial form of contagion. Elaborating on the work of Shaler, she notes that the communicable bond of cofeeling that obtains between middle-class, native-born (white) Americans is an infection to which blacks, characterized as "internal immigrants," are pronounced both naturally and socially immune.[45]

These formulations about the "democratic" contagion of sympathy and

its connection to issues of social inclusion and exclusion have suggestive implications for the late-eighteenth-century context in which Charles Brockden Brown produces his four most important novels. While a serious epidemic of yellow fever in fact attacks the coastal northeast in the 1760s, it is
in the 1790s that the infectious transmission of this pestilence becomes
tangled with political discussions of race, citizenship, and national identity.
In an uncanny historical confluence, the plagues of 1793 and 1798 break out
at moments of great international tension, the effects of which ripple across
the Atlantic and disturb the domestic arena of early republican government.
Occurring first during the Reign of Terror, itself figured as a rampant and
evil infection,[46] yellow fever erupts again at a period when the wars of the
French Revolution have elevated levels of American xenophobia.

Brown's representations of nativism and racial conflict in a time of pestilential illness, while seeming to operate at the periphery of his works or to
be claustrated within the digressive tangents that riddle novels like *Wieland*,
Arthur Mervyn, and *Ormond*, actually are central to his brooding vision of the
tenuous legitimacy of the Founding.[47] These overtly political meditations
take place largely on the margins: in Brown's inverted narratology, the edge
of representation marks the space in which the author's richest cultural observations unfold.[48] In that regard Baxter's irrational notions about susceptibility to and exemption from the spread of the fever articulate divisive social
fantasies at work in the 1790s. By succumbing to madness immediately before being leveled by infection, Baxter becomes another of Brown's characters
whose private paranoia—indeed, whose incipient psychosis—is also in some
sense a symptom of public disorder.

The peculiar evolution of Baxter's vocational history is emblematic, as
well, of the larger post-Revolutionary social transformation Brown charts in
Ormond. Once a member of an elite British infantry corps fighting on the
front lines of several European wars,[49] Baxter is presumably too old to serve
in the American Revolution, and, given his rabid Francophobia, one imagines he might have taken the Tory side during the War for Independence.
Now a civilian, Baxter has worked as a porter until the time of the plague. As
Philadelphia's citizenry flee the fever, conventional modes of commercial
activity and attendant mechanisms of social regulation grind to a halt. Un-
employed as a result of such upheaval, the former soldier enlists with the
Guardians of the city to guarantee the "preservation of property" during the
epidemic (64–65). In becoming a watchman, Baxter elects to invest his martial spirit in the protection of private wealth rather than of public virtue.

While the veteran's odd career raises interesting questions about the place of violence in a culture whose political identity is constituted through the savagery of war, his ultimate fate dramatizes the paradoxes of liberty that result when "ideals" are actualized by means of bloodshed.[50] If in the name of nation building such insurgent ferocity must be renounced as it was in the post-Revolutionary period, what happens to the brutal energies and impulses that have made such social legitimation possible?[51] What is the role of the warrior in a society that no longer requires defending? And what are the effects on revolutionary "fraternity"—on masculine identity itself—when the arena for performing feats of male valor suddenly vanishes?

As he moves from the role of agent on the field of battle to intermediary in the realm of commerce and finally to instrument in a project of social supervision, Baxter experiences heroic diminishment that symbolizes a larger shift in the social values of the young nation. Collective civic endeavor—the communal effort of waging the Revolution itself—yields to individualistic economic enterprise, the isolation of private selves engaged in the bustle of trade. During the chaos of the fever, citizens excluded from prosperity in the burgeoning marketplace express their material *ressentiment,* some going so far as to reclaim the violence repressed in the post-Revolutionary settlement and unleash it on the community in the form of vandalism and looting. As political conflict yields to social and economic unease, the former warrior-*cum*-watchman, fated to survey and inform on his compatriots from behind the front lines of capitalism, can take no vital action.

Significantly, Baxter's performance of "duty" has little to do with maintaining the public good, perhaps *the* primary value of republican culture. By the late eighteenth century, the Puritans' brotherly watch, Frank Shuffelton's term for spiritual vigilance endowed with civic import, has devolved into something less honorable—a shift exemplified in the discipline exerted in the name of virtue by the unfeeling patriarchal chorus in *The Coquette.* How else are we to understand Baxter's unauthorized surveillance of his own neighbors, members of the working poor who have little to fear from the looters who threaten the elite of the city? As an activity formerly endowed with spiritual import by civically oriented Americans, "watching" undergoes a degraded materialization in *Ormond* that carries with it multiple and untoward valences. This discussion obviously evokes Michel Foucault's analysis of eighteenth-century cultures of discipline, which employ technologies of vision to survey, police, and regulate inmate and captive populations, be they prisoners, patients diseased in body and in mind, or the poor. While my reading of voyeurism in *Ormond* takes a decidedly different direction, focusing on the way Brown's poetics of visibility and invisibility inflect his characters' experience of sympathy, my notions of a regulatory gaze and of surveillance have been greatly informed by Foucault's work.[52]

Writing in a culture founded on the Enlightenment's central epistemology of vision, the skeptical Brown uses the episode with Baxter to interrogate the Lockean dictum that "to see is to know."[53] This digression provides a focal point for meditating on the abiding obsession in *Ormond* with acts of perception and operations of sight: not only does the book feature surveillance, voyeurism, and blindness as central motifs and even formal principles, but one of its more remarkable subplots concerns a nearly idolatrous fixation on a miniature portrait, the fate of whose complex peregrinations from obscurity to visibility constitutes a story of its own.

Brown's critique of Locke inheres in the idea that vision is an utterly fallen if not a tragic sense. In his fiction, people's unobstructed access to the external world of objects and others is largely overwritten by traces of mind.[54] His characters, including minor figures like Baxter, largely fail to see with any objective clarity—actually *cannot* perceive—what lies before them; their vision of a world beyond the self is almost completely occluded by preexisting thoughts, attitudes, beliefs, and feelings. The former soldier shares affinities with Brown's Theodore Wieland, who is unable to distinguish between voices deployed by the ventriloquist Carwin and the psychotic ravings at work inside his own brain. Like Wieland, whose sanity is undone by this sensory confusion, Baxter is "unmanned" and maddened by the spectacle he witnesses in the Monrose garden. As Martinette herself later affirms, "The rueful pictures of my distress and weakness, which were given by Baxter, existed only in his own fancy" (209).

Baxter's poetics of projection originate in an earlier encounter with "Miss Monrose." Neither returning the watchman's gaze nor employing his native language when she meets him in the street, the inscrutable woman provides a perfect tabula rasa on which the former soldier can launch his fantasy of her travail. From the distance initially required by his Francophobia, Baxter observes the Frenchwoman, whose eyes are "always fixed on the ground." After being moved by what he (incorrectly) deduces to be her sorrowful expression, he attempts conversation, but when Martinette answers in French his question about her father, the former soldier determines that "his words" are "not understood" and says "no more" (64).

At work in this brief exchange are a set of assumptions about the French character and female sentiment that remain utterly uncorroborated by the other on whom they are thrust. Baxter's knowledge of Miss Monrose rests almost exclusively on private fantasies about her compatriots, themselves based solely on hostile wartime encounters and informed by a level of antipathy that makes impossible any authentic understanding of French cultural or kinship practices. There is no evidence that Baxter can either speak or understand the language, suggesting that his assessment of linguistic "failure" must be attributed to his own incomprehension. Indeed, his erroneous appraisal of Miss Monrose's facility for language will be utterly discredited when it comes to light that Martinette's unaccented English is marked by "unrivalled fluency. Her phrazes [sic] and habits of pronouncing, [are] untinctured with any foreign mixture, and [bespeak] the perfect knowledge of a native of America" (189). Marveling to Sophia over Martinette's expressive gifts, Constantia wonders that the Frenchwoman "should talk English with equal fluency and more correctness than a native" (192). The statement raises suggestive questions about the connection between the uses of language and the foundation of national identity—the problem of determining who indeed "is the alien" in the early republic.[55]

Deputized to discover acts of trespass against the property he guards, Baxter is particularly hostile to the intrusion of the stranger, be it local vandal or foreign inhabitant; either figure inserts the troubling dimension of altierity into a social space whose homogeneity it is the watchman's job to protect. In light of his prejudice, what kindles Baxter's surprising impulses of "sympathy" toward Martinette? Neither her proximity nor her visibility determine his response; instead, it is her reclusive absence from the public scene that allows the watchman to call up the tableau of the Frenchwoman's suffering, an image with which he identifies and by which he is moved. The narrator reports:

Something like compassion was conjured up in his heart by the figure of the lady, as he recollected lately to have seen it. It was obvious to conclude that sickness was the cause of her seclusion. The same, it might be, had confined her father. If this were true, how deplorable might be their present condition! Without food, without physician or friends, ignorant of the language of the country, and thence unable to communicate their wants or solicit succor; fugitives from their native land, neglected, solitary, and poor. His heart was softened by these images. . . . He stepped into the porch, and put his eye to the key-hole. All was darksome and waste. He listened and imagined that he heard the aspirations of grief. The sound was scarcely articulate, but had an electrical effect upon his feelings. He retired home full of mournful reflections. (65)

Only after conjuring this sentimental spectacle and effectively interpolating himself within its frame does the former soldier embark on his "sympathetic" quest to discover the fate of the family.[56]

In doing so, Baxter is aroused less by humanitarian principles than he is by impulses inspired and immediately mystified by his own fantasia. He interprets the "scarcely articulate" sounds of the silent house as "the aspirations of grief," transforming essentially inaudible tones into a plaint so powerful that it excites "an electrical effect upon his feelings." That the information quickening his perceptions emanates from his imagination does not diminish Baxter's capacity to pity Mlle Monrose. In fact, the stirrings of compassion must issue from within if they are to override Baxter's abiding prejudice—which operates in the imaginary and is little remedied by experience of the symbolic *or* of the real. I invoke Lacan's categories here to emphasize that Baxter's fantasies remain unmediated by the interposition of culture, represented by his conversations with and contiguity to the Monrose family. In that regard, his view through the keyhole into the darkness might be understood as a metanarrative meditation in which Brown highlights the way projections of pity and terror become potent sources for fiction making itself—the moment in which the reader receives a glimpse of the author's self-conscious rumination on the creative process itself. Brown's most fascinating maniacs and villains are also, tellingly, his most trenchant figures for the artist, a connection to which we will return. Thus, the spectral images and haunting sounds that provoke Baxter's "mournful reflections" (65) are not summoned by the (fictive) world he inhabits; instead, they radiate from and reverberate in the mirror of his own mind.

Like the younger Harrington's voyeuristic exercise in *The Power of Sympathy*, the watchman's fantasies of compassion constitute a disturbing gloss on, if not a grim parody of, Adam Smith's discussion of sympathy in *The Theory of Moral Sentiments*. According to Smith, fellow feeling is a faculty predicated on the workings of vision and imagination, the ability to leave oneself behind in order to take another's part:

As we have no immediate experience of what other men feel, we can form no idea of the manner in which they are affected, but by conceiving what we ourselves should feel in the like situation. Though our brother is upon the rack, as long as we ourselves are at our ease, our senses will never inform us of what he suffers. . . . By the imagination we place ourselves in his situation, we conceive ourselves enduring all the same torments, we enter as it were into his body and become in some measure the same person with him, and thence form some idea of his sensations, and even feel something which, though weaker in degree, is not altogether unlike them.[57]

In *The Theory of Moral Sentiments*, selfhood is always constituted by and contingent on sympathetic relations with others: identity, never an isolated quantum, invariably has social implications. Smith's inquiry offers a proof text for approaching the problems of self at the heart of Brown's fiction, suggesting that such instabilities of identity bear a vital connection to the crisis of collective cohesion operating in early national culture. This emphasis on figurative emigration from the isolated private body and imaginative communion with the feelings of another has suggestive implications for deciphering Baxter's "contamination" as a fatal failure of sympathy.

In the introduction to his study of the social operations of sympathy in eighteenth-century Anglo-America, Michael Meranze performs a powerful reading of the scene in Laurence Sterne's *Sentimental Journey through France and Italy* where Yorick imagines "the miseries of confinement," which inspires William Hill Brown's digression on the slave woman. Conjuring the image of a languishing prisoner on whom he gazes in his mind's eye through an imaginary dungeon window, Yorick is stricken by the vision of pain and must flee from the scene of his own invention. Meranze remarks that,

in Sterne's imaginary picture of Yorick's imaginary compassion, the gestures of eighteenth-century sympathy pour forth: the hope of capturing the intensity of suffering in the mind's eye; the turning from multitudes to the individual; the fascination (which drew Yorick even closer) of the suffering body. But at the same time, Sterne, in his critical parody of sensibility, highlights the paradoxes of sympathy itself—in his efforts at compassionate reflection, Yorick effectively blocks what little light the prisoner has, and as he tries to bring the experience of confinement within his comprehension, the imagined pain proves unbearable, and he escapes his own picture. The pleasures and pain that structure sympathy, it seems, were the pleasures and pain of the sympathetic *subject*. Sympathy could only be sustained at a suitable distance; if sympathy's object was too intense or too near, the subject of sympathy fled.[58]

Meranze's observations about sympathy's poetics of distance and contiguity shed important light on what Brown explores in *Ormond:* the reality that certain expressions of fellow feeling are not necessarily motivated by the impulse of humanity and might be better understood as projections, indices of a failure to imagine with compassion the altierity of the other.

Central to the former grenadier's disastrous midnight encounter is his inability to recognize Martinette or to decode her affective experience. The watchman cannot see the alien woman in all her otherness, a vital precondition for ultimately imagining the humanity they share. Instead, he looks through her, projecting fantasies about Frenchness and femininity on the space cleared by his imperious vision, illusions bearing virtually no relation to her actual plight but reflecting his own in powerful ways. This show of egoism evokes the distinction between the altruistic and selfish origins of fellow feeling Smith notes at the very end of his treatise. There he responds to Hobbes and Mandeville, who argue that sympathy derives from love of self rather than from regard for others. Such detractors, counters Smith, confuse the operations of identification at work in the sympathetic imagination with identity itself:

> [T]hough sympathy is very properly said to arise from an imaginary change of situations with the person principally concerned, yet this imaginary change is not supposed to happen to me in my own person and character, but in that of the person with whom I sympathize. When I condole with you for the loss of your only son, in order to enter into your grief I do not consider what I, a person of such a character and profession, should suffer, if I had a son, and if that son were unfortunately to die: but I consider what I should suffer if I was really you, and I not only change circumstances with you, but I change persons and characters. My grief, therefore, is entirely upon your account, and not the least upon my own. (*Theory of Moral Sentiments*, 317)

He then asserts that Hobbes and Mandeville do not account for the transformation of being underwriting his own conception of sympathy, which David Marshall identifies as "a loss of self, a transfer, and a metamorphosis."[59]

Sympathy is the faculty through which one comes to understand another's anguish through imaginative inhabitation—an impulse that in

Charlotte Temple has democratizing force and that in *The Coquette* exposes, by its failure, the limits of republican fellow feeling. In *Ormond*'s watchman, compassion's fundamental properties undergo a peculiar distortion. Baxter's initial "encounter" on the evening of the scene in question takes place not with a real woman but rather with his own fantastic and melodramatic projection of Miss Monrose. Indeed, even the appellation by which her undiscerning neighbors identify the Frenchwoman is a fiction, concocted on the basis of mistaken assumptions—which nevertheless gives vivid expression to the nativist leanings of Baxter's associates. When Martinette finally tells her version of the midnight story, she identifies her surrogate kinsman as "Roselli" (209): the community, it becomes clear, has turned an Italianate floral noun into a homophone for Monroe, transforming a generic symbol of old-world romance into a pointed allusion to the republic's Founding Fathers. While his neighbors recast the Frenchwoman as an American with decidedly patriotic ties, the watchman evokes another set of cultural associations to the heroines of eighteenth-century literature. Baxter conjures an absent tormented other who does not exist outside the purview of gothic and sentimental novels, and, simultaneously, he erases the reality of the actual woman who resides in his own backyard. In so doing, the watchman deviates from the first step in Smith's dynamics of sympathy: placing clear vision at the beginning of a sequence of mental activity in which the imagination's substitution of subject for object immediately follows. Accurate sight is crucial to fellow feeling; if the sympathetic agent cannot identify the object before him or her as worthy of compassion, the entire process short-circuits or irreparably miscarries.

While Baxter believes that impulses of sympathy drive his interest in Miss Monrose—and not the compulsion to bolster his flagging self-conception—he stages what becomes a disavowal of fellow feeling in a paradigmatic Brownian moment of sensory *misconaissance:* confusing the movements of a mysterious figure, who passes into the Monrose house bearing an unusual light, for the intrusions of a robber. That on the very evening he has extensively imagined her agony the watchman not only fails to recognize his own neighbor but actually misconstrues her as a thief are important symbolic features of this xenophobic drama.

The details at work in Baxter's misrecognition of Martinette add up to a nativist parable about the malevolent intentions of European émigrés to the new republic. An unknown criminal—who stands in figurative relation to the alien so feared by the Federalists in the late 1790s—attempts to break and enter into a dwelling associated with the history of the young nation itself. The "plunder" this offender seeks symbolizes the nation's material wealth, a prize rightfully belonging to its legitimate (native) citizens alone. Yet the malefactor of Baxter's fantasy is utterly innocent of the charges leveled against her. Far from being thieves, Martinette and her "father" are legal occupants of the house next door and pose no material or political threat to the community. In light of these facts, Baxter's fantasy of "housebreaking" elaborates a series of passionately held xenophobic prejudices about the intrusion of foreigners into the polity and economy of early republican America.

In addition to inscribing his political inclinations, the watchman's faulty "vision" exposes related forms of bias. Most striking is his inability to decipher the gender of the shadowy form crossing his gaze:

> His eye . . . caught a glimpse of an human figure, passing into the house . . . The person had a candle in his hand. . . . The person disappeared too quickly to allow him to say whether it was male or female. This scrutiny confirmed, rather than weakened the apprehensions that first occurred. He reflected on the desolate and helpless condition of this family. The father might be sick; and what opposition could be made by the daughter to the stratagems or violence of midnight plunderers. This was an evil which it was his duty, in an extraordinary sense, to obviate. (66)

Baxter takes his second furtive glimpse into the Monroses' affairs as he observes this androgynous figure recede from view through the frame of another modest aperture. It is particularly arresting that a professional watchman should be confounded by a vision of his own neighbor; equally telling is the fact that, under the conditions of public crisis, the figure has become so defamiliarized that Baxter cannot ascribe to it a sex, much less determine whether the person is stranger or acquaintance, alien or native.

The former soldier's disorientation tells us less about the object of his vision than it does about its subject. Uncertainty over the gender identity of the flitting specter quickens the watchman's anxiety, occasioning a series of melodramatic fantasies about the precarious fate of the Monrose family— fantasies strongly inflected by sexual formulae derived from the popular gothic, sentimental, and melodramatic narratives that dominate the imaginations of readers in both England and America at the end of the eighteenth century.[60] Such novelistic conventions hold that patriarchy is weak, afflicted, perhaps even moribund; in the absence of proper paternal protection, daugh-

ters are helpless, imperiled by the menacing impulses of miscreants who invariably lie in wait.

Given the bloodthirsty military history of the protagonist of Baxter's
story, it is particularly ironic that he casts her in the role of frantic victim.
Despite Brown's emphasis on the savage and violent appearance, "the mus-
cular form, and rugged visage, scarred and furrowed into something like ferocity" (67) that Baxter brings to his voyeurism, the true hysteric of the piece
is the watchman himself. It is not Martinette who is terrified of contracting
the fever—quite the contrary: at the end of the novel the woman warrior
reveals that she has remained a stalwart companion and nurse to her "father"
during his final illness, the nature of which, curiously, remains unspecified.
Neighbors like Whiston, a brother who abandons his afflicted sister at the
height of the epidemic, expose the tenuous nature of American kinship relations under conditions of public crisis. In contrast, the Frenchwoman's loyalty to her surrogate parent endures beyond his life; under virtually impossible circumstances, she summons the energy to inter his corpse with a
modicum of dignity. It is the Anglo-American Baxter, mesmerized and horrified by the fruits of his scopophilic enterprise, who is driven to madness,
infection, and death, on his retreat from the ocular field.

Baxter's erasure of gender from the picture he sees through the window—the blankness that registers where his "vision" of sexual difference
should abide—is a failure to experience his own identity as a soldier and as a
man. In the era of the 1790s, when even George Washington's heroic war
record becomes a metaphor for charismatic leadership rather than its own
badge of honor, Baxter's investment of his masculinity in a military persona
comes to seem largely irrelevant.[61] No longer able to affirm his virility as a
function of vocation, the former soldier shores up his identity by other less
palpable means, through the creation of a strategic fiction.[62] Employing what
Derrida has termed "the logic of the supplement" when he imagines Martinette de Beauvais, née "Monrose," as a damsel in distress languishing at the
hands of criminals,[63] Baxter resembles those chivalric figures in Burke's *Reflections* whose heroism is not only produced by but actually could not exist
without immoderate exhibitions of women's anguish. Writing of Burke's poetics of gender, Claudia Johnson argues that "the spectacle of immanent and
outrageous female suffering may not be the unthinkable crime which chivalric sentimentality forestalls, but rather the one-thing-needful to solicit male
tears and the virtues that supposedly flow with them."[64]

Such heroic masculine identity is necessarily constructed against a feminized or feminine other who exists in essential proximity. Consequently, the scene in which the specter is revealed to be none other than Martinette proves thoroughly and fatally destabilizing. Rather than demonstrating hysterical emotion, the Frenchwoman is dispassionately detached—a lack of affect that puts her entirely at odds with the behavior conventionally coded as feminine in the eighteenth-century novels that inspire Baxter's chivalric ideals. Having evacuated the gender role culturally assigned to women, Miss Monrose leaves the quantum differential of sexual identification vis-à-vis the watchman dangerously out of balance.[65] Far from making a spectacle of her womanliness, or dramatizing her femininity as masquerade,[66] she is unaware (in contrast to Harriot in *The Power of Sympathy*) of the potential presence of an observing audience. So it is that this figure of self-sufficient stoicism unwittingly foils the watchman's sentimental dream of effecting her rescue, a plan on which his masculine identity depends.

Brown structures the midnight tableau in which Martinette inadvertently thwarts Baxter's illusions as an extended moment of mirroring gone awry. As such, the episode unfolds according to the dynamics Kimberly W. Benston describes in his essay on facing scenes in African American literature. There, "the *face* catch[es] its reflection in some version of the other (be it racial, familial, or even psychical). This primary speculation of an alternative configuration of the self comprises several scenarios: the shock of one's reflection in the father's or mother's face, the glance of self-discovery or dissociation in the mirror, the confrontation with the face of mastery, the encounter of some emblem of communal visage."[67] Although, as a Caucasian, Brown obviously shares little cultural experience with the writers whose tradition Benston charts, it is nevertheless true that his work uniquely brings racial and nativist conflict into the early American novel. Moreover, Brown is deeply interested in exploring the dynamics of inequality at work in the post-Revolutionary period, as illuminated in the facing scene between Baxter and the Frenchwoman.

In spite of seeming to embody the position of intellectual domination and mastery that structures the dynamic of looking in the voyeuristic relation,[68] this viewing subject in fact becomes seduced before, held, and ultimately contaminated by the object of his vision—a female body refusing to be fetishized stonily returns his gaze. The voyeurism that initiates this tableau functions within Brown's mimesis at the level of plot, inflecting the transmission of the story and configuring Baxter in relation to the narrator, who operates as a double for both Brown and the fictive audience.[69] As a "secret witness" to the primal scene in the Monrose garden—Sophia writes that "he was solicitous to obtain some information by silent means" (67)—the ex-soldier violates the sanctity of Martinette's solitary rites; so, too, his wife repeats the intrusion by relating it to her employer, who informs the narrator who speaks for Brown who creates the novel that is *Ormond.* Doubling Baxter's inappropriate gaze, we witness the hidden drama of the alien other through the metaphorical keyhole of Brown's concentric narrative structure, his much-derided, little-understood, signature technique. Scopophilia thus becomes a tainted figure for the reading process itself; in this fictive universe, neither character nor reader has direct access to the events being represented.

The claim that underwrites the homology between voyeurism and the act of reading is itself a gothic formulation, intimating that, in the paranoid, xenophobic scopophiliac Baxter (who emerges into representation for ten brief pages before being dispatched to a mass grave as a yellow-fever victim), Charles Brockden Brown inscribes a surrogate figure for a sector of his readership. We will return, at the end of the chapter, to the connection between the author's representations of the crazed voyeur who lurks and dies within his novel and the fantasies Brown projects about the audience who reads—or *misreads*—his fiction at the close of the eighteenth century. The implications are central to any conclusions we might draw about cultural prognostications in *Ormond.*

For now, we must note that the tableau does resolve at once the question of gender that had so confused the watchman in his initial moments of speculation: "The kitchen door at length opened. The figure of Miss Monrose, pale, emaciated, and haggard, presented itself. . . . [The] illumination, faint as it was, bestowed a certain air of wildness on features which nature, and the sanguinary habits of a soldier, had previously rendered, in an eminent degree, harsh and stern" (68). Martinette and Baxter are figured as apparent opposites: while she looks wan, skeletal, and careworn—a character evoking pathos and pity—he appears savage, severe, and forbidding—a pillar of martial strength. Yet appearances in this post-Lockean fictive world are necessarily deceptive. Martinette's ostensible frailty bears no relation to her ideological zeal for liberty or the performance of martial deeds into which her passions translate. Indeed, the Frenchwoman later details the way in which she has "assume[d] the male dress," "acquire[d] skill at the sword" (201), and seen service in the American and French Revolutions. Baxter's robust physicality, in contrast, proves no safeguard against the trauma that costs him his life. Because these images of defenseless femininity and rugged manhood originally emanate from Baxter's point of view, they merely reprise his sentimental construction of a potentially heroic relation to Miss Monrose. Absent from this manifest narrative of sexual difference but latent in its uncanny particulars is any notion that the Frenchwoman could also be—that in fact, she is—a fellow veteran of foreign wars, Baxter's unlikely but bone fide adversary as well as compatriot in arms.

As if to underscore that the drama being played out by candlelight is one of *identity* rather than distinction, a motif I have noted in *Wieland*'s homicidal tableau, the confrontation between the ex-grenadier and the revolutionary woman foregrounds the question of who in the scene is the subject and who is the object of the look. The visual details suggest that the contrast remains uncertain, suspended in flux. Martinette's taper sheds enough anterior light to reveal her identity to Baxter, and, ostensibly, it illuminates the view before her, leading directly to the face of the neighbor peering over the fence—who is yet unseen. But the odd visual effects intimate that, although the woman warrior has not yet registered his presence, the voyeur himself has already become the object of *narrative* speculation well in advance of the look that Martinette will imminently return, rendering him a victim indeed.

Framing the gaze of the peeping tom and effectively trumping his action at the level of storytelling is none other than Sophia. In addition to being identified with Martinette by virtue of gender, education, and shared feminist sensibility, the narrator of *Ormond* carefully attends to the dynamics of power underwriting the act of surveillance. Incarnating Brown's critique of post-Revolutionary fraternity, Sophia—as the abiding voice and consciousness of *Ormond*—must expose all males who wield an illicit gaze, from Mr. Dudley, whose relatively righteous spying leads to blindness, to Ormond, whose transgressive scopophilia engenders psychotic and homicidal consequences. In her detailed representation of the scene's peculiar optical dynamics, Sophia replays formally what the Frenchwoman enacts dramatically inside the fictive world. There, Medusa-like, Martinette returns Baxter's gaze, penetrates his equanimity, and opens him up to the energies of madness and infection—a distinctly feminizing metamorphosis.[70]

While the watchman endows what is phantasmagoric with life and meaning, he denies the reality of what lies visibly before him—the dynamics of disavowal suffuse this passage. The narrator explains that "death is familiar to the apprehensions of a soldier" and notes that "Baxter had assisted at the hasty interment of thousands, the victims of the sword or of pestilence." Yet inexplicably, the former trooper does not recognize what Sophia describes as routine military procedure for disposing of the dead. Even if, as he comes to fear, the corpse Miss Monrose buries is a yellow-fever victim, why does Baxter's veteran experience with death by "pestilence" fail to domesticate the terror that he feels? The narrator continues,

> Whether it was because this theatre of human calamity was new to him, and death, in order to be viewed with his ancient unconcern, must be accompanied in the ancient manner, with halberts and tents, certain it is, that Baxter was irresolute and timid in everything that respected the yellow fever. The circumstances of the time suggested that this was a grave, to which some victim of the disease was to be consigned. His teeth chattered when he reflected how near he might now be to the source of the infection: yet his curiosity retained him at his post. (67)

Without the buttressing of "halberts and tents," the martial props that inscribe masculinity on this "theatre of human calamity," the impromptu grave becomes both defamiliarized and irresistible, eerie and strangely mesmerizing.

That death could attack the home front in martial fashion is a reality that confounds the watchman's comprehension, for his worldview is organized by a gendered separation of spheres in which domesticity guarantees a safe haven against belligerent threats. As a soldier mindful of such essential données of military life as the distance of a musket shot or the known trajectory of a grenade, Baxter has been trained to keep the possibility of annihilation at an appropriately sanitized distance, but the veteran is no longer a member of the ranks. Without the regimental context through which he might at least rationalize, if not defend against, his encounters with death, the ex-grenadier's apprehensions intensify; as the fever crosses the perimeter delineating neighbor from stranger and "sickness" menaces "his own family" (64), he begins to unravel.

Under the inverted, nightmarish conditions of the epidemic, Baxter's binary paradigms—feminine and masculine, home front and battlefield, civilian and soldier—lose their meaning.[71] An "invisible enemy," yellow fever collapses the distinction between what is domestic or indigenous and what is foreign or imported, categories that recur in both medical arguments over the etiology of the disease and political contention surrounding anxiety over the alien.[72] In the face of such a breakdown of systems of classification, the boundaries that guarantee identity become increasingly burdensome to patrol. Home and hearth become arenas in which victims struggle against violent death. Gardens metamorphose into makeshift graveyards, and women, far from being undone by the unfolding calamity, preside over the demise of the community. Baxter cannot translate his martial experience to combat the domestic invasion, but Martinette, veteran of revolutionary conflict, proves a brilliant soldier on every front. In the context of this overturning of the social and sexual order, it is Baxter who becomes unmoored from the identity of warrior: as the field of battle on which he seeks to serve becomes ungendered, so too does he.

Despite the fact that he arms himself with his grenadier's "hanger" before venturing on his midnight foray, the watchman cannot confront the truth that he is no longer a soldier or, more precisely, that his presence on this dreamlike field of battle is irrelevant to its outcome. The horror of the epidemic, which has sent him tumbling down the economic chain of being, only underscores the reality of his degraded place. And, far from playing the part of Baxter's damsel in distress, Martinette remains a figure of imperturbable valor, seeming to possess the very quantum of heroic (and masculine) identity the watchman appears to have lost.

Confounding Baxter's vision of a besieged and helpless heroine of sentiment, the Frenchwoman more aptly recalls Edmund Burke's portrait of Marie Antoinette—complete with a near homophonic name—who symbolizes stoic courage.[73] In 1790, the Irish conservative writes elegiacally of the suffering queen,

> the great lady . . . has borne that day . . . [and] bears all the succeeding days, . . . she bears the imprisonment of her husband, and her own captivity, and the exile of her friends, and the adulation of addresses, and the whole weight of her accumulated wrongs, with a serene patience; . . . she has lofty sentiments; . . . she feels with the dignity of a Roman matron; that in the last extremity she will save herself from the last disgrace, and that if she must fall, she will fall by no ignoble hand. (169)

Burke's vision of eighteenth-century female heroism remains a fascinating touchstone for Brown's imagination in *Ormond*, despite the fact that Martinette's politics situate her on the opposite side of the French Revolution from Marie Antoinette: she is, after all, interring the corpse of a Gallic patriarch in what Bill Christophersen terms "a symbolic drama of regicide transpir[ing] in a neighbor's yard"[74]—a reading that Baxter's reactionary inter-pretation of events supports. While Martinette drags Monrose's corpse to-ward burial, Baxter's "blood [runs] cold" at the "spectacle." And as the Frenchwoman bears up under the burden of her duty, the former grenadier's "horror increase[s] in proportion as she [draws] nearer to the spot where he [stands]" (69). Conjuring an image of the soldier that he used to be, Marti-nette proves an uncanny mirror for Baxter; what he cannot see reflected in her impassive visage is the truth of their shared experience and, with it, the possibility of sympathy along decidedly unsentimental lines, a fellowship based on belligerence rather than on grief, as in *Charlotte Temple*.

In the struggle for identity that unfolds in this scene, the terms of battle are inscribed in the contrast between Baxter's heightened affect and Mar-tinette's definitive failure to demonstrate feeling; their emotions exist in asymmetrical relation not only to each other but, more emblematically, to conventional cultural expectations about gender and passion. Against Bax-ter's hysteria, the Frenchwoman's insensibility threatens to unsettle the watchman. Following an observation that could only have come from Baxter himself, the narrator pointedly emphasizes that Martinette's "tears were ei-ther exhausted or refused to flow, for none were shed by her" (69). The for-mer soldier does eventually register the fleeting if "genuine expression of sor-row" (69) that momentarily crosses Miss Monrose's tired face, but, in spite of this concession to her potential humanity, the watchman experiences Martinette's failure of tears—her dramatic withholding of the very senti-ment that could mark her as a feeling woman—as a personal affront. This (mis)perception reveals Baxter's increasing paranoia, for the Frenchwoman has no knowledge of the figure who remains hidden from view.

Martinette's disengagement from the arena of emotion calls up a recip-rocal but inverted response in the voyeur. While she sits "buried in reverie, her eyes scarcely open and fixed upon the ground" (69), utterly unreceptive to the world around her, Baxter becomes an affective sponge, reabsorbing the excessive emotion projected onto Martinette as it ricochets off the self-enclosed Frenchwoman and rebounds on him. By withholding feeling at what is in Baxter's eyes the crucial moment of trauma—she is about to place an unidentified but most likely "paternal" body in the ground—the woman warrior strikes terror in the heart of the watchman. When the shroud cover-ing the nameless corpse is accidently "drawn aside," it "exhibit[s], to the startled eye of Baxter, the pale and ghastly visage of the unhappy Monrose" (69). As if endowed with animation and agency, the ghoulish countenance of the dead patriarch appears to fix on the watchman's look in an instant of identificatory horror. Baxter is deeply shaken by the specter of this "father's" dissolution, particularly as it contrasts with the reality of the "daughter's" power. Embodying authority in an unlikely form, Martinette seems to sap Baxter of the vital potency that lies at the center of his self-conception. Riveted by the uncanny gaze of extinguished paternal command, finding himself in the vacant stare of the corpse of her "father," the former soldier, himself a parent of daughters, finally catches a glimpse of the reflection that has until now eluded him. Martinette, disturbed by the sounds of the peeping tom as he "hastily withdr[aws] from the fence" (69), only then returns a horrified look to the voyeur who surveys her silent sorrow. Breaking up the scene of specularity with a piercing shriek, she drives the watchman from the visual field. Fatally identified with the "unhappy" M. Monrose, Baxter is as good as dead.

In the final movement of this intricate spectacle, the watchman becomes the transgressive witness to nothing less than an early republican primal scene: in the plague-ridden context of post-Revolutionary America, the death of the father and his burial at the hands of the daughter prove even more threatening than any glimpse of his erotic life could be. This is not to ignore the lurid quality of a midnight scene in which an unmarried woman, presumably clothed in a nightdress, stands astride the dead body of an older man who is not her biological father to prepare for his burial. It is only to suggest that the political ethos of the episode is even more provocatively disturbing than its sexual content. Put another way, while the passage certainly evokes the incestuous thematics explored in Greek tragedy that inspired Freud's notion of the Oedipus complex, it also summons up dynamics that he will create and elaborate in *Totem and Taboo*, a metapsychological work more pertinent to my discussion of primal scenes of the Founding.[75]

Figured and defamiliarized in this bizarre tableau is the well-known Revolutionary paradigm Lynn Hunt evokes from Freud's *Totem and Taboo*.[76] As gothically reworked by Charles Brockden Brown, the American version of the fable rings a fascinating change on the Freudian myth of murder, incorporation, and the birth of conscience: after dispatching the patriarch, the primal brother in the American story *fails to inherit* his mantle because, instead of identifying with the father's *power*, he internalizes his own patricidal aggression and is himself destroyed. Thus, the primal sister, invisible to representation in Freud's version of the story but commandingly present in Brown's,[77] comes forward as a warrior in her own right to assume the father's prestige and seize power over the horde. The episode powerfully reverses the primal scene we have been tracing throughout this study: here, the female other disinters herself—comes into visibility—in the process of burying the patriarch, while Baxter, in his voyeurism, imitates the rites of social burial, but ends up dead himself.

Even the vaguest outlines of the Baxter digression conjure up a rich series of associations to the political and cultural context of Brown's novel. Underscoring the problematic nature of masculinity and fraternity as figures for social identity and communal cohesion, the embedded tale of his demise points evocatively in the direction of *Ormond*'s feminist and female homosocial ending but at the same time raises important questions about the prospect and limits of sympathy as an affect extending outward from persons to collectives. What is the prognosis for the health of the community when, at a time of civic emergency, compassion among ostensibly "generous and intrepid spirit[s]" (67) becomes implicated with infection itself?

The story of the veteran's "contamination" reworks, as well, the drama of American identity formation that Jared Gardner details in his reading of *Edgar Huntly*. Arguing that in the late 1790s both the selfhood and the stability of the republican national (read white, middle-class, Anglo-Saxon, male) are figured in binary terms, he notes that the citizen's identity as an American depends on the recognition and reprobation of the alien other.[78] Extending the Enlightenment impulse to classify and categorize, the Founders and their Federalist successors actually legislate the forced invisibility, if not the hygienic removal,[79] of figures whose nonwhite, nonprivileged, nonnativeborn, nonmale status differentiates them from the authorized political subjects of the nation. Thus, African American slaves, females under coverture, and foreigners and dissenting democratic-republicans subject to arrest and imprisonment under the Alien and Sedition Acts and members of the lower classes become sacrificial figures in the drive to consolidate republican homogeneity.[80] Erased from official forms of political representation, they comprise the gothic residue of eighteenth-century American Enlightenment culture. *Ormond* dramatizes the irony that underlies this sanitary construction of the citizen's identity under the conditions of contagious disease.

In Brown's fictive universe, the citizens of the infant nation are constituted over against a series of black, female, alien, and indigent bodies, and patriotic identification is the purview of a small and privileged male elite. That Brown incarnates this white, male, Anglo-Saxon citizen in the reactionary, paranoid, and diseased Baxter raises intriguing questions about the author's vision of a republican future built on such ground. As a critical medi-tation on the mechanisms of the Founding, Brown's novel dramatizes the dynamics of exclusion and violence that guarantee, if only at the manifest level of official culture and at great collective expense, a seemingly homoge-neous American citizenry. *Ormond* asks whether the cost of such investments may actually exceed the value of the enterprise itself.

Portraits

In the embedded tale of the watchman's contamination, Brown offers a nar-rative rendition of "historical" tableaux, the most demanding and compli-cated genre of painting in the Anglo-American canon. In subtle but equally important ways, both miniatures and more elaborate portraits inform the structure and content of the book: a series of minute character sketches and several more extended biographical interludes join Brown's historical render-ing to create the disjunct, atemporal contours of the greater novel, imagining a domestic realm threatened, like the public world, by the infectious rupture of sympathetic relations, the contamination of fellow feeling. As a self-referential nod to such narrative procedures, Brown places a (fictive) minia-ture painting at the center of the plot in *Ormond* and creates an extended digression around its shifting career.

The inset tale of the dislocation, alienation, and recovery of Sophia's portrait highlights the fact that, in *Ormond*, identifications are made and iden-tity is established through acts of reflective vision extending beyond the pur-view of embodied relations, per se.[81] The episode of the itinerant miniature suggests that, in a culture whose own origins remain inchoate, fragile, and insecure, even two-dimensional images that cannot return their bearer's gaze wield the power to constitute and authorize a certain form of selfhood. In that regard, the facing scenes dramatizing and underscoring the specular na-ture of self-construction do not require that the persons involved be mutually aware in order to establish or disturb identity; as the story of Baxter reveals, the watchman's most powerful "sympathetic" visions unfold *phantasmagori-cally*, before Martinette catches a glimpse of his voyeuristic stare and shatters his projections. Nor must such encounters even include the image of a hu-man face: written descriptions of character are sufficient—enabling the con-struction of the other without requiring a tangible presence. One has only to think of the example of Franklin, who negotiates a world in which selfhood is coterminous with authorizing documents (letters of introduction and credit), to understand that the issues Brown demarcates here are pervasive problems in late-eighteenth-century American culture.[82]

The incident involving the loss and reclamation of Sophia's miniature portrait is one in a series of important episodes in *Ormond* featuring imposture, forgery, counterfeiting, and masquerade, practices of dissimulation in which identity comes unmoored from traditional foundations and proliferates cancerously. Perversions of both representation and fellow feeling, these acts involve taking "the place of someone else" without "taking someone else's part." That is, the deliberate falsification of letters of reference, the circulation of fraudulent bank notes, and the performance in disguise of an identity not one's own parody David Marshall's definition, *pace* Adam Smith, of the operations of sympathy. Superficial resemblance substitutes for human connection or material collateral, the authentic "documentation" that underwrites public assertions of self.[83]

The narrative of the dislocated miniature recounts the story of Martyne, an émigré English confidence man who purchases the tiny likeness of an absolute stranger in order to buttress a fraudulent tale of origin. The imposter's masquerade unfolds apart from any personal desire for the woman in the picture who, in keeping with the uncanny coincidences that mark Brown's fiction, is none other than Sophia.[84] Prominently displaying the image of his "absent beloved," he makes a bogus attachment into a public spectacle. Sophia writes, "He had suffered a portrait which hung at his breast, to catch [her proxy's] eye. On her betraying a desire to inspect it more nearly, he readily produced it" (241). Operating here is a voracious social ambition completely detached from the workings of sympathy: the rascal weaving the narrative deploys Sophia's image to substantiate the story of his prospects, a tale of identity constructed at the expense of an unknown woman's innocent reputation. The narrator notes that her intermediary "easily drew from him confessions that this was the portrait of his mistress. He let fall sundry innuendoes and surmises tending to impress her with a notion of the rank, fortune and intellectual accomplishments of the nymph, and particularly of the doating fondness and measureless confidence, with which she regarded him" (241). In his flaunting of the miniature, Martyne tries to trumpet the reality of a romantic fiction bought and paid for with cash.

Like other rogues in the author's oeuvre, Martyne resembles Brown's ventriloquist Carwin, who, according to Fliegelman, "is seducer less of women than of opinion."[85] To a character, Brown's scoundrels are far more successful at self-promotion than sexual conquest. As such, they serve as prescient cultural barometers, embodying forms of consumerism and publicity that in the late 1790s, several decades before the advent of advertising and other phenomena of the nineteenth-century marketplace, remain relatively unknown. It is as if, in imagining a character who points toward the commercial face of liberal individualism,[86] Brown could eerily prognosticate the aesthetic and social trends of the Jacksonian future, per se, for Martyne's dramatic exhibition of Sophia's likeness is sharply incongruent with genteel conventions governing the exchange of miniature portraits at the turn of the nineteenth century. The imposter's impulse to flaunt his "connection" to Sophia—to wear his devotion literally on his sleeve—reflects more about Martyne's market-minded hucksterism than it does about the romantic codes of the epoch in which *Ormond* is set.

This rascal's schemes are unwittingly abetted by a goldsmith who traffics in intimate artifacts-*cum*-commodities, objects that have distinguished the privacy of an era and the self-enclosure of an economy, both on the verge of passing away. Although Constantia's ruthlessly acquisitive landlord M'Crea describes the jeweler as one whose "character and place of abode" are "universally known" (219), only the landlord, a figure from the late-eighteenth-century melodramatic repertoire, can attest to this reputation. With the exception of Sophia, the novel's genteel characters have no dealings with the jeweler. Even the bankrupted heroine knows nothing of the workings of such an individual, essentially a pawnbroker, who serves the needs of an impoverished gentry at a time of social turmoil. In contrast to the goldsmith, Martyne prefigures the nineteenth-century American consumer in all his or her brazen vulgarity. Taken together, the confidence man and the jeweler represent two sides of a commercial coin. Circulating in a republican world not yet able to recognize the vision of the liberal future for which they stand, the goldsmith and the impostor augur the development of a new sort of American marketplace twenty years ahead of its time.[87]

If, for Martyne, the miniature portrait is a public commodity, a means to upward mobility, for Sophia it is a private souvenir, conjuring the emotional exchange of happier days. Such likenesses, according to Robin Bolton-Smith and Dale Johnson, are not openly displayed until the Victorian era; in the Federalist period, they take part in rituals of courtship that are distinctly private. Set behind the hinged covers of pendants, such images are worn discreetly by women as lockets and by men in the pockets of vests or frock coats—embodying what art historians characterize as an art of "concealment," the very term that Werner B. Berthoff uses to describe Charles Brockden Brown's narrative technique. Bolton-Smith and Johnson write,

> The miniature portrait, made to be set in a piece of jewelry or secreted in a drawer for private viewing, conveys a . . . private message to lovers, family, and friends. . . . This small likeness, so closely bound to the private lives of its participants, was a tiny distillation of the time in which it was created . . . It was this small, conservative, discreet miniature that found its way to the shores of the New World during the last half of the eighteenth century, along with the tradition of exchanging miniatures to mark life's important moments.[88]

In the late eighteenth century, the tiny portrait is an artistic form meant, like letters, to promote sympathy between private individuals—to bridge distance, absence, and even death. As a colleague of the famed American miniature painter Edward Green Malbone writes, Malbone's special virtuosity involves

> a style particularly congenial to the benevolence of [the] feelings . . . such striking resemblances . . . will never fail to perpetuate the tenderness of friendship, to divert the cares of absence, and to aid affection in dwelling on those features and that image, which death has forever wrested from it.[89]

A precursor to the daguerreotype and the photograph, the painted likeness is a memento "designed to be carried" or, if worn, "turned inward to preserve the privacy of grief" or the intimacy of love. Symbolizing "bonds of loyalty, friendship, or affection," they become particularly important as relics—aids to memory and objects of succor—in periods of extended cultural dislocation such as the Revolutionary era and its aftermath.[90]

At stake in Martyne's exhibition of the miniature he acquires for money—a display incongruent with the romantic rituals of the caste he aspires to join—is the spurious assertion of a sympathy to which he has no authentic claim. The goldsmith who sells him the likeness remarks to Sophia, as she hunts the "owner" of her lost portrait, "I should imagine that the young man was acquainted with the original. To say the truth, I hinted as much at the time, and I did not see that he discouraged the supposition. Indeed, I cannot conceive how the picture could otherwise have gained any value in his eyes" (221). Although Martyne is far from being "acquainted with the original," the jeweler's phrase is redolent of the Brownian refrain "do you know the author?" that haunts *Wieland*'s narrative.[91] Such emphasis on tracing the source of the image back to an authoritative precursor underscores Brown's obsession in *Ormond* with the problem of origin as an essential feature of identity. As William Scheick notes in the definitive essay on this subject, "concern with origination informs the central meaning of the work."[92]

Looby's discussion of the recurrent search for origins in *Wieland* powerfully illuminates this issue. Noting that characters obsessively attempt to determine the causes of baffling events in the novel, as well as locate the sources of their present circumstances in a historical past, Looby remarks on Brown's apprehension "concerning the apparent groundlessness of American political legitimacy that makes him at once wish for a connection to a determinate and authoritative Saxon origin, and at the same time despair of reclaiming it."[93] This preoccupation with returning to what, following Looby, I characterize as primal scenes of *origin* in *Wieland* marks Brown's attempt to bind his anxiety about the soundness of the nation's Founding. As Looby suggests, when an act of commencement is factitious and arbitrary, when legitimacy is suspect, the search for origins proliferates beyond control, whether the subject of that quest is an individual, a family, or a nation. In *Wieland*, the three are connected.

That Brown sets *Wieland* in a pastoral suburb of pre-Revolutionary Philadelphia, a quasi-Jeffersonian milieu, while he locates *Ormond* in the urban heart of the Federalist capital of the republic speaks to the author's darkening vision of the American future. Rather than reiterating *Wieland*'s precarious attempts to ground or locate origins, the even more pessimistic *Ormond* challenges the idea that any source—be it self or nation—might prove stable or authoritative. Instead, the novel dramatizes a proliferation of false appellations, forged epistles, alienated portraits, and counterfeited bills that figure the fluid and protean nature of identity in a shifting and seemingly groundless post-Revolutionary world, where even the origins of epidemic illness—the etiology of yellow fever—remain unclear.

While the identity of the portrait's subject remains a mystery, the aesthetic merit of the image is perfectly evident to Martyne, reflecting not only the beauty of the sitter and the artistry of the maker but something even more provocative and ineffable; it provides "a tiny distillation of the time in which it was created," the promise of a world beckoning alluringly to a man as imaginative as he is opportunistic. Far from seizing on Sophia's picture in a random moment of captivation, Martyne has actually searched for such an artifact to exploit for his imposture. In his eyes the value of the min-

iature transcends its material worth. As the narrator learns when she negotiates to recuperate the trinket for a costly sum, he has been willing to pay
"a price for it, at least double its value, as a mere article of traffic" (243).
Martyne envisions the likeness as an economic passport, endowed with the
power to ferry its owner beyond the limits of his station. As the exclusive
prop in a somewhat improvised but effective display of illusion, the portrait
not only supplements but actually confers identity as a positive presence.
Thus, through the designated offices of a two-dimensional icon, an unknown
and unconnected alien comes to magnify himself from virtual invisibility into
public perception.

Since in the final decades of the eighteenth century, only Americans
of the privileged and the upper-middle classes send their daughters to be
painted, the mere *appearance* of an attachment to a handsome and affluent
woman would seem to situate this placeless émigré in a world from which he
would otherwise be debarred. Purportedly, parents of such advantaged young
women also continue to supervise their offspring's romantic associations,
despite the relative liberalizing of prerogatives of courtship in the post-
Revolutionary period.[94] Theoretically then, the impostor's amorous association has been certified by an approving and affluent republican father, a
phantasmal doppelgänger for the figure he longs to become.[95] Martyne's social pretensions literally *depend* on the transparency of Sophia's portrait, its
legibility as an emblem of class and position in the eyes of his privileged
audience. This fact becomes immediately clear in the narrator's report of her
conversation with the imposter's landlady, who highlights the tenuousness of
his ties to any community whatsoever. The woman affirms that the fellow is
"a man of specious manners and loud pretensions. He came from England,
bringing with him forged recommendatory letters, and after passing from
one end of the country to the other, contracting debts which he never paid,
and making bargains which he never fulfilled, he suddenly disappeared. It is
likely that he returned to Europe. Had he no kindred, no friends, no companions? He found none here. He made pretences to alliances in England,
which better information has, I believe, since shewn to be false" (221–22).
Lack of origins or of ties to the Anglo-American social fabric does not
obstruct Martyne's assimilation into republican life. In fact, his experience
recalls Benjamin Franklin, who in *The Autobiography* initially asserts the importance of being well connected only to explode the notion as an inhibiting
myth when he details the treachery of Governor Keith; falling under the spell
of this high-ranking and notorious confidence man who never delivers on

his promised letters of *credit,* the young printer learns an object lesson in the limited value of paternal patronage and the enabling powers of liberty.[96] So, too, Martyne's unrootedness affords him imaginative freedom to rewrite his past, construct a more compelling narrative of self, and market it to the world.

In that regard, both the imposter and the more ominous forger Craig, whose story I will explore in a moment, evoke the post-Revolutionary "new men . . . of paper" against whom classical republicans notoriously inveigh.[97] Like the stock jobbers and speculators who threaten the virtue of the infant nation and consequently imperil its fragile cohesion, both Craig and Martyne traffic in various forms of credit. What distinguishes Brown's villains from these other economic opportunists is the nature of what they are willing to risk. Martyne, Craig, and Ormond himself repeatedly hazard their fortunes on fraternal trust, a commodity that, once possessed, returns dividends of immeasurable worth and, if lost, leaves ruin and even violence in its wake. In a period in which many Americans greet cries of "liberty," "equality," and "fraternity" with equivocal approval, treachery against public confidence committed in the name of brotherhood leaves wounds that are especially galling and deep.

The denouement of the Martyne digression, in which a furious Sophia confronts and exposes the imposter, suggests that liberty and fellow feeling do not easily coexist in post-Revolutionary culture. In the world of *Ormond,* at least, freedom and sympathy seem to operate according to the principles of a zero-sum economy, where one man's individual independence and private pleasure come at the expense of another's (or a woman's) public character and personal tranquility. Violating late-eighteenth-century codes of courtship and privacy, Martyne discloses a view of compassion that is, itself, bizarrely askew.

The inset story of Martyne's specular relationship with a tiny portrait likeness becomes, like the Baxter digression, a fitting microcosm for the vicissitudes of identity and sympathy that plague the characters in *Ormond.* The locket functions as an emblematic touchstone of selfhood in a novel that turns around problems of constructing both personal and national character in the uncertain decades following national legitimation. If sympathy as defined by Smith is ideally an exchange that takes place face to face, collapsing the distance and difference that divide individual members of the social body, the affair of the displaced miniature unfolds as another Brownian parody of fellow feeling and sociality.

Forgery

Martyne's deed resonates with the acts of the other forgers, counterfeiters, and masqueraders who abound in Brown's novels, proliferating false sympathy, contaminating and ravaging their fellows. Beyond the titular villain himself, the most prominent of these figures is Thomas Craig, master manipulator of credit and credibility. Craig's fraudulent letters of introduction and subsequent embezzlement from Mr. Dudley's business ultimately destroy the apothecary's fortunes, while his aspersions on Constantia's reputation nearly cost the young woman her good name. The man's seemingly incomprehensible metamorphosis into Mr. Dudley's murderer at the end of the narrative marks his stunning shift from acquisitive scoundrel into blatant sociopath, a transformation for which no detail of *Ormond*'s plot could possibly prepare the reader. Known for his compulsion to commit fraud—a serious breach of the social contract—at any opportunity, the young man becomes a homicidal maniac without a word of warning. This inexplicable turn of events provides ample evidence to support the persistent charges that Brown's mode of composition is "hasty," "careless," and "improvised." [98] Indeed, such a radical amplification of the character's malevolence marks an evolution seemingly incongruent with Brown's initial portrayal of Craig. [99]

In fact, Craig's ultimate crime is not discontinuous with his earlier offenses. While incommensurate with homicide, forgery and counterfeiting still constitute virulent transgressions against the social order, violating public faith in the operations of representation itself, without which there can be no culture of print, no economy of credit, and no republican political process. Notwithstanding the grievous nature of his assaults against the collective, it nevertheless remains true that, until the end of *Ormond*, Craig refrains from the physical violation of bodies, per se. Instead, he acts out his rancor by employing an extended scheme of fraternal seduction and filial betrayal along economic, as well as personal, lines. The forger's conspiracy is driven by his keen understanding of a common misperception, the origins of which can be attributed not to Smithian sympathy but to Mandavillian selfishness: the confusion arising when personal projection is mistaken for apparent social knowledge of an unfamiliar other, as in the case of Baxter's distorted apprehension of Martinette de Beauvais. Craig's genius lies in his ability to orchestrate and exploit such dynamics, which Daniel E. Williams characterizes as "*transactions of belief.*" [100]

In his work on the *Memoirs of Stephen Burroughs* (1798), an infamous

late-eighteenth-century American masquerader and counterfeiter whose resemblance to Brown's Craig is in some ways remarkable, Williams coins this
double-barreled conceit to characterize the machinations of a protean figure
who, despite his dubious sincerity, speaks eloquently for his times. As his
autobiography aptly shows, Burroughs's distinctive form of behavior, his capacity to incarnate conviction and fidelity in an audience of doubters, marks
him as uniquely American.[101] To describe the intricate way this dissimulator
preys on and manipulates the credulous faith of his victims, Williams formulates the notion of "transactions of belief." This seemingly paradoxical
expression evokes the lexicons of trade and theology, domains that, even with
the equivocal acceptance of commercial republicanism by the end of the
eighteenth century,[102] exist and operate in concerted tension. In the seventeenth century, of course, these realms are vitally interconnected. In that regard, Williams's language both echoes and collapses the basic polarity that
distinguishes American thought of the late eighteenth century, the divorce
between economic and religious matters embodied in such antithetical figures as Benjamin Franklin and Jonathan Edwards. Of course, this bifurcated
description of the vexed relationship ostensibly obtaining between the material and spiritual worlds vastly oversimplifies the ways in which, even in the
age of Enlightenment, the two traditions borrow from and leak into one
another.[103] Thus, the conjunction of materialism and spirituality conjured by
Williams's telling phrase aptly reflects the extraordinary and paradoxical moment at which Burroughs lives, lies, and writes: an era steeped in nostalgia
for the security afforded by communal religious enthusiasm and one that
simultaneously points toward liberal individualism, a market economy, and
the commercial future.

The notion of "transactions of belief" enables Williams to explore questions of identity—physical and metaphysical—evoked by the multiple meta-
morphoses Burroughs alleges having undergone and comes to represent in
his book. Among his other crimes, he steals sermons written by his father, a
well-respected Presbyterian minister, and for nearly six months passes himself off as a clergyman. Burroughs's documentary account of a fraudulent life,
composed at the very historical moment when Brown turns to fiction, is also
inflected by a serious literary sensibility manifested in an expert use of the
picaresque as narrative form and vehicle for social criticism.

Burroughs's autobiography turns around the very conundrums of self-
construction that so preoccupy Brown in *Ormond.* In a passage from the
Memoirs frequently discussed by critics,[104] the confidence man comes face to

face with a physician who begins to regale him with apocryphal stories concerning the notorious rogue. As if in simply discoursing about this imposter the doctor becomes infected by a contagious impulse to dissimulate, he claims to have been "acquainted with a certain character by the name of Stephen Burroughs, who, of all others, was the most singular . . . he was a person possessed of the greatest abilities of any man he ever knew."[105] Not only has this man never met Burroughs; he also has no idea that his interlocutor is the very scoundrel in question. Williams writes of the doctor:

> Complacently self-assured, he was confident that he knew Burroughs. Ironically, he did not; he did not even know the man with whom he was speaking. His perception was based on a set of beliefs, an assurance that he knew both the man he was talking about and the man he was talking to. Knowing, then, was a form of believing. Yet as seen here and throughout the narrative, all forms of identity identification were unstable and unreliable. The perception of self was based on external transactions of belief, and, as Burroughs repeatedly illustrated, beliefs could easily be manipulated.[106]

Burroughs's masquerade proves an evocative analogue for Craig's misrepresentations in *Ormond*. While crimes against belief seem incommensurate with homicide, the initial offenses committed by Brown's forger nevertheless eat away at notions of credibility and communal trust that enable a nascent commercial society to survive and prosper.

Craig's abuses unfold along a continuum that begins with an extensive epistolary dissimulation regarding his origins and ends with the murder of a man who has served as his surrogate father. His mysterious offstage slaying of Mr. Dudley, the effects of which erupt into representation without warning, is the closest thing to patricide Brown will (decline to) dramatize in *Ormond*. Scholars traditionally gloss over the dissimulator's culpability for the murder, identifying him instead as simply the instrument of Ormond, whom they condemn as the agent and mastermind of the killing, but their displaced attribution of guilt, however accurate from the point of view of the law, obscures a central feature of the national fantasy at work in the novel. By ascribing this assassination to a figure identified with the French Revolution, such imputation of responsibility muddles two important facts: that the crime features an indigenously American cast (despite his fraudulent claim about having emigrated from Yorkshire, Craig hails from rural New Hampshire) and that, beyond expressing Ormond's maniacal desire for revenge against

Mr. Dudley (who would obstruct the libertine's sexual designs on his daughter), the murder of Constantia's father by his former apprentice bears a decidedly oedipal and therefore political resonance.

What critics call "murder" becomes more fully explicable as "patricide," once we restore Craig to his rightful place as agent, as well as instrument, of the crime. The killing of the father of a woman who symbolizes the innocence of the young republic is a powerful symptom of social disorder, a potent metaphor for the internecine conflicts that divide post-Revolutionary culture. To hold Ormond and, by extension, the immoderate spirit of European insurrection solely responsible for this assault against a progenitor—to erase Craig's principal role in the killing—is to disregard the reality that the roots of post-Revolutionary America's social problems are largely and disturbingly domestic.

This observation might appear to echo a Jeffersonian diagnosis of the nation's condition at the turn of the eighteenth century, resonating with well-known contemporary forms of partisan analysis, the sort of propaganda deployed by Democratic-Republicans eager to dominate a political universe still controlled, however insecurely, by John Adams and the Federalist party. Instead, it is meant to suggest something much more fundamental about the difficulties plaguing the infant nation, since crises like the yellow-fever epidemic cut across a vastly wider human landscape than would seem to be implied by the party-oriented characterizations of social disruption.[107] The manichean analysis of the period cannot fully acknowledge two basic facts: that what divides Americans on the eve of the new century are always already *internal* affairs and that the pull of contrasting allegiances to embattled European powers functions as a grand displacement through which the citizens of the republic disavow and rechannel ideological differences too ugly to own as indigenously American.[108]

Thus, criticism indulges the impulse to demonize Ormond as the European and, in particular, the French other for crimes that are clearly also Craig's, abuses endemic to early national society. In so doing, scholars themselves echo the dualistic post-Revolutionary impulse for dealing with contention, which reaches a height in the 1790s. At all levels of culture, from the debate over the etiology of the yellow fever to controversies surrounding immigration and the problem of the alien, Federalist era politicians and commentators identify the origins of American social conflict in sources either outside the individual bodies of citizens or beyond the collective borders of the nation. This fact, of course, scarcely exonerates Ormond for a variety of outrages: indeed, there is no question that by the end of the novel Brown's titular character is a thoroughly reprehensible fiend. It is only to note that, at every level of the work, within his depiction of characters, in major dramatic episodes, and, in particular, through extended digressions, Brown imaginatively reenacts the ideological strife threatening to unravel the republic's fragile cohesion.

It is in this context that the final, murderous, exploit of Thomas Craig, the one malefactor in *Ormond* who is also a native-born American citizen, must be seen as a crime with decidedly political implications. But before we turn to the forger's assassination of Mr. Dudley, which marks the homicidal swan song to an already nefarious career, we must examine the initial scenes in which Craig's attack against legitimacy and singularity—his assault on authentic origins—begins to unfold.

In the drama of the forger's attack on the livelihood of the apothecary, Brown enacts his ongoing concern with the morality of the Revolution. Craig symbolically reoccupies the structural position of the archetypal patriot in the years leading up to 1776 when he violently casts off the rule of his (surrogate) father in order to make his own way in the world. While the miscreant's quest to unseat and destroy the patriarch's economic sovereignty, his appropriation and devastation of Mr. Dudley's fortunes, appears to be motivated by unadulterated acquisitiveness that knows no ideological bounds, with every gesture of dissimulation, Craig expresses a rabid and thorough going antagonism to established forms and figures of authority. Aside from these resonant parallels between the patriot cause and what we might call Craig's "rebellion," the two cases remain incommensurate in larger terms. Beyond the obvious fact that Constantia's parent is far from a tyrant, the apprentice's assault against Dudley's "government" unfolds in isolation. Craig can justify his injurious deeds according to no greater ideal than simple avarice itself; the lone principle guiding the forger's beliefs, beyond the dictate to grow rich, is a ruthless compulsion to remain free from any social bond, a precept to which Craig remains devoted until he is slain by Ormond.

Thus, despite some interesting resemblances to the struggle for American independence, the extended episode of sincerity betrayed, authority repulsed, and liberty achieved must be seen as a distinctly *post*-Revolutionary parable of individualism run amok. Craig's departure from a fictive English home, Dudley's symbolic adoption of the young man, the latter's feigned devotion and years of purported service, and his ultimate treachery and flight to Jamaica on being suspected of fraud constitute a highly ironic, if not pa-

rodic, and ultimately unworthy analogue for the patriot experience of freedom. If anything, Brown figures the apprentice's rebellion as not only unrighteous but actually unnatural: in destroying his ties to a family into which
he might have married, Craig scorns the legitimate channels through which
he could have acquired Dudley's property. By invoking the category of the
"natural" in the context of questions about legitimate as opposed to unrighteous inheritance, I pointedly conjure the specter of Edmund Burke, whose
ideas that organic, evolutionary modifications in the social order are superior
to artificial, revolutionary transformations influenced not only Brown but an
entire post-Revolutionary generation.[109]

Of course, the legitimate path to such accession would necessitate
Craig's submission to the bondage of marriage, which Brown himself cri-
tiques in *Ormond* through several extended tirades on the disempowerment
of wives and the utility of free love. These digressions mark the novel as one
of the earliest protofeminist productions in the history of American literature. Although Constantia's alleged hostility to matrimony as an institution
is deployed through the lens of Sophia's narrating consciousness and is thus
inflected by the latter's profoundly antipatriarchal and homosocial attitudes,
her views nevertheless resonate with statements Brown also makes in *Alcuin;
A Dialogue,* his bizarre and intriguing feminist treatise.[110]

Instead, the apprentice-*cum*-embezzler seeks unbridled aggrandizement
detached from the claims of law or sympathy, the accumulation of wealth
unfettered by any obligation to the past, be it parent, benefactor, or beloved.
Foregrounding the dangers of excessive liberty—the price paid by the
Founding generation for the legacy of freedom and material possibility they
have forged for their offspring—Craig's story dramatizes the way the Revolution's children may be unwilling, unfit, or simply unable to take up the
burden of their freighted inheritance.[111]

Both Craig's scheme to seduce the Dudleys into what Constantia later
calls the "protect[ing] and foster[ing] [of his] youth" (93) and the opportunity for embezzlement that results from his sympathetic infiltration of the
business ring a change on the traditional modus operandi of the confidence
man who rises to prominence in the early national period. According to
Karen Halttunen, this figure habitually preys on "raw country youth[s] entering the city to seek [their] fortune[s]."[112] A character thought to be based
in part on Benjamin Franklin,[113] Arthur Mervyn, the eponymous hero of
Brown's best-known novel exploring the connection between commerce and
sincerity, personifies the classic dupe of Halttunen's paradigm. Hailing from

rural origins, Mervyn is discovered and mentored by the urbane and duplicitous Welbeck, a paternal figure who capitalizes on the boy's naïveté in the most literal sense. The forger, in contrast, exploits age and purported experience, attacking and supplanting the father instead of assuming his part. In *Ormond*, Brown inverts what Halttunen details as the well-established scheme of the trickster in order to press his point about the deeply unnatural, unabashedly political character of Craig's incursions against authority. Such reversal suggests that, notwithstanding the powerful legacy the revolutionary generation bequeaths, this heroic cohort (which includes Constantia's father if only by virtue of age) proves far from invulnerable to failure or defeat, much less to the radical challenges of its young.

Though Halttunen's study focuses on the nineteenth-century incarnation of the confidence man, it illuminates the way in which Brown presciently foresees the liberal individualism lying just beyond the horizon of his culture and represents it as a nightmare. Halttunen argues that the confidence man occupies the center of antebellum anxieties about establishing and recognizing social identity in a republic theoretically based on the boundless potential of the individual and nineteenth-century concerns about securing success in the anonymous "world of strangers" that was the antebellum city.[114] She goes on to note that the "intellectual framework" of such nineteenth-century schemes to manipulate the faith of innocent young Americans is "eighteenth-century republican ideology":

> [T]he struggle between liberty and power, the danger of corruption and decay, the ultimate threat of tyranny and enslavement—were [all] present in the nineteenth century confidence game. In it, the passive liberty of the American youth falls victim to the self-aggrandizing power of the confidence man. The youth loses his liberty because he surrenders his vigilance and abandons his republican virtue for a riotous life of luxury and sin. Once the liberty of the rising generation was lost, the advice writers feared, the American republic would be in grave danger.[115]

In *Ormond*, the bad son is the figure who swindles the good father, usurping his estate, contaminating his security, and ultimately taking his life; indeed, the plot of Craig's deception details in progressively literalizing fashion what Halttunen delineates as the eighteenth-century republican drama of liberty lost. But the novel marks a shift in the archetypal scheme of confidence by casting the surrogate son as the villain of the piece. This inversion hints at

Brown's uneasiness with the Founders's vision of the Revolution as an un-ambiguously righteous and consecrated event; though such received wisdom marks his inheritance as a republican "son," it is also an endowment that Brown's Quaker upbringing and skeptical sensibility cause him to interro-gate, rather than celebrate, in his fiction.

With this in mind, we can better decode the meaning of Craig's inau-gural crime: the fabrication of letters that, taken together, detail the specious story of his purportedly honest beginnings, a tale crafted to play directly on Mr. Dudley's heartstrings and manipulate his social self-conception. In a novel premised on epistolary sincerity, forgery—a form of seduction enacted through the medium of words—is a particularly resonant offense. It is sig-nificant that *Ormond* promotes itself as an extended and detailed letter, com-posed in candid response to an interested inquiry about Constantia Dudley made by the mysterious I. E. Rosenberg. Brown provides no details about the man: from the preface we can infer only that he is a German and possibly a Jewish alien. Denied a body and a voice, the narrator's correspondent re-mains unrealized as a character. Levine, among other critics, speculates that Rosenberg functions in the capacity of Constantia's potential suitor;[116] as such, this silent and dematerialized cipher fulfills Sophia's wish that no male of substance compete with her for the young woman's affection. Existing solely as the discursive effect of Sophia's text, Rosenberg nevertheless makes a tacitly intriguing foil for Ormond. Neither French nor English, he eludes the Anglo-Franco political binary dividing *Ormond'*s characters and sche-matizing their allegiances. If anything, as a German and a Jew, Rosenberg incarnates the spirit of pure otherness, the disruptive "third term" Margery Garber invokes in her work on the cultural role of the transvestite. In that regard, the man's political function in the novel is exclusively diacritical: as a figure for the implied reader of *Ormond,* as the object of Sophia's epistolary and Constantia's (possible) romantic desire, Rosenberg incarnates Brown's impulse, however undeveloped, to imagine an ending that would take his characters beyond the Federalist versus Jeffersonian schism that so divides his era. This inclination, of course, bears neither literal nor figurative fruit: by the end of the novel, Constantia and Sophia have departed for England and Martinette has returned to France.[117]

While letters ultimately enable Craig's plot to ravage the Dudleys' for-tunes, they set into motion only the second phase of an elaborate three-part strategy. For its overall success, Craig's scheme depends on incarnating the apothecary's belief in his personal integrity, a transaction best effected via face-to-face exchange. In addition to this scoundrel's virtuosity as a writer, he is equally adept at theatrical dissimulation: performing the role of the eager and honest youth, Craig projects the seemingly transparent essence of a self that, in fact, is the calculated product of dramatic art. Craig's technique evokes Diderot's theory that the actor must lose himself in creating a role.[118] That the trickster gains the apothecary's trust and receives an invitation to become the man's apprentice *before* offering to share the letters ostensibly documenting both his origins and his history is a fact little noted about *Ormond*. Whether as a simple oversight or as a blunder more symptomatic of his feeble powers of perception, Mr. Dudley declines to request references verifying Craig's identity. By afflicting the patriarch with a cataract that blinds him immediately after dispatching him into bankruptcy and ruin, Brown nicely literalizes Dudley's failure of discernment about Craig. Remaining oddly reticent about the unprofessional nature of their initial interview, Sophia simply reports that according to the apothecary, Craig's "veracity appeared liable of no doubt" (8).

The forger's proficiency at writing constitutes the first and only achievement he might legitimately claim in *Ormond*. Indeed, the narrator goes on to note the one detail that immediately impresses Stephen Dudley about his future apprentice and eventual partner: the way in which Craig reveals himself to be "master of his book and pen . . . [with] more than the rudiments of Latin" (8). Better than any other artist-villain in the canon of Brown's novels, with the possible exception of Welbeck, the forger and counterfeiter in *Arthur Mervyn*, Craig comprehends the nature of textuality and the power of dissemination. He also understands the way epistolarity enables the construction of self and other through the dialectic of writing and exchange: indeed, his composition and circulation of bogus letters functions as a limiting case for Terry Eagleton's ideas about epistolary fiction itself.[119] So brilliantly shines the light of Craig's literacy that it utterly obscures his lack of credentials; in the apothecary's eyes, Craig's enfranchisement in the "republic of letters"—his mastery of writing's forms—overshadows the fact that he possesses nothing substantial to corroborate claims about his identity. Duped by the technology of writing—mistaking the supplement for an originary and authentic presence—Dudley becomes the perfect gull for the forger's misrepresentations.

Only after gaining his employer's trust does this dissimulator, proceeding on his own initiative, come to orchestrate the epistolary drama of his self-accreditation. Between the apprentice's original appearance in Mr. Dudley's shop, his installation in the bosom of the patriarch's family, and his voluntary display of "copies" of the earliest letters he claims to have received from his kin, there exists a small but suggestive temporal gap. The chronological discrepancy between Craig's advent and his "authentication" provides an early clue regarding the character of Mr. Dudley's employee, a hint that the transaction of belief cementing their bond might be premised on a lie.

Indeed, as Sophia recounts the story of Craig's fraudulent dealings with the Dudleys, Brown's prose takes on the zeal of a legal argument for the prosecution, reconstructed from evidence gathered in the wake of the crime and deployed with a spirit of vengeance.[120] The narrator notes that the forger

> maintained a punctual correspondence with his family, and confided to his patron not only *copies* of all the letters which he himself wrote, but those which, from time to time, he received. He had several correspondents, but the chief of those were his mother and his eldest sister. The sentiments contained in their letters breathed *the most appropriate* simplicity and tenderness, and flowed with the *nicest propriety, from the different relationships of mother and sister.* The style and even the penmanship *were distinct and characteristical* [*sic*]. (9, my emphasis)

This description of purported epistolary authenticity appears at the very beginning of a novel written in the form of a letter,[121] a book consumed with issues of originality, personal and public authority, and social legitimacy. Thus, it is remarkable that Craig passes off epistles scripted *ex nihilo* as facsimile "*copies*" of missives alleged to be genuine but which, in fact, have no material existence at all; they abide in the forger's imagination alone, in some kind of Platonic form, the illusory precursors of the so-called duplicates he shares with the Dudley family. In other words, this assaulter of origins makes a point of disseminating as "copies" (9) letters that in their own way are absolutely original. Always preferring the reproduction over the prototype, the artificial to the authentic, Craig lives by a principle that guides everything from his crafting of letters to his counterfeiting of bank notes to his invention of an evil twin on whom he can project culpability for his crimes.

The mechanistic nature of the forger's art prefigures the relation Walter Benjamin evokes in his famous essay "The Work of Art in the Age of Mechanical Reproduction" (1936) between a proliferating textuality and modernity itself. Benjamin writes that "the technique of reproduction detaches the reproduced object from the domain of tradition. By making many reproductions it substitutes a plurality of copies for a unique existence. And in permitting the reproduction to meet the beholder or listener in his own particular situation, it reactivates the object reproduced. These two processes lead to a tremendous shattering of tradition which is the obverse of the contemporary crisis and renewal of mankind." [122] Craig's fraudulent writing indeed leads to a small if not a "tremendous shattering of tradition," personified in Constantia's father, Stephen Dudley, whose business he ravages and whose life he ruins. It is hardly insignificant that the apothecary is also a painter by training and vocation. Dudley represents that side of the dichotomy between artistic authenticity and mechanical reproduction that Benjamin would associate with the "aura" of the original work of art. Earlier in the same passage, Benjamin notes that

> the authenticity of a thing is the essence of all that is transmissible from
> its beginning, ranging from its substantive duration to its testimony to
> the history which it has experienced. Since the historical testimony rests
> on the authenticity, the former, too, is jeopardized by reproduction when
> substantive duration ceases to matter. And what is really jeopardized
> when the historical testimony is affected is the authority of the object.
> One might subsume the eliminated element in the term "aura" and go
> on to say: that which withers in the age of mechanical reproduction is
> the aura of the work of art. [123]

Pitting Dudley, who incarnates a kind of artistic originality utterly unable to cope with the demands of the world, against Craig, who embodies a form of mechanistic genius undaunted if not actually inspired by the vicissitudes of life, Brown takes up the cultural conflict Benjamin would explore so movingly in an essay written more than one hundred years later.

The malefactor's gifts find their most brilliant expression in written improvisation, his epistolary invention from limited materials at hand. Here, Tzvetvan Todorov's ideas about the significance of writing as a technology that enables the dynamics of conquest offer an interesting paradigm for thinking about the forger's craft, notwithstanding the many incongruities that underwrite the analogy. Such a comparison is obviously overstated: Todorov details an historical act, the imperialist European invasion of the New World, while Brown describes the fictional exploits of an evil character, the destructive career of a figure existing in a book. Yet these indisputable differences do not diminish the fact that Brown, like Todorov, is examining the contact and conflict of disparate cultures, questions "of the other."

Indeed, this early American novelist is deeply concerned with the nature of identity as a product of confrontations between individuals of disparate privilege living in a society that—while theoretically premised on equality—excludes a substantial proportion of its inhabitants from basic rights and institutions. Brown most directly interrogates this dynamic in *Edgar Huntly*, where Native Americans and citizens of the new republic, reciprocally perceiving each other as invading aliens, literally *hunt* and attempt to destroy one another, but the operations of conquest and devastation pertain to *Ormond*, as well, if in more metaphorical form. They extend from Thomas Craig's despoliation of the Dudley family, to the scenes of yellow fever permeating and decimating the community that immediately follow in the narrative as if by contagious magic, to the ravages of Ormond's sexual appetite, with its homicidal reverberations. The entire novel, in other words, details diverse but related processes of infiltration and blight, providing the background for the author's abiding refrain: what constitutes American identity in the post-Revolutionary period?

In light of Brown's interest in the way "invasion" at both the individual and collective levels is made possible through writing, the description of what Todorov terms the "technology of conquest" is highly evocative: "Masters in the art of ritual discourse, the Indians are inadequate in a situation requiring improvisation, and this is precisely the situation of the conquest. Their verbal education favors paradigm over syntagm, code over context, conformity-to-order over efficacy-of-the-moment, the past over the present. Now, the Spanish invasion creates a radically new, entirely unprecedented situation, in which the art of improvisation matters more than that of ritual."[124] This paradigm of cultural contact provides a suggestive set of terms for thinking about conflicts of class and generation dividing early republican society from within. However incongruent with transformations that result from the winning of independence, in particular the substitution of fraternal equality for paternal supremacy at the level of social theory, Mr. Dudley's vision of a post-Revolutionary world order remains dominated by the fathers. The patriarch inhabits a sphere in which custom and respect for the experience of "the past over the present" remain highly valued. Despite his misguided delegation of economic authority to a youth, a step that results in the loss of his resources, this paternalistic gesture underscores the apothecary's wish that the old social hierarchies persist. Thomas Craig, in contrast, occupies an entirely other sphere, a universe being created anew by the post-Revolutionary era's "new men of paper" who scorn the significance of tradition. To such figures as the forger, "the art of improvisation matters more than that of ritual."

The success of Craig's deception depends on an ability to improvise from a fund of private knowledge: in this case, Stephen Dudley's prejudices about the workings of the Anglo-American social order in the late eighteenth century. The forger's own epistolary self-construction is geared to mirror—however phantasmagorically—an approximate notion of his employer's ideas about gender, class, and national identity, what he can infer regarding Dudley's beliefs about the nature of the apprentice's background. Thus, the missives deployed by his "mother" and "sister" in a hand "appropriate" and "characteristical" are fittingly emblematic of nothing more than Craig's approximate reflections—the educated guesses he makes about the apothecary's imagination of working-class women from the north of England and the way their letters should sound.[125]

Craig's ploy could be said to unfold as a monstrous parody of what David Marshall characterizes as the "mirror of sympathy,"[126] Smith's outline for the specular, reflexive workings of human fellow feeling. In order to create for the Dudleys a moving narrative of his antecedents, a tableau of origins so compelling that his own sincerity could never be doubted, the forger enlists the dynamic charted by the Scotsman in *The Theory of Moral Sentiments:*

> In order to produce this concord, as nature teaches the spectators to assume the circumstances of the person principally concerned, so she teaches this last in some measure to assume those of the spectators. As they are continually placing themselves in his situation, and thence conceiving emotions similar to what he feels; so he is as constantly placing himself in theirs, and thence conceiving some degree of that coolness about his own fortune, with which he is sensible that they will view it. As they are constantly considering what they themselves would feel, if they actually were the sufferers, so he is as constantly led to imagine in what manner he would be affected if he was only one of the spectators of his own situation. As their sympathy makes them look at it, in some measure, with his eyes, so his sympathy makes him look at it, in some measure, with theirs, especially when in their presence and acting under their observation: and as the *reflected* passion, which he thus conceives, is much weaker than the original one, it necessarily abates the violence of what he felt before he came into their presence, before he began to

recollect in what manner they would be affected by it, and to view his situation in this candid and impartial light. (*Theory of Moral Sentiments*, 23)

Craig's anticipation and manipulation of Dudley's feelings constitute a grotesque misapplication of Smith's paradigm of compassion, for what the forger pointedly omits from his version of the equation is the possibility of fellow feeling itself. Adopting the principles of imaginative projection and speculation that Smith elaborates in his theory, but completely unhinging these dynamics from either the world of affect or the reality of others, the sociopath mimics the forms of sympathy evacuated of all content.

The forger's letters deceive at a double remove from the truth, enacting a parasitic but emotionless relation to the structures of fellow feeling: they are "written" by a male author in the voices of women who do not exist, functioning as a fascinating metanarrative signature for Brown's larger procedures in *Ormond*, and they are "sent" to a character who is equally fictional—Craig's "English émigré" self. In the scheme to seduce the apothecary into relinquishing his fortune, the forger ultimately dispenses with the pretense of sharing letters from his alleged home, missives he purports to receive at "punctual" (9) intervals. Instead, Craig suggests that the master himself engage in a personal, purportedly trans-Atlantic correspondence with his so-called mother. With that turn of the screw, the evil dissimulator lures the apothecary into a final transaction of belief, the epistolary alliance that ultimately insures his family's material ruin.

The exchange between Craig and Dudley is triangulated and disembodied, circulating through the purported writing of a (fictional) woman, and thus endowed with a homosocial energy peculiar to Brown's narratives.[127] The apothecary's phantasmagoric correspondence with "Mrs. Craig" provides a direct channel through which the wicked apprentice can lubricate his employer's vanity: fraudulent letters provide a capacious forum for mirroring the patriarch's vision of himself as virtuous republican mentor. Craig applauds the master for upholding the values of the Revolution, extolling his patriotic fostering of a humble English youth whose pursuit of happiness he single-handedly enables. It is through hard work and Mr. Dudley's beneficent offices that this mother's son might eventually become a citizen of the infant nation—or so Craig affirms in his fabricated missives.

In assuming the voice of his supposed female parent, the textual embodiment of a maternal ideal, Craig acts out a series of personal and political fantasies. First, he attempts to erase all connections to his actual mother, an impoverished and illiterate woman living in rural New Hampshire. Merely growing up in the shadow of such a progenitor would seem to prove contaminating. Second, he deconstructs the authority of the fathers and replaces it with an alternative sort of power. In that regard, Craig echoes the narrative strategy of the author who creates him: for, in both *Wieland* and *Ormond,* Brown assumes the female voice as an antipatriarchal gesture, enacting the dream that "the word" in the post-Revolutionary nation might emanate from off center.[128] Finally, and perhaps most important for the forger, the fiction of Mrs. Craig, maternal imago as eloquent epistolarian, embodies his ultimate desire: to reject his own origins in illiteracy itself, to be self-created. Because the youth's imaginary mother is a forbearer he begets in writing, she also becomes the figure through whom he creates himself anew. Brought to representational life by her so-called son, a young man who is in fact her author and father, the imaginary Mrs. Craig enables the forger's literary parthenogenesis.

Given this connection in *Ormond* between self-creation, writing, and misrepresentation, it is poetically just that the forger's plot should be exposed by the primitive epistolary impulses of a loathed parent. Mr. Dudley's suspicions of his partner belatedly arise when he opens and reads a letter seemingly misaddressed to Thomas Craig from a Mary Mansfield of New Hampshire. So thoroughly ignorant is the youth's correspondent that she enlists a functional illiterate to act as her amanuensis. Mrs. Mansfield's complaint about her son's desertion of his mother (13), an abandonment that precipitates her into grinding poverty and chronic illness, proves particularly confounding in light of Craig's apparent devotion to the Dudley family. Notwithstanding the ostensible incongruence between her claims about disloyalty and the youth's seemingly faithful performance of professional duty, the primitive portrait of filial ingratitude resonates in troubling ways. Only after perusing her missive does it dawn on the apothecary that Craig's dedication, his extraordinary *investment* in the success of their business, may be criminal in nature.

The revelation of the forger's coarse beginnings sheds a fascinating light on the possible motives for his scheme against the Dudleys, a design for self-aggrandizement that, as we have noted, might have been achieved by lawful and felicitous means. In rejecting his biological precursors, in claiming affiliation to origins that are entirely imaginary, in endowing writing with nearly sacred generative powers, the evil youth attempts to flee from a legacy of ignorance and despair. Pathological son of the Enlightenment, Craig at once anticipates and exaggerates, to an eventually patricidal degree, Thomas Jefferson's sentiments about "each generation" functioning "as a distinct nation, with a right, by the will of its majority, to bind themselves, but none to bind the succeeding generation, more than the inhabitants of another country."[129] In a moment of Brownian irony, Craig is obstructed by the very agent of tradition from whom the extended plot is meant to free him. Thus, while *Ormond* may deconstruct and interrogate the sufficiency and validity of origins, the past exerts a pull on Brown's characters that is not easily evaded. Instead, history returns with the vengeance of all things repressed to impede and destroy such figures in their imaginative efforts at self-recreation.

The exchange of forged correspondence is *Ormond*'s metaphor for fraudulent relations between private individuals. By extension, the transmission of counterfeit bank notes becomes the novel's figure for perversion of public forms of association and cooperation, a collective infection that pervades the entire community.[130] While phony letters violate the transactions of belief around which all meaningful epistolary interchange is predicated, bogus money destroys material trust, unraveling the connections that bind the world of commerce and make economic enterprise possible. Brown's novel details the way both sympathetic and mercantile exchange, while obviously unfolding in different arenas of "the social," not only depend on but cannot exist without the principle of credit, the very commodity Thomas Craig seeks to control.[131]

When this culprit moves from forgery to counterfeiting his corruption of fellow feeling merely expands in scope, coming to harm the many instead of to injure the few. At this point in *Ormond*, the Dudleys have removed in disgrace from New York to Philadelphia, while the now prosperous Craig, having returned from his fugitive's flight to Jamaica, also surfaces in the City of Brotherly Love—a new venue for the violation of fraternal trust. In "coincidental" Brownian fashion, Constantia glimpses the forger on a local street, though Craig remains unaware of his former victim. Seeking reparations for his sins against her father, who is now blind, impoverished, and on the verge of suicide, the young woman determines to confront the malefactor, making him face the consequences of the destruction he has wrought.

Inaugurating the second act in a drama of persecution, credit abused, and sympathy betrayed, the forger offers Constantia a fraudulent fifty dollar bill. This "gift" of cash is meant to "repay" the girl "with interest" (97) for his rape of the Dudley's fortunes. Predictably, after she traces the rogue to Ormond's home, Craig refuses to meet the virgin in a personal encounter. His act of disavowal forces Constantia to resort to intercourse by letter, the communicative form through which the scoundrel most successfully dominates his adversaries. But fully expecting that Craig will deny her request for an audience, the young woman composes a note affirming her charitable intentions: she promises to avoid employing legal means to vindicate her father's claims against the embezzler if he will extend financial succor in this moment of duress.

Banking on the notion that a thousand words are more palatable than a single affecting picture, Craig makes a brilliant calculation. By refusing to see Constantia, he effectively avoids being compelled to bear witness to the moving tableau of distress she is certain to conjure, and so the touching scene of entreaty is restricted to the private theater of her imagination. Employing the grammar of melodrama, Sophia gives voice to her friend's aborted fantasy of arousing the man's compassion, "Craig, perhaps, was accessible. Might she not, with propriety, demand an interview, and lay before him the consequences of his baseness? He was not divested of the last remains of humanity. It was impossible that he should not relent at the picture of those distresses of which he was the author" (92). By circumventing this spectacle and remaining invisible, the forger returns the conflict to the textual ground on which he knows he will prevail. Language trumps the power of ritual performance here—for the motif of supplication is as old as Western theater—but only because dramatic display itself is disallowed. In order to defuse the danger of an embodied encounter, the potential consequences of which could explode his sinister machinations, Craig demands that writing take the place of speech.

Extemporizing on an act of improvisation, the forger then makes a gesture that takes the powers of textuality and dissemination to their zero degree of communicability, instructing Ormond's servant to present Constantia with a fraudulent bank note wrapped in a piece of blank paper. It is not enough for the forger simply to deny the possibility of a face-to-face encounter. To avenge the indignity of having been identified, Craig determines to withhold the exchange of any words *altogether*, entirely silencing all communication—spoken or penned. By substituting an empty page for an explicit message in writing, the villain effectively covers over the space in which sympathy or repentance could be inscribed, actually making empathic expression impossible, interdicting even the most generic or conventional gestures of human compassion.

The dissimulator's silent "gift" ensures that the Dudleys' chain of economic relations will be thoroughly and utterly shattered, for counterfeit money infects and contaminates credit in cancerous fashion. While the "interest" Craig anticipates being repaid for his deed signifies the final ruination of the family's affairs, the invisible hand of counterfeiting only brings to a dramatic conclusion the sequence of destructive effects that forgery and embezzlement so potently inaugurate. In the eyes of the malefactor, destitution is just punishment for Constantia's threat to expose the fraudulent claims on which he bases his script for a new beginning. Earlier, Brown reveals that despite Craig's pretense of making a capital contribution to Dudley's business as a partner, this so-called cash, like the villain's fictive identity itself, has no independent origin. Instead, the money in question "had been previously purloined from the daily receipts of his shop" (16), effectively recycled according to Craig's compulsion to reject the authentic for the artificial. Through counterfeiting, the forger continues to circulate his poisonous influence across the sector of the community that is the heroine's domain, causing a cascade of reverberations that redound on Constantia throughout the remainder of *Ormond*.

Indeed, it is not enough to ruin the Dudleys's economic present and to contaminate all future credit as well: in his penultimate act of violence against the family, Craig disseminates a story about Constantia's despoiled virtue, naming his own make-believe brother as coconspirator in the crime against her virginity—for, far from being a seduced and abandoned maiden, the former virgin of Craig's demonic fable is a "willing" participant in her own sexual ruin. The scoundrel eventually communicates this lie to Ormond, who investigates its veracity and becomes Constantia's benefactor, at least until the libertine himself determines to possess the woman at any cost. In the meantime, the story of Craig's "brother" marks the ultimate example of the criminal's procreative fantasies, a dream of parthenogenesis that is fully gothic in its implications. And just as the forger has given this "sibling" life— a narrative existence in any case—so too does he control his fictive demise. Along the way, Craig *frère* displays a brutal lack of fellow feeling entirely in keeping with his "sibling's" pathological character.

In this final episode of ingenious misrepresentation, the forger reproduces himself imaginatively in the form of the evil twin on whom he projects all agency for the various crimes he commits against the Dudleys. The outrages perpetrated by this wicked brother, while largely concocted from the story of Craig's dishonest life, could fill a catalog worthy of an eighteenth-century novel villain. Indeed, in his fallacious claim about the brother's successful sexual corruption of Constantia, among other boasts, the youth borrows a leaf from Carwin's book, mimicking the ventriloquist's specious assertions about his erotic exploits, transgressions that never take place in *Wieland*. Thus, the miscreant's "brother," after "robbing" the Dudleys of their worldly goods, absconds to Jamaica where he mysteriously "dies."

The West Indian destination of Craig's fugitive "brother" can be seen as an important feature of Brown's realism in *Ormond*, given the fact that trade with the islands remains a significant aspect of late-eighteenth-century Anglo-American commerce, despite the legal prohibition against it.[132] Stanley Elkins and Eric McKitrick note that "the British West Indies, though closed by law, had in fact again become remarkably accessible to enterprising American shippers. With the connivance of local planters, governors, and customs officials, through *forged papers* and other stratagems, virtually regularized, the wants of the sugar islands were being almost as well supplied as ever by 1789."[133] As the forger's history with the Dudleys suggests, the prospect of navigating legal barriers with falsified documents is perfectly compatible with Craig's particular notion of enterprise.

There is, however, another and a far darker valence to this allusion, one that points to the twin specters of slavery and Revolution, to the black uprising against white colonial power in San Domingo. While banished to the margins of Brown's book, the mass rebellion of that island's slaves nevertheless haunts the political heart of *Ormond*. Against this background, what does it mean that Craig's "brother" flees to Jamaica, an island geographically contiguous to Haiti? Elkins and McKitrick assert that "the failure of the French authorities to crush the slave uprising in St. Domingue and the anarchic conflict there among whites and mulattoes presented not only a threat—to nearby Jamaica with its 300,000 slaves—but also an opportunity."[134] In scripting a (phantasmagoric) West Indian itinerary for the forger, the author underscores the moral guilt in which his villain is immersed. Brown sends Craig back to what we might call the "primal scene" of American traffic in African flesh, the terminus of the notorious Middle Passage of slavery's triangular trade.

While the nature of his affairs in Jamaica remains unknown, Craig's own malevolent history and *Ormond*'s international political context imply that any business he has in the Islands is at best ethically questionable. We have speculated that the forger represents the utter corruption of the post-

Revolutionary man. On the continuum of morally dubious transactions that could take place in Jamaica at the turn of the nineteenth century, slavery certainly would figure prominently.[135] Brown links the sinister Craig with an unspecified but nevertheless ominous form of Island "trade." In doing so, he subtly suggests that American mercantilism in the era following the Revolution is based on economic practices of a decidedly unfraternal, if not an ethically contaminated, nature. It is no accident that the shadow of slavery haunts the forger's gothic fiction of "brotherhood." Reckoned among the other unspeakable abuses perpetrated by his wicked sibling, Craig's mysterious interlude in Jamaica provides an ambiguous if nevertheless evocative touchstone for Brown's vision of the darker side of masculine fellowship. If the family functions as a metaphor for the state, as several recent critics of the early American novel have suggested,[136] *Ormond*'s detailed delineation of the failure of fraternity proves a sad commentary on the prospect that brotherly cohesion might ground the social order in post-Revolutionary America.

It is against the background of these crimes against fathers, daughters, and even the notion of brothers that Thomas Craig apparently assassinates Stephen Dudley. Brown gives his readers no details about why the forger makes the leap from fraud, a serious but exculpable crime, to patricide, perhaps the most heinous and certainly the most reprobated form of murder in Western culture.[137] As we have been suggesting, however, the roots of the villain's seemingly gratuitous homicide are everywhere apparent in his criminal résumé. In retrospect Craig's final deed seems almost anticlimactic. In comparison with the scheme to endlessly torture Mr. Dudley economically, simply ending the patriarch's life would appear to be an act of relative benevolence.[138] In that regard, the forger's ultimate realization of patricidal wishes, his actual killing of Mr. Dudley, at once embodies and ironically ends the unlimited regime of antioedipal violence that constitutes his nefarious career. Without a father figure to molest and destroy, this son of liberty run amok has lost his function in Brown's plot, and so he is slain by Ormond in the novel's final pages.

Blackface Masquerade

Craig personifies the monstrous implications of ascendent liberalism unrestrained. His criminal self-authorization through forgery, counterfeiting, patricide, and mysterious business dealings in Jamaica presage a future where the lure of the marketplace supplants familial and communal bonds, traffic in human flesh remains a viable form of enterprise, respect for authority bears little on the progress of industry, and civic virtue itself has become an anachronism. Manipulating the dynamics of sympathy, approximating the forms of fellow feeling but possessed of no compassion himself, such a predator sees his neighbors as potential quarry rather than as brothers or citizens united in collective endeavor. Craig's perversions of fellow feeling represent the excesses of freedom that endanger the nation's social and material fabric in the final years of the eighteenth century.

The scoundrel's malevolent assault on one family and its minions, however emblematic of future economic and cultural developments, nevertheless remains a private incursion. While corrosive of affective and economic ties, forgery in its various manifestations is morally incommensurate with Ormond's extraordinarily idiosyncratic abuse of sympathy—a racial counterfeit bearing not only ideological but ethical implications. Darkening his skin, initiating himself into what one historian of nineteenth-century theater calls the "mysteries of cork,"[139] the villain undergoes a transformation unprecedented in the history of the early American novel: he publicly comports himself in the guise of an African American chimney sweep. Sophia explains:

> There was a method of gaining access to families, and marking them in their unguarded attitudes more easy and effectual than any other: It required least preparation and cost least pains: The disguise, also, was of the most impenetrable kind. He had served a sort of occasional apprenticeship to the art, and executed its functions with perfect ease. It was the most entire and grotesque metamorphosis imaginable. It was stepping from the highest to the lowest rank in society, and shifting himself into a form as remote from his own as those recorded by Ovid. In a word, it was sometimes his practice to exchange his complexion and habiliments for those of a negro and a chimney-sweep, and to call at certain doors for employment. This he generally secured by importunities, and the cheapness of his services. (133–34)

However temporary, this Protean "class abdication" "through cross-racial immersion" enables the libertine to obtain intimate information about his inferiors[140]—social knowledge to which Ormond has no legitimate claim.[141]

Such crossing of the color line constitutes an act of cultural "theft" without the attendant "love," "admiration," or "envy" that Eric Lott describes as structuring the complex dialectical exchange of blackface minstrelsy in antebellum America.[142] Rather than reflecting an interest in African American cultural practices, much less revealing a sympathy for the numerous tribulations faced by blacks in the early national period, Ormond's abject disguise actually serves to fortify his position of social domination. Indeed, his expropriation of a bondsman's color, garb, and labor would seem to repeat in theatrical form the very dynamic of exploitation and commodification that marks slavery itself;[143] the libertine clearly profits from assuming the (negative) power of blackness.

Paradoxically, however, it is through the trope of African American masquerade that Brown most dramatically exposes the Janus face of republican freedom—liberty for the few constituted over against the bodies of the many—those Americans who do not "figure" as citizens and who thus are excluded from freedom's embrace: aliens, Native Americans, the poor, women, and, most pointedly, those of African descent both slave and free. Ormond assumes the mask of blackness without remotely imagining the subjective experience that accompanies such embodiment. Much less does the character take on any forms of political consciousness attending this wretched fate—for, according to social historians, not only do African American chimney sweeps constitute the lowest echelons of the free black labor force, they compose the most degraded cohort of slaves whose masters hire their time for profit.[144] Given these socioeconomic details, Ormond's gesture of what Lott would call "cultural theft" opens up a fascinating space in Brown's novel for meditation on post-Revolutionary America's associated dilemmas of race and class. Ironically, the libertine's masquerade discloses both the excesses of freedom at work in the new republic—represented by figures like Craig; and the tragic limitations of liberty—symbolized by the faceless and nameless human referents of Ormond's extraordinary transracial disguise.

Viewed in isolation as another metanarrative miniature, the pathetic tableau in which the villain publicly descends into blackness telegraphs those unrealized promises that haunt American claims about life, liberty, and the pursuit of happiness in the Federalist era. But unfolding in relief against the libertine's own peculiar history—his blending of political radicalism with economic privilege—Ormond's plaintive petition for employment at Constantia's door takes on an ominous resonance. Never one to invent a figure whose evil signifies in politically legible fashion—a villain whose ideas we could recognize easily—the author imagines a scoundrel of particularly unintelligible views: indeed, both the generic radicalism of this protean male-

Woodcut of African American chimney sweeps, ca. 1800. (Courtesy the Beinecke Library)

factor (he is probably a member of the Illuminati) and his nationalistic allegiances seem to shift shape in the novel almost as often as does he. Ormond's beliefs about the world of political economy and international revolution are incoherent at best, but, in tracing Brown's allusions to the radical European intellectual background informing the libertine's vision, scholars have almost entirely overlooked the book's exploration of problems plaguing America in the 1790s, internal social dilemmas of the post-Revolutionary era such as slavery and racial strife.

While Ormond's masquerade as an African American bondsman and chimney sweep has been critically ignored, it is precisely in the novel's representation of slavery—a distinctly domestic crisis—and not in the villain's phantasmagoric international schemes that *Ormond*'s real "political" interest lies. While his disguise brings the plight of black slave labor into fictive representation, the novel provides no evidence that Ormond shares any fraternal, abolitionist, or revolutionary fellow feeling with African Americans, bound or free. How then are we to read the politics of racial cross-dressing in the novel? What is the cultural meaning of Ormond's "blacking up?" Does

the villain's gesture represent a carnivalesque moment of utopian identification, or is his deed a reactionary manifestation—an effort to consolidate his
position atop the ladder of color and class? Considering the possibility that
blackface can express either of these attitudes, as well as many others, Lott
cites the work of various historians who discuss cross-race masquerade as a
constitutive feature of American working-class rioting and revelry, transgressive public displays often underwritten by racial animus. He notes one scholar's reading of an 1834 Philadelphia race riot in which some of the antiabol-
itionist mob "wore black masks and shabby coats" and quotes another's
characterization of such uprisings as "blackface-on-Black violence." [145]

These facts illuminate Brown's fictive deployment of blackface masquerade in an eighteenth-century context. Far from gesturing toward what Lott
calls minstrelsy's "sympathetic identification" with African American culture
or its expressive forms in the antebellum era, Ormond in fact "obstructs the
visibility of black" experience. [146] In that regard, the villain's spectacular transformation follows more closely Lott's notion that "in such a conflictual racial
scene [as the working-class riot] the mask was increasingly used for reactionary purposes." Nevertheless, Lott also notes "a feature of American blackface
masking that critics have been slow to recognize: an unstable or indeed *contradictory power,* linked to social and political conflicts that issue from *the
weak, the uncanny, the outside.*" [147] Ormond's supremacist attitudes about distinctions of race and class may be reactionary indeed, but such politics are a
function of a reprehensible character and take place within a fictive world.
Brown's narrative use of blackface masquerade, in contrast, comes closer to
Lott's notion that minstrelsy can evoke "contradictory power," issuing a critique from a place "outside" the purview of elite white culture. Such racial
cross-dressing, while affording the libertine a certain social invisibility, paradoxically enables his unlimited access to the private sphere; the very property
that makes blackness a liability can also prove a source of intimate knowledge
about white culture that, for those African Americans who possess it, translates into a form of gothic power. Brown's deployment of the motif of racial
counterfeiting brings sharply into focus the idea that blackness in the new
republic is the site of cultural rupture. [148]

Ormond's brilliant mimicry of African American dialect and the chimney sweep's craft, taken in concert with his cunning disguise, constitute an
affectively compelling veneer. But the performance is underwritten by theatrical genius alone. Whether he is dressed in the garb of the slave or adorned
in the rich accoutrements of his rightful identity, Ormond remains curiously

detached from and unmoved by the plight of the bondsman, disinterested in the evolving, negative sense of the term. In the course of laboriously outlining the libertine's radical philosophy, Sophia makes no mention of his position on the institution of slavery, never suggesting that the villain finds it morally repulsive or intellectually problematic. Such indifference to African American abjection in no way diminishes the villain's ability to create a moving impression of the slave's suffering humanity—his power to elicit in his female auditor a genuinely compassionate response.[149]

Possessed of and celebrated for gifts of theatrical dissimulation that emerged in childhood, Ormond easily masters the forms of supplication purged of all political or moral content. His ability to evoke in a potential benefactress latent sentiments of pity for the "Negro" marks nothing more than a calculated performance. As such, the libertine's blackface impersonation raises disturbing questions about the moral efficacy of representation, per se. Indeed, the ethical ground on which his cross-racial masquerade is constructed is precarious at best: underlying the dubious morality of Ormond's ruse is an entire antitheatrical tradition that parallels the history and development of Western philosophy itself, beginning with Plato's hostility to dramatic mimesis in Book X of the *Republic*. Jonas Barish asserts that this antitheatrical prejudice reaches a new level of complexity in the mid- to late eighteenth century, when two contradictory theories of the relationship between acting and feeling take center stage. Barish characterizes the first, which he traces to the seventeenth century, as an "anachronistically Stanislavskian" or "sensibilist" mode,[150] a form of "emotional identification or self-effacing alienation."[151]

Rousseau's famous antitheatrical diatribe in the "Letter To M. D'Alembert on the Theatre" takes up this reading and pursues its negative implications to their logical conclusion: "What is the talent of the actor? It is the art of counterfeiting himself, of putting on another character than his own, of appearing different than he is, of becoming passionate in cold blood, of saying what he does not think as naturally as if he really did think it, and finally, of forgetting his own place by dint of taking another's."[152] The danger of theatrical identifications for Rousseau lies in "nothing less than the self-annihilation of the actor."[153]

Denis Diderot makes the opposite case in *Paradoxe sur le comédien*, a tract he writes in response to Rousseau's "Letter." According to Marshall, Diderot refutes "the argument that the ideal actor is a *comédien sensible* (an actor of sensibility) whose talent consists in his ability to . . . 'forget himself and become distracted from himself,' and to 'render the exterior signs of sentiment so scrupulously that you might be deceived.' With such a knowledge of the exterior symptoms of feeling, rather than of any special depth of feeling itself, this actor can . . . 'address himself to the sensations of those who are watching and listening to him.'"[154] A "cool, detached, manipulative counterfeiter of feelings," Diderot's ideal actor is a figure who "is not supposed to forget anything, least of all his effect on the audience."[155] In consonance with the new dramatic style developed by practitioners such as David Garrick, "which depended less on sensibility or declamation than on mimicry,"[156] Diderot proposes that acting is a form of hypocrisy, "the deception of others through the imitation of the signs and symptoms of sentiments that are not really there."[157]

It is only because, following Rousseau, Ormond is able to become "passionate in cold blood," "saying what he does not think as naturally as if he really did think it," that his descent into blackness signifies, but, in contrast to Rousseau's hypothetical actor, the libertine never forgets his own place "by dint of taking another's." In an important sense he comes closer to embodying Diderot's notion, elucidated by Marshall, that the dramatic performer, "in order to coolly impersonate a character, . . . must lack a self (or at the very least put aside his self)."[158] Like Thomas Craig, Ormond is a gifted actor precisely because he is also a sociopath, a man without feelings. In that regard, he exposes the danger of the eighteenth century's semiotics of sympathy—the fact that, as indices of sincerity, physical manifestations of compassion are sorely unreliable.[159]

What source inspires Ormond's compelling rendering of "importunity" in blackface? If mimicry's origins lie not in the depth of human feelings but in the plasticity of the human face and form, what visual prototypes animate the libertine's performance as a slave? It is clear that the local accents of Philadelphia's African American chimney sweeps provide one point of departure for his feint, but, given the narrative premium Brown places on things visual in *Ormond*—his emphasis on specular rather than dynamic exchanges, on phantasmagorical projections rather than impartial reflections, on miniature portraits rather than embodied relations—the badge of antislavery worn in eighteenth-century Philadelphia offers another interesting referent for the villain's mise-en-scène.

Indeed, Ormond's gesture of entreaty broadly mimics the affecting tableau Josiah Wedgwood designs as an emblem for the London Society for the Abolition of Slavery in 1787, which Philadelphia abolitionists begin to display on their lapels in the years that follow. The potter's cameo depicts "an African . . . in chains in a supplicating posture, kneeling with one knee upon the ground, and with both his hands lifted up to Heaven, and round the seal . . . the following motto, as if he were uttering the words himself—'Am I not a Man and a Brother?'"[160] The description comes from the British abolitionist leader and historian Thomas Clarkson, who serves on the committee that commissions Wedgwood's cameo. In 1787, Wedgwood sends a package of the emblems to Benjamin Franklin in his capacity as president of the Pennsylvania Abolition Society for distribution to antislavery advocates in Philadelphia. In a letter that has become a famous artifact of eighteenth-century American abolitionist history, Franklin writes to Wedgwood in the spring of that year: "I have seen in their countenances such a Mark of being

Josiah Wedgwood's 1787 antislavery medallion, "Am I Not a Man and a Brother?" (Courtesy the Wedgwood Museum, Barlaston, UK)

affected by contemplating the Figure of the Suppliant (which is admirably executed) that I am persuaded it may have an Effect equal to that of the best written Pamphlet in procuring favour [*sic*] to those oppressed People." [161]

We must substitute the dirty and degraded "habiliments" of the chimney sweep's apprentice for the loincloth and chains of Wedgwood's kneeling bondsman in order to imagine the way Ormond perversely brings the abolitionist emblem to life. By contrast, in the highly stratified social context of eighteenth-century Anglo-America, to wear the discarded garb of the gentry—its tattered tailcoat and black hat—marks one as a scavenger as well as a slave, a double degradation. [162] The noble exoticism of Wedgwood's ceramic icon is of little relevance to the dissimulating libertine as he plays out his scene of supplication in the urban heart of Philadelphia. As a local image of outcast and abject humanity, the African American chimney sweep provides a far more compelling protagonist for Ormond's tableau vivant than does the English potter's majestic slave—for in republican America, the former figure is the object of enormous cultural pathos. [163]

By "importuning" the maiden for work in her chimney, Ormond would seem to be echoing the emblem's moving refrain, "Am I Not a Man and a Brother?," a query that underscores the powerful ethos of fraternity marking the abolitionist movement. [164] In light of his plaint it is not insignificant that Brown represents Constantia as the only white character in the novel who can claim meaningful ties to the black community. During the epidemic, she meets and renews her bond to a black woodcarter who had worked for her father; this "gentle and obliging" man, known for his "kindness" (53–54), now labors in the ranks of the African American nurses and hearse drivers exhorted to serve the sick and the dead by the white community. He is also the only figure in her district, black or white, rich or poor, who will help the maiden care for her afflicted neighbors. This nameless character could have been lifted directly out of Absalom Jones and Richard Allen's 1794 *A Narrative Of The Proceedings Of The black People, During The Late Awful Calamity In Philadelphia, In The Year 1793*, written by Philadelphia's two leading black ministers to refute racist charges that the African American community engaged in mercenary behavior during the epidemic. [165] The tract, to which I will return in my coda, contains a fascinating portrait gallery of heroic black eighteenth-century Philadelphians. The dramatic show of fellow feeling these African Americans extend to their white brethren during the plague constitutes a remarkable moment in the annals of early American race relations.

Offering fellowship that transcends the limits of race, Constantia Dudley is deputized as the exclusive white embodiment of universal fellow feeling in *Ormond;* she alone is capable of responding as "a woman and a sister"[166] to the libertine's act of (spurious) supplication. When he steps temporarily into the condition of the slave, Ormond literalizes Marshall's description of Smith's vision of sympathy—the act of "putting oneself in the place of someone else."[167] Despite the remarkable nature of his metamorphosis, the libertine nevertheless manages to violate the basic principle of compassion: enduring his "brother's" physical pain, Ormond refuses to take a "fraternal" part. In withholding pity, Brown's villain utterly disavows what might have been an epiphany of antislavery consciousness, uniquely felt from the interior vantage of a so-called brother under the skin, but the prospect of cementing bonds of fellowship—be they cross-racial, affective, or even biological—is the furthest thing from the villain's mind.

Far from evincing a fraternal sentiment that transcends the divisions of color and economic strata in post-Revolutionary America, Ormond's blackface cross-class masquerade bears a reactionary significance to the novel's internal politics: Sophia notes that "we should never have believed, what yet could be truly asserted, that he had frequently swept his own chimneys, without the knowledge of his own servants. It was likewise true, though equally incredible, that he had played at romps with his scullion, and listened with patience to a thousand slanders on his own character" (134). In this extraordinary tableau of the "master" blacking up and behaving as a slave in order to spy on the very people who labor in his service, Ormond literalizes two important notions about the "peculiar institution." The first is that household slavery functions as the gothic underbelly of domesticity itself. In the intimate nature of the cross-racial social relations that obtain under slavery—connections policed from both sides of the color line by a mutually paranoid reciprocal surveillance—slavery shows its uncanny aspect as a grotesque parody of the forms of bourgeois family life.[168]

The second notion, following Orlando Patterson's formulation, is that the relations between master and slave enact a dynamic of human parasitism in which the language of paternalism reverses and mystifies the identities of the dominant and the subordinate. Patterson writes:

> To all members of the community the slave existed only through the parasite holder, who was called master. On this intersubjective level the slaveholder fed on the slave to gain the very direct satisfactions of power

over another, honor, enhancement, and authority. The slave, losing in the process all claim to autonomous power, was degraded and reduced to a state of liminality. The slaveholder camouflaged his dependence, his parasitism, by various ideological strategies. Paradoxically, he defined the slave as dependent.[169]

The scene of cross-class voyeurism in *Ormond* literalizes the dialectical exchange Patterson outlines in his analysis, a dynamic in which the roles of dominated and dominator are infinitely reversible: the master, dressed as a slave, feeds off the social expansiveness of his laboring fellow, all the while feigning the degradation of a figure whose suffering is to him only theoretical. According to Patterson's examination of the theatrical role playing that slavery itself instates, Ormond's taking on of the mantle of blackness and its attendant abjection only exaggerates dramatically what we might call the "performative aspect" of slavery's social face. Patterson notes that "all slaves, like oppressed peoples everywhere, wore masks in their relations with those who had parasitized them."[170] Thus, when the libertine spies on his own servants in blackface disguise, he brings the dual aspect of slavery's "mask"— bondage as both hideous reality and factitious social role—into full ideological view. In addition, by costuming his villain as a chimney sweep whose soot-covered visage serves as a second dusky veil obscuring his already corked up skin, Brown would seem to be making the point all the more emphatic.

Yet, at the level of narrative, Ormond's descent into blackness creates a politically disruptive effect. When the privileged white alien disappears behind the facade of the youth of color, he is taking the place of a figure who is always already socially invisible—thus, the twofold process of erasure enabling his blackface masquerade exposes the gothicism underlying the early republic's multiracial culture. One year before Brown writes *Ormond*, Absalom Jones and Richard Allen make their foray into print in order to counter the aspersions leveled by printer Mathew Carey, among other propagandists, that blacks have extorted exorbitant prices for nursing white fever victims, driving hearses, and burying the dead. In their tract, they discuss the problem of African American social invisibility, the way in which blacks are excluded from the community's imagination of sympathy. *A Narrative* provides a fascinating contemporary commentary on the problems of personal and national identity, fraternity, and sympathy that Brown also meditates on in *Ormond*, offering an African American companion piece (and possibly an inspiration for) the white author's fictional account of the crisis.

Addressing and dispelling the fantasy at work in plague-ridden Philadelphia that blacks and French émigrés are invulnerable to the fever, Jones and Allen also connect this idea about the "immunity" of the cultural other to the way in which African Americans are excluded from the perceptible purview of the community. Patterson's notion of slavery as a form of social death finds a powerful eighteenth-century antecedent in *A Narrative*. The authors state, "Early in September, a solicitation appeared in the public papers, to the people of colour to come forward and assist the distressed, perishing, and neglected sick; with a kind of assurance, that people of our colour were not liable to take the infection" (*A Narrative*, 3). By a paradoxical process of racialist dialectic, the invisible African American, an absent presence in terms of social and political representation, comes visibly into view in order to aid and support an afflicted white community whose own numbers are threatened with erasure by the plague.

Underscoring the peculiar figurative inversion at work in descriptions of the black community during the epidemic, Jones and Allen continue: "We wish not to offend, but when an unprovoked attempt is made, to make us blacker than we are, it becomes necessary to be over cautious on that account; therefore we shall take the liberty to tell of the conduct of some of the whites" (*A Narrative*, 8–9). In the blink of an eye, Philadelphians of color shift from imperceptibility to hyperembodiment. Toward the end of their pamphlet, the ministers note that, "When the people of colour had the sickness and died, we were imposed upon and told it was not with the prevailing sickness, until it became too notorious to be denied, then we were told some few died but not many" (*A Narrative*, 15). In the racist psychic economy of post-Revolutionary Philadelphia, to be thought to be "immune" means to be seen as living beyond the pale of the human community, to be excluded from the circle of sympathy that identifies white Philadelphians as brethren in common affliction.[171] Such a double deletion of identity for African Americans—their social death and live burial—brings into dramatic prominence the failures of fraternity and sympathy that threaten to strip liberty of its moral meaning in the new nation.

However fleetingly, *Ormond* represents blackness in America as a powerful social problem—a predicament that directly intersects with the discourses of identity, fraternity, and sympathy around which the novel unfolds. Those critics who disregard the elusive pull of race in *Ormond* unwittingly and uncannily repeat the perception at work in early republican culture itself that blacks remain largely invisible.[172] Imbedded in the gothic metaphors of social death and live burial are persistent longings that the quandaries created by slavery, manumission, and the debate around emancipation would themselves simply disappear. *Ormond*'s rhetoric of visibility refracts this impulse in fascinating ways.

By raising the prospect of sympathy for the plight of the slave only to shut it down, Brown inaugurates his assault on the notion that fraternity remains a civic value in post-Revolutionary America. His critique extends across the novel's range of characters and incidents, thematic motifs, and formal strategies. Familial ties in *Ormond* turn out to be just as shifty and elusive as the names that fail to inscribe identity. In fact, fictional siblings and siblinghood take on more life and reality than do actual fraternal relations. Inspired by tropes from gothic fiction, Craig invents a "brother"—a scapegoat to blame for his fraud against the Dudleys. Just as easily as the forger gives his brother life, he brutally takes it away. By sentencing his "sibling" to die a fictive and mysterious death in Jamaica against a background of racial strife and the threat of black rebellion, Craig manages to implicate himself—if only in fantasy—in his culture's guilty entanglement with slavery.

Thus, in *Ormond*, ties to one's brother prove only a matter of convenience, for, at the merest whim, siblings can be created through invention and denounced in fact. Just as Constantia's neighbor Whiston denies his bond to his dying sister once she is afflicted with yellow fever, Ormond suppresses the truth that he is Martinette's real brother, while simultaneously indulging in a fraternal fiction at the expense of Helena Cleves, his cast-off mistress. On rejecting the pathetic woman who for love of him has sacrificed her integrity and reputation, Ormond promises to become for her sake "an impostor." He vows to Helena that he "will guard thy ease and thy honor with a father's scrupulousness. Would to heaven a sister could be created by adoption. I am willing, for thy sake, to be an imposter. I will own thee to the world for my sister, and carry thee whither the cheat shall never be detected" (163). But all such "fraternal" relations in this novel translate irreducibly to death: Mary Whiston is forsaken by her brother and dies, and Helena responds to "brotherly" abandonment by committing suicide.

As if to emphasize that fraternity remains his crucial figure for social cohesion, Brown avenges Whiston's betrayal of his sister by dispatching the man to a hideous demise and worse: the egotistical brother is fated to remain unburied. Like the carcass of a dishonored hero from the *Iliad* left as food for the dogs, the lifeless and neglected body of Whiston signals the breakdown of civilized cultural norms.[173] Sophia recounts:

It appeared that Whiston had allowed his terrors to overpower the sense of what was due to his sister and to humanity. On discovering the condition of the unhappy girl, he left the house, and instead of seeking a physician, he turned his steps toward the country . . . He was discovered [in a hay-rick] in the morning by the inhabitants of a neighboring farm house. These people had too much regard for their own safety to accommodate him under their roof, or even to approach within fifty paces of his person. A passenger whose attention and compassion had been excited by this incident, was endowed with more courage. He lifted the stranger in his arms, and carried him from this unwholesome spot to a barn. This was the only service which the passenger was able to perform. Whiston, deserted by every human creature, burning with fever, tormented into madness by thirst, spent three miserable days in agony. When dead, no one would cover his body with earth, but he was suffered to decay by piecemeal. (48)

By a retributive narrative logic worthy of Dante, Brown condemns the unaccommodated Whiston to suffer fatal consequences for his failure of sympathy by infecting him with the disease he so cravenly fled. Utterly abandoned, the man languishes in agony, dies horribly, and is left to rot. The spectacle of Whiston's emotional and material disintegration—his loss of humanity as a kinsman and of physical integrity as a corpse—dramatizes the nearly total collapse of communal bonds in the City of Brotherly Love: more powerfully than any other image in the novel, the fragmented and decomposing body of this citizen figures the virtual unraveling of republican culture itself. If "fraternity" has any meaning in *Ormond*, it is an ironic and dark one indeed, masking under its rhetoric of care and devotion the most unfilial modes of human relations. Thus, Brown exposes the way "brotherhood"—purported watchword of republican ideology—becomes one of the first principles to fall victim to post-Revolutionary disorder.[174]

If, for the white Anglo-American males in the novel—Baxter, Craig, Whiston—fraternal ties bear neither familial nor social import, for the alien female—Martinette de Beauvais—brotherhood retains residual value as a political category, constituting an essential component of the French Revolution's tripartite rallying cry: liberté, égalité, fraternité. But for this woman warrior, filial associations are devoid of affective content; instead, brotherhood functions exclusively as a nationalist principle. When Constantia inquires about where Martinette turned for succor, on the death of M. Roselli, the Frenchwoman scornfully indicates that comfort and compassion are sentimental notions in which she does not trade, explaining that "having finished the interment of Roselli (soldier-fashion) for he was the man who suffered his foolish regrets to destroy him, I forsook the house" (209). Martinette's description of bereavement is both remarkably clinical and actively hostile to the very ideas of attachment, grief, and feeling itself; in an account suffused with irritation rather than sorrow, she complains about having to tolerate the nostalgically romantic illusions of a paternal figure who in his impotence could be Baxter's doppelgänger. Martinette plays Thomas Paine to Roselli's Edmund Burke when she brutally characterizes her surrogate father's sentimental investment in his country's traditions, a depth of fellow feeling she deigns excessive, maudlin, and unmanly. Her indictment recalls Paine's notorious disparagement in *Rights of Man* of what he sees as Burke's self-indulgent theatricality, when he assails Burke for representing the events of the French Revolution in melodramatic tones that appeal to the most primitive emotions of his audience:

> [As] to the tragic paintings by which Mr. Burke has outraged his own imagination, and seeks to work upon that of his readers, they are very well calculated for theatrical representation, where facts are manufactured for the sake of show, and accommodated to produce, through the weakness of sympathy, a weeping effect. But Mr. Burke should recollect that he is writing History, and not *Plays;* and that his readers will expect truth, and not the spouting rant of a high-toned exclamation. When we see a man dramatically lamenting in a publication intended to be believed, that, *"The age of chivalry is gone!"* that *"The glory of Europe is extinguished for ever!"* that *"The unbought grace of life"* (if anyone knows what that is), *"the cheap defence of nations, the nurse of manly sentiment and heroic enterprise, is gone!"* and all this because the Quixote age of chivalry nonsense is gone, what opinion can we form of his judgement [*sic*], or what regard can we pay his facts? In the rhapsody of his imagination, he has discovered a world of windmills, and his sorrows are, that there are no Quixotes to attack them. But if the age of aristocracy, like that of chivalry, should fall, (and they originally had some connexion [*sic*]), Mr. Burke, the trumpeter of the Order, may continue his parody to the end, and finish with exclaiming, *Othello's occupation's gone!"* [175]

Martinette's critical representation of Roselli's nostalgic yearnings, a reading that could have been inspired by Paine, constitutes an indirect but energetic protest against the sentimentalization and feminization of masculine virtue in the post-Revolutionary period. In that respect, the woman warrior also recalls Mary Wollstonecraft in *Vindication of the Rights of Woman,* a work Claudia Johnson characterizes as "militantly antisentimental." Going on to argue that in her book Wollstonecraft "protests the masculinization of sensitivity Burke had celebrated," Johnson notes that the *Vindication* "denounces the collapse of proper sexual distinction as the leading feature of her age, and as the grievous consequence of sentimentality itself. The problem undermining her society in her view is feminized men, and they are not to be corrected by easy seducements, but by bracing and even humiliating, exhortations to manlier duties and sterner pleasures." According to Johnson, such heroic females as Burke's Marie Antoinette and Wollstonecraft herself (a list to which the French queen's namesake in *Ormond*—Martinette de Beauvais—must be included) resist and invert the eighteenth-century paradigm of sex-gender-performance; in their decidedly unsentimental and unfeminine behavior, these women deconstruct the premises of the sexual norm, and thus "appear in a sort of affective counter-drag. Exemplifying a self-possession and effectuality that make them superior to calamity in an irrational world, they are utterly isolated figures, bent on a course of self-determination that tragically dooms them even as it proves that the 'true heroism of antiquity' has fallen onto their worthy shoulders. . . . sentimental masculinity will oblige them too to be equivocal beings, like Wollstonecraft and Marie Antoinette, the best men around." [176] Brown's Martinette makes a fitting addition to this cohort of antisentimental heroines, figures whose stoic valor puts them at odds with received notions of gender in eighteenth-century culture.

With nationalistic contempt, the Frenchwoman then addresses the question of brotherly ties, "Hast thou forgotten that there were at that time, as least ten thousand French in this city, fugitives from Marat and St. Domingo? . . . Supposed thou that there were none among these, who would receive a countrywoman, even if her name had not been Martinette de Beauvais? Thy fancy has depicted strange things, but believe me, that, without a farthing and without a name, I should not have incurred the slightest inconvenience" (209). When catastrophe strikes the republican polity in the decade after the Founding, the American brothers fly in horror from their afflicted fellows. Such comportment provides a stunning contrast to the behavior of the dispossessed French refugees, a community standing fast in commitment to the Revolution's values, particularly notions of equality and fraternity. The extraordinary case of Martinette de Beauvais somewhat complicates the more general observation that in *Ormond* the spirit of fraternity exists in almost mutual exclusion to the workings of liberty. Incarnating the excesses of post-Revolutionary independence, Craig and Ormond, both sociopaths and libertines, exemplify this assertion, but Martinette alone bears a Revolutionary pedigree underwritten by a fervent belief in the social value of freedom: infected by the zeal of her English husband, a "political enthusiast, who esteemed nothing more graceful or glorious than to die for the liberties of mankind" (201), the woman warrior evinces a passion for liberty unmatched by fictional peers of either sex.

Brown formally underscores Martinette's ideological preeminence when he deputizes her to tell her own story in the first person: the Frenchwoman's interpolated account of her life marks the only moment in *Ormond* when Sophia yields narrative authority to another—and it is hardly insignificant that this other is also a woman. Like the author who imagined her into being,[177] Martinette also takes on the tones of the opposite sex to assert the cause of liberty. The character may have been based on the historical Deborah Sampson, a woman who in 1782 adorned herself in a uniform and enlisted in the Continental Army under the name of Robert Shurtliff. Sampson fought in the American Revolution until, after being wounded in the groin, she was discovered by a military surgeon. On ultimately securing an honorable discharge, she became the first woman in the history of the new nation to receive a soldier's pension.[178] As we have seen, Martinette's unusual name also evokes associations to the former queen of France who, in the prophetic if decidedly partisan eyes of Edmund Burke, will become an heroic martyr to Revolutionary hardheartedness. The appellation, in addition, suggests a kind of mechanistic rigidity. Indeed, in her ability to pass herself off as a man, Martinette does strictly "adhere to the details of forms and methods" of soldierly comportment,[179] which in her case translates as a life purged of emotional connection. Martinette's obdurate severity makes her unique in *Ormond:* she is the only character who remains truly free.

The Frenchwoman's narrative of life on the front lines of the battle for liberty underscores that, though her allegiances are kindled out of passion for a spouse, they quickly transmute into an abiding and transcendent political passion. Martinette relates that, when her husband "tendered his service to the Congress as a volunteer" in the "third year of the Revolutionary War in America," she vowed to accompany him in every danger, to vie with him in military ardour [*sic*]; to combat and to die by his side. I delighted to assume the male dress, to acquire skill at the sword, and dexterity in every boisterous exercise. The timidity that commonly attends women, gradually vanished. I felt as if imbued by a soul that was a stranger to the sexual distinction. (201)

The cross-dressing soldier goes on to note that

I am an adorer of liberty, and liberty without peril can never exist. . . . Have I not been three years in a camp? What are bleeding wounds and mangled corpses, when accustomed to the daily sight of them for years? Am I not a lover of liberty, and must I not exult in the fall of tyrants, and regret only that my hand had no share in their destruction. . . . My hand never faltered when liberty demanded the victim. (206)

In exchange for the freedom in which she clearly revels and for which she remains willing to die, Martinette forswears the claims of sympathy—no small price to pay.

Near the end of her first embedded monologue, the woman warrior affirms her intention "henceforth to keep my liberty inviolate by any species of engagement, either of friendship or marriage" (204). To be absolutely free in *Ormond*'s terms means to embody self-reliance; but it also suggests being closed off, invulnerable, beyond the reach of infection, compassion, and feeling itself. As Brown imagines the wages of independence in the new republic, the apparent cost of freedom would seem to be a life without personal ties. Indeed, the brilliant woman warrior, known for her "conversation and comportment," also "exhibit[s] no tendencies to confidence, or traces of sympathy" (190). Personifying Liberty, she is a lady who sheds no tears. Martinette explains that the "death of Roselli I foresaw, because it was gradual in its approach, and was sought by him as good. My grief, therefore, was exhausted before it came, and I rejoiced at his death, because it was the close of all his sorrows. The rueful pictures of my distress and weakness, which were given by Baxter, existed only in his own fancy" (209–10). The Frenchwoman cannot allow herself to imagine that fellow feeling might constitute a social good. In order to preserve her hard-won independence, she must vigorously deny the very sort of sympathy that—because she is a woman—her surrogate father and Baxter mistakenly project on her.

If compassion in the post-Revolutionary period is not to be found between brothers, fathers, and surrogate daughters, where does it reside? The
answer, in *Ormond*, lies in the bond of sisterhood, in both female homosociality and romantic love between women. With Constantia's feminist overturning of Ormond's seduction plot, sisterly love provides the last resort for
sympathy in Brown's novel.[180] Sophia's account of the reunion with her beloved friend certainly suggests no other reading: "The ordinary functions of
nature were disturbed. The appetite for sleep and food were confounded and
lost amid the impetuosities of a master passion. To look and to talk to each
other afforded enchanting occupation for every moment. I would not part
from her side, but ate and slept, walked and mused and read, with my arm
locked in hers, and with her breath fanning my cheek" (250). Like many
scenes in *Ormond*, Brown organizes this tableau around the dynamic of specularity, but the nature of the look Sophia records exchanging with Constantia marks the singularity of the episode, which turns around a mutuality
of vision manifested by none of the other gazers in the novel. Unlike the
book's recurring moments of potential sympathy gone awry, the reunion is
suffused with a thoroughgoing reciprocity of feeling, affection embodied in
the graphic images of physical fusion Sophia so passionately describes.

When the libertine spies on this scene of homosocial pleasure—a spectacle of fellow feeling in almost the literal sense (the women who compose it
are virtually twins)—it is the last moment in *Ormond* where the act of looking makes a mockery of the workings of sympathy. The episode stands apart
from the novel's earlier moments of voyeurism, however, where a character's
failure to identify with the object of vision reflects a deficit within the gazing
self. In the final scene of surveillance, there is truly no one and no thing in
Ormond's ocular field with whom or which he might identify. His furtive
attempt to insert himself into a picture from which he is clearly excluded—a
glass that erases rather than mirrors his look—ultimately obliterates the villain's self-conception. Such illicit surveillance explodes the moral premise underwriting Smith's poetics of vision—that sympathetic observation and recognition of the social other enable a powerful form of affective knowledge
precisely because they are activities premised on mutuality.

When the libertine acts as a secret witness, he colonizes the place of the
other without taking his object's part. Seeing without feeling, physically contiguous and emotionally aloof, Ormond parodies the structures of fellow
feeling rather than inhabits them from within. Encoded in this perversion of

reflective vision, this one-way perceptual dynamic, is the risk of mistaking a telescopic vista for a glance into the mirror. From Baxter to Ormond, all of the novel's unrighteous gazers ultimately become contaminated by the view of self they witness or fail to find reflected in voyeurism's uncanny glass: vision in *Ormond* proves polluting when what one sees is not the other but a defamiliarized, disavowed version of oneself.

Like the watchman, Ormond becomes deranged by the sight of a female who appears neither submissive nor sentimental, who fails to conform to conventional eighteenth-century norms of gender.[181] Surreptitiously viewing a scene in which he can play no romantic or erotic part—a configuration that by definition erases the very (masculine heterosexual) space in which he envisions himself an active agent—Ormond becomes infected by what he sees. So blinded, the villain is driven to assault Constantia's virtue, to which he enjoys no romantic claim. Miscalculating her heroic valor, he attacks the maiden's purity and thereby guarantees his own destruction.

Coda

Ormond ends with what seems a stunningly barren vision of the early national future. Its white male characters are blind, dead, or permanently banished to England. While the heroic women of the novel survive and endure, the author disperses them from the American strand precisely along those factional lines that separate figures like the hostile neighbors Baxter and Monrose, who replay the strife of the domestic political parties to which they stand in symbolic relation. Constantia and Sophia retreat to England, and Martinette returns to face the aftermath of the Terror in post-Revolutionary France.

In concluding his tale with a female homosocial coupling, Brown does imagine a space for sympathy in the Federalist period that transcends the purview of a failed fraternity, but this vista is not quite utopian: for as much as a community of women offers an alternative to patriarchal authority, it does not solve the problem of exactly how difference is to figure and be consolidated into an intricately patterned early national fabric. Constantia and Sophia conjure a powerful vision of fellow feeling with potentially representative resonance, but their disavowal of the mother country remains largely a symbolic gesture; as women they possess no legal citizenship, which reduces their expatriation to ambiguous protest at best. There is an additional limitation to reading this couple in any emblematic fashion: theirs is a bond in which otherness remains unintegrated into the mirror of sympathy if only because no difference or altierity obtains between them; that these women are twinned almost incestuously effectively collapses the distance that always exists between any two separate persons—however sympathetic or harmonious they may be. It is difficult to consider Constantia and Sophia's union as a viable model for the renovated social body—and, in that regard, the national crypt would seem to be inescapably sealed.

But as *Ormond* draws to its sorry close, Brown peoples his narrative landscape with the human residue of a fractured polity, those who, paradoxically less privileged and mobile than the heroines, have more at stake in the American future. While Constantia and Sophia withdraw from the scene of Ormond's crimes, the invisible Americans the novel brings into fleeting view tacitly come to preside over the bleakness of its ending: the white washerwoman Sarah Baxter, representing the working classes; Constantia's significantly nameless African American friend, formerly a carter of wood and a nurse and driver during the fever; and the magistrate Melbourne, a white male incarnation of the law, who constitutes the remaining emblem of authority in a world that has lost most such figures. This motley assortment of characters—both ciphers and citizens—comprises the only group in *Ormond* to survive the travails of 1793 to remain in Philadelphia. For economic reasons—the poverty and bondage that paralyze movement or the wealth and status that obviate escape—the working-class women, the black nurses, and the magistrate Melbourne himself all continue to identify themselves as Americans. Speaking at a distance from Brown's manifest narrative of expatriation, they channel a range of republican voices: those enfranchised as well as those interred in the funereal rites of the Founding.

This peculiar social remnant, for all its apparent randomness, takes on a powerful symbolic force at the end of the novel. In a strangely vital way, such figures mark the future of America in all its difference and self-division, a prospect that Brown presciently glimpses decades before its time. With the exception of the magistrate, these are the very disenfranchised characters who populate Jones and Allen's *A Narrative* and make the pamphlet a curious gothic doppelgänger of Brown's disturbing book.

Reaching across the divide of race, class, and citizenship that polarizes fever-stricken Philadelphia in manichean fashion, splitting the population into natives and aliens, comrades in suffering and exiles from communal fellowship, these anonymous African Americans extend the bond of sympathy to a white community that disavows their status as brethren. The ministers record that

> it was a rare instance to see one [white] neighbor visit another, and even friends when they met in the streets were afraid of each other, much less would they admit into their houses the distressed orphan that had been where the sickness was; this extreme seemed in some instances to have the appearance of barbarity; with reluctance we call to mind the many opportunities there were in the power of individuals to be useful to their fellow-men, yet through the terror of the times was omitted. A black man riding through the street, saw a man push a woman out of the house, the woman staggered and fell on her face in the gutter, and was not able to turn herself, the black man thought she was drunk, but observing she was in danger of suffocation alighted, and taking the woman up found her perfectly sober, but so far gone with the disorder that she was not able to help herself; the hard hearted man that threw her down, shut the door and left her—in such a situation, she might have perished in a few minutes: we heard of it and took her to Bush-hill [the plague hospital established by the Guardians of the city for the indigent afflicted]. Many of the white people, that ought to be patterns for us to follow after, have acted in a manner that would make humanity shudder. (*A Narrative*, 19)

Inadvertently underscoring the pathos of antislavery's central question (which, of course, fails rhetorically to challenge the gender barrier)—"who in the human community should be considered a man and a brother?"—white Philadelphians reveal their essential savagery in this inverted enactment of abolitionism's refrain. In exhibiting such monstrous callousness, these citizens raise important doubts about the righteousness of their own enfranchisement in the circle of sympathy.

In an additional tableau that unfolds toward the end of the historical portion of their narrative, a scene that foreshadows what will become Brown's central themes, Jones and Allen offer an image of humanity that counters *Ormond*'s dark prognosis:

> We can with certainty assure the public that we have seen more humanity, more real sensibility from the poor blacks, than from the poor whites. When many of the former, of their own accord rendered services

where extreme necessity called for it, the general part of the poor white people were so dismayed, that instead of attempting to be useful, they in a manner hid themselves—a remarkable instance of this—A poor afflicted dying man, stood at his chamber window, praying and beseeching every one that passed by, to help him to a drink of water; a number of white people passed, and instead of being moved by the poor man's distress, they hurried as fast as they could out of the sound of his cries—until at length a gentleman, who seemed to be a foreigner came up, he could not pass by, but had not resolution enough to go into the house, he held eight dollars in his hand, and offered it to several as a reward for giving the poor man a drink of water, but was refused by everyone, until a poor black man came up, the gentleman offered the eight dollars to him, if he would relieve the poor man with a little water. "Master," replied the good natured fellow, "I will supply the gentleman with water, but surely I will not take your money for it" nor could he be prevailed upon to accept his bounty: he went in, supplied the poor object with water, and rendered him every service he could. A poor black man, named Sampson, went constantly from house to house where distress was, and no assistance without fee or reward; he was smote with the disorder, and died, and after his death his family were neglected by those he had served. (*A Narrative*, 10–11)

Who will come to the rescue of a suffering citizen during the epidemic? Only an alien and an African American prove willing to succor a brother when the white residents of Philadelphia turn away from the tableau of anguish. In this poignant moment, the contorted logic and political justification both for the Alien and Sedition Acts and for slavery itself crumble under their own ponderous weight. The ministers's narrative goes beyond exposing the speciousness of arguments that foreigners menace the native social body and that blacks cannot compete with white labor or contribute to the well-being of the community; it actually documents the essential error of nativist and racist principles.

Rather than ending with such an image of sympathetic exchange across the lines of color, class, and national origin, *Ormond* concludes with what could be read as a reactionary fantasy of dissent from that radical vision. If narrative closure functions as wish-fulfillment (dream or nightmare) in representational form, then Constantia's flight to the mother country speaks to the part of Brown despairing for the American future. Nevertheless, the scene of interracial benevolence punctuating the author's account of the fever silently haunts the novel's later episodes of failed compassion for the female, black, or alien other. The generosity one African American extends to Constantia and her white neighbors—his offer of aid in removing Mary Whiston's corpse when no one else will come forward—marks the only moment in *Ormond* in which the sympathy of an outsider *would seem* to embody disinterest in the ideal eighteenth-century sense of the word as well as to transcend the meanings it begins to accrue at the dawn of the nineteenth century. As a category of virtue, "disinterest" initially signifies the surmounting of bias and as such is a watchword of republican ideology, but, by the time Brown writes *Ormond* the term has come to denote the disengagement from feeling, per se.

Far from emanating from disinterest's transcendent position of judgment, the magnaminity of Constantia's African American compatriot more precisely reflects what I have called "emerging liberal sympathy," a form of fellow feeling based on imaginative recognition of and emotional response to the suffering of another. The black man helps the white woman because he remembers her kindness and comprehends her pain; cross-racial relations are marked neither by republican disinterest nor by the human parasitism of slavery but by an authentic understanding of distress and a willingness to offer relief: a reflexive compassion whose benefits have come full circle. The concept of disinterested virtue cannot capture the political complexity of the woodcarter's benevolence, because such purportedly lofty detachment emanates strictly from above, the exclusive purview of the affluent, white male. Always already implicated in structures of race, class, gender, and economic privilege, republican disinterest is never, finally, dis-interested. Thus, the virtue of *Ormond*'s most compassionate, if also most marginalized, American remains politically invisible, as its agent suffers the burden of social death, live burial, and permanent exclusion from the fraternity of fellow feeling.

While *Ormond* contains the early American novel's most sophisticated rendering of foreclosed political possibility, its darkening view is not unique to the fiction of the era; as I hope to have shown, such skepticism underwrites the literary tradition Charles Brockden Brown inherits from William Hill Brown, Susanna Rowson, and Hannah Webster Foster. Inaugurating this legacy, *The Power of Sympathy* seems to offer a democratizing vision of public life in its antislavery tableau and egalitarian sentiments, but W. H. Brown's reactionary subtext reveals that those most vigorously asserting claims of transcendent fellow feeling are in fact pursuing decidedly interested and less-than-virtuous agendas. *Charlotte Temple*, on the other hand, unabashedly re-routes benevolence through interest and identification, away from republican emotional forms and toward democratic structures of feeling. But Rowson's efforts to expand the franchise of sympathy, to forge a national community based on readerly compassion, run aground on the shoals of excess—through the melancholia of a narrator whose extravagant grief blurs her ideological program for transparent social relations. Virtuous disinterest gives way to immoderate investment—which exacts its own form of tyranny—and ulti-mately to the blockage of pathological mourning.

If excessive interest compromises democratic prospects in *Charlotte Temple*, undue disinterest crushes fanciful dissent from republican hegemony in *The Coquette*. Indeed, it is in the name of transcendent judgment that Foster's patriarchal chorus interdicts the heroine's murmurs of freedom, deni-grating such talk as "a play about words" (31). From such elevated heights, the community abandons Eliza Wharton to suffer and die below, the victim of a culture that puts virtue—less moral absolute than restrictive social in-vestment—before the call of sympathy. Finally, in *Ormond*, Charles Brockden Brown charts the way republican disinterest becomes eclipsed by emerging liberal enterprise as the collective good of the commonwealth yields to specu-lation and specularity, the malignant one-way vision the book so trenchantly exposes.

The novel also tacitly suggests that the remedy to such ills lies in another form of "transmission": the storytelling central to *Ormond*'s very structure and that stands for reparative forms of social contact and human interchange. It is no accident that, within the fictive universe, Sarah Baxter's tale plays such a crucial and compelling part. In just this way, the historical account that precedes Brown's book by five years, Jones and Allen's pamphlet, proves enor-mously powerful as well: its modern editor asserts that *A Narrative*, "was the first public defense of free blacks who were drawn into the vortex of one of the worst plagues in the history of the United States," [182] was widely distrib-uted among whites. The fictional washerwoman and the real-life ministers exchange their tales across those lines of class and race and gender that sun-der Americans in the post-Revolutionary period and beyond; their narrative efforts re-circulate the blood of sympathy throughout the public body—both imagined and real.

In contrast, Baxter, Craig, and Ormond engage in a perverted form of vision and projection, parodying the structures of fellow feeling and speaking to a certain unenlightened sector of the audience—those Americans who read novels for sexual titillation rather than moral edification. Engaging in dangerous acts of imagination, these men all double for the author who creates them: peering through the keyhole, Baxter stands for the writer as voyeur; constructing his masculine heroism against the fantasy of Martinette as damsel in distress, Baxter suggests Brown's ambivalent and phantasmagorical relationship to the literary foremothers in whose wake he writes. In the scene with which I began the discussion of *Ormond*, we look at Brown pondering Sophia reporting on Sarah recounting Baxter watching Martinette burying Roselli; through this infinite regress of vision and voice, Brown implicates Baxter, the narrator, himself, and the audience for wielding an unrighteous gaze.

The tableau offers a thunderous "no" to *Charlotte Temple's* vision of sympathetic relations: Rowson's dream of transparent communion between narrator and reader has devolved into a nightmare of degenerate, contaminated, even deadly analogy. Recalling *Ormond's* fictive origin in epistolarity itself, the forger's fateful plot unfolds in similar fashion; his letters cast an indelible taint on the link between correspondence and sincerity in eighteenth-century Anglo-American culture. And Ormond's forays as a peeping Tom, hiding behind a stretched sheet of canvas to watch Constantia Dudley from a gap in the adjacent wall, evoke parallels between painterly and writerly vision, suggesting a troubling correlation between artistic proclivity and inherent perversion. As we attempt to understand Brown's renunciation of his novelistic career in the early years of the nineteenth century, it is difficult to ignore the author's self-conscious apprehension over the power dynamics underlying his own aesthetic impulses—inclinations that *Ormond's* villainous artists so vividly replay.[183]

While the creative energies of Brown's fictive doppelgängers—Baxter, Craig, and Ormond—remain morally problematic in *Ormond*, the storytelling of Sarah Baxter and Jones and Allen, who gather their material from the margins of republican culture, offers a subtle antidote. Oscillating between these discordant figures in his identifications as a writer, Brown conjures Sophia as his ultimate proxy. Although affluent and white, like Ormond, Constantia's companion is also female and disenfranchised, like the washerwoman and the ministers, and, as such, she speaks from a unique position of antipatriarchal privilege. Representing dissent from "the regime of the brother,"[184] Sophia suffers little compunction about borrowing his scopophilic tactics, turning her scrutiny back on the villainous Ormond in the damning account of his designs that becomes the novel itself.

In inhabiting this female narrative persona who would recuperate the gaze as a decidedly homosocial and sympathetic rather than heterosexual and voyeuristic gesture, Brown makes a nod to Rowson and Foster, who begin their novels by idealizing the prospect of a women's community. While Rowson's feminized audience, comprised of both male and female readers of feeling, eagerly anticipates her promise of democratic sympathy, this vista is significantly clouded by the narrator's melancholia. Writing after Rowson, and dissenting from her dream of fellowship, Foster systematically defeats Eliza Wharton's fanciful, utopian, and impossible vision of a women's world of compassionate communion folded into the Federalist hegemony. It is only—ironically—in *Ormond*, arguably the darkest of these novels, that female sympathy is allowed to survive the horrors of seduction, disease, and death, though not on American soil. But as *Ormond*'s discourse of infection suggests, such sentimental fellow feeling itself unfolds on an affective continuum also occupied by cohabitation, inhabitation, and, ultimately, possession. Verging precariously close to parasitism, heightened sympathy can blur into dispossession, estrangement, and alienation—social death and live burial—for the overtaken host.

What then might this imply for Charles Brockden Brown as the male literary inheritor and inhabiter of a female fictive tradition? Is it not inevitable that his re-vision of his imaginative foremothers must be both defamiliarizing as well as sympathetic? Does Brown recognize the powerful value of feminized representations of feeling—do they ground and mirror his own transvestite novelistic productions?[185] Like Baxter, does he disavow, erase, and flee from such reflections in an act of *misconaissance* that uncannily repeats the funereal rites of the Founding by burying alive this maternal legacy?

Only in the gaze that Brown turns on himself, in his searching inquiry into the possibility of true Smithian transmigration, do the most tentative answers to these questions lie. So often in *Ormond* fellow feeling degenerates into something like the self-serving experience of theatricality Rousseau describes: an act that the viewing subject conceives of as compassionate, but that actually obliterates real others in order to sustain the self-conception of the subject who looks. Far from recirculating the blood of sympathy, such gazing comes closer to a form of social vampirism. Thus, we understand why the early American novel's sentimental structures are shot through with gothic energies, why tropes of transparency and reflection devolve into images of projection and collapse, and why the figure of live burial pertains less to the protodemocratic *Charlotte Temple* than it does to the firmly republican

Power of Sympathy and *Coquette,* as well as to the protoliberal *Wieland* and *Ormond.*

Ormond's primal scene of patriarchal interment provides a potent metaphor for my final ruminations about post-Revolutionary political foreclosure and the encryptment of social possibility in the novels of the Federalist period. In its closing pages, a powerful strand of early American fiction also comes to an end. Through Sarah Baxter and the unnamed African American woodcarter, Brown represents the economically excluded, the socially dead, and the politically invisible, providing a mournful picture of America's uncounted "many" on the eve of the nineteenth century. In Melbourne, he embodies a vestigial trace of the virtuous republican "few." What authority does Brown imagine coming into the breach to direct this diverse and inchoate remnant of community he depicts? By leaving that prerogative in the hands of a man who is deputized to uphold the law—an institution whose mechanisms Brown views with hesitation at best—the author concludes his book on an equivocal if not a despondent note. Yet his ending is also prophetic. Witness the enormous social force of *Uncle Tom's Cabin* (1852) and its (symbolic) connection to the drafting of the Emancipation Proclamation (1862) and to the Thirteenth Amendment to the Constitution, which abolished slavery (1865). Indeed, it is exclusively through the power of narrative and the intervention of the law—both of which by 1802 Brown has thoroughly renounced—that those invisible Americans haunting the margins of *Ormond* begin to emerge from the gothic shadows of the Founding. Less an actual place than a conceptual space, their destination also marks an incomplete enfranchisement—a bittersweet induction into the community of citizenship, if not yet the circle of sympathy.

Notes

CHAPTER ONE

1. Historian Marshall Smelser first articulates the idea that to understand the disorder of the 1790s one must appreciate the centrality of affect and its excesses in his "The Federalist Period as an Age of Passion," *American Quarterly* 10.4 (winter 1958): 391–419, especially 391. See also John R. Howe, Jr., "Republican Thought and Political Violence of the 1790s," *American Quarterly* 19.2 (summer 1967): 147–65.

2. The first three terms are Smelser's. See also Linda K. Kerber, *Federalists in Dissent: Imagery and Ideology in Jeffersonian America* (Ithaca: Cornell University Press, 1970). I add the notion of grief in order to thicken the affective description of the period and to telegraph the central concern of *The Plight of Feeling*.

3. In using spatial figures with explicitly hierarchical implications to describe a stratified social reality that is in fact more complex than such metaphors would suggest, I risk the charge that I am imposing an anachronistic Freudian model on events that predate the development of psychoanalytic thought by almost one hundred years. But the topographical imagination is not the exclusive domain of Freud and his followers. Indeed, the entire notion of the "Founding" of the republic is in fact predicated on its own architectural—spatial, hierarchical, and topographical—formulation. Thus, in talking about undersides, foundations, and crypts, I take as much from the language of the Framers and the historians who create the notion of the Founding as I do from psychoanalysis.

4. Literary histories identify William Hill Brown's *The Power of Sympathy* as the first American novel; *Wieland,* Charles Brockden Brown's earliest work of fiction, is classified as the first novel written by a professional man of letters in the United States.

5. See Claudia L. Johnson, *Equivocal Beings: Politics, Gender, and Sentimentality in the 1790s: Wollstonecraft, Radcliffe, Burney, and Austen* (Chicago: University of Chicago Press, 1995), 3. Jay Fliegelman notes Thomas Paine's derision of Burke's excessively dramatic rep-

resentational practices; in *The Rights of Man,* Paine opines that "as to the tragic paintings by which Mr. Burke has outraged his own imagination, and seeks to work upon that of his readers, they are very well calculated for theatrical representation, where facts are manufactured for the sake of show, and accommodated to produce, through the weakness of sympathy, a weeping effect." See Fliegelman, *Declaring Independence: Jefferson, Natural Theatricality, and the Culture of Performance* (Stanford: Stanford University Press, 1993), 78–79; quoting Paine, *The Rights of Man,* ed. Eric Foner (1791; Harmondsworth: Penguin Books, 1984), 49–50.

6. The peculiarly transatlantic genealogy of *Charlotte Temple,* written and published in England in 1791 by a British-born émigré to America and reprinted there in 1794 on her return to the new republic, requires the dual publication date and the claim of an Anglo-American origin.

7. Cathy N. Davidson registers an exception to this otherwise uniform disenfranchisement: "in only one state, New Jersey, and only briefly, were propertied women (both black and white) granted the vote." See *Revolution and the Word: The Rise of the Novel in America* (New York: Oxford University Press, 1986), 120.

8. Thomas Jefferson, "First Inaugural Address" (March 4, 1801), in *Writings,* ed. Merrill D. Peterson (New York: Library of America, 1984), 493.

9. I borrow this language from Laura Rigal's analysis of Bartram's *Travels* (1791) in *Meeting Places: Rhetoric, Ritual, and Text in the North American Interior, 1700–1812,* work in progress.

10. This dynamic approximates the so-called mirror of sympathy Adam Smith elaborates in *The Theory of Moral Sentiments* (1759), which I discuss in my analysis of *The Power of Sympathy* at the end of this chapter. Jefferson's image of such fluid political identifications recalls Smith's description of the circulation and transformation of feeling he sees as essential for sympathetic understanding and which is crucial to his liberal theory, with its attendant vision of social and economic exchange. See also Terry Mulcaire, *The Aesthetics of Laissez-Faire,* work in progress.

11. Paul Downes observes that, "given [the] climate" of "American political culture in the 1790s," "Brown's reputation as a master of gothic suspense seems more like an achievement of realism." See "Sleep-Walking out of the Revolution: Brown's *Edgar Huntly,*" *Eighteenth Century Studies* 29.4 (summer 1996): 413–31, especially 413.

12. See Nathaniel Hawthorne, "The Custom-House," in *The Scarlet Letter,* vol. 1 of *The Centenary Edition of the Works of Nathaniel Hawthorne,* eds. William Charvat, Roy Harvey Pearce, and Claude M. Simpson (1850; Columbus: Ohio State University Press, 1962), 36. Jonathan Arac offers a trenchant explication of Hawthorne's "neutrality," which he characterizes as Hawthorne's failure to take action in both political life and narrative art. See Arac's important essay "The Politics of *The Scarlet Letter,*" in *Ideology and Classic American Literature,* eds. Sacvan Bercovitch and Myra Jehlen (Cambridge: Cambridge University Press, 1986), 247–66.

13. I take my language here from Davidson, who articulates and explores this concept of female nonrepresentation in a range of critical works, including her introductory essays to modern editions of such texts as *Charlotte Temple* (New York: Oxford University Press, 1986) and *The Coquette* (New York: Oxford University Press, 1986).

14. See Ann Jessie Van Sant, *Eighteenth-Century Sensibility and the Novel: The Senses in Social Context* (Cambridge: Cambridge University Press, 1993).

15. See Jean-Jacques Rousseau, "Letter to M. D'Alembert on the Theatre," in *Politics and the Arts: "Letter to M. D'Alembert on the Theatre,"* trans. Alan Bloom (1758; Ithaca: Cornell University Press, 1968); Adam Smith, *The Theory of Moral Sentiments,* eds. D. D.

Raphael and A. L. Macfie (1759; Indianapolis: Liberty Classics, 1982); and Edmund Burke, *Reflections on the Revolution in France,* ed. Connor Cruise O'Brien (1790; Harmondsworth: Penguin Books, 1968). Hereafter, these works will be cited parenthetically in the text.

16. The spectacular is, of course, the domain of melodrama, a theatrical mode that enacts manichean moral conflict through spectacles of visibility. My definition of the form is indebted to Peter Brooks, *The Melodramatic Imagination: Balzac, Henry James, Melodrama, and the Mode of Excess* (1976; New York: Columbia University Press, 1984). Feminist film theory elaborates Brooks's formulations by putting the crucial category of gender at the center of the discussion; it also theorizes the same incongruences between the auditory and visual registers of narrative that interest me in the early American novel. See Christine Gledhill, ed., *Home Is Where the Heart Is: Studies in Melodrama and the Woman's Film* (London: British Film Institute, 1987); and John Fletcher, "Melodrama: An Introduction," *Screen* 29.3 (summer 1988): 1–12. For important work on melodrama that predates Brooks, see David Grimsted, *Melodrama Unveiled: American Theatre and Culture, 1800–1850* (Chicago: University of Chicago Press, 1968).

17. The secondary literature on sentiment and sensibility in the eighteenth-century Anglo-American narrative tradition is vast. For the best recent extended treatment of the subject, see G. J. Barker-Benfield, *The Culture of Sensibility: Sex and Society in Eighteenth-Century Britain* (Chicago: University of Chicago Press, 1992). See also Barbara M. Benedict, *Framing Feeling: Sentiment and Style in English Prose Fiction* (New York: AMS Press, 1994); Ann Jessie Van Sant, *Eighteenth-Century Sensibility and the Novel;* John Mullan, *Sentiment and Sociability: The Language of Feeling in the Eighteenth Century* (Cambridge: Cambridge University Press, 1988); David Marshall, *The Surprising Effects of Sympathy: Marivaux, Diderot, Rousseau, and Mary Shelley* (Chicago: University of Chicago Press, 1988); and Janet Todd, *Sensibility: An Introduction* (London: Methuen, 1986). For what is now a classic treatment, see R. F. Brissenden, *Virtue in Distress: Studies in the Novel of Sentiment from Richardson to Sade* (London: Macmillan, 1974). See also Jean H. Hagstrum, *Sex and Sensibility: Ideal and Erotic Love from Milton to Mozart* (Chicago: University of Chicago Press, 1980).

Much of my thinking about the relationship between the feeling that characterizes sentimentality and the pathological disturbance of mourning that takes shape in melancholia is inspired by Mitchell R. Breitwieser's remark that, in "a recent work on Melville and mourning in antebellum America, Neal L. Tolchin has identified the centrality of a blocking and channeling of mourning in genteel culture, and the consequent production of an underground melancholia. Tolchin's extensive and perspicacious investigation of Melville's America suggests to me that sentimentalism is a reappearance of the Puritan sublimation of mourning, promoting quite different social values, but availing itself of Puritanism's legacy of social technique." See *American Puritanism and the Defense of Mourning: Religion, Grief, Ethnology, and Mary White Rowlandson's Captivity Narrative* (Madison: University of Wisconsin Press, 1990), 210 n. 61. Also see Neal L. Tolchin, *Mourning, Gender, and Creativity in the Art of Herman Melville* (New Haven: Yale University Press, 1988), xiii, 5–7, and 12.

In an essay that discusses Breitwieser's book as a theoretical jumping-off point for the notion that an unresolved or pathological grief lies at the heart of American literature, I make a case that adumbrates the concerns developed in *The Plight of Feeling:* "mourning is the central subtext of much American sentimental women's writing in the eighteenth and nineteenth centuries; multivocality plays a crucial role in communicating what such sublimated narrative material represses. In both Susanna Rowson's *Charlotte Temple* and Susan Warner's *The Wide, Wide World,* moral prescription and sentimental piety function as smokescreens for the deep and unresolved maternal mourning that cannot be voiced because to open the channel of such grief into direct expression is to violate a cultural taboo." See Julia Stern, "To Represent Afflicted Time: Mourning as Historiography," *American Literary History* 5.2 (summer 1993): 378–88, especially 385.

18. My understanding and application of gothicism largely derive from the work of Eve Sedgwick, who contends in her first book that two central features involve "literal, figural, or structural" uses of "live burial" and the notion of the "unspeakable." Though much that is relevant to my concerns has been written about the connection between gothicism and women's narrative, Sedgwick's work remains, to my mind, the most imaginative and capacious theoretical account. See *The Coherence of Gothic Conventions* (New York: Methuen, 1986), 5. For recent feminist studies of gothicism, see, for example, Susan Wolstenholme, *Gothic (Re)Visions: Writing Women as Readers* (Albany: State University of New York Press, 1993); Michelle A. Massé, *In the Name of Love: Women, Masochism, and the Gothic* (Ithaca: Cornell University Press, 1992); Kari J. Winter, *Subjects of Slavery, Agents of Change: Women and Power in Gothic Novels and Slave Narratives, 1790–1865* (Athens: University of Georgia Press, 1992); Eugenia Delamotte, *Perils of the Night: A Feminist Study of Nineteenth-Century Gothic* (New York: Oxford University Press, 1990); and Kate Ferguson Ellis, *The Contested Castle: Gothic Novels and the Subversion of Domestic Ideology* (Urbana: University of Illinois Press, 1989). For a reading that traces links between Edmund Burke's gothic portrait of the French Revolution and British fiction of the 1790s, see Steven Bruhm, *Gothic Bodies: The Politics of Pain in Romantic Fiction* (Philadelphia: University of Pennsylvania Press, 1994).

It is important to note that *The Plight of Feeling* enacts a form of gothicism in its own narrative methods. While this study centers around extensive readings of *Charlotte Temple, The Coquette,* and *Ormond,* it also draws from the private correspondence, political orations, and biographies and autobiographies of George Washington, John Adams, James Madison, Alexander Hamilton, Thomas Jefferson, and Benjamin Franklin. But, in the spirit of reversing the hierarchical relation that obtains between the master and counternarratives circulating throughout early national culture, I bring the language of the Founders into *subtextual* representation, through the notes that underwrite *The Plight of Feeling.* Thus, these two discourses, one feminized and fictive, the other masculinized and historical, speak contrapuntally, dialogically, and palimpsestically, just as they do in the 1790s, but with an inversion of the emphasis between melody and harmony, call and response, text and subtext.

19. Freud's notion of the primal scene, first formulated in the case study of the "Wolf Man," involves the young child's traumatic observation of *his* parents' erotic activity, which, according to Laplanche and Pontalis, provides "a representation of, and solution to, the major enigmas that confront the child." (The child in Freudian theory is always figured male unless Freud is exploring questions of female psychosexual development.) See Marshall, *Surprising Effects of Sympathy,* 51; citing Laplanche and Pontalis, "Fantasy and the Origins of Sexuality," *International Journal of Psychoanalysis* 49 (1968): 11, a translation of "Fantasme originaire, fantasie des origines, origine des fantasmes," *Les Temps modernes* 215 (1964): 1833–68.

20. Following Marx, Douglas argues that the sort of fetishism that springs up around both Charlotte and *Charlotte Temple* is the very dynamic that inaugurates mass culture itself. See Ann Douglas, introduction, Susanna Rowson, *"Charlotte Temple" and "Lucy Temple,"* ed. and introd. Ann Douglas (Philadelphia, 1794; New York: Penguin Books, 1991), vii–xliii, and *The Feminization of American Culture* (1977; New York: Avon Books, 1978). See also Cathy N. Davidson, "The Life and Times of *Charlotte Temple:* The Biography of a

Book," in *Reading in America: Literature and Social History,* ed. Cathy N. Davidson (Baltimore: Johns Hopkins University Press, 1989), 157–79; and Eva Cherniavsky, *That Pale Mother Rising: Sentimental Discourses and the Imitation of Motherhood in 19th-Century America* (Bloomington: Indiana University Press, 1995), 28–40.

21. For a richly suggestive explication of the notion of "nobody" as it applies to women writers and the rise of the English novel, see Catherine Gallagher, *Nobody's Story: The Vanishing Acts of Women Writers in the Marketplace, 1670–1820* (Berkeley and Los Angeles: University of California Press, 1994).

22. In registering a dynamic whereby a hegemonic collective identity is constituted at the expense of a heterogeneous difference that is noted, localized, and cast out, I borrow the concept of fetishism from psychoanalysis, arguing that the physics or poetics of fetishism can be extended beyond the level of intrapsychic symptomology and applied to illuminate interpsychic, as well as social and cultural, dynamics. The chorus's fetishistic operations against Eliza Wharton in *The Coquette* unfold in just this manner.

23. See Louise J. Kaplan, *Female Perversions: The Temptation of Emma Bovary* (New York: Doubleday, 1991), 123. Robert Stoller notes that, in fetishism, "objects take the place of narratives." See *Observing the Erotic Imagination* (New Haven: Yale University Press, 1985), 155, quoted in Valerie Steele, *Fetish: Fashion, Sex, and Power* (New York: Oxford University Press, 1996), 168.

24. See Douglas, *Feminization of American Culture.* Literary scholars and historians of the Anglo-American eighteenth century such as Terry Eagleton, Claudia Johnson, and G. J. Barker-Benfield note, as well, the increasing feminization of middle-class sociality in the period between 1750 and 1800. See, for example, Eagleton, *The Rape of Clarissa: Writing, Sexuality, and Class Struggle in Samuel Richardson* (Minneapolis: University of Minnesota Press, 1982), 13–15 and 95; Johnson, *Equivocal Beings,* 3–17; and Barker-Benfield, *Culture of Sensibility,* 37–103 and 154–214.

25. For a discussion of the epistolary continuum, see Janet Gurkin Altman, *Epistolarity: Approaches to a Form* (Columbus: Ohio State University Press, 1983). For recent feminist readings of epistolary fiction, see Nicola J. Watson, *Revolution and the Form of the British Novel, 1790–1825: Intercepted Letters, Interrupted Seductions* (Oxford: Clarendon Press, 1994); Peggy Kamuf, *Fictions of Feminine Desire: Disclosures of Heloise* (Lincoln: University of Nebraska Press, 1987); and Linda S. Kauffman, *Discourses of Desire: Gender, Genre, and Epistolary Fictions* (Ithaca: Cornell University Press, 1986).

26. Though grounding itself in male homosociality, *The Power of Sympathy* partakes of a feminist discourse as well. Significantly, such material is gothicized—buried alive—in the four interpolated tales regarding Miss Elizabeth Whitman (the historical figure whose story of seduction and abandonment is fictionalized in Foster's *The Coquette*), Ophelia, Fidelia, and Maria. Yet, as in the work of Charles Brockden Brown, particularly *Ormond*'s female homosocial discourse, in *The Power of Sympathy* digressions prove far more compelling than does the narrative proper.

William Hill Brown's feminist impulses have historical roots. In her discussion of his oblique criticism of the Federalist patriarchy of late-eighteenth-century Boston, Cathy N. Davidson strongly implies that the young novelist was sympathetic to the plight of women. She notes that the ruling cohort defended Perez Morton, a real-life seducer who is figured in the novel under the slightly veiled name of "Martin," against charges of culpability in the suicidal death of Frances Apthorp, his sister-in-law and paramour and the mother of his illegitimate child. Davidson argues that in the four inset narratives of seduction and abandonment (kidnapping, rape, and betrayal) that punctuate and refract the central plot of *The*

Power of Sympathy, the novelist clearly takes up the cause of the wronged woman. See *Revolution and the Word,* 101, and *"The Power of Sympathy* Reconsidered: William Hill Brown as Literary Craftsman," *Early American Literature* 10 (1975): 14–29.

27. See William Hill Brown, *The Power of Sympathy; or, The Triumph of Nature, Founded on Truth,* in *"The Power of Sympathy" and "The Coquette,"* ed. William S. Osborne (1789 and 1797; New Haven: College and University Press, 1968), 31; hereafter, cited parenthetically in the text.

28. See Hannah Webster Foster, *The Coquette,* ed. Cathy N. Davidson (1797; New York: Oxford University Press, 1986), 156; hereafter, cited parenthetically in the text.

29. I refer here to theoretically inflected readings of eighteenth-century American fiction written in the wake of Derrida's meditations on textuality and supplementarity, Lacan's explorations of the subject of the unconscious, and Foucault's interrogations of identity as constructed within and routed through disciplinary circuits of power and knowledge. In what follows, I draw on the work of Michael Warner, Jay Fliegelman, and Christopher Looby, the three scholars of early national literature whose work is most obviously informed by these continental influences.

30. The narrative manner of *Charlotte Temple* departs from direct epistolary form. In fact, Rowson uses multiple modes of storytelling in the novel: first-person narrative interjections intrude on a third-person dramatic presentation, which is also interlarded with a significant number of letters.

31. So Fliegelman characterizes Warner's argument. See *Declaring Independence,* 128. Warner's reasoning follows that of Jürgen Habermas in *The Structural Transformation of the Public Sphere: An Inquiry into a Category of Bourgeois Society,* trans. Thomas Burger (Cambridge, Mass.: Massachusetts Institute of Technology Press, 1992).

32. See Christopher Looby, *Voicing America: Language, Literary Form, and the Origins of the United States* (Chicago: University of Chicago Press, 1996), 3.

33. Describing an entire range of post-Revolutionary cultural forms inflected by voice or by the performance of affect, Fliegelman argues that Jefferson personifies the principle of charismatic vocality; Franklin plays a similar role for Looby. The abiding paradox that runs through *Declaring Independence* and *Voicing America* is the fact that voice for Jefferson and for Franklin is both an organic property of the physical body and a construction of textual performance: what Fliegelman characterizes as Jefferson's "pauses" in the Declaration of Independence and what Looby terms Franklin's various "interruptions" in the *Autobiography* become constitutive features of the doubly *embodied* nature of oral language in the period following the Founding, its sonorous origins in living beings and its textual articulation in printed form. For the impersonality of writing as a disembodied phenomenon, see Michael Warner, *The Letters of the Republic: Publication and the Public Sphere in Eighteenth-Century America* (Cambridge, Mass.: Harvard University Press, 1990), 38–42, 48, 62, and, in particular, 39. See also Larzer Ziff, *Writing in the New Nation: Prose, Print, and Politics in the Early United States* (New Haven: Yale University Press, 1991), in particular 90–106. And see Grantland S. Rice, *The Transformation of Authorship in America* (Chicago: University of Chicago Press, 1997), especially 1–13.

34. For a compelling discussion of letter writing as a central cultural form in the pre-Revolutionary and Revolutionary periods, see Virginia Stewart, "The Intercourse of Letters: Correspondence and American Identity in the Eighteenth Century" (Ph.D. diss., Northwestern University, 1997). My own reading of epistolarity in the post-Revolutionary period is indebted to Eagleton's formulations about the connection between letter writing and identity formation. See *Rape of Clarissa,* 52.

35. Epistolary novels cannot of course represent the physicality of pen and ink with

anything approximating mimetic fidelity. Nevertheless, it is an abiding convention that the extratextual audience is in a metaphorical sense reading over the shoulders of those fictional characters who receive handwritten missives, which bear the material traces of the "bodies" of their "authors" in the intratextual world—ink blots, excised passages, and even the stains of blood, sweat, and, most often, tears.

36. Habermas writes: "The literary form of [purely human relations] at the time was the letter. It is no accident that the eighteenth century became the century of the letter: through letter writing the individual unfolded himself in his subjectivity. . . . In the jargon of the time . . . the letter was considered an 'imprint of the soul,' a 'visit from the soul'; letters were to be written in the heart's blood, they practically were to be wept. From the beginning, the psychological interest increased in dual relation to both one's self and the other; self-observation entered a union partly curious, partly sympathetic with the emotional stirrings of the other I. The diary became a letter addressed to the sender, and the first-person narrative became a conversation with one's self addressed to another person. These were experiments with the subjectivity discovered in the close relationships of the conjugal family. Subjectivity, as the innermost core of the private, was always already oriented to an audience (*Publikum*)." See *Structural Transformation of the Public Sphere*, 48 and 49.

37. Outside the realm of epistolarity, the connection between gender and genre is most powerfully evident in the fiercely (male) homosocial universe of the picaresque fiction of the period, works like Royall Tyler's *Algerine Captive* (1797) and Hugh Henry Brackenridge's *Modern Chivalry* (1792–1819). Tabitha Tenney's *Female Quixotism* (1801) stands as a striking exception to this observation, but her book is a comedy and thus falls beyond my purview here.

38. For an explication of emblematic thinking as it originates in Puritan theology and particularly as it inflects American women's writing of the seventeenth and eighteenth centuries, see Breitwieser, *American Puritanism and the Defense of Mourning*, 17–70 and 210.

39. See Selzer's important "Saying Makes It So: Language and Event in Brown's *Wieland*," *Early American Literature* 12 (1978): 81–91. For a more detailed discussion of the relation between inner and outer voices, self and other, and problems of identity and identification in *Wieland*, see Julia Stern, "Parsing the First-Person Plural: Transformations of Gender and Voice in the Fiction of Charles Brockden Brown and Edgar Allan Poe" (Ph.D. diss., Columbia University, 1991), 19–28. Looby makes a similar argument about ventriloquism in his study of the connection between distortions of voice and processes of national legitimation in *Wieland;* he also notes the way in which Brown's generic borrowings, his conscription of the literary forms of the Old World, constitute another level of novelistic "ventriloquism." See *Voicing America*, 171.

40. For a compelling treatment of the problem of legitimation in *Wieland*, see Looby's reading in *Voicing America*, 146–74.

41. Brown is also clearly influenced by Ann Radcliffe and Mary Wollstonecraft, to name only the two most obviously influential British women writers whose works he read. I am grateful to Christopher Looby for providing me with this powerful language for thinking about Brown's emotional and narrative inhabitation of the American fictional forms developed by Rowson and Foster.

42. For a discussion of the claims for the *first*ness of Brown's novel, see Cathy N. Davidson, "Commodity and Communication: The First American Novel," in *Revolution and the Word*, 83–109.

43. Sterne's book marks the high-water moment of eighteenth-century Anglo-American fellow feeling as represented in novel form. By deploying contempt for Sterne's miniature masterpiece through the discourse of a vulgar and uneducated daughter of the

nouveau riche, Brown underscores the significance of *A Sentimental Journey* to his own development as a writer: "'I do not like the *title*,' said Miss Bourn. 'Why, my dear!' apostrophized the mother, 'you are mistaken; it is a very famous book.' 'Why my dear!' retorted the daughter, 'it is sentimental. I abominate everything that is sentimental—it is so unfashionable too.' 'I never knew before,' said Mr. Holmes [a minister], 'that wit was subject to the caprice of fashion.' 'Why Squire Billy,' returned Miss Bourn, 'who is just arrived from the center of politeness and fashion, says the bettermost geniuses never read any sentimental books; so you see sentiment is out of date'" (51). See Sterne, *A Sentimental Journey through France and Italy*, ed. Graham Petrie (1768; Harmondsworth: Penguin Books, 1986), 97–98.

44. David Marshall uses the "mirror of sympathy" as a controlling metaphor in his reading of Smith. See *Surprising Effects of Sympathy*, 5. See also Smith, *Theory of Moral Sentiments*, 22–23.

45. David Marshall explains that Rousseau, "arguing against the defenders of the stage who evoke catharsis and speak of the moral and sentimental education of audiences, . . . insists that the theater teaches us how to replace real sympathy with a painless representation or imitation of sympathy. This occurs not so much through an aestheticization of other people's suffering as through a false sense that one has fulfilled one's responsibilities toward others by responding in the playhouse. . . . Rousseau objected to the self-congratulatory sympathy that turns people into passive spectators both inside and outside the theater." See *Surprising Effects of Sympathy*, 143.

46. This reading of Brown's digression on the horrors of slavery is indebted to Michael Meranze, who generously shared with me his explication of "The Captive" in manuscript form.

47. In *Ormond*, Charles Brockden Brown plays out the drama of the white male citizen's transcendent privilege—the luxury of his physical disembodiment in the language of politics and government—and the political agency such release from the body entails. This peculiar state, one of liberation from the limitations of a particularized identity and, paradoxically, one of vast public authority, profoundly contrasts with the black slave's burden of hyperembodiment and social death, the weight of an identity that exacts not only strict exclusion from the fraternal community of citizens but also social invisibility. When Ormond, the villainous libertine, masquerades as an African American chimney sweep in order to spy on both his servants and the heroine, he collapses the seeming conflict between white male disembodiment and black social death in a fascinating moment that literalizes the citizen's transcendent subjectivity while it specifically exploits—on multiple levels—the slave's fatal embodiment. See chap. 4 for an elaboration of this remarkable scene and for a discussion of its metacritical significance as a commentary on taxonomies of race, class, and political privilege in the post-Revolutionary era. For the notion that the black self is hyperembodied in literary and cultural representations, see Lauren Berlant, "National Body/ National Brand: *Imitation of Life*," in *Comparative American Identities: Race, Sex, and Nationality in the Modern Text*, ed. Hortense J. Spillers (New York: Routledge, 1991), 110–40, in particular 112–14.

48. Surely Brown has not chosen at random the name Harrington for both democratic youth and libertine father: it evokes James Harrington (1611–77), the English political philosopher whose work on republicanism, particularly notions about reposing power in a landed gentry, plays a central role in the "ideological origins" of the American Revolution. The thwarting of the younger Harrington's "democratic" impulses suggests that Brown remains critical of Harrington's views—views that, though instrumental to the republican ideology of revolution, are ultimately conservative, contradicting the concepts of social

equality and liberty for which the new nation theoretically stands. See Bernard Bailyn, *The Ideological Origins of the American Revolution* (Cambridge, Mass.: Harvard University Press, 1967); and J. G. A. Pocock, *The Machiavellian Moment: Florentine Political Thought and the Atlantic Republican Tradition* (Princeton: Princeton University Press, 1975), especially 401–61.

49. See James B. Twitchell, *Forbidden Partners: The Incest Taboo in Modern Culture* (New York: Columbia University Press, 1987), 204.

50. Charles Brockden Brown, *Wieland; or, The Transformation: An American Tale*, vol. 1 of *The Novels and Related Works of Charles Brockden Brown: Bicentennial Edition*, eds. Sydney J. Krause and S. W. Reid (1798; Kent, Ohio: Kent State University Press, 1977), 87; hereafter, cited parenthetically in the text.

51. This application of manicheanism, which is central to my discussion of forging early American identity through a dialectic of difference, comes from Abdul R. Jan Mohamed's important essay "The Economy of Manichean Allegory: The Function of Racial Difference in Colonialist Literature," in *"Race," Writing, and Difference*, ed. Henry Louis Gates, Jr. (Chicago: University of Chicago Press, 1986), 78–106. The dualism of manicheanism pertains as well to melodramatic formations of identity, with which *The Plight of Feeling* is also concerned.

52. The phrase is Carroll Smith-Rosenberg's; see "Dis-covering the Subject of the 'Great Constitutional Discussion,' 1786–1788," *Journal of American History* 79 (December 1992): 841–73.

53. The incestuous circle is one from which the characters never fully extricate themselves: Clara marries, after all, a man with whom she has been raised as a sibling.

54. One could also argue, of course, that Theodore Wieland's transmutation into a murderous maniac constitutes the ultimate version of an otherness opening up within identity, a rift that far transcends distinctions of class and national origin (with which the novel is also concerned). Under the incestuous pressures of the inverted world of *Wieland*, a future based on identity proves impossible. As Tony Tanner notes: "incest not only involves a chaotic confusion of generations by sexuality bringing together precisely the two figures who should be kept apart when it comes to sexuality and mating; it also effectively refuses and nihilates that transaction, or interfamilial exchange of the daughter in marriage, on which society depends. It is the ultimate travesty of endogamy from which no healthy future can come. . . . The murder of the child by the father [is] a particularly vivid demonstration of a past violently destroying the future . . . What we witness is a hopeless and destructive conflation of people and bodies that should remain separate and unviolated if the family, and by extension society itself, is to have any clearly defined ongoingness." See *Adultery and the Novel: Contract and Transgression* (Baltimore: Johns Hopkins University Press, 1979), 28.

CHAPTER TWO

1. For this anthropological reading of the meaning of Indian captivity, see Richard Slotkin, *Regeneration Through Violence: The Myth of The American Frontier, 1600–1860* (Middletown, Conn.: Wesleyan University Press, 1973); see also Christopher Castilgia, *Bound and Determined: Captivity, Culture-Crossing and White Womanhood From Mary Rowlandson to Patricia Hearst* (Chicago: University of Chicago Press, 1996). For an important exploration of the connection between captivity and sentimental narratives of the seventeenth and eighteenth centuries, see Nancy Armstrong, "Why Daughters Die: The Racial Logic of American Sentimentalism," *The Yale Journal of Criticism* 7.2 (1994): 1–24.

2. My summary here is indebted to the extended discussion of eighteenth-century

French writings on the ethics of the drama in David Marshall, *The Surprising Effects of Sympathy: Marivaux, Diderot, Rousseau, and Mary Shelley* (Chicago: University of Chicago Press, 1988), particularly 105–77. Jay Fliegelman explores the implications of "natural theatricality" in American culture during roughly the same period; see *Declaring Independence*, especially 79–93.

Although we have no information about what Rowson read as she was working as a professional actress and playwright, we can speculate that Rousseau's charges that the drama encourages artificiality and promotes corruption, leveled in his antitheatrical writings of the late 1750s and early 1760s (which range beyond the "Letter To M. D'Alembert on the Theater" to include his "Discourse on the Origins of Inequality" and *The Social Contract*; indeed, Marshall suggests that Rousseau's entire oeuvre marks an extended reflection on the dangers of theatricality), were not unfamiliar to late-eighteenth-century Anglo-American intellectuals, artists, actors, and dramatists.

3. See "Letter to M. D'Alembert on the Theatre," in *Politics and the Arts: "Letter to M. D'Alembert on the Theatre,"* trans. and introd. Allan Bloom (1758; Ithaca: Cornell University Press, 1968), 34 and 131, note.

4. This discussion relies on Marshall's account of Diderot in *The Surprising Effects of Sympathy*, 133–34.

5. See Patricia L. Parker, *Susanna Rowson* (Boston: Twayne Publishers, 1986), "Chronology."

6. For the most imaginative recent account of this struggle as it manifests itself in fiction, see Christopher Looby, *Voicing America: Language, Literary Form, and the Origins of the United States* (Chicago: University of Chicago Press, 1996), 145–202.

7. For a selection of recent readings of *Clarissa* that foreground issues of gender, politics, and culture, see Lynda Zwinger, *Daughters, Fathers, and the Novel: The Sentimental Romance of Heterosexuality* (Madison: University of Wisconsin Press, 1991); Janice Hanley-Peritz, "Engendering the Exemplary Daughter: The Deployment of Sexuality in Richardson's *Clarissa*," *Daughters and Fathers*, eds. Lynda E. Boose and Betty S. Flowers (Baltimore: Johns Hopkins University Press, 1989), 181–207; Frances Ferguson, "Rape and the Rise of the Novel" *Representations* 20 (fall 1987): 88–112; Terry Eagleton, *The Rape of Clarissa: Writing, Sexuality, and the Class Struggle in Samuel Richardson* (Minneapolis: University of Minnesota Press, 1982); Terry Castle, *Clarissa's Ciphers: Meaning and Disruption in Richardson's "Clarissa"* (Ithaca: Cornell University Press, 1982); and William Beatty Warner, *Reading "Clarissa": The Struggles of Interpretation* (New Haven: Yale University Press, 1979).

8. See Jay Fliegelman, *Prodigals and Pilgrims: The American Revolution Against Patriarchal Authority, 1750–1800* (Cambridge: Cambridge University Press, 1982); Cathy N. Davidson, *Revolution and the Word: The Rise of the Novel in America* (New York: Oxford University Press, 1986); Shirley Samuels, "The Family, the State, and the Novel in the Early Republic," *American Quarterly* 38.3 (1986): 381–95 and *Romances of the Republic: Women, the Family, and Violence in the Literature of the Early American Nation* (New York: Oxford University Press, 1996); and Jane P. Tompkins, *Sensational Designs: The Cultural Work of American Fiction 1790–1860* (New York: Oxford University Press, 1985).

9. Those two tyrannies are explicated in the subtitle of the nonepistolary American versions of the novel: *The Arts of a Designing Villain* and *The Rigours of Parental Authority*. Fliegelman identifies five surviving early American imprints of *Clarissa*, all of which were published in the 1790s and four of which were based on the Philadelphia edition of 1791. He postulates that a chapbook edition of 1772 and an abridged edition (1786) were literally "read to pieces"—neither version of the novel survives. See *Prodigals and Pilgrims*, 86–87.

10. I use the term "Anglo-American" to emphasize the interconnectedness of the

trans-Atlantic British-colonial and postcolonial world in the period 1760–99, as well as to describe the dual national identity of Susanna Rowson. Rowson emigrated from England to America to join her father, an officer in the British Navy stationed in Boston, when she was five years old; she returned to England in 1778, after living under house arrest during the Revolution. *Charlotte Temple* was written in England in 1791, where it achieved almost no recognition or readership; it was only with the American publication of the novel in 1794, a year after Rowson returned to the new republic where she was to live the rest of her life, that the book took hold of the popular imagination and became a best-seller. Since the tale itself concerns the dangers of emigration, of leaving both mother and mother country, the fact of its international genealogy and its rejection by the English reading audience adds an interesting element to the maternal drama that, as I shall argue, the novel works out in both its plot and its narrative form. See Dorothy Weil, *In Defense of Woman: Susanna Rowson (1762–1824)* (University Park: Pennsylvania State University Press, 1976); and Patricia Parker, *Susanna Rowson.*

11. For an extended meditation on the subject of rebellious children figuring revolution in the early American novel, see Fliegelman, *Prodigals and Pilgrims,* particularly 83–92 and 261–64. For a reading of Charlotte Temple's "sin" as a "betrayal of what she herself calls her 'filial duty,'" see Zwinger, *Fathers, Daughters, and the Novel,* 52.

12. Zwinger sees a heterosexual rather than a homosocial Oedipal dynamic at work in *Charlotte Temple,* which she characterizes as a function of the father-daughter romance plot that grounds the sentimental novel. See *Fathers, Daughters, and the Novel,* 50–51.

13. Criticism of American sentimental novels of the late-eighteenth and mid-nineteenth centuries has so overemphasized the heterosexual father-daughter Oedipal plot that an equally powerful homosocial mother-daughter Oedipal dynamic has gone almost unrecognized. Scholars treating *Charlotte Temple* have neglected this central relationship precisely because Rowson's maternal principle remains disembodied and absent from the world of the framed narrative; instead, it operates as a vocal representation, working through the frame.

Late-eighteenth and mid-nineteenth-century American sentimental narratives written by women represent and foreground female subjectivity in ways that Freudian and Lacanian psychoanalysis have failed to account for theoretically; it has only been since the late 1970s that feminist psychoanalytic theorists have begun to rethink the "problem" of female subject formation. One of the central figures of this movement is Kaja Silverman, who highlights the significance of mother-daughter homosexual desire as a function of the negative Oedipal complex in *The Acoustic Mirror: The Female Voice in Psychoanalysis and Cinema* (Bloomington: Indiana University Press, 1988), 123–24. See also Marianne Hirsch, *The Mother/Daughter Plot: Narrative, Psychoanalysis, Feminism* (Bloomington: Indiana University Press, 1989), 50, 54, 57.

Alone in the criticism of *Charlotte Temple,* Blythe Forcey suggests the significance of the maternally figured narrator. Her focus, however, is on the role this persona plays in directing and diverting the audience's attention away from the potentially corrupting letters that circulate in the novel; she does not read the narrator's maternal intrusions as constituting their own independent narrative matter that would require a separate mode and method of exegesis. See Forcey, "*Charlotte Temple* and the End of Epistolarity," *American Literature* 63.2 (June 1991): 225–41.

14. In invoking Lacanian categories to talk about the relationship between fictive parents and children, and particularly, in making a case for a maternal figure who operates in the symbolic rather than in the imaginary, I follow Kaja Silverman. In *The Acoustic Mirror,* Silverman qualifies a central tenet of Lacanian theory, relocating maternal power away from

an ahistorical pre-Oedipal imaginary relation and onto a negative Oedipal symbolic dynamic that operates within the historical world of language and signification. Rowson's narrator, functioning as a *speaking* mother, would seem to disrupt Lacan's theoretical classification of the symbolic as the exclusive domain of the father. To postulate a maternal presence in the symbolic, or, as Diana Fuss puts it, "to symboliz[e] the female imaginary" is to qualify Lacan's reading of sexual difference in important ways. Feminist psychoanalytic critics have begun to deconstruct Lacan's formulations about the binary relationships between male/female and symbolic/imaginary on precisely these grounds. See Silverman, 123, and Fuss, *Essentially Speaking: Feminism, Nature, and Difference* (New York: Routledge, 1989), 60.

15. This important phrase was coined by Jane Tompkins in her discussion of the antebellum American novel. See Tompkins, *Sensational Designs*, xi–xix. The ongoing cultural power of *Charlotte Temple* may be attributed, in part, to its compelling representation of a fully rational speaking mother, the narrator of the frame.

16. Just as a film narrative has both visual and acoustic tracks, so too can a book, although it is important to add that readers receive such effects through the mediation of the graphic mode, via print, and not directly, as in film. Clearly, cinematic narrative is more literally and immediately mimetic of sensory detail than an unillustrated literary text could be. Despite this important distinction, I want to argue that the early American novel, in general, and *Charlotte Temple*, in particular, partake of a generic polymorphousness that features mimetic realism, epistolarity, and, most important, a melodramatic theatricality based on the centrality of descriptive visual tableaux. With the exception of Ann Douglas, who writes about *Charlotte Temple*'s connections to melodrama in her introduction to the Penguin edition of the novel, critics of *Charlotte Temple* have failed to acknowledge the complex generic multiplicity at work in what has been misread as an excruciatingly simple novel. While Charlotte's *story* may in fact be primitive, Rowson's *narratology* is anything but, and the building blocks of her tale derive from a rich and diffuse compendium of literary and theatrical sources.

In attempting to theorize how the narrator of *Charlotte Temple* performs her intrusive operations, I have borrowed from film studies the notions of the voice-over and of the visual and the acoustic regimes. Kaja Silverman writes compellingly of the gendered relationship between embodiment and cultural power. Following Mary Ann Doane, she argues that in classic Hollywood cinema, women are figured as being in overly close relationship to their own bodies, always associated with the physical and thus represented as claustrated within a relentlessly corporeal identity. Women rarely narrate the "voice-over," or disembodied vocal track, that punctuates and frames the visual regime of classic cinema. Instead, women are sunk in the body, while men enjoy a transcendent, quasi-theological relationship to the cultural symbolic by paradoxically coming into representation in disembodied form, as pure voice. Silverman writes: "the voice-over is privileged to the degree that *it transcends the body*." See *The Acoustic Mirror*, 49 and 164. See also Mary Ann Doane, *The Desire to Desire: The Woman's Film of the 1940s* (Bloomington: Indiana University Press, 1987). Rowson's literary use of the "voice-over" marks a departure, 150 years before the advent of talking pictures, from the gendered vocal identifications Silverman theorizes in *The Acoustic Mirror*. In *Charlotte Temple*, it is symbolic maternal subjectivity that "approaches a kind of theological threshold" (Silverman, 164) and that achieves its fullest power precisely by being disembodied.

17. The following circumstances significantly complicate any simple attempt to apply biographical material to a political exegesis of *Charlotte Temple*'s disapproval of unrighteous rebellion. Consider Rowson's British birth, her American childhood and adolescence before

and during the Revolution, and her mixed loyalties and allegiances as a prisoner of war under house arrest in Massachusetts, when she and her Tory father's family endured two years as captives who were, paradoxically, aided and abetted by patriot neighbors. Rowson's hostility to things French, personified in the portrait of the villainess La Rue, could support an antirevolutionary reading of the novel, but the politics with which I am concerned in *Charlotte Temple* pertain to gender and culture and not to party or even to nation—beyond the ways in which they point to a larger and more unified Anglo-American notion of nationalism that, in the 1790s, was finally eroding once and for all—though figures like Rowson who embraced trans-Atlantic affiliations were reluctant to relinquish either set of ties. By the early years of the nineteenth century, when Rowson began writing textbooks for her female academy, her allegiances could be said to be firmly American. For a detailed account of the author's complex negotiation of nationalist identifications, see Parker, *Susanna Rowson*, 67–82.

18. Susanna Rowson, *Charlotte Temple*, in *"Charlotte Temple" and "Lucy Temple,"* ed. and introd. Ann Douglas (Philadelphia, 1794; New York: Penguin Books, 1991), 26, my emphasis. All future references to this work will be made parenthetically in the text.

19. I will return to the subject of the narrator's tyrannical proclivities at the end of the chapter. Thanks to Jana Argersinger for this potent expression.

20. Benedict Anderson coins this phrase in his discussion of nationalism as a phenomena that begins affectively and, in a crucial sense, fictively. See *Imagined Communities: Reflections on the Origin and Spread of Nationalism* (1983; London: Verso, 1991), 6.

21. See Jean-Jacques Rousseau, *Julie, or the New Eloise. Letters of Two Lovers, Inhabitants of a Small Town at the Foot of the Alps*, trans. and abridged Judith H. McDowell (1761; University Park: Pennsylvania State University Press, 1968), 357–59.

22. See Jean Starobinski, *Jean-Jacques Rousseau: Transparency and Obstruction*, trans. Arthur Goldhammer (1971; Chicago: University of Chicago Press, 1988), 97.

23. Starobinski, 99.

24. See Jean-Jacques Rousseau, "A Discourse on the Origin of Inequality," in *The Social Contract and Discourses*, trans. and introd. G. D. H. Cole (London and New York: J. M. Dent and E. P. Dutton, 1973), 27–113.

25. The phrase "gendering of melancholia" is Juliana Schiesari's, as is the notion that affects can have "a cultural status" or, in the case of the sentimental, melodramatic, and gothic American novel about which I write, a cultural and representational history. See Schiesari, *The Gendering of Melancholia: Feminism, Psychoanalysis, and the Symbolics of Loss in Renaissance Literature* (Ithaca: Cornell University Press, 1992), ix.

26. The sexual downfall of the heroine of Hannah Foster's 1797 novel *The Coquette*, another tale of seduction, abandonment, and death based on the real life of Elizabeth Whitman, a woman poet from Connecticut, is also linked to excessive reading practices. In both the novel and the contemporary reports about Whitman herself, detractors attempting to trace the etiology of her ruin repeatedly point to the woman's overindulgence in certain (depraved) forms of reading; an imagination overworked and overheated by sensational novels has no defense against the seductive strains of the libertine. For extended treatment of the sentimental politics at work in *The Coquette*, see chap. 3.

27. The affective strata that organize *Charlotte Temple*—the way the novel's manifest narrative of rationality overlays its latent discourse of melancholy—are not unique to eighteenth-century American women's writing; in fact, they may be constitutive features of Enlightenment accounts of maternity and loss, found in both the fiction of sensibility and in biographical and autobiographical writings of the early Romantic period. Deployed in measured prose, William Godwin's extraordinary *Memoirs of the Author of the Rights of Woman*

(1798), an agonized personal meditation on the brilliant life and untimely death of Mary Wollstonecraft, who succumbed to postpartum septic infection days after delivering their daughter Mary (Godwin Shelley), marks a fascinating case in point. In this book, Godwin imagines his union with Wollestonecraft as the fusion of rationality and sensibility—a strategy meant to domesticate his wife before an unforgiving, moralistic middle-class audience. Ironically, Godwin's attempt to make her career appear more conventional than transgressive has a violent and destructive outcome: in doing so he disavows Wollestonecraft's own passionate commitment to female rationality—the cornerstone of *Vindication*. Compartmentalizing sense from sensibility at the level of both theme and narrative, the author of *The Enquiry Concerning Political Justice* reveals a mind steeped in the manichean politics of genre that suffuse his era and that I explore throughout this study.

In the tenth and final chapter of the *Memoirs*, Godwin exercises extraordinary efforts of control to ward off the gothicism of Wollstonecraft's story and the melancholia underwriting his response. He does so by conscripting the vocabulary of clinical gynecology, the language of science and reason, to articulate what is clearly emotional, horrific, and heartwrenching: the medical complications surrounding Wollstonecraft's delivery, and specifically, the account of her incompletely expelled placenta, the embedded fragments of which grow toxic and ultimately cause her death. Underlying Godwin's rendering of Wollstonecraft's demise are the mutiny and betrayal of the female reproductive functions which, as a result of the trauma of childbirth, become agents of the mother's own destruction, a monstrous fact that no amount of authorial restraint can rationalize away. Godwin writes: "and it was not till after two o'clock on Thursday morning, that I received the alarming intelligence, that the placenta was not yet removed, and that the midwife dared not proceed any further, and gave her opinion of calling a male practitioner. I accordingly went for Dr. Poignand, physician and man-midwife to the same hospital, who arrived between three and four hours after the birth of the child. He immediately proceeded to the extraction of the placenta, which he brought away in pieces, till he was satisfied that the whole was removed. In that point however it afterwards appeared that he was mistaken." The bereaved husband goes on to detail—in carefully tempered language—his growing sense of disaster and the attendant desperation, a despair that must be anatomized ("death does not always take place by that gradual process I had pictured to myself") in order to be survived. Though Wollstonecraft's physician (mistakenly) informs him that "the patient was surprisingly better," the philosopher

> now sought to suppress every idea of hope. The greatest anguish I have any conception of, consists in that crushing of a new-born hope which I had already two or three times experienced. If Mary recovered, it was well, and I should see it time enough. But it was too mighty a thought to bear being trifled with, and turned out and admitted in this abrupt way. I had reason to rejoice in the firmness of my gloomy thoughts, when, about ten o'clock on Thursday evening, Mr. Carlisle told us to prepare ourselves, for we had reason to expect the fatal event every moment. To my thinking, she did not appear to be in that state of total exhaustion, which I supposed to precede death; but it is probable that death does not always take place by that gradual process I had pictured to myself; a sudden pang may accelerate his arrival. She did not die on Thursday evening.

While Godwin's final utterance seems almost aphasic in its understatement, it is to my mind the most devastating locution in the entire *Memoirs*, suffused with the unspeakability—entire worlds of feeling disallowed from expression—that Eve Sedgwick identifies lying at the heart of gothic narrative. See Godwin, *Memoirs of the Author of the Rights of Woman*, ed.

and introd. Richard Holmes (1798; Harmondsworth: Penguin Books, 1987), 266, and 269–70; see also Sedgwick, *The Coherence of Gothic Conventions,* 4–5. Thanks to Faye Lederman, whose work on Godwin's *Memoirs* for my humanities seminar on the early American novel inspired these meditations.

28. See Susan K. Harris, *Nineteenth-Century American Women's Novels: Interpretive Strategies* (New York: Oxford University Press, 1990), 39–50.

29. In her introduction to the 1986 Oxford University Press edition of *Charlotte Temple,* Cathy N. Davidson asserts that the novel's foregrounding of separation anxiety during a period of widespread political upheaval goes far toward explaining the great psychological appeal of the novel. Davidson writes that "*Charlotte Temple* addressed the insecurities rampant in the early republic" (xii). My reading of the novel attempts to explore the psychological and cultural ramifications of Davidson's insight in specifically feminist (maternal) terms by focusing on the way that separation anxiety relates to mourning and operates at the level of novelistic form, particularly through narrative voice.

30. See Forcey, "*Charlotte Temple* and the End of Epistolarity," 241, for a different reading of the role of epistolarity in *Charlotte Temple.* While Forcey argues that epistolarity reaches the end of its historical efficacy as a viable narrative form in Rowson's book, it is my sense that the letter form operates as one of several cooperative generic discourses, all of which achieve full semiosis within *Charlotte Temple*'s framed narrative.

31. *Charlotte Temple*'s narrative functions textually through its embedded epistolarity, the inclusion and representation of multiple letters. The novel operates aurally in its employment of dialogue, in its use of narratorial interruption, and in its depiction of an oral tradition about Charlotte (the living legend) that springs up at the end of the novel and is passed from character to character by word of mouth. Finally, much of the power of *Charlotte Temple* is produced by the brilliant visual set pieces that punctuate the novel. Scenic tableaux proliferate: we see Charlotte swooning into the carriage at her elopement; we follow the pregnant and consumptive Charlotte, dressed in rags, as she makes her way through a blinding snowstorm to New York City; and we witness Montraville in the act of virtually throwing himself on Charlotte's open grave. At the end of the chapter, I will return to this claim about the relationship between generic multiplicity and Rowson's narrative strategy. For now, it is sufficient to note that the repetitive redeployment of the story of loss through multiple embedded genres within the novel form marks a crucial way in which this narrative moves between mourning and melancholia.

32. See Sigmund Freud, "Mourning and Melancholia," 1917, in *The Standard Edition of the Complete Psychological Works of Sigmund Freud,* trans. and ed. James Strachey, in collaboration with Anna Freud, assisted by Alix Strachey and Alan Tyson. 24 vols. (London: Hogarth Press, 1953–74), 14:237–58.

33. In "Mourning and Melancholia," Freud argues that the latter condition is a pathological disturbance of the mourning process in which the ego, unable to decathect from the lost object, introjects that object (incorporates the object cathexis) into the ego. The superego, enraged over the abandonment suffered in the external world, turns its fury against the encrypted lost object, which, by virtue of the process of introjection, has now become part of the survivor's self; melancholia is the process of internal self-devouring, the replaying of loss and punishment that occurs in the inner world of the mourner who cannot let go in order to carry on.

34. See Linda K. Kerber, *Women of the Republic: Intellect and Ideology in Revolutionary America* (Chapel Hill: University of North Carolina Press, 1980) for a discussion of the post-Revolutionary conditions that initially opened up and soon afterward shut down American optimism over expanded opportunities for women in the late-eighteenth century.

Many factors contributed to cultural anxiety in the period. Among the most important were discontent over the ratification of the Constitution among Republicans; Federalist dread of faction; xenophobia in the face of the sudden emigration of Continental refugees in flight from European revolution; Federalist fear of French Jacobin influences infecting the new republic; a series of yellow fever epidemics in the Northeast; and concern over the possibility of an economic depression.

35. Kaja Silverman's theories about gender, the Oedipal phase, and melancholia are pertinent here. In *The Acoustic Mirror*, Silverman argues that, for females, the Oedipal phase, in which the girl child must relinquish her homosexual object cathexis to the mother in order to embrace a heterosexual identification, involves a melancholic form of loss. Since the girl must give up her connection to that which she also *is*, the loss constitutes a *loss of self* and thus never can be mourned fully. Instead, the loss is taken inside the self, incorporated as a central feature of female identity. For Silverman, to be a heterosexual female is to be, by definition, melancholic (155–59). While this hypothesis demands historicization, it nevertheless constitutes a compelling theoretical backdrop to my speculations about why the melancholic substrate of *Charlotte Temple* has appealed to readers across different historical eras. This is not to suggest that female melancholia is a transhistorical phenomena; rather, I am attempting to locate its particular social construction within the formation of the excluded American subject during the post-Revolutionary period. In that regard, women constitute the test case of melancholic subject formation as routed through "otherness," from which the cases of African Americans, Native Americans, and aliens would follow.

36. J. Laplanche and J.-B. Pontalis, *The Language of Psychoanalysis*, trans. Donald Nicholson-Smith (New York: W. W. Norton, 1973), 488.

37. The phrase comes from Mitchell Breitwieser's discussion of mourning in *American Puritanism and the Defense of Mourning: Religion, Grief, Ethnology, and Mary White Rowlandson's Captivity Narrative* (Madison: University of Wisconsin Press, 1990). My understanding of Freud's "Mourning and Melancholia" has been enriched by Breitwieser's powerful meditation on the operations and reprobation of grief in early American culture.

38. Another species of repetition goes on at the symptomatic level, in the lived life of the patient, which Freud calls "acting out" and which he contrasts with "working-through" in the "Remembering, Repeating" essay. "Acting out" refers to the compulsive dramatization and repetition of conflict that remains resistant to treatment or "working-through." *Charlotte Temple* encompasses both principles in its narrative method, staging episodes of "acting out" in its melodramatic tableaux. Such theatrical moments resist incorporation into the fantasy of transparent relations at work in *Charlotte Temple*. In contrast, the narrator's perseverative narrative manner—her obsessive retelling of Charlotte's story through the multigeneric discourses that lace the novel—is itself symptomatic, functioning as a "represented" principle of working-through within the fictive universe. We can thus juxtapose the theatricality of "acting out" with the mournfulness of "working-through," a division that clarifies the conflicting affective impulses contained within *Charlotte Temple*, though it is important to add that the working-through is never actually achieved—that mourning becomes melancholia.

39. Ann Douglas was the first critic to note Charlotte's arrested psychic development, "But, at bottom, Charlotte is looking for a parent, not a lover; she is a child in years and even more so in mind. Her enormous pathos in the later portions of the story comes from our sense of her as a helpless child, a trapped and defenseless animal, looking frantically to see where it can reattach and be safe. . . . Without love—without, to be more precise, symbiosis—the child must die." See Douglas's introduction to *"Charlotte Temple" and "Lucy*

Temple," xxviii. My reading takes off from Douglas's formulations, which she generously shared with me in manuscript form prior to the publication of her introduction to the 1991 Penguin edition of *Charlotte Temple.*

40. In *The Acoustic Mirror,* Silverman goes on to assert that, in a stunning act of reversal and cooptation, the patriarchal symbolic, represented by and through classic Hollywood cinema, has seized on what rightly belongs to the female subject dwelling in the Lacanian imaginary and enlisted it in the task of shoring up *male* subjectivity in the symbolic. Thus, the cinematic voice-over, almost exclusively enunciated by a male speaker, attempts to re-conscript the maternal envelope for patriarchal aggrandizement (72, 76, 164).

Without wanting to seem unmotivated in my use of what might, on first appearance, look like disparate or eclectic feminist film theories mustered for the sake of making local points, I have chosen to rely on the work of Kaja Silverman and E. Ann Kaplan with a specific purpose in mind. Silverman's claims are powerfully illustrated by examples from film narrative, but such illustrations are not limited to the cinematic text. Her readings hold equally true for exegesis of gothic literary narrative, which, like *Charlotte Temple*'s hybrid sentimental-melodramatic form, constitutes another popular eighteenth-century mode of women's writing.

Kaplan's work interests me primarily because her theorization of melodramatic "wom-en's films" originates with readings of female-authored sentimental and melodramatic novels of this period and because her focal emphasis is on cultural representations of mater-nity. In a chapter entitled "The 'Resisting' Text Within the Patriarchal 'Feminine': Nine-teenth-century Women's Writing and the 'Maternal Woman's Film' in the Silent Era," Kap-lan performs a literary analysis on *Uncle Tom's Cabin,* the most mother-centered American novel of the mid-nineteenth century, before proceeding to explore the ways in which its sentimental and melodramatic features were adopted by silent film directors like Griffith and Vidor.

A historical logic motivates both my interest in a feminist film theory that derives from a literary understanding of melodrama and my use of such theory to reread an eighteenth-century sentimental novel that deploys the central motifs of melodrama. As a theatrical genre that originated in post-Revolutionary France, the melodramatic form comes into cul-tural prominence at the very moment that the post-Richardsonian Anglo-American senti-mental novel is taking hold in the new republic. Susanna Rowson's experiences as an actress and a playwright in late-eighteenth-century Britain and America help account for her thor-ough knowledge of the structure of melodrama and make sense of the ease with which she embraces melodramatic plotting and tableaux in *Charlotte Temple.* See Kaplan, *Motherhood and Representation: The Mother in Popular Culture and Melodrama* (London: Routledge, 1992), 124–48 and Peter Brooks, *The Melodramatic Imagination: Balzac, Henry James, Melodrama, and the Mode of Excess* (1976; New York: Columbia University Press, 1984), 14–20. See also Christine Gledhill, "The Melodramatic Field," in *Home is Where the Heart Is: Studies in Melodrama and the Woman's Film,* ed. Christine Gledhill (London: British Film Institute, 1987), 14–22, 24–25, and 33–34.

41. Susanna Rowson's own biography constitutes a haunting background for the ma-ternal object relations I am attempting to trace: her mother, Susanna Musgrove Haswell, died of puerperal fever shortly after her daughter's birth; when the child Rowson joined her father in America five years later, he had married a woman whom she did not like. During the Revolutionary War, the Haswell family were interned as loyalists, which so demoralized both Haswell and his second wife that they were incapable of earning a living for the family; thus, it fell to the adolescent Rowson to care for and support the woman who had taken her

mother's place. In her own marriage, years later, Rowson was ultimately the sole financial provider, as a writer of novels, plays, and patriotic songs and as the successful headmistress of a girls' school that was open for over twenty years; having no children of her own, Rowson nevertheless supported her husband William's illegitimate son with her earnings and, toward the end of her life, took in two surrogate teenage daughters, one the child of a relative, the other the orphaned daughter of a theatrical colleague. For recent biographies of Rowson, see Weil and Parker.

I would assert that the aura of wish-fulfillment enveloping the maternal-filial object relations in *Charlotte Temple* constitutes Rowson's imaginative effort to work through her significant psychic losses via the figure of the narrator. The multiple subject positions I have attempted to unveil in this passage speak to the complexity of her own identifications in such a mother-daughter hierarchy; one could argue that, in some crucial way, Susanna Musgrove Haswell Rowson was never allowed to be *either* the young daughter of a mother *or* the mother of a young daughter and that the maternal grief that so suffuses *Charlotte Temple* is a projection of sorrow for herself.

42. Charlotte will die after giving birth to her baby daughter; the cause of death is unspecified, but we know that she has been wasting away during her pregnancy, both from the hunger and want and from the despair caused by Montraville's neglect. The unmarried, "uncovered" woman, whose education is incomplete and whose middle-class origins make the prospect of undertaking manual labor unlikely, cannot fend for herself. La Rue will ultimately die of the pox, contracted, so it would seem, through sexual contact. These two diametrically opposed female constructions of a male-dominated culture, patriarchy's purest and most-depraved products, are ultimately destroyed by the system that has both created them and that ultimately has used them up.

43. The ethos of female homosociality suffusing *Charlotte Temple* extends from the characterological dynamics at work within its realist narrative to the theological universe governing the story; the narrator enumerates a pantheon of deities, all of whom are women: "Benevolence," "Misfortune" (xlix), "chaste Queen of Night" (5), "Madam Prudence" (17), "Love," "Hymen," "Plenty," her handmaid "Prudence," "Hospitality" (21), "Peace," "Health," "Content," "Love" [again] (22), "giddy flutterers," "thoughtless daughters of folly," "children of dissipation," "Humility," "Filial Piety," "Conjugal Affection," "Industry," "Benevolence" and "yonder lovely Virgin . . . Content" (32), "her parent Religion," "her sisters Patience and Hope" (33), "Charity" (69), "the syren [sic] Hope" (75), artful "Circe" (76), "Medusa," and "Gorgon" (112). The narrator's epic catalogue of goddesses embodies the entire spectrum of virtues and vices: her female pantheon is not purely benevolent. Most significantly, the narrator displaces the Christian family romance of heavenly father and human child and substitutes a mother and child relation that represents the bond between herself and the reader. Thus, these female deities pluralize the singular patriarchal God and thereby evoke a revolution on a grand scale, forwarding the campaign against brutal patriarchy by deposing the male God and the attendant social order authored by human incarnations of male power. Thanks to Jana Argersinger for help with these formulations.

44. See Kathleen W. Jones, "Mother's Day: The Creation, Promotion, and Meaning of a New Holiday in the Progressive Era," *Texas Studies in Language and Literature* 22.2 (summer 1980): 175–196; and Leigh Eric Schmidt, "The Commercialization of the Calendar: American Holidays and the Culture of Consumption, 1870–1930," *The Journal of American History* 78.3 (December 1991): 887–916.

45. Kaplan continues by noting that "the indulgent mother takes something for herself by satisfying needs for love, nurturance and merging through the child; while the phallic mother satisfies needs for power that her ideal function prohibits. . . . Like the master-slave

psychic phenomenon analyzed by Hegel and then Franz Fanon, in which those who are (or were) slaves identify with the master position once freed, mothers take out their subjection to their husbands [La Rue will take out her subjection under patriarchy itself] on their children. They identify with the Law of the Father when interacting with the child, who is now given over to the 'slave' position." See Kaplan, *Motherhood and Representation*, 47–48, my interpolation.

46. See Madelon Sprengnether, *The Spectral Mother: Freud, Feminism, and Psychoanalysis* (Ithaca: Cornell University Press, 1990), 5, and 219, for discussion of the fusional desire for the mother that is the death instinct. See also Douglas, who writes, "The power of [Charlotte's] story comes from a kind of death wish; for what is the death wish but the drive to escape separation, individuation, and maturation?" (introduction, xxx).

47. See Forcey, "*Charlotte Temple* and The End of Epistolarity," 231–32, 234.

48. Louisa May Alcott, *Little Women*, ed. Elaine Showalter (1868; New York: Penguin Books, 1989), 437.

49. It is important to distinguish Rowson's use of embedded letters as inner texts in *Charlotte Temple* from the correspondence that constitutes the exclusive narrative matter of works like *The Power of Sympathy* and *The Coquette*. In *Charlotte Temple*, letters fall on the textual side of the continuum in the early American novel that unfolds between embodied voice and disembodied writing. At the opposite side of this spectrum lies the voice of the narrator, which depends on the fantasy of presence that underlies the Rousseauvian poetics and politics of Rowson's book. Chap. 3 will explore the ways in which voice in *The Coquette* can also be a function of a textualized signature, the fiction that the handwritten letter is itself a form of affective transparency.

50. See the preface and first chapters of Brooks, *The Melodramatic Imagination*, ix–23.

51. Rowson's narrator informs us at the beginning of the novel that La Rue had eloped from a French convent with a young officer and had lived openly with several men before experiencing the "repentance" that convinced Mme Du Pont to employ her as the teacher of girls (23).

52. Rousseau elaborates his theory of natural compassion in "A Discourse on the Origin of Inequality," 66–67.

53. I stress *apparent* unfeelingness to emphasize that La Rue's insensibility is itself a performance, a function of her unwavering theatricality; far from being devoid of feeling for her former pupil, the Frenchwoman "had ever been fully sensible of Charlotte's sense and virtue" (121). Nevertheless, she emphatically maintains that the raving girl is a stranger, dramatically denying the fact of any prior relation. Ignoring her own stirrings of humanity, La Rue elects to remain as consistently "unnatural" in the Rousseauvian sense as she has throughout her depraved career. But in so doing she commits the ultimate act of hubris for an actor: disregarding the feelings of the audience. So enmeshed is La Rue in the web of her own artifice that she brazenly spurns the desires of those assembled in the Crayton home who crave nothing less than a spectacular display of compassion.

In an editorial aside striking for its absence of emotion, the narrator describes La Rue's disavowal of Charlotte not as a failure of mercy but as a strategic misjudgment of the power of sympathy inhering in those who bear witness to her cruelty. Characterizing the deed an improper "reflection," the narrator evokes the images of maternal mirroring that punctuate the novel's discourse of fellow feeling. Few would argue that disclaiming recognition of a child one has mentored marks a chilling betrayal of sympathy. But in even more pragmatic terms, the Frenchwoman has miscalculated the fundamental values of the community in which she has artfully risen to prominence, failing to reckon how in the eighteenth-century Anglo-American world, compassion figures as a beneficial investment: "Had she reflected properly, she would have afforded the poor girl protection; and by enjoining her silence, ensured it by acts of repeated kindness" (121). Following Adam Smith, Rowson would seem to suggest that fellow feeling and profitability, far from being at odds, actually flourish in the service of each other.

How, finally, do we explain the narrator's uncharacteristic withholding of venomous outrage as she contemplates La Rue's hardheartedness or understand her hyperrationality in the face of the Frenchwoman's gothic absence of maternal impulses? Rowson's narrator leaves such eruptions of outraged sensibility to Mrs. Crayton's servants and hangers-on because, at this very late moment in *Charlotte Temple*, she has already deputized the internal auditors of the story to do her emotional work. Excessive sentiment is circulated through appropriate channels (from the domestics to Mrs. Beauchamp to the doctor) and safely framed within the world of the tale, or so it would seem. But because the narrator's feelings are suffused with melancholia, this affective division of labor can never be successfully transferred or, finally, concluded, and, in that regard, *Charlotte Temple* remains a novel that does not close. Thanks to Mitchell Breitwieser for several important exchanges about this passage.

54. See Rousseau, "A Discourse on the Origins of Inequality," 67.

55. See Philip Fisher, *Hard Facts: Setting and Form in the American Novel* (New York: Oxford University Press, 1985), 104–107.

56. See Rousseau, "A Discourse on the Origins of Inequality," 66.

57. In considering Rowson's intellectual debt to Rousseau, it is hardly irrelevant to note that, at the end of the extended passage on spectacles of suffering from the "Discourse on Inequality," Rousseau characterizes compassion as a "gentle voice" (68), an association that evokes the narrator, Rowson's ultimate incarnation of "natural" and transparent relations. I will return to this connection in the following pages.

58. See *The Surprising Effects of Sympathy*, 105–34.

59. Marshall describes the problem succinctly: "Theater, in Rousseau's view, does more than mirror the theatrical representations and relations of cosmopolitan life. It reproduces these representations and relations outside as well as inside the playhouse. Theater is especially dangerous for women, according to Rousseau, because it plays on their already enured character. . . . In addition to using her arts to disguise her thoughts and desires, a woman (in Rousseau's terms) seems condemned to live outside herself, in the regards and the judgments of others. . . . Once on the stage, then, women seem unbearably theatrical as they double what Rousseau sees as their inherent dissimulation, *amour-propre*, and exhibitionism." See *The Surprising Effects of Sympathy*, 140.

60. "Discourse on the Origins of Inequality," 86.

61. "Discourse on the Origins of Inequality," 86–87.

62. See Davidson, "The Life and Times of *Charlotte Temple:* The Biography of a Book," in *Reading in America: Literature and Social History*, ed. Cathy N. Davidson (Baltimore: Johns Hopkins University Press, 1989), 157–79; Douglas, introduction, xxxvi; and Cherniavsky, *That Pale Mother Rising: Sentimental Discourses and the Imitation of Motherhood in 19th-Century America* (Bloomington: Indiana University Press, 1995), 24–25.

CHAPTER THREE

1. While never rivaling *Charlotte Temple*'s popularity, *The Coquette* nevertheless becomes an impressive steady seller in its own right: William S. Osborne notes in his preface to the text that there were thirty editions of the novel by 1840. See "Note on the Texts," in William Hill Brown, *The Power of Sympathy,* and Hannah W. Foster, *The Coquette,* in *"The*

Power of Sympathy" and "The Coquette," ed. William S. Osborne (1789 and 1797; New Haven: College and University Press, 1968), 25. For the history of *Charlotte Temple*'s nearly universal appeal and for the notion of the steady seller, see Cathy N. Davidson, *Revolution and the Word: The Rise of the Novel in America* (New York: Oxford University Press, 1986), 17; see also Davidson, "The Life and Times of *Charlotte Temple:* The Biography of a Book," in *Reading in America: Literature and Social History*, ed. Cathy N. Davidson (Baltimore: Johns Hopkins University Press, 1989), 157–79.

2. See René Girard, *Violence and the Sacred*, trans. Patrick Gregory (1972; Baltimore: Johns Hopkins University Press, 1977). See also Susan L. Mizruchi, *The Science of Sacrifice: American Literature and Modern Social Theory* (Princeton: Princeton University Press, 1997).

3. I borrow this phrasing from David Marshall. See his *The Surprising Effects of Sympathy: Marivaux, Diderot, Rousseau, and Mary Shelley* (Chicago: University of Chicago Press, 1988), 3.

4. Eva Cherniavsky similarly asserts that Eliza "envisions her power to feel not as the medium of social interpellation, but as the medium of social relations between women." Cherniavsky's notion of social interpellation comes from Louis Althusser's formulation "that ideology 'acts' or 'functions' in such a way that it 'recruits' subjects among the individuals (it recruits them all), or 'transforms' the individuals into subjects (it transforms them all) by that very precise operation which I have called *interpellation* or hailing, and which can be imagined along the lines of the most commonplace everyday police (or other) hailing: 'Hey, you there!.'" The Althussarian dynamic Cherniavsky identifies approximates my notion of "republican sympathy," while what she characterizes as social relations between women comes closer to what I term "protoliberal sympathy." The distinction, with all its attendant ideological freight, would suggest that republican sympathy is coercive and tyrannical, while protoliberal sympathy enables freedom. While such facile comparisons are to a large degree congruent with the general contours of Foster's novel, the brilliance of *The Coquette* inheres in its representation of the limits and dangers of liberty as well as of social restriction. See Cherniavsky, *That Pale Mother Rising: Sentimental Discourses and the Imitation of Motherhood in 19th-Century America* (Bloomington: Indiana University Press, 1995), 39. See also Althusser, *Lenin and Philosophy and Other Essays*, trans. Ben Brewster (New York: Monthly Review Press, 1971), 174.

5. For the republican reading, see Kerber, *Women of the Republic: Intellect and Ideology in Revolutionary America* (Chapel Hill: University of North Carolina Press, 1980), 248–49; Pettengill, "Sisterhood in a Separate Sphere: Female Friendship in Hannah Webster Foster's *The Coquette* and *The Boarding School*," *Early American Literature* 27.3 (1992): 185–203; Lewis, "The Republican Wife: Virtue and Seduction in the Early Republic," *William and Mary Quarterly* 44 (October 1987): 689–721; and Carroll Smith-Rosenberg, "The Female World of Love and Ritual," *Signs* 1 (1975), reprinted in *Disorderly Conduct: Visions of Gender in Victorian America* (New York: Oxford University Press, 1985). For the protoliberal interpretation, see Davidson, introduction to *The Coquette*, by Hannah Webster Foster, ed. Cathy N. Davidson (New York: Oxford University Press, 1986); and Smith-Rosenberg, "Domesticating 'Virtue': Coquettes and Revolutionaries in Young America," in *Literature and the Body: Essays on Persons and Populations*, ed. Elaine Scarry (Baltimore: Johns Hopkins University Press, 1988). For two essays that provide an authoritative overview of this debate, see Robert Shalhope's "Toward a Republican Synthesis: The Emergence of an Understanding of Republicanism in American Historiography," *William and Mary Quarterly* 29 (January 1972): 48–80; and his "Republicanism and Early American Historiography," *William and Mary Quarterly* 39 (April 1982): 334–56.

6. Pettengill argues against a reading that would "demonize, in Foucauldian fashion,"

the "complex function of sisterhood" in *The Coquette*. This impulse to reject as demonic a reading the text fully supports points to the odd manicheanism that haunts criticism of the early American novel, a criticism that repeats at the level of interpretive practice the very conflicts that split the political figures of the Federalist era itself. See Pettengill, "Sisterhood in a Separate Sphere," 199.

7. Michael T. Gilmore identifies this ideological double vision in the post-Revolutionary novel as a feature of the genre itself: "The letters of the early Republic should be described as republican and communal as much as pre-Romantic." He continues, "native fiction contained its own volatile mixture of progressive and premodern features." See Gilmore, "The Literature of the Revolutionary and Early National Periods," in *The Cambridge History of American Literature, Volume I: 1590–1820*, ed. Sacvan Bercovitch (Cambridge: Cambridge University Press, 1994), 544, 620.

8. For a discussion of emerging versus dominant culture, see Raymond Williams, *Marxism and Literature* (Oxford: Oxford University Press, 1977), 121–27. At this early moment in my argument, I borrow from Smith-Rosenberg the distinction between emerging liberalism as an economic theory and republicanism as a political vision in order to emphasize a particular dichotomy. At other points in the chapter, however, I will allude to republican economic thinking and protoliberal political ideology as well. Rather than being precise terms with fixed meanings, republicanism and liberalism constitute the subjects of an ongoing historical debate. See Carroll Smith-Rosenberg, "Red, Black, and Female: Constituting the American Subject," *Social Science Information* 30 (June 1991): 341–57, particularly 342; and "Dis-covering the Subject of the 'Great Constitutional Discussion,' 1786–1789," *Journal of American History* 79 (December 1992): 841–73. See also Joyce Appleby, *Liberalism and Republicanism in the Historical Imagination* (Cambridge, Mass.: Harvard University Press, 1992).

9. See Cherniavsky, *That Pale Mother Rising*, 40.

10. Hannah Webster Foster, *The Coquette*, ed. Cathy N. Davidson (1797; New York: Oxford University Press, 1986), 44. Hereafter, all citations will be to this edition of the novel and will be noted parenthetically in the text.

11. Eve Kosofsky Sedgwick, *The Coherence of Gothic Conventions* (New York: Methuen, 1986), 5. Sedgwick notes that a constitutive relationship exists between formal dynamics in gothic narrative and the issues of content that "haunt" the genre.

12. See Ann Douglas, *The Feminization of American Culture* (1977; New York: Avon Books, 1978), 7–13, 17–49.

13. See Frank Shuffelton, "Mrs. Foster's *The Coquette* and the Decline of the Brotherly Watch," *Studies in Eighteenth-Century Culture* 16 (1986): 211–24. Sharon M. Harris cites Michel Foucault's *Discipline and Punish* in her description of the surveillance of the community, evoking the panopticon as "an architectural structure that 'induce[s] in the [prison] inmate a conscious and permanent visibility that assures the automatic functioning of power,'" and arguing that, "[w]hile Eliza does not confront a tangible structure," "like this," "the social panoptic of everyone observing and commenting on her actions also produces what Foucault terms 'homogenous effects of power.'" The concerns of Harris's article, with its emphasis on women's subversive political voice, come very close to my own; my argument diverges in its reading of the novel's conclusion, which I see as a relatively bleak prognosis for women's freedom in the post-Revolutionary era. Harris's interpretation, in contrast, is based on an optimistic understanding of the intentions of the female chorus as they are expressed in the final letter of the novel. See Foucault, *Discipline and Punish: The Birth of the Prison*, trans. Alan Sheridan (New York: Viking, 1979), 201, 222, quoted in Harris, "Hannah Webster Foster's *The Coquette:* Critiquing Franklin's America," in *Redefining The*

Political Novel: American Women Writers, 1797–1901, ed. Sharon M. Harris (Knoxville: University of Tennessee Press, 1995), 15.

14. See Richard L. Bushman, *The Refinement of America: Houses, Persons, Cities* (New York: Vintage, 1992), 81. Mrs. Laiton's query about Eliza's loss, while in keeping with certain prevailing concepts of sensibility, violates all notions of delicacy and taste as Bushman describes them, particularly the idea that delicacy seeks to "protect people from every hurt"—a veneer of sensibility obscures the essentially hostile nature of her remarks.

15. David Waldstreicher makes a similar observation in "'Fallen Under My Observation': Vision and Virtue in *The Coquette*," *Early American Literature* 27.3 (1992): 204–18, especially 210.

16. Cherniavsky argues that the reader incorporates Charlotte Temple; here, I extend her analysis of female introjection to include the audience's incorporation of the narrator as well. See *That Pale Mother Rising*, 38.

17. See Smith-Rosenberg, "Domesticating 'Virtue,'" 169.

18. In a maneuver that is probably far from her manifest intentions in *The Coquette*, Foster inverts Jeffersonian fantasies about Federalist ideology. The Jeffersonian opposition to the Federalist hegemony remains convinced that in the eyes of Adams, Hamilton, and other national leaders, the good of the country depends on the preeminence of an elite group of natural aristocrats, the only figures fit to govern the republic and thereby safeguard its virtue. The anti-Federalists, in contrast, believe that in the name of such policy the Federalists sacrifice the good of the many for the domination of the few. In the contracted social universe of Foster's novel, the privileged chorus oddly represents the "many," while that majority ultimately figures Eliza Wharton (who technically numbers herself among them), as one of the "few." According to Foster's reversal of the logic of Federalism, the will and the life of the "few" must be sacrificed to preserve the coherence and virtue of the "many," despite the fact that those "many" represent a powerful cultural elite. More typically, scholars read Eliza as a figure for the Jeffersonian individual who suffers from the tyranny of the Federalist majority, as rarified and tiny as that majority might be. I am indebted to Michael Meranze for bringing this provocative reversal to my attention.

19. See Smith-Rosenberg, "Domesticating 'Virtue,'" 171.

20. David Hume writes: "Where two orders of men, such as the nobles and people, have a distinct authority in government, not very accurately balanced and modelled, they naturally follow a distinct interest; nor can we reasonably expect a different conduct, considering that degree of selfishness implanted in human nature. It requires great skill in a legislator to prevent such parties." See "Of Parties in General," in *Essays: Moral, Political, and Literary*, ed. Eugene F. Miller (Indianapolis: Liberty Classics, 1985), 59.

James Madison, the principal American disciple of Hume, writes several essays on faction in the late 1780s that are published in *The Federalist*, the most famous of which is Number 10. In these essays he argues, *pace* Hume, that a multiplicity of interests would be represented by a multiplicity of parties, which would act as checks on each other. Approximately five years later (1792–93), in a very different political mood, Madison returns to the subject in a series of pieces for Philip Freneau's republican newspaper, the *National Gazette*. No longer identifying himself as a Federalist, Madison asserts that party divisions are based on principle, not interest, and must be accepted as such. He then goes on to identify the danger of factionalism not in the dynamic of conflict, per se, but in one of the two parties (reduced from many). In the words of Stanley Elkins and Eric McKitrick, "the struggle [is] hardly less than one between good and evil. The 'evils' of party have thus been drastically relocated. They reside not in 'parties' but in *one* of the parties, and the real evil—no longer figurative but palpable and visible—is even more monstrous than imagined." The very language with which Elkins and McKitrick describe this conflict, particularly the notions of "palpable and visible evil" and of monstrosity itself, supports my gothic characterization of the affective ethos of the period. See Elkins and McKitrick, *The Age of Federalism: The Early American Republic, 1788–1800* (New York: Oxford University Press, 1993), 266, 268.

21. See Elkins and McKitrick, *The Age of Federalism*, 487, 263, 266, 265.

22. See Albert Furtwangler, *American Silhouettes: Rhetorical Identities of the Founders* (New Haven: Yale University Press, 1987), 85–114.

23. See Elkins and McKitrick, *The Age of Federalism*, 292.

24. Mrs. Richman warns Eliza against joining the major in his "party formed avowedly for pleasure" (14), and, later, she rails poetically against "Confed'racies in vice, or leagues in pleasure" (25).

25. See Abdul Jan Mohamed, "The Economy of Manichean Allegory: The Function of Racial Difference in Colonialist Literature," in *"Race," Writing, and Difference*, ed. Henry Louis Gates, Jr. (Chicago: University of Chicago Press, 1985), 82. Smith-Rosenberg makes a comparable point about the early republic as a peculiarly postcolonial site in her essays "Red, Black, and Female," 343, and "Dis-covering the Subject," 847–48.

26. See Davidson, introduction to *The Coquette*, xiv.

27. Smith-Rosenberg writes, "Familial and community spokesmen have become spokeswomen, the feminized Greek chorus of Richman, Freeman, and Eliza's widowed mother, who at the end can only mouth hollow platitudes" ("Domesticating 'Virtue,'" 178). One year after publishing *The Coquette*, Foster makes her own foray into the genre that specializes in such bromides. In *The Boarding School* (Boston: Isaiah Thomas, 1798), she takes the voice of *The Coquette's* patriarchally identified female chorus, which dominates but does not absolutely totalize the discursive landscape of her novel, and makes it even more monologic. See Nancy Armstrong and Leonard Tennenhouse, "The Literature of Conduct, The Conduct of Literature, and the Politics of Desire," in *The Ideology of Conduct: Essays in Literature and the History of Sexuality*, eds. Nancy Armstrong and Leonard Tennenhouse (New York: Methuen, 1987), 1–24; Nancy Armstrong, *Desire and Domestic Fiction: A Political History of the Novel* (New York: Oxford University Press, 1987); and Sarah Emily Newton, "Wise and Foolish Virgins: 'Usable Fiction' and the Early American Conduct Tradition," *Early American Literature* 25 (1990): 139–67.

The secondary literature on the republican discourse of virtue and early American hostility to luxury is voluminous. Among the most important works on the subject are J. G. A. Pocock, *The Machiavellian Moment: Florentine Political Thought and the Atlantic Republican Tradition* (Princeton: Princeton University Press, 1975), particularly 462–552; Drew McCoy, *The Elusive Republic: Political Economy in Jeffersonian America* (Chapel Hill: University of North Carolina Press, 1980), particularly chaps. 1–5; and Joyce Appleby, *Capitalism and a New Social Order: The Republican Vision of the 1790s* (New York: New York University Press, 1984). See also Bernard Bailyn, *The Ideological Origins of the American Revolution* (Cambridge, Mass.: Harvard University Press, 1967); and Gordon Wood, *The Creation of the American Republic: 1776–1787* (New York: W. W. Norton, 1969).

28. Caryl Emerson and Michael Holquist, glossary to *The Dialogic Imagination*, by M. M. Bakhtin, trans. Caryl Emerson and Michael Holquist (Austin: University of Texas Press, 1981), 426–27.

29. See Smith-Rosenberg, "Domesticating 'Virtue,'" 163–64.

30. Thanks to Terry Mulcaire, whose work on the relationship between sentimentalism and capitalism has been helpful in my formulation of these arguments.

31. See David Marshall, *The Figure of Theater: Shaftesbury, Defoe, Adam Smith, and George Eliot* (New York: Columbia University Press, 1986), 165–92.

32. Both heroine and libertine boast that they have "perfectly adapted" their conversation "to the taste" of another (Eliza 12, Sanford 23). Both Eliza and Sanford complain about "confinement" (Eliza 29, 47, 53, 61; Sanford 65, 66, 116) and being shackled (Eliza 13, Sanford 23). And both call on the powers of "charity" to "blot out with a tear" (Eliza 9), "obliterate" (Eliza 20), and "draw a veil" (Sanford 37) over their faults.

33. See Irene Fizer, "Signing as Republican Daughters: The Letters of Eliza Southgate and *The Coquette*," *The Eighteenth Century* 34.3 (1993): 243–63; Lewis, "Republican Wife"; and Kerber, *Women of the Republic*, 265–88.

34. See Terry Eagleton, *The Rape of Clarissa: Writing, Sexuality, and Class Struggle in Samuel Richardson* (Minneapolis: University of Minnesota Press, 1982), 52.

35. Evoking Eagleton's idea that epistolarity is "speech-for-another"—that letter writing comes closer to dramatic artifice, in the Rousseauvian sense, than it does to transparency, Mitchell R. Breitwieser notes that "the illicitly acquired letter titillates Valmont because it seems to allow him to see the woman's interior. This is perhaps why he is so attracted to a pious woman, because she might be supposed to write truthful letters. But every letter is a theatrical act, even Tourvel's (as opposed, perhaps to a Shakespearian monologue) as we learn gradually when it occurs to us that Valmont's letters to Merteuil are far from candid." Electronic-mail communication with the author, July 19, 1996.

36. See Davidson's introduction to the Oxford University Press edition of *The Coquette*, xix.

37. For an important overview of the early American understanding of fancy, see Terence Martin, *The Instructed Vision: Scottish Common Sense Philosophy and the Origins of American Fiction* (Bloomington: Indiana University Press, 1961), 95–97, 107–108, 153–57; see also Thomas McFarland, *Originality and Imagination* (Baltimore: Johns Hopkins University Press, 1985), who locates the European origins of the debate about fancy and imagination in the work of Kant and who traces the unfolding of the conflict through the work of Coleridge.

38. See John Locke, *An Essay Concerning Human Understanding*, ed. A. D. Woozley (1690; New York: New American Library, 1964), 234.

39. See Julie Ellison, "The Politics of Fancy in the Age of Sensibility," in *Re-Visioning Romanticism: British Women Writers, 1776–1837*, eds. Carol Shiner Wilson and Joel Haefner (Philadelphia: University of Pennsylvania Press, 1994), 228.

40. See Ellison, "Politics of Fancy," 230, 250.

41. See Ellison, "Politics of Fancy," 241.

42. Kerber's analysis of the novel operates within this register. See *Women of the Republic*, 235–64.

43. Even Susanna Rowson confronts this anxiety, deploying the Wollstonecraftian narrator of *Charlotte Temple* to caution her audience against casting reason to the winds when reading romantic fiction. Michael Warner addresses the republican prejudice against fiction in the final pages of his book on print culture and the public sphere in eighteenth-century America. See *The Letters of the Republic: Publication and the Public Sphere in Eighteenth-Century America* (Cambridge, Mass.: Harvard University Press, 1990), 175–76. And for compelling treatment of these issues in the female-authored English novel of precisely the same period, see Claudia L. Johnson, *Equivocal Beings: Politics, Gender, and Sentimentality in the 1790s: Wollstonecraft, Radcliffe, Burney, Austen* (Chicago: University of Chicago Press, 1995).

44. Jay Fliegelman argues that the Declaration is written to be performed vocally, and Michael Warner describes the central linguistic trope of the Constitution as "the fictive speaking voice of the written constitution." According to Fliegelman, however, Warner's

"analysis ignores the degree to which eighteenth-century print culture, unable to stand apart from the politics of sincerity and authenticity, rejected the notion of 'power embodied in special persons' only to redefine those special persons—not by office, but by sensibility." Fliegelman is arguing that affect and presence—what I am calling *voice*—function as a supplement that haunts the disembodiment of writing in the period of the Founding; his book powerfully illustrates the *spokenness*, the theatricality, of the written word in late-eighteenth-century America. This qualification of Warner's thesis has been instrumental in my own thinking about the centrality of voice as the umbrella term for a certain form of affective language characteristic of this period, occurring in both written and spoken discourses. See Fliegelman, *Declaring Independence*, especially 128–29; and Warner, *Letters of the Republic*, 96.

45. See Bailyn, *The Ideological Origins of the American Revolution*; and Thomas Gustafson, *Representative Words: Politics, Literature, and the American Language, 1776–1864* (Cambridge: Cambridge University Press, 1992). Bailyn shows that the intellectual inspiration for rebellion springs not from Lockean liberalism but from the literature of classical republicanism, both the Roman sources and its late-seventeenth- and early eighteenth-century British Country–party elaboration in the works of Milton, Trenchard, Gordon, and others. This thesis is now undergoing a critique by more economically minded historians such as Joyce Appleby and T. H. Breen.

46. See Cherniavsky, *That Pale Mother Rising*, 39–40.

47. See Richard Poirier, *A World Elsewhere: The Place of Style in American Literature* (New York: Oxford University Press, 1966), ix.

48. See Davidson, introduction to *The Coquette*, x; and Smith-Rosenberg, "Domesticating 'Virtue,'" 169.

49. See Warner, *Letters of the Republic*, 173.

50. Warner, *The Letters of the Republic*, 173.

51. See James Turner, "The Properties of Libertinism," in *T'is Nature's Fault: Sexual Underworlds of the Enlightenment*, eds. G. S. Rousseau and Roy Porter (Chapel Hill: University of North Carolina Press, 1988), 75–87; for the quotations, see 81.

52. See Eagleton, *Rape of Clarissa*, 52.

53. See Eagleton, *Rape of Clarissa*. See also Terry Castle, *Clarissa's Ciphers: Meaning and Disruption in Richardson's "Clarissa"* (Ithaca: Cornell University Press, 1982), 19–20.

54. See Pettengill, "Female Friendship in a Separate Sphere," 194.

55. See Edmund Burke, *Reflections on the Revolution in France*, ed. Connor Cruise O'Brien (1790; Harmondsworth: Penguin Books, 1973), 175. Although imagination and passion are not precisely congruent in *Vindication* and *Reflections*, both Wollstonecraft and Burke write about the efficacious power of the affective faculties.

56. See Waldstreicher, "'Fallen Under My Observation,'" 207; and Adam Goldgeier, "*The Coquette* Composed," *Constructions* 1 (1990):1–14.

57. For the origins of this phrase, see Joan Riviere, "Femininity as Masquerade," *International Journal of Psychoanalysis* 10 (1929): 303–13. For a postmodern feminist elaboration of Riviere's psychoanalytic formulations, see Judith Butler, *Gender Trouble: Feminism and the Subversion of Identity* (New York: Routlege, 1990), especially 47–56.

58. In *Declaring Independence*, Fliegelman takes the theatricality of politics and the politics of theatricality as one of his primary subjects. See, in particular, "Natural Theatricality," 79–94.

59. Kenneth Silverman remarks that Shakespeare's drama of star-crossed lovers is also the "play most frequently performed at Covent Garden's Drury Lane Theatre in London."

The transatlantic fame of *Romeo and Juliet* is a phenomenon that, on its own terms, tells us little: the taste of pre-Revolutionary Anglo-American theatergoers is largely determined by the British theatrical domination of the colonies. It is nevertheless interesting that colonies and mother country share, even if by necessity, a cultural imagination that embraces the dramatic exploration of a factional conflict that ends with the death of its central figures. See Silverman, *A Cultural History of the American Revolution: Painting, Music, Literature, and the Theatre in the Colonies and the United States from the Treaty of Paris to the Inauguration of George Washington, 1763–1789* (1976; New York: Columbia University Press, 1987), 62.

60. Dating the events of the novel from its range of historical allusions proves an interesting challenge. Elizabeth Whitman, the historical figure whose story forms the basis for Foster's tale, dies in 1788. Bowen's Museum debuts in Boston in 1791 and accumulates its collection until 1795, when it assumes the name of the Columbian Museum. The most frequently mentioned early American female equestrian is a Mrs. Spinacuta, who appears in Rickett's Circus, usually considered the first professional circus to play in the early republic, in Boston in 1796. R. W. G. Vail writes that competing for the title of the first equestrienne in the history of the American circus is a Miss Venice, or Vanice, who appears in Lailson's Circus, also in Boston in 1796. Assuming that Foster's fictional practices involve a protorealist form of historical representation, we can date her story as beginning in 1796, providing that people conventionally continue to refer to the museum in Boston as Mr. Bowen's, despite its renaming. On Bowen's Museum, see William W. Clapp, Jr., *A Record of the Boston Stage* (Boston: James Munroe and Co., 1853), 87; Ethel Stanwood Bolton, *American Wax Portraits* (Boston: Houghton Mifflin Co., 1929), 16–21; and Wayne Craven, *Sculpture in America* (New York: Thomas Y. Crowell, 1968), 28–29. On Mrs. Spinacuta, see John Culhane, *The American Circus: An Illustrated History* (New York: Henry Holt and Co., 1990), 4. On Miss Venice, see Vail, "Random Notes on the History of the Early American Circus," in *Proceedings of the American Antiquarian Society*, New Series 43. April 19, 1933–October 18, 1933 (Worcester, Mass.: American Antiquarian Society, 1934), 176.

61. For two short but incisive treatments of Tyler's comedy, see Davidson, *Revolution and the Word*, 212–15; and Jeffrey H. Richards, *Theater Enough: American Culture and the Metaphor of the World Stage, 1607–1789* (Durham: Duke University Press, 1991), 272–79.

62. *Romeo and Juliet* is performed as a moral lecture in Boston in 1792; in fact, Susanna Rowson actually plays the part of Juliet's nurse in a production at Boston's Federal Street Theater before she retires from the stage in 1797. See Clapp, *Record of the Boston Stage*, 8; and Dorothy Weil, *In Defense of Women: Susanna Rowson (1762–1824)* (University Park: Pennsylvania State University Press, 1976), 4.

63. Shakespeare and Richardson, in addition to Laurence Sterne, whose language is sprinkled throughout the libertine's villainous letters, constitute the most important literary precursors for *The Coquette*. The author's allusions to *Romeo and Juliet*, *Othello*, and *Twelfth Night*, as well as *Clarissa*, provide a rich set of clues for unpacking the latent, antididactic narrative that runs against the grain of Foster's manifestly moralizing intentions.

64. Literally featuring the live burial of its heroine, *Romeo and Juliet* functions as potent background against which the funereal dynamics of Foster's novel unfold. Thanks to Martin Müeller for his insights on the significance of this play to an eighteenth-century audience.

65. See Jane Tompkins, *Sensational Designs: The Cultural Work of American Fiction, 1790–1860* (New York: Oxford University Press, 1985).

66. See Edmund Burke, *Reflections*, 176.

67. See Fliegelman, *Declaring Independence*, 91.

68. Also see Warner, *Letters of the Republic,* 64.

69. On the power of dramatic representation to obliterate the externality of the beholder and draw him or her inside the fictive world, a condition that he equates with the experience of sympathy, see Michael Fried, *Absorption and Theatricality: Painting and Beholder in the Age of Diderot* (Berkeley and Los Angeles: University of California Press, 1977), 104.

70. See Marshall, *Surprising Effects of Sympathy,* 148.

71. See Jean-Jacques Rousseau, "Letter to M. D'Alembert on the Theatre," in *Politics and the Arts: "Letter to M. D'Alembert on the Theatre,"* trans. Allan Bloom (1758; Ithaca: Cornell University Press, 1968), 16–17.

72. See also Jonas Barish, *The Antitheatrical Prejudice* (Berkeley and Los Angeles: University of California Press, 1981), 269–70; and Marshall, *Surprising Effects of Sympathy,* 135–77.

73. See letter 194 of Samuel Richardson, *Clarissa; or, The History of a Young Lady,* ed. Angus Ross (1747–48; Harmondsworth: Penguin Books, 1985), 618.

74. For Adams's letter to William And, March 15, 1804, see *Correspondence between the Hon. John Adams and the Late William And, Esq.* (Boston: 1823), 19; quoted in Jay Fliegelman, *Prodigals and Pilgrims: The American Revolution against Patriarchal Authority, 1750–1800* (Cambridge: Cambridge University Press, 1982), 237. For details about Richardson's correspondence with his readers, see Eagleton, Castle.

75. I am grateful to Helen Deutsch for this insight.

76. Thanks to Jana Argersinger for sharing Prof. Alexander Hammond's observations about the politics of narrative in *Charlotte Temple.*

77. See *Othello* 3.3.155–61, in *The Riverside Shakespeare* (Boston: Houghton Mifflin, 1974), 1221.

78. See Culhane, *American Circus,* 4.

79. Culhane, *American Circus,* 5.

80. Jefferson is quoted in Culhane, *American Circus,* 4.

81. In fact, Ricketts is a known admirer of Washington, who seeks the company of the Scottish riding master to discuss the relative gates of indigenous American horses. See Culhane, *American Circus,* 4.

82. See Faye E. Dudden, *Women in the American Theatre: Actresses and Audiences, 1790–1870* (New Haven: Yale University Press, 1994), 21.

83. The third is a Miss Johnson of Swann's circus; see Stuart Thayer, *Annals of the American Circus, 1793–1829* (Manchester, Mich.: Rymack Printing Co., 1976), 7.

84. *Columbian Centinel* [*sic*], August 31, 1796. See Thayer, *Annals of the American Circus,* 13.

85. See Adam Smith, *The Theory of Moral Sentiments,* eds. D. D. Raphael and A. L. Macfie (Indianapolis: Liberty Classics, 1982), 10.

86. A recurring refrain among scholars and students of Foster's novel regards the author's failure to imagine, much less to represent, a viable economic alternative to marriage for Eliza Wharton. While I am not suggesting Foster believes that a genteel woman like her heroine, who hails from the elite Federalist community, could go to work managing a theater, it is interesting to note that, in the period immediately following the publication of her novel, a few American middle-class women do just that. The most famous of them is Anne Brunton Merry, who after the death of her husband manages the "Chestnut Street Theatre in Philadelphia between 1803 and 1805" (Dudden, *Women in the American Theatre,* 12). See also Gresdna Ann Doty, *The Career of Mrs. Anne Brunton Merry in the American Theatre* (Baton Rouge: Louisiana State University Press, 1971); Glenn Hughes, *History of*

the *American Theatre, 1700–1950* (New York: Samuel French, 1951), 121; and George C. D. Odell, *Annals of the New York Stage* (New York: Columbia University Press, 1927–49), 2:598.

87. See G. J. Barker-Benfield, *The Culture of Sensibility: Sex and Society in 18th-Century Britain* (Chicago: University of Chicago Press, 1992); and Janet Todd, *Sensibility: An Introduction* (London: Methuen, 1986).

88. See Marie-Hélène Huet, *Monstrous Imagination* (Cambridge, Mass.: Harvard University Press, 1994), 212–14, and 188.

89. Lucy does not describe Daniel Bowen's museum as a display of waxworks; nor does she detail the contents of the collection. Such omissions suggest that Bowen's establishment is well known to Foster's audience, functioning as a part of its collective *mentalité*. Although the museum probably figures in what we might term eighteenth-century America's repertoire of cultural literacy, little information about it survives in the historical record. Those few remaining sources that however incompletely document portions of Bowen's collection can be found scattered in Boston newspapers from the period as well as in early nineteenth-century histories of the American theater and circus and twentieth-century studies of wax sculpture in America. For an advertisement for Bowen's museum from the beginning of the 1790s, see *Columbian Centinel* [*sic*], June 1, 1791, 91. For an anonymous review of the collection that appears during the (roughly approximate) period in which the novel is set, see *Boston Gazette,* December 28, 1795, 3.

90. Isaac J. Greenwood, *The Circus: Its Origin and Growth* (1889; Washington, DC: Hobby House Press, 1962), 82.

91. See the *Boston Gazette,* December 7, 1795, 3.

92. See Carroll Smith-Rosenberg, "Dis-covering the Subject"; and "Subject Female: Authorizing American Identity," *American Literary History* 5.3 (fall 1993): 481–511. See also Jared Gardner, "Alien Nation: Edgar Huntly's Savage Awakening," *American Literature* 66.3 (September 1994): 429–61; and see chap. 4 below.

93. Looby writes of another instance in which George the Third is figuratively linked with George Washington. This is the moment when the King's visage transforms into the face of the American general, Founding Father, and first President on the sign in front of the local inn in Washington Irving's "Rip Van Winkle." Looby argues that what is "decisive" about this detail is "Rip's *recognition* of the change as one of semiotic substitution, his immediate demystification of the new order of signs of authority." See *Voicing America,* 43 and 94–96. In Foster's representation of Bowen's Museum, in contrast, there is no dissenting spectator from outside the Federalist majority who could demystify the reactionary, indeed the nostalgic, political aura that surrounds these doppelgängers in wax. In fact, this contiguity carries a decidedly conservative ideological charge, suggesting that the differences between the two figures are easily collapsed.

94. Elkins and McKitrick note that "Adams laid himself open to charges, which he never fully lived down, of secretly favoring monarchy" (*Age of Federalism,* 46). Looby suggests, however, that "George Washington's construction as a charismatic symbolic presence was largely a posthumus, retroactive phenomenon, part of a long and contested process of creating out of an ambiguous revolutionary past usable political myths and traditions; and to the extent that the cult of Washington existed during Washington's life and during the immediate postrevolutionary consolidation, it was a deeply ambivalent phenomenon, marked by bombastic inflations and the widespread dissemination of his idolized image on the one hand, and on the other hand by such public demurrals as that of John Adams, who in Congress in 1777 said he was 'distressed to see some of our members disposed to idolize an image which their own hands have molten. I speak here of the superstitious veneration

which is paid to General Washington'" (*Voicing America*, 43). See also Adams, quoted in Barry Schwartz, *George Washington: The Making of an American Symbol* (New York: Free Press, 1987), 22.

95. Liberalism as a political philosophy does not reject patriarchal authority; indeed, Carole Pateman, Joyce Appleby, Lynn Hunt, Margaret Jacobs, Smith-Rosenberg, and others have argued that the de facto liberal subject is a white male of the privileged classes. It is nevertheless true that the Lockean model of individualism is less inflected by gender than is the male homosocial republican formulation that originates in classical theory. See, in particular, Appleby, *Liberalism and Republicanism in the Historical Imagination* (Cambridge, Mass.: Harvard University Press, 1988). See also Pateman, *The Sexual Contract* (Stanford: Stanford University Press, 1988).

96. Although allegedly originating in the horrors of the French Revolution, Marie Tussaud's waxworks actually postdate the figures in Bowen's Museum by at least a decade. It is not until 1802 that Tussaud makes her debut at the Lyceum Theater in London, as part of Philipstal's Phantasmagoria, a magic lantern show. Fliegelman chronicles an earlier example of waxworking that has its origins in pre-Revolutionary America in his relation of Patience Wright's story. Wright leaves the colony of New York for London in 1772 in order to practice her extraordinary art of "utterly realistic, fully in the round, life-size wax portraiture modeled from life." See Huet, *Monstrous Imagination*, 194–95; and Fliegelman, *Declaring Independence*, 84–85, 87.

97. *Merriam-Webster's Collegiate Dictionary*, 10th ed., sv "resort."

98. Pettengill makes a related observation: "It is important to remember that Eliza is not the only character who completes a major transition in the novel. Her two best friends, Lucy Freeman and Mrs. Richman, also undergo critical changes—Lucy marries, and Mrs. Richman bears and loses a child" ("Sisterhood in a Separate Sphere," 193).

99. Harris reads the plague on the infants in the novel as a reverberation "of the death of innocence" that she argues Eliza experiences on recognizing that "there is no place in late-eighteenth-century America for her opinions." Harris's essay foregrounds the political critique at work in Foster's novel, and, as such, it echoes my own arguments in important ways. Our interpretations differ, however, in their assessments of the female community's response to Eliza's death. Harris sees in the emerging cohesion of the chorus members a potentially positive vision of a female future, while I read their exercise of sympathy as an ominous extension of the fetishizing process that creates community at the cost of the transgressive individual. See "Critiquing Franklin's America," 5.

100. The term is discussed at greatest length by Fizer. While her essay offers a lively account of female possibility in the wake of the American Revolution, the reading of Eliza as a figure of excessive sexual appetite flattens Foster's nuanced portrait of the heroine's desires and thereby overlooks the cultural significance of her struggle; in important ways, Fizer's treatment of *The Coquette* partakes of the monocular vision of the chorus. See "Signing as Republican Daughters."

101. Although both Smith-Rosenberg and Lee Virginia Chambers-Schiller locate the origins of the dynamic at the turn of the eighteenth century, the bulk of the substantiating data derives from early nineteenth-century sources. It is my contention that the dominant energies of Foster's novel, embodied in the feminized patriarchal chorus, look backward to a real eighteenth-century ethos, while Eliza's desires point to the opening possibilities of the nineteenth century. But, as much as the heroine would revel in a female world of love and ritual, such a space is precisely what is missing in Foster's novel. See Smith-Rosenberg, "Female World of Love and Ritual"; and see Chambers-Schiller, *Liberty, a Better Husband*.

Single Women in America: The Generations of 1780–1840 (New Haven: Yale University Press, 1984).

102. Scholars such as Harris, "Critiquing Franklin's America," Smith-Rosenberg, "Domesticating 'Virtue,'" and Shuffelton, "Brotherly Watch," note the parallels that exist between the chorus and the patriarchy. For the historical origins of this alliance, see Douglas, *Feminization of American Culture*, 94–139.

103. See Smith-Rosenberg, "Female World of Love and Ritual," 64, 74.

104. Harris charts the waning of Lucy's intimate attention to Eliza; see "Critiquing Franklin's America," 11–12.

105. Fizer similarly notes that "Eliza's final acts of fornication" "mark at once the libertinous nature of her sexuality and its redomestication" ("Signing as Republican Daughters," 244).

106. On the issue of emblematic monumentality and its destructive interpretive valence, see Mitchell R. Breitwieser, *American Puritanism and the Defense of Mourning: Religion, Grief, and Ethnology in Mary White Rowlandson's Captivity Narrative* (Madison: University of Wisconsin Press, 1990), particularly 17–70.

107. Louise Kaplan writes, "A fetish is designed to keep the lies hidden, to divert attention away from the whole story by focusing attention on the detail." See *Female Perversions: The Temptations of Emma Bovary* (New York: Doubleday, 1991), 34 and 35. For the original psychoanalytic formulation of the concept, see Sigmund Freud, "Fetishism" (1927), in *The Standard Edition of the Complete Psychological Works of Sigmund Freud*, trans. and ed. James Strachey, in collaboration with Anna Freud, assisted by Alix Strachey and Alan Tyson. 24 vols. (London: Hogarth Press, 1953–74), 21:149–57. See also Elisabeth Bronfen, *Over Her Dead Body: Death, Femininity, and the Aesthetic* (New York: Routledge, 1992), 95–97.

108. See George Forgie, *Patricide in the House Divided: A Psychological Interpretation of Lincoln and His Age* (New York: W. W. Norton, 1979), in particular chap. 1, "The Founding Heros and the Post-Heroic Generation," 13–53. Mason Weems's biography of Washington constitutes the original textual instantiation of this dynamic. See *The Life of Washington*, ed. Marcus Cunliffe (Cambridge, Mass.: Harvard University Press, 1962).

109. Kaplan, *Female Perversions*, 35.

110. See Looby, *Voicing America*; see also Warner, *Letters of the Republic*; and Fliegelman, *Declaring Independence*.

111. Harris traces much of the chorus's platitudinous language to the proverbs and aphorisms of Benjamin Franklin. See "Critiquing Franklin's America," 4, 6.

112. For a different reading that suggests Eliza's is indeed the editorial hand behind her posthumous anthology but that sees this gesture as her radical assertion of independence from the patriarchal voice, see Goldgeier, "*Coquette* Composed," 8.

113. Identifying the connection between the consumption of women as sexual commodities and the self-wasting disease of anorexia nervosa that fictional victims of seduction and abandonment inflict on themselves, Maud Ellmann writes, "[I]t is unclear from Clarissa's syntax whether she is dying of the illness or the ethic of consumption, and whether she is suffering or perpetrating her decline. The ambiguity is telling, since her illness both resists her family and acquiesces in its *woman-eating* values." See *The Hunger Artists: Starving, Writing, and Imprisonment* (Cambridge, Mass.: Harvard University Press, 1993), 82, my emphasis. See also Gillian Brown, "Anorexia, Humanism, and Feminism," *Yale Journal of Criticism* 5.1 (1991): 189–215.

114. See Elkins and McKitrick, *The Age of Federalism*, 482.

115. I here borrow the language of Christopher Castiglia, "In Praise of Extravagant Women: *Hope Leslie* and the Captivity Romance," *Legacy* 6 (1989): 3–16.

116. Franklin's textual transcription in *The Autobiography of Benjamin Franklin* of the tombstone he erects for his parents' grave bears comparison here. Particularly interesting is the way in which both Franklin and Foster's chorus create monuments that glorify themselves far more than they honor their beloved dead. Inscribing their own autographs in stone becomes the ultimate signature of possession, the most permanent form of rewriting the past in the interest of a future posterity. See *Franklin: Writings,* ed. J. A. Leo Lemay (New York: Library of America, 1987), 1315–16.

117. Major Sanford believes that Eliza has chosen to suffer her seclusion and confinement in Salem, the site in early America most famous for the repression and extermination of female "eccentricity" and "waywardness" during the witchcraft delusions of the 1690s. She will actually die in Danvers, but the libertine's mistaken association marks another occasion of the patriarchal impulse to demonize female nonconformity. Harris also notes this connection: "That Eliza's final destination is Salem, the symbolic place of persecution, should not be overlooked. The fallen Eliza's fate differs from that of the 'witches' only in the manner of death. The finger has been pointed, and society willingly listens to her accusers. Foster extends the painful irony of this allusion by including Eliza, who has now internalized her society's values, as one who joins in the process, damning herself" ("Critiquing Franklin's America," 16).

118. See Helen Deutsch, "'Is It Easier To Believe?': Narrative Innocence from *Clarissa* to 'Twin Peaks,'" *Arizona Quarterly* 49.2 (summer 1993): 137–58.

119. In the *Poetics,* pity and terror are precisely the reactions that tragic drama is said to evoke in its audience. See Aristotle, *Poetics,* trans. Richard Janko (Indianapolis: Hackett Publishing Co., 1987), 17.

120. Pettengill notes, "Ironically, Eliza's friends continue busily to communicate with one another for and about Eliza. When she stops writing, her conversations and actions are reported at second hand, passed around from friend to friend" ("Sisterhood in a Separate Sphere," 198).

CHAPTER FOUR

1. Charles Brockden Brown, *Ormond, or The Secret Witness.* Vol. 2 in *The Novels and Related Works of Charles Brockden Brown,* eds. Sydney J. Krause and S. W. Reid (1799; Kent, Ohio: Kent State University Press, 1982), 190. Further references to this edition of the novel will be cited parenthetically in the text.

2. Much of my current thinking about the problem of alien-ness in *Ormond* has been informed by Jared Gardner's important essay "Alien Nation: Edgar Huntly's Savage Awakening," *American Literature* 66.3 (September 1994): 429–61, especially 430, 432, 436, 450.

3. Adams to Jefferson, June 30, 1813, *The Adams-Jefferson Letters: The Complete Correspondence between Thomas Jefferson and Abigail and John Adams,* ed. Lester J. Cappon, (Chapel Hill: University of North Carolina Press, 1959), 2: 347.

4. See Werner B. Berthoff, "The Literary Career of Charles Brockden Brown" (Ph.D. diss., Harvard University, 1954), 146.

5. The unknown etiology of the illness provokes rabid controversy within Philadelphia's medical community in the 1790s. Martin S. Pernick notes that "it was not until 1901 that Walter Reed demonstrated the process by which the *Aedes aegypti* mosquito transmits yellow fever from an infected person to a healthy one." See "Politics, Parties, and Pestilence: Epidemic Yellow Fever in Philadelphia and the Rise of the First Party System," *William and*

Mary Quarterly 3d ser., 29 (1972): 559–85, 562. For the definitive documentary account and social history of the epidemic, see J. H. Powell, *Bring out Your Dead: The Great Plague of Yellow Fever in Philadelphia in 1793*, introd. Kenneth R. Foster, Mary F. Jenkins, and Anna Coxe Toogood (1949; Philadelphia: University of Pennsylvania Press, 1993). See also Eve Korngold, "Crisis in the Capital: The Cultural Significance of Philadelphia's Great Yellow Fever Epidemic," *Pennsylvania History* 51.3 (1984): 189–205; Mark Workman, "Medical Practice in Philadelphia at the Time of the Yellow Fever Epidemic," *Pennsylvania Folklife* 27.4 (1978): 33–39; Carl Binger, M.D., *Revolutionary Doctor: Benjamin Rush, 1746–1813* (New York: W. W. Norton, 1966); and Chris Holmes, "Benjamin Rush and the Yellow Fever," *Journal of the History of Medicine and Allied Sciences* 21.3 (1966): 246–63.

The following references constitute only a sampling of the vast contemporary literature on the epidemic: Dr. Benjamin Rush, *An Enquiry Into the Origin of the Late Epidemic Fever in Philadelphia* (Philadelphia: Mathew Carey, 1793); and *An Account of the Bilious Remitting Yellow Fever, As It Appeared in the City of Philadelphia, In the Year 1793*, 2d ed. (Philadelphia: Thomas Dobson, 1794); The College of Physicians of Philadelphia, *Facts and Observations Relative to the Nature and Origin of the Pestilential Fever, Which Prevailed in This City, in 1793, 1797, and 1798* (Philadelphia: Thomas Dobson, 1798); Mathew Carey, *A Short Account of the Malignant Fever Which Prevailed in Philadelphia in the Year 1793*, 5th ed., in Mathew Carey, *Miscellaneous Essays* (1793; Philadelphia: Carey and Hart, 1830), iii–97; William Currie, *A Description of the Malignant, Infectious Fever Prevailing at Present in Philadelphia* (Philadelphia: Thomas Dobson, 1793) and *An Impartial Review, of That Part of Dr. Rush's Late Publication, Entitled 'An Account of the Bilious Remitting Yellow Fever, As It Appeared in the City of Philadelphia'* (Philadelphia: Thomas Dobson, 1794); and *Memoirs of the Yellow Fever, Which Prevailed in Philadelphia, and Other Parts of the United States of America, in the Summer and Autumn of the Present Year, 1798* (Philadelphia: Thomas Dobson, 1798).

6. See William S. Kashatus III, "Plagued! Philadelphia's Yellow Fever Epidemic of 1793," *Pennsylvania Heritage* 19.2 (1993): 32–37, especially 32.

7. See Bill Christophersen, *The Apparition in the Glass: Charles Brockden Brown's American Gothic* (Athens: University of Georgia Press, 1993), 61–62, 65.

8. The metaphor of the nation as virtuous woman is an eighteenth-century commonplace; from early on, Brown scholars have drawn such allegorical correspondences between his female characters and the republic. In cultural representations, "Liberty" is almost always figured with feminine iconography; in America, "she" evolves from Indian Princess to Columbia. See E. McClung Fleming, "The American Image as Indian Princess 1765–1783," *Winterthur Portfolio II* (1965): 65–81; and "From Indian Princess to Greek Goddess: The American Image 1783–1815," *Winterthur Portfolio III* (1967): 37–66. See also Robert S. Levine, "Villainy and the Fear of Conspiracy in Charles Brockden Brown's *Ormond*," *Early American Literature* 15 (1980): 124–40, especially 136. For the French version of this iconography, see Joan B. Landes, *Women and the Public Sphere in the Age of the French Revolution* (Ithaca: Cornell University Press, 1988); see also Lynn Hunt, *The Family Romance of the French Revolution* (Berkeley and Los Angeles: University of California Press, 1992), 82–84.

9. Insisting on the value of genuine feeling along with the virtue of rationality, personifying what I call in chap. 2 the "sympathetic Enlightenment," the narrator of *Charlotte Temple* tries to bring within the circle of illumination those who have been occluded by the male-authored Enlightenment; as such, she marks an important exception.

10. See *Alcuin, A Dialogue* (1798) in "*Alcuin, A Dialogue and The Memoirs of Steven Calvert.*" Vol. 6 in *The Novels and Related Works of Charles Brockden Brown*, eds. Sydney J.

Krause and S. W. Reid (Kent, Ohio: Kent State University Press, 1987). See also *Wieland; or, The Transformation: An American Tale*. Vol. 1 in *The Novels and Related Works of Charles Brockden Brown;* Cathy N. Davidson, "The Matter and Manner of Charles Brockden Brown's *Alcuin*," in *Critical Essays on Charles Brockden Brown,* ed. Bernard Rosenthal (Boston: G. K. Hall, 1981), 71–87; and Linda K. Kerber, *Women of the Republic: Intellect and Ideology in Revolutionary America* (Chapel Hill: University of North Carolina Press, 1980), 185–233.

11. The epistolary form proves an exception to this rule. William Hill Brown undertakes such crossings in *The Power of Sympathy* (1789). Likewise, women writers such as Hannah Webster Foster take up male narrative personae.

12. See Madeline Kahn, *Narrative Transvestism: Rhetoric and Gender in the Eighteenth-Century English Novel* (Ithaca: Cornell University Press, 1991). See also Fliegelman, introduction to *Wieland and Memoirs of Carwin the Biloquist* (1798; Harmondsworth: Penguin Books, 1991), xxii–xxiii.

13. These master narratives include the Declaration of Independence, *The Federalist Papers,* and the Constitution, as well as a series of artifacts Jay Fliegelman catalogs in his evocative study of Jefferson and his culture: Paul Revere's engraving of the Boston Massacre, images of the Continental Congress voting for independence, and portraits of the Founding Fathers, including Washington crossing the Delaware and Thomas Jefferson in thoughtful meditation. See Fliegelman, *Declaring Independence,* 71, 76–77, 84.

14. See Hunt, *The Family Romance of the French Revolution,* 71. My analysis of fraternity in Brockden Brown's *Ormond* is indebted to Hunt's richly provocative reading of the meaning of brotherhood during the French Revolution and its aftermath. Hunt is careful to distinguish the French from the American Revolutionary case and to differentiate between the familial mythology that each post-Revolutionary republic adopted. Thus, "in contrast to the Americans, the French did not mythologize a living leader"; "they did not successfully represent themselves either collectively or individually as fathers of their country." Hunt also notes that "the expression 'Founding Fathers' may in fact be a relatively modern one" (71). See *Family Romance* 70–71; see also Wesley Frank Craven, *The Legend of the Founding Fathers* (Ithaca: Cornell University Press, 1956), 2, n. 1.

15. See Fliegelman, *Declaring Independence;* and Looby, *Voicing America: Language, Literary Form, and the Origins of the United States* (Chicago: University of Chicago Press, 1996).

16. I take this term from Michael Warner, *The Letters of the Republic: Publication and the Public Sphere in Eighteenth-Century America* (Cambridge, Mass.: Harvard University Press, 1990), 34–72.

17. See Kaja Silverman, *Male Subjectivity at the Margins* (New York: Routledge, 1992). Eva Cherniavsky makes a similar point about the use of the white middle-class maternal body as a limiting case in the establishment of white male republican identity. See *That Pale Mother Rising: Sentimental Discourses and the Imitation of Motherhood in 19th-Century America* (Bloomington: Indiana University Press, 1995), 2.

18. See Terry Castle, *Clarissa's Ciphers: Meaning and Disruption in Richardson's "Clarissa"* (Ithaca: Cornell University Press, 1982).

19. Among the first to celebrate rather than deny the significance of this dynamic in *Ormond* is Lillian Faderman; see her groundbreaking study *Surpassing the Love of Men: Romantic Friendship and Love Between Women from the Renaissance to the Present* (New York: William Morrow, 1981), 112–15, 434 n. 12–435 n. 14. For a selection of the more traditionally homophobic readings, see Ernest Marchand, introduction to *Ormond* (New York: American Book Co., 1937), xxxii; Harry R. Warfel, *Charles Brockden Brown: American*

Gothic Novelist (Gainesville: University of Florida Press, 1949), 132; Leslie Fiedler, *Love and Death in the American Novel* (1959; New York: Stein and Day, 1966), 103–104; Donald A. Ringe, *Charles Brockden Brown* (New York: Twayne Publishers, 1966), 60–61; and Norman S. Grabo, *The Coincidental Art of Charles Brockden Brown* (Chapel Hill: University of North Carolina Press, 1981), 47–50. Historian Steven Watts is the most recent Brown critic to acknowledge the prominence of lesbian desire in *Ormond;* yet his interpretation of women's homoeroticism seems both oddly out of tune with contemporary theories of sexuality and strangely limited to (representations of) the intrapsychic life of Brown's characters, never reaching out to interpret the connection between the emotional and the historical and cultural realms. He writes of Constantia: "as her rational faculties steadily proved less able to illuminate the social and moral atmosphere, she turned to the attractions of female homoeroticism. This theme, although muted because of eighteenth-century convention, ran deep in the novel." See *The Romance of Real Life: Charles Brockden Brown and the Origins of American Culture* (Baltimore: Johns Hopkins University Press, 1994), 97.

20. Christopher Looby observes that Brown defines his identity and art in terms of what each is *not,* arguing that the author's self-conception is forged against a peculiar series of double negatives: he is not *not* a Federalist; not *not* a radical; not *not* a bohemian; not *not* a literary man; not *not* a capitalist, etc. Offered during discussion of my readings of forgery and masquerade in *Ormond* (preliminary versions of the second part of this chapter) at the University of Chicago's American Studies Workshop meeting of February 2, 1996, Looby's dialectical formulation advances the most incisive account yet articulated of the novelist's fluid identity, uncertain politics, and professional self-fashioning.

21. This notion is the thesis of Christopher Looby's chapter on *Wieland* in *Voicing America,* 145–202.

22. Christophersen notes this tendency toward overdetermination in Brown's employment of the plague motif, remarking on the author's "ambitious use of diction to complement, if not to achieve, a symbolic dimension. Brown's diction lends itself, as often as not, to parody and criticism; yet there are passages in which his melodramatic rhetoric camouflages allusions—hence the baroque renderings." See *Apparition in the Glass,* 60.

23. See Robert A. Ferguson, "'What is Enlightenment?': Some American Answers," *American Literary History* 1.2 (summer 1989): 245–72, particularly 251; and "The American Enlightenment, 1750–1820," in *The Cambridge History of American Literature, Volume I: 1590–1820,* ed. Sacvan Bercovitch (Cambridge: Cambridge University Press, 1994), 345–538. For an extensive treatment of the subversive and countersubversive dimensions of the novel, see Robert S. Levine, *Conspiracy and Romance: Studies in Brockden Brown, Cooper, Hawthorne, and Melville* (Cambridge: Cambridge University Press, 1989), 15–57.

24. For a recent and thorough account of Godwin's influence on Brown, see Pamela Clemit, *The Godwinian Novel: The Rational Fictions of Godwin, Brockden Brown, Mary Shelley* (Oxford: Oxford University Press, 1993), 35–69, 105–38.

25. For the most comprehensive and incisive treatment of Brown's vocational struggles, and particularly for the way in which his abandonment of the law enabled his career as a creative writer, see Robert A. Ferguson, *Law and Letters in American Culture* (Cambridge, Mass.: Harvard University Press, 1984), 129–49. See also Looby, *Voicing America,* 180–92.

26. The term is coined by Frank Shuffelton in "Mrs. Foster's *The Coquette* and the Decline of the Brotherly Watch," *Studies in Eighteenth-Century Culture* 16 (1986): 211–24.

27. For an overview of this reassessment of the novel of the 1790s, see Claudia L. Johnson, *Equivocal Beings: Politics, Gender, and Sentimentality in the 1790s: Wollstonecraft, Radcliffe, Burney, Austen* (Chicago: University of Chicago Press, 1995). See also Nicola J.

Watson, *Revolution and the Form of the British Novel, 1790–1825: Intercepted Letters, Interrupted Seductions* (Oxford: Oxford University Press, 1994); Gary Kelly, *Women, Writing, and Revolution, 1790–1827* (Oxford: Oxford University Press, 1994), *English Fiction of the Romantic Period, 1789–1830* (London and New York: Longman, 1989), and *The English Jacobin Novel, 1780–1805* (Oxford: Oxford University Press, 1976); Marilyn S. Butler, *Romantics, Rebels, and Reactionaries: English Literature and Its Background, 1760–1830* (Oxford: Oxford University Press, 1981); and Robert Kiely, *The Romantic Novel in England* (Cambridge, Mass.: Harvard University Press, 1972).

28. Thus, a figure like Charles Wilson Peale begins his professional life as an artist by painting miniatures, before moving on to portraits and history paintings, the three ascending levels of skill required of accomplished painters in eighteenth-century Anglo-American culture. For a discussion of Peale's practice of the different genres in relation to the evolution of his career, see Joseph Ellis, *After the Revolution: Profiles of Early American Culture* (New York: W. W. Norton, 1979), 46.

Dale T. Johnson, cocurator of "Tokens of Affection: The Portrait Miniature in America," the first comprehensive exhibition of American miniature painting since 1927, which ran from March 29 through June 16, 1991 at Washington's National Museum of American Art, notes that portrait miniatures are "the most neglected area in American art." The exhibition cocurated with Robin Bolton-Smith, however, represents the current revitalization of interest in this nearly forgotten genre of early republican painting. Johnson is quoted in John A. Cuadrado, "Portrait Miniatures—Captivating Glimpses into History," *Architectural Digest* 48 (April 1991): 54. See also Robin Bolton-Smith and Dale T. Johnson, "The Miniature in America," *Antiques* 138 (November 1990): 1042–55; and Dale T. Johnson, *American Portrait Miniatures in the Manney Collection* (New York: Metropolitan Museum of Art, 1990).

29. Like Defoe, perhaps the most influential eighteenth-century picaresque novelist in English, Brown uses the first-person voice and an episodic structure to tell his stories; like Defoe, and unlike virtually every other important Anglo-American author of the latter eighteenth-century, Brown adopts a female persona to narrate two of his four most important works. The parallel breaks down, however, once we consider that picaresque fiction is a decidedly comic form, while Brown's work is explicitly tragic.

30. Watts characterizes *Ormond* as "a highly melodramatic story of passion, sexuality, and sociopathy," a work that "at the same time" unfolds as a "rather wooden novel of ideas. Caught up in political and intellectual agitation of the late-eighteenth-century Atlantic world, the author constructed his characters as somewhat mechanical representations of clashing ideas and ideologies." See *Romance of Real Life*, 89.

31. Martinette ultimately reveals that M. Roselli, who goes by the "French" name of Monrose, has an Italian sister. This strange detail leaves the question of his European antecedents somewhat ambiguous. Politically, however, the patriarch identifies himself as French, an affiliation that links him in important ways to the political struggles of the era.

32. While officially aligned with Great Britain as a result of the Jay Treaty and demurring from actual continental hostilities, the new republic rehearsed this European conflict domestically through the factional battles fought between Federalists and Republicans in the second half of the 1790s. See Stanley Elkins and Eric McKitrick, *The Age of Federalism: The Early American Republic, 1788–1800* (New York: Oxford University Press, 1993) for the most recent comprehensive treatment of the conflict. One of the few current scholars of Brown's work to draw on these important connections is Christophersen, *Apparition in the Glass*, 65.

33. Paul C. Rodgers, Jr., notes that, far from being indigenous to *Ormond*, the Baxter

digression is spliced into the novel virtually without alteration from its original form in Brown's "Man At Home" magazine series. Using this fact to argue that the episode introduces "material" "irrelevant" to *Ormond*'s plot or symbolic meaning, Rodgers misses the obsessive significance of the tableau in Brown's overall imaginative schema, the idea that the scene of the watchman's contamination and subsequent unmooring of identity becomes Brown's persistent metaphor for the problems plaguing early republican culture. That the author determined to reuse the episode suggests the absolute relevance of the material. Rodgers also fails to decode the "intimate connection" between the Dudleys and the Monroses; he concludes that "all indications suggest the Monrose material was thrown into the text as a stopgap to meet an editorial deadline, after which it became an embarrassment." As should become apparent, I take very seriously Brown's assertion about the digression, deployed through Sophia: "[h]owever foreign the destiny of Monrose may at present appear to the story of the Dudleys, there will hereafter be discovered an intimate connection between them" (*Ormond,* 62). See Rodgers, "Brown's *Ormond:* The Fruits of Improvisation," *American Quarterly* 26.1 (March 1974): 13, 18. See also Charles Brockden Brown, "The Man at Home," *Weekly Magazine,* (February, 24, 1788): 99–103 and (March 3, 1788): 133–36, in *"The Rhapsodist and Other Uncollected Writings by Charles Brockden Brown,"* ed. Henry R. Warfel (New York: Scholars Facsimiles and Reprints, 1943), 47–56.

34. Martinette de Beauvais, Miss Monrose of the Baxter tableau, counts these refugees at "at least ten thousand . . . fugitives from Marat and St. Domingo" (209). For more on the French émigré presence in eighteenth-century Philadelphia, see Francis Sergeant Childs, *French Refugee Life in the United States, 1790–1800: An American Chapter of the French Revolution* (Baltimore: Johns Hopkins University Press, 1940); and David Lee Clark, *Charles Brockden Brown: Pioneer Voice of America* (Durham: Duke University Press, 1952), 12–13.

35. See the historical notes to *Ormond* in the Kent State edition, 408–409.

36. See Edmund Burke, *Reflections on the Revolution in France,* ed. Connor Cruise O'Brien (1790; Harmondsworth: Penguin Books, 1973), 170–72. I am indebted to Johnson's *Equivocal Beings,* 1–19, for my understanding of Burke's centrality to the English novelistic tradition of the 1790s.

37. See Peter Kafer, "Charles Brockden Brown and Revolutionary Philadelphia: An Imagination in Context," *Pennsylvania Magazine of History and Biography* 116.4 (October 1992): 467–98, especially 468–73 and 479–81. See also Looby, *Voicing America,* 201, 205. Looby's discussion of Brown's complex historical imagination of the Revolution has been central to my understanding of the double vision at work in his recurring representations of patricide, where the father's violent death is always the subject of sorrowful narration.

38. Brown's critics remain divided about exactly when the author cast off his radical Godwinianism to assume the stance of a staunch Federalist propagandist. The outer limit for dating this significant political shift is 1803, when, in the guise of a French counselor of state, he writes the notorious pamphlet entitled *An Address to the Government of the United States on the Cession of Louisiana to the French, and on the Late Breach of Treaty By the Spaniards, Including the Translation of a Memorial, on the War of San Domingo, and the Cession of Mississippi to France, drawn up by a Counsellor of State* (Philadelphia: C. and A. Conrad, 1803). For a historical review of the debate, see the bibliographic essay that appends Watts's cultural biography of Brown, *Romance of Real Life,* 225–41.

39. See Looby, *Voicing America,* 202.

40. In coining this phrase, I ring a change on Eve Sedgwick's articulation of the notion of "homosexual panic." See Sedgwick's *Between Men: English Literature and Male Homosocial Desire* (New York: Columbia University Press, 1985), particularly 83–96; and *Epis-*

temology of the Closet (Berkeley and Los Angeles: University of California Press, 1990), 182–212.

41. See Sacvan Bercovitch, *The American Jeremiad* (Madison: University of Wisconsin Press, 1978), 8, 11.

42. See Powell, *Bring out Your Dead*, 95.

43. See Pernick, "Politics, Parties, and Pestilence," 571.

44. See Powell, *Bring out Your Dead*, 95, 107, 110; and Korngold, "Crisis in the Capital," 189–205.

45. See Susan L. Mizruchi, "Neighbors, Strangers, Corpses: Death and Sympathy in the Early Writings of W. E. B. Du Bois," in *Centuries' Ends, Narrative Means*, ed. Robert D. Newman (Stanford: Stanford University Press, 1996), 313–42 and 592–602; "Cataloguing the Creatures of the Deep: 'Billy Budd, Sailor' and the Rise of Sociology," *Boundary 2* 17.1 (spring 1990): 285; and *The Science of Sacrifice: American Literature and Modern Social Theory* (Princeton: Princeton University Press, 1997).

46. See Shirley Samuels, "Infidelity and Contagion: The Rhetoric of Revolution," *Early American Literature* 22 (1987): 183–91.

47. Looby explores Brown's obsession with legitimation as a problem of both politics and epistemology in "'The Very Act of Utterance': Law, Language, and Legitimation in Brown's *Wieland*," chap. 3 in *Voicing America*, 145–202.

48. *Edgar Huntly* constitutes an obvious exception. Brown's last major novel is deeply enmeshed, from start to finish, in questions of race, national origin, and the problem of citizenship, particularly in its depiction of Native American warfare and Irish immigration in the 1790s. For a detailed reading of these issues, see Gardner, "Alien Nation," 429–61.

49. See textual notes to *Ormond*, 409.

50. See Christophersen, *Apparition in the Glass*, 78.

51. Lynn Hunt's reading of the French Revolution takes off from the parable about the founding of civilization in Freud's *Totem and Taboo: Some Points of Agreement between the Mental Lives of Savages and Neurotics*, *The Standard Edition of the Complete Psychological Works of Sigmund Freud* (henceforth, *SE*), trans. and ed. James Strachey, in collaboration with Anna Freud, assisted by Alix Strachey and Alan Tyson. 24 vols. (London: Hogarth Press, 1953–74), 13: 1–161. See Hunt, *Family Romance*, 6–12.

52. See, in particular, *Discipline and Punish: The Birth of the Prison*, trans. Alan Sheridan (New York: Vintage Books, 1979); and *The Birth of the Clinic: An Archaeology of Medical Perception*, trans. A. M. Sheridan Smith (New York: Vintage Books, 1975).

53. Ferguson formulates this phrase in "'What is Enlightenment?'," 252; see also 251.

54. For Brown's critique of Locke, see Fliegelman, introduction to *Wieland*, xiii and xix. See also Joan Dayan, *Fables of Mind: An Inquiry Into Poe's Fiction* (New York: Oxford University Press, 1987), which rigorously reconceptualizes the relations between the English and continental philosophical traditions of the seventeenth and eighteenth centuries and the work of theologically and epistemologically oriented American writers from Edwards through Poe.

55. See Gardner, "Alien Nation," 436.

56. This dynamic calls up and reverses Denis Diderot's account of the absorptive effects of certain eighteenth-century French genre paintings by Chardin and Greuze. According to Michael Fried, Diderot observes that these works so powerfully evoke sympathy that the fictive figures seem to reach out from the picture frame to incorporate the viewer within their tableaux, thus collapsing and thereby erasing the distance between beholder and object of vision. Diderot describes exactly the process of breaking the frame that *Charlotte Temple's*

narrator desires. See Fried, *Absorption and Theatricality: Painting and Beholder in the Age of Diderot* (Berkeley and Los Angeles: University of California Press, 1980), 92.

57. See *The Theory of Moral Sentiments*, eds. D. D. Raphael and A. L. Macfie (1759; Indianapolis: Liberty Classics, 1982), 9. All further references will be cited parenthetically in the text.

58. I am grateful to Michael Meranze for sharing with me his unpublished manuscript on Sterne and the politics of sympathy.

59. See David Marshall, *The Figure of Theater: Shaftesbury, Defoe, Adam Smith and George Eliot* (New York: Columbia University Press, 1986), 179.

60. For an astute elaboration of the politics of affect at work in the novels of excess I allude to here, works by such figures as Mary Wollstonecraft, Ann Radcliffe, and Frances Burney, see Johnson, *Equivocal Beings*, especially 1–46.

61. Thanks to Robert A. Ferguson for pointing out that, by making Baxter an ex-soldier, the Quaker Brown—a pacifist—is setting him up for a fall.

62. Ferguson's work on Brown's vocational anxiety is highly suggestive here; just as he argues that Brown worked through his apprehensions over giving up a legal career by writing fiction, I am proposing that Baxter—and to some extent the author for whom he stands—augment their self-conceptions as men by spinning stories. See Ferguson, *Law and Letters*, 129–49. See also Watts, *Romance of Real Life*.

63. Noting the way in which the supplement signals the absence that always already exists within presence, Derrida writes: "But the supplement supplements. It adds only to replace. It intervenes or insinuates itself in-the-place-of; if it fills, it is as if one fills a void. If it represents and makes an image, it is by the anterior default of a presence. . . . As a substitute, it is not simply added to the positivity of presence, it produces no relief, its place is assigned in the structure by the mark of an emptiness." See Jacques Derrida, *Of Grammatology*, trans. Gayatri Chakravorty Spivak (Baltimore: Johns Hopkins University Press, 1976), 145.

64. See Johnson, *Equivocal Beings*, 15.

65. Johnson writes, "the conservative insistence upon the urgency of chivalric sentimentality fundamentally unsettled gender itself, leaving women without a distinct gender site. Under sentimentality, all women risk becoming equivocal beings." Like the heroines of Radcliffe and Burney about whom Johnson writes, Martinette "must . . . shoulder the once-masculine virtues of stoic rationalism and self-control" (*Equivocal Beings*, 11, 16).

66. See Joan Riviere, "Femininity as Masquerade," *International Journal of Psychoanalysis* 10 (1929): 303–13.

67. See Kimberly W. Benston, "Facing Tradition: Revisionary Scenes in African American Literature," *PMLA* 105.1 (January 1990): 99.

68. See Sigmund Freud, "'A Child is Being Beaten': A Contribution to the Study of the Origin of Sexual Perversions" (1919), *SE* 17:175–204; Mary Ann Doane, "Film and Masquerade: Theorizing the Female Spectator," *Screen* 23.3–4 (September–October 1982): 74–88, and *The Desire to Desire: The Woman's Film of the 1940s* (Bloomington: University of Indiana Press, 1987); and Michelle A. Massé, *In the Name of Love: Women, Masochism, and the Gothic* (Ithaca: Cornell University Press, 1992).

69. We might think of this metanarrative collapse—where character, narrator, writer, and reader all mirror each other's activity—as a contaminated reprise of the narrator's efforts to incorporate the reader in *Charlotte Temple*, Brown's cynical reworking of Rowson's dream of sympathy as a waking nightmare marked by perversion, disease, and death rather than by transparent relations.

70. For a reading of the relationship between "male penetration or 'opening up'" and "the remapping of the masculine in the occult film," an investigation that has been highly suggestive for my work on Brown, see Carol Clover, *Men, Women, and Chainsaws: Gender in the Modern Horror Film* (Princeton: Princeton University Press, 1992), 70, 105. Clover's meditation on what I would call the "gendered narrative physics" of the horror film resonates in important ways with Johnson's work on gender as a narrative quantum in English fiction of the 1790s. Although my linking of these two studies would seem an ahistorical gesture, it in fact makes sense from the vantage point of *literary* history: in her reading of horror cinema, Clover explores narrative forms that originate in the gothic, sentimental, and melodramatic novels that Johnson reads so astutely in *Equivocal Beings*. See also Tania Modleski, *Loving with a Vengeance: Mass-Produced Fantasies for Women* (New York: Methuen, 1984), 59–84.

71. Levine notes that "during the 1790s the fever was regularly portrayed as a duplicitous form of foreign infiltration and subversion." Levine cites a letter written on October 25, 1796 by Brown to his brother James, which "describe[s] his own encounter with the fever: 'Plague operates by invisible agents, and we know not in what quarter it is about to attack us.'" Brown's anthropomorphic imaging of fever as *a martial corps* of stealthy saboteurs conveys a social anxiety similar to that of numerous contemporaneous countersubversive texts, particularly Federalist texts warning Americans to beware 'the foul contagion of French principles.'" See Levine, *Conspiracy and Romance*, 34, my emphasis. Brown's letter continues: "No shield, therefore, can be lifted up against [the epidemic]. We fear it as we are terrified by dark in which tho much of our panic be, doubtless, owing to the influence of education, and may be removed by habitual exposure to it, yet our defenseless condition and the invisible approaches of danger may contribute to our alarms." For the complete text of this letter, see Clark, *Pioneer Voice of America*, 156.

72. See Pernick, "Parties, Politics, and Pestilence," 561–86.

73. Levine makes a similar observation about the connection between the French queen executed by the revolutionaries and Brown's fictive woman warrior: "As her name suggests, Martinette during the French Revolution becomes a stalwart revolutionary and victim as well, both a martinet and Marie Antoinette." See *Conspiracy and Romance*, 51.

74. See Christophersen, *Apparition in the Glass*, 65.

75. I am grateful to Robert A. Ferguson for early discussions about the complex implications of this passage, both erotic and political. See also Carole Pateman, *The Sexual Contract* (Stanford: Stanford University Press, 1988), 109.

76. See Hunt, *Family Romance*, 6–7.

77. According to Freud, the competition that originally sets the primal father and the primal brothers at odds involves the possession of women. Thus, I take it that the primal horde includes the presence of "sisters." See *Totem and Taboo*, 141–44.

78. See Gardner, "Alien Nation," 432, 437.

79. It is, of course, one of Foucault's central insights that the notion of segregating "alien" populations for disciplinary purposes—including scientific or medical inquiry—is a legacy of the Enlightenment.

80. Mizruchi argues that sacrifice is a mechanism of social control in late-nineteenth- and early twentieth-century American literature and social thought. See *Science of Sacrifice*.

81. The pertinent passages in the novel are on 221–22 and 241–43.

82. For a brilliant discussion of the printer's negotiation of his "origins" through the use of textuality, see the section of Looby's chapter on Franklin entitled "Verbal Imposture," chap. 2 in *Voicing America*, 118–24.

83. See David Marshall, *The Surprising Effects of Sympathy: Marivaux, Diderot, Rousseau, and Mary Shelley* (Chicago: University of Chicago Press, 1988), 3.

84. Norman Grabo's study of Charles Brockden Brown centers on the pattern of "accidental" concurrence that pervades the fiction. See *The Coincidental Art of Charles Brockden Brown.*

85. See Jay Fliegelman, *Prodigals and Pilgrims: The American Revolution against Patriarchal Authority, 1750–1800* (Cambridge: Cambridge University Press, 1982), 38.

86. In contrast to Brown's sophisticated imagination of the marketplace, Foster's rendering of protoindividualist aspirations, which has been identified with emerging liberalism, remains inchoate in *The Coquette,* where gossip has not yet yielded to advertising.

87. See Jean-Christophe Agnew, *The Market and the Theater in Anglo-American Thought, 1550–1750* (Cambridge: Cambridge University Press, 1986); and Stuart Blumin, *The Emergence of the Middle Class: Social Experience in the American City, 1760–1900* (Cambridge: Cambridge University Press, 1989).

88. See Bolton-Smith and Johnson, "Miniature in America," 1043–44; and Werner B. Berthoff, "'A Lesson on Concealment': Brockden Brown's Method in Fiction," *Philological Quarterly* 37 (1958): 45–57.

89. *Charleston Times,* May 27, 1807, quoted in Ruel Pardee Tolman, *The Life and Works of Edward Greene Malbone, 1777–1807* (New York: 1958), 62.

90. See Cuadrado, "Portrait Miniatures," 42; and Bolton-Smith and Johnson, "Miniature in America," 1045. Cuadrado writes that "for Washington's officers in the Revolution [portrait miniatures] served [particularly] personal ends. They were remembrances made to be cherished by worried spouses far away from the fields of battle" (42).

Miniature portraits figure in all the novels explored in this study. See chap. 1 for the fetishistic import of such portraits and chap. 2 for the equivocal role they play in the personal and cultural climate of upheaval that marks the post-Revolutionary period. Susanna Rowson's *Charlotte Temple,* itself a fetishistic miniature bounded by a powerful and compelling frame, could be said to turn around the link between a culture's need for relics and a recurrent nostalgia that is in fact a form of melancholia.

91. For a trenchant discussion of themes of authorship, agency, and origination in *Wieland,* see Walter Hesford, "'Do You Know The Author?': The Question of Authorship in *Wieland,*" *Early American Literature* 17 (1982–83): 239–48.

92. See William J. Scheick, "The Problem of Origination in Brown's *Ormond,*" in *Critical Essays on Charles Brockden Brown,* ed. Bernard Rosenthal (Boston: G. K. Hall, 1981): 126–41, 127. Names in *Ormond* multiply as wildly as do fraudulent selves: the Dudleys of New York are also the Acworths of Philadelphia; Craig is really Mansfield; Martinette is known throughout the first half of the novel as Ursula Monrose, though her name is really Ormond by birth and Wentworth by marriage; and her surrogate father is called Monrose by the Baxters, who have performed an act of Frenchification on the Italian Roselli. Ormond's mistress Helena Cleves attempts to disguise her nonvirginal but unmarried state with the pseudonym "Mrs. Eden," as if the name itself reassigned innocence to her exploited person. Renomination becomes another facet of disguise and impersonation, supporting the notion afoot in the novel that the self is ever recreatable. As Scheick asserts, names in *Ormond* "are fictions. . . . Each [name] reflects not only the deceptions of the human mind but also the protean, creative capacity of the human will" (135).

93. Looby, *Voicing America,* 157.

94. See Marybeth Norton, *Liberty's Daughters: The Revolutionary Experience of American Women: 1750–1800* (Boston: Little Brown, 1980), 229–31. See also Lee Virginia

Chambers-Schiller, *Liberty, A Better Husband: Single Women in America, The Generations of 1780–1840* (New Haven: Yale University Press, 1984), 35–36.

95. My claim here regarding the native and therefore citizen status of the families whose daughters could sit for miniature portraits is meant to be suggestive. While it is certainly possible that royalist émigrés from the French Revolution might have carried assets such as jewels and gold in their flight to America, it is unlikely that even aristocratic refugees could underwrite the commissioning of family portraits in the months immediately following their exodus. More probably, these people, like the fictional French exiles in *Ormond*, are figures of "tarnished splendour" (63).

Francis Sergeant Childs devotes an entire chapter of her study of French refugee life in Philadelphia to the economic status of these exiles. She notes that "the economic position of the refugees was determined by the circumstances of the emigration. Granted this basic fact, they seem, economically speaking, to have formed three major divisions. One consisted of those arriving absolutely destitute and therefore needing assistance of some sort for the moment at least. Another included those who, arriving with little or modest means, nevertheless somehow or other struggled along on their own resources, capitalizing on their accomplishments, such as music, painting, dancing and drawing, as did the socially privileged, or on their craftsmanship, as did the butchers and bakers. . . . The third group, smaller and more prominent socially, consisted of individuals who had some resources and were consequently able to go into business in the United States, to invest in land, and in general to maintain a somewhat higher standard of living. These divisions were by no means determined by social distinctions—wealthy and fortunate San Domingo planters were among the destitute, while some tradesmen evidently saved enough to carry on in the New World." See Childs, *French Refugee Life*, 84.

Newspaper evidence from the period reveals that, beyond the privileged amateurs who gave painting lessons to genteel Philadelphians, actual artists of French extraction from the Continent and the West Indies established themselves in the new republic, particularly in the South, following the revolutions in France and San Domingo. As members of the artisan class, neither such figures themselves nor their offspring were the likely *subjects* of such portraiture. As the political privileges of republicanism turned on the ownership of property, the most economically advantaged inhabitants of America were also often native citizens. For the French artists, see Bolton-Smith and Johnson, "Miniature in America," 1045.

96. See Benjamin Franklin, *The Autobiography*, in *Benjamin Franklin: Writings*, ed. J. A. Leo Lemay (New York: Library of America, 1987), 1332–33, 1338, and 1342–44. For an interesting reading of Keith as an eighteenth-century forerunner of the nineteenth-century confidence man, see Karen Halttunen, *Confidence Men and Painted Women: A Study of Middle-Class Culture in America, 1830–1870* (New Haven: Yale University Press, 1982), 3. Halttunen's important study oddly overlooks the way in which Franklin himself actually fits the paradigm of the confidence man she details. As he relates his schemes in his memoir, of course, Franklin's designs appear beneficent and generally productive for the development of early national culture, while those of a figure like Keith are merely disruptive. It is important to remember, however, that the narrative is itself a material product of Franklin's inventive mind—and in that regard it actually constructs rather than passively awaits the confidence he seeks to win from his reading public. For the designing side of Franklin's character, see Gary Lindberg, *The Confidence Man in American Literature* (New York: Oxford University Press, 1982), 76.

97. See Jane Tompkins, *Sensational Designs: The Cultural Work of American Fiction, 1790–1860* (New York: Oxford University Press, 1985), 52, who notes that the phrase is coined by James Otis and quoted by John Eliot to Jeremy Belknap in the *Belknap Papers*

(January 12, 1777), 104, all of which are cited by Gordon S. Wood, *The Creation of the American Republic, 1776–1787* (New York: W. W. Norton, 1969), 477. Tompkins goes on to remark that "on this phenomenon Wood himself makes the following pronouncement, which accords well with Brown's picture of the post-Revolutionary era: 'The most pronounced social effect of the Revolution was not harmony or stability but the sudden appearance of new men everywhere in politics and business'" (*Sensational Designs*, 210 n. 29). See also Carroll Smith-Rosenberg, "Domesticating 'Virtue': Coquettes and Revolutionaries in Young America," in *Literature and the Body: Essays on Persons and Populations*, ed. Elaine Scarry (Baltimore: Johns Hopkins University Press, 1988), 163–64.

98. See Rodgers, "Fruits of Improvisation," 7. His essay, suffused by a tone of irritation at those *Ormond* scholars making claims for the novel's narrative unity and integrity, puts forward an interesting case for the incoherence of the work, which he chalks up to the "fruits of improvisation" noted in his title. Arguing that Brown wrote against a pressing deadline, Rodgers asserts that the author's motives were primarily to entertain. While the essay cuts through much of the overly allegorical analysis the book has sustained, it effectively obviates the possibility that Brown's novel *means* at all, challenging particularly the notion that *Ormond* constitutes a significant cultural artifact of Federalist Philadelphia in the throes of post-Revolutionary crisis. My point is that, while sections of *Ormond* do not come together in the way that conventional eighteenth-century Anglo-American fiction is purported to do (a premise that much current criticism of this material surely would contest), its disparate parts and digressive tableaux indeed constitute a fascinating picture of a nation on the verge of collapse. For an important reading of Brown's work as a barometer of social disorder in the post-Revolutionary period, see Emory Elliott, *Revolutionary Writers: Literature and Authority in the New Republic, 1725–1810* (New York: Oxford University Press, 1982), 218–70.

99. That the forger is not identified as the killer until the end of the novel does blunt the impact of Brown's apparently drastic reconception.

100. Smith's model of perception and imaginative translation is predicated on this notion. Daniel E. Williams coins the phrase "transactions of belief." See "In Defense of Self: Author and Authority in the *Memoirs of Stephen Burroughs*," *Early American Literature* 25.3 (1990): 97, my emphasis.

101. For a detailed background on the evolution of the trickster, a universal literary archetype who transgresses boundaries and taboos, into the confidence man, a distinctly American figure who is culturally representative rather than marginal, see Lindberg, *Confidence Man*, 8.

102. See Joyce Appleby, *Capitalism and a New Social Order: The Republican Vision in the 1790s* (New York: New York University Press, 1984); and "Republicanism and Ideology," in *Liberalism and Republicanism in the Historical Imagination* (Cambridge, Mass. Harvard University Press, 1992), 277–90; see also Smith-Rosenberg, "Domesticating 'Virtue,'" 163, and 182 n. 10.

103. This is particularly true in the case of Franklin, who characteristically adopts Calvinist categories and reinvents Puritan practices: both are evidenced in his keeping of "accounts" on the tablet of virtues detailed in *The Autobiography*, 1384–89. For the classic statement and exposition of the dynamic, see Max Weber, *The Protestant Ethic and the Spirit of Capitalism*, trans. Talcott Parsons, introd. Anthony Giddens (1920; New York: Charles Scribner's Sons, 1958). For a dialectical reading of the operations that underlie this dichotomy, and for an analysis of its deconstruction within the work of the very figures who emblematize the divide, see Mitchell R. Breitwieser, *Cotton Mather and Benjamin Franklin: The Price of Representative Personality* (Cambridge: Cambridge University Press, 1984).

104. Such scholars include Larzer Ziff, *Writing in the New Nation: Prose, Print, and Politics in the Early United States* (New Haven: Yale University Press, 1991), 66; and Fliegelman, *Declaring Independence*, 37. See also Daniel A. Cohen, *Pillars of Salt, Monuments of Grace: New England Crime Literature and the Origins of American Popular Culture, 1674–1860* (New York: Oxford University Press, 1993), 155–62; and Christopher W. Jones, "Praying Upon Truth: *The Memoirs of Stephen Burroughs* and the Picaresque," *Early American Literature* 30.1 (1995): 32–50.

105. See Stephen Burroughs, *Memoirs of Stephen Burroughs*, ed. Philip F. Gura (1798, 1804, 1811; Boston: Northeastern University Press, 1988), 224. The three dates given for the narrative's original publication indicate parts I and II, which in 1811 were combined into one volume attached with new appendices.

106. See Williams, "In Defense of Self," 92.

107. While an imaginative work of speculative historiography, Pernick's "Politics, Parties, and Pestilence," which attempts to connect the civic response to yellow fever and the development of party politics in Philadelphia of the 1790s, partakes of the dualistic forms of analysis I am concerned with uncovering here. Cornfield elaborates this criticism in "Crisis in the Capital."

108. In that regard, the pervasive figure of incest in the early American novel takes on a dynamic significance, emblematizing the way in which what are perceived as disturbances from without are themselves always already operative within the nation. Thus, what the party manichees of the period would denounce as exogamous philandering—the nation's flirtation with European political allegiances—is in fact a virulent form of endogamous contention that cannot be acknowledged. See Anne Dalke, "Original Vice: The Political Implications of Incest in the Early American Novel," *Early American Literature* 23 (1988): 188–201; and James B. Twitchell, *Forbidden Partners: The Incest Taboo in Modern Culture* (New York: Columbia University Press, 1987), 194, 200–5.

109. Burke sounds this note very early in *Reflections*, when he writes that "A state without the means of some change is without the means of its conservation." Ten pages later, he continues, "The very idea of the fabrication of a new government, is enough to fill us with disgust and horror. We wished at the period of the Revolution, and do now wish, to derive all we possess as *an inheritance from our forefathers.* Upon that body and stock of inheritance we have taken care not to inoculate any cyon [*sic*] alien to the nature of the original plant. All the reformations we have hitherto made, have proceeded upon the principle of reference to antiquity; and I hope, nay I am persuaded, that all of those which possibly may be made hereafter, will be carefully formed upon analogical precedent, authority, and example." See Burke, *Reflections*, 106, 117.

110. Early in *Ormond*, Sophia notes the antimatrimonial attitudes of her beloved friend: "Now she was at least mistress of the product of her own labour [*sic*]. Her tasks were toilsome, but the profits, though slender, were sure, and she administered her little property in what manner she pleased. Marriage would annihilate this power. Henceforth she would be bereft even of personal freedom. So far from possessing property, she herself would become the property of another" (84). For Ormond's hostility to marriage and thoughts about the liberation of women from the sexual shackles of matrimony, see 122–23.

111. For a detailed reading of the "post-heroic" generation, see George B. Forgie, *Patricide in the House Divided: A Psychological Interpretation of Lincoln and His Age* (New York: W. W. Norton, 1979), in particular 13–53.

112. See Halttunen, *Confidence Men and Painted Women*, 3.

113. I briefly discuss Franklin's own early experience as gull above. For a sampling of the criticism that draws the connection between Mervyn and Franklin, see James H. Justus,

"Arthur Mervyn, American," *American Literature* 42 (1970): 304–24; William Hedges, "Charles Brockden Brown and The Culture of Contradictions," *Early American Literature* 9.2 (Fall 1974): 136–38; Elliott, *Revolutionary Writers*, 244, 259; Grabo, *Coincidental Art*, 85; Alan Axelrod, *Charles Brockden Brown: An American Tale* (Austin: University of Texas Press, 1983), 144, and 147–48; Robert S. Levine, "Arthur Mervyn's Revolutions," *Studies in American Fiction* 12.2 (autumn 1984): 149; and Watts, *Romance of Real Life*, 104.

Although it is in *Arthur Mervyn* that Brown makes most obvious use of this Founder's "representative personality," Franklin also personifies the Enlightenment interest in mechanical invention; it is as a *printer*, a proliferator of writing, that Franklin also haunts *Ormond* in decidedly ominous ways. In particular, Franklin's own impulse toward textual dissimulation in his early career makes him an interesting prototype for the forger Craig. In a range of episodes recorded in the *Autobiography*, Franklin describes the way he claims authorship for a series of literary texts written by others: the incident when, in a distinctly *fraternal* pre-Revolutionary gesture of political solidarity, he signs his name to a newspaper piece authored by his brother who has been jailed for libel by the Tory authorities; or the episode involving James Ralph and the Junto, when at his friend's behest, but taking zealous pleasure in the deception, Franklin declares that it is he who composes the poem that in fact Ralph himself writes, in order that the verse receive an unbiased hearing; or even the description of erecting a gravestone for his parents, where he essentially takes credit for their greatest creative act—the engendering of Benjamin Franklin himself—when he signs his name on their tomb as the author of its text. In all these ways and in several others noted by Looby, for Franklin, textuality supplements and enables a form of public authority that shores up identity itself. See Looby, *Voicing America*, 118–24.

Emory Elliott notes that, while in the 1790s, "Franklin's *Autobiography* had not yet been published, its existence and content were known among Philadelphia intellectuals who had read the section completed before 1789 and had urged Franklin to print it." See *Revolutionary Writers*, 298 n. 20. See also Mary E. Rucher, "Benjamin Franklin," in *American Literature 1764–1789: The Revolutionary Years*, ed. Everett H. Emerson (Madison: University of Wisconsin Press, 1977), 105–25. For the notion of representative personality, see Breitwieser, *Price of Representative Personality*, 1–6.

114. See Halttunen, *Confidence Men and Painted Women*, xvi.

115. See Halttunen, *Confidence Men and Painted Women*, 8, 9.

116. See Levine, *Conspiracy and Romance*, 33.

117. For the significance of a "third term" for the rejection of binary thinking, see Marjorie Garber, *Vested Interests: Cross-Dressing and Cultural Anxiety* (New York: Routledge, 1992), 10. For the importance of Germany to Brown's imagination, see Looby, *Voicing America*, 151–52, 154–58. For an expanded reading of the way in which Brown maps geography onto politics at the conclusion of *Ormond*, see below.

118. See Marshall, *Surprising Effects of Sympathy*, 109. On the notion of natural transparency and its connection to new theatrical forms in the eighteenth century, see Fliegelman, "Natural Theatricality," in *Declaring Independence*, 79–94.

119. Eagleton asserts that "the letter can never forget that it is turned outwards to another, that its discourse is ineradicably social. Such sociality is not just contingent, a mere matter of its destination; it is the very material condition of its existence. The other to whom the letter is addressed is included within it, an absent recipient present within each phrase. As speech-for-another, the letter must reckon that recipient's likely response into its every gesture." See *The Rape of Clarissa: Writing, Class Struggle, and Sexuality in Samuel Richardson* (Minneapolis: University of Minnesota Press, 1982), 52.

120. In light of Brown's almost entirely negative characterization of the legal profession

in *Ormond*—those passages where Constantia contemplates pressing suit against Thomas Craig for embezzlement and fraud—such argumentative language deployed by a novelist who has only recently abandoned his study of law is particularly arresting. In fact, the charges Brown levels against the early national judicial process prove hauntingly resonant almost two hundred years later. Thus, Sophia writes: "But the law was formal and circuitous. Money itself was necessary to purchase its assistance. Besides, it could not act with unseen virtue and instantaneous celerity. The cooperation of advocates and officers was required. . . . It was enough that justice must be bought, and that she had not the equivalent. Legal proceedings are encumbered with delay, and her necessities were urgent. Succour [*sic*], if withheld till the morrow, would be useless. Hunger and cold would not be trifled with. What resource was there left in this her uttermost distress? . . . All that he had, according to the principles of social equity, was her's [*sic*]; yet he, to whom nothing belonged, rioted in superfluity, while she, the rightful claimant, was driven to the point of utmost need. The proper instrument of her restoration was law, but its arm was powerless, for she had not the means of bribing it into activity. But was law the only instrument?" (91–92). While in her indictment of Craig Sophia sounds like a prosecuting attorney, the larger narrative reads as an extended brief for the defense, undertaken with the object of exonerating Constantia Dudley of charges of murder. As an exhaustive and elaborate, and circuitous, case, made to extenuate Ormond's killing as an act of self preservation, *Ormond* constitutes a remarkably thorough "vindication." This fact suggests that Brown's training continued to inflect his thinking and writing well after he cast off the thought of practicing law.

121. Inspired by the texts of continental political thinkers seizing the American imagination in the early 1790s, Brown turns to the writing of fiction and, in less than three years, creates a quartet of works that take up the difficulty of forging personal and political identity in the wake of Revolution. Brown's four major novels are narrated in the first-person voice; with the exception of *Arthur Mervyn*, which is constructed explicitly as a memoir, *Wieland*, *Ormond*, and *Edgar Huntly* purport to be extended epistles composed and transmitted to unnamed or unrepresented European correspondents. These works constitute "letters from the front" of American national identity formation, republican dispatches to a nonrepublican world that is eager and curious to be introduced "to scenes to which [it has] been hitherto a stranger" (Epistolary Preface "To I. E. Rosenberg," 3). I am grateful to Jonathan Arac for the early suggestion that Burke's *Reflections* would provide an important key to the contorted politics and peculiar narrative strategies of Charles Brockden Brown.

122. See Benjamin, "The Work of Art in the Age of Mechanical Reproduction," *Illuminations*, trans. Harry Zohn, ed. and introd. Hannah Arendt (New York: Schocken Books, 1969), 221.

123. See Benjamin, "Art in the Age of Mechanical Reproduction," 221.

124. See Tzvetan Todorov, *The Conquest of America: The Question of the Other*, trans. Richard Howard (New York: Harper and Row, 1984), 87.

125. Brown provides no evidence of course that either Dudley or Craig knows anything about the scriptive practices, much less the dialect, of working-class women from Yorkshire. Thus, the forger's letters ultimately emanate from a purely imaginary space. They are nevertheless inflected by Craig's general knowledge of Dudley's beliefs about gender, class, and national identity, notions to which his missives *correspond* as closely as possible, as Sophia's testimony suggests.

126. See Marshall, *Surprising Effects of Sympathy*, 5.

127. See Sedgwick, *Between Men*.

128. I here invoke Cathy N. Davidson's term and by extension her important argument

about the central role that writing plays in the formation of early national culture. See Davidson, *Revolution and The Word.*

129. Somewhat later in this letter, Jefferson notes, "[S]ay at this moment, a new majority have come into place, in their own right, and not under the rights, the conditions, or laws of their predecessors. Are they bound to acknowledge the debt, to consider the preceding generation as having had a right to eat up the whole soil of their country, in the course of a life, to alienate it from them . . . and would they think themselves either legally or morally bound to give up their country and emigrate to another for subsistence? Every one will say no; that the soil is the gift of God to the living, as much as it has been to the deceased generation; and that the laws of nature impose no obligation upon them to pay this debt." Jefferson's meditations here about the precedence youth should take over age are neatly summarized in the famous statement from this letter's second paragraph: "The earth belongs to the living, not to the dead." See Jefferson's letter to John Wayles Eppes, June 24, 1813, in *Thomas Jefferson: Writings.* ed. Merrill D. Peterson (New York: Library of America, 1984), 1280, 1281–82, and 1280.

130. Thanks to Robert A. Ferguson, who suggested that Blackstone considers counterfeiting as a form of treason.

131. Current scholarship on the corpus of Adam Smith's works suggests just this. See Marshall on Smith in *Figure of Theater,* 165–92; and see Mulcaire, *Aesthetics of Laissez Faire,* work in progress.

132. Brown's father and brothers were merchants whose knowledge of—if not commerce with—the island trade gave him a personal context for meditating the evil of slavery. A Quaker upbringing in Revolutionary and post-Revolutionary Philadelphia would certainly expose someone like Brown to abolitionist ideas.

133. See Elkins and McKitrick, *The Age of Federalism,* 73.

134. See Elkins and McKitrick, *The Age of Federalism,* 651.

135. See Winthrop D. Jordan, *White Over Black: American Attitudes Toward the Negro, 1550–1812* (New York: W. W. Norton, 1968), 375–91; and Eugene D. Genovese, *From Rebellion To Revolution: Afro-American Slave Revolts In The Making Of The Modern World* (Baton Rouge: Louisiana State University Press, 1979).

136. Fliegelman's *Prodigals and Pilgrims* offers an extended meditation on this relation; see also Tompkins, *Sensational Designs,* 60; and see Shirley Samuels, *Romances of the Republic: Women, the Family, and Violence in the Literature of the Early American Nation* (New York: Oxford University Press, 1996), 3–22, and "The Family, The State, and the Novel," *American Quarterly* 38.3 (1986): 381–95.

137. See Freud, *Totem and Taboo,* and Hunt, *Family Romance.*

138. This reading of Mr. Dudley's final fate simplifies what are in fact the more equivocal details of his later days: after Ormond hires a Continental eye surgeon to restore the patriarch's vision, he comes to enjoy a brief respite of health and relative well-being before he is murdered by Craig. Nevertheless, Mr. Dudley remains financially dependent on Constantia's inheritance from Helena Cleves, Ormond's former mistress. Before committing suicide after being thrown over by the libertine in favor of Constantia herself, Helena bequeaths the girl her annuity and property, entitlements provided by her lover. And so it is that the family's economic restoration remains indirectly contingent on the offices of Ormond alone, a fact that Mr. Dudley deplores as much as he loathes the libertine and seeks to free Constantia from his influence. While the patriarch would seem to enjoy the (short-lived) return of his sight, his vision of his daughter's future nevertheless remains utterly blighted.

139. T. Allston Brown, *History of the American Stage*, (1870; New York: Benjamin Blom, 1969), 202, quoted in Eric Lott, *Love and Theft: Blackface Minstrelsy and The American Working Class* (New York: Oxford University Press, 1993), 50.

140. See Lott, *Love and Theft*, 51.

141. As a resident alien living in a republic whose Bill of Rights protects against unlawful searches and seizures, Ormond quite literally violates the Dudley's privileges under the Constitution; his voyeurism is not only unethical but also illegal.

142. For an elaboration of the cross-racial phantasmagoria that organize such expropriations, see Lott, *Love and Theft*, 38–62.

143. See Lott, *Love and Theft*, 57.

144. Historian George Lewis Phillips, whose pioneering work on English and American chimney sweeps remains definitive, writes: "If Negro boys had not displaced white boys in our flues, the American public might have shaken off its apathy, as the English did, and put down the employment of youngsters serving as corkscrews in loosening the soot. Because of the influence of slavery, the young Africans, regarded as an inferior race of beings, were considered as expendable in performing menial work, and so accustomed was the public to seeing them wandering about the streets that it gave little thought to their pitiful condition. . . . Life for them as Negroes was hard enough, but when they were chimney-sweeping apprentices as well, it was doubly difficult." See Phillips, *American Chimney Sweeps: An Historical Account of a Once Important Trade* (Trenton: Past Times Press, 1957), 73.

In their singular study of African American chimney sweeps in post-Revolutionary and antebellum New York, Paul A. Gilje and Howard B. Rock note that, "in New York, where slavery was well entrenched in the eighteenth century, the bondage [of black chimney sweeps] was real. Sometime before 1800, slaveowners began to hire out their slaves, including children, for this work. Given the high demand for labor in New York, there was little competition from free white workers, who had no taste for difficult tasks in a notorious and degrading trade. Although whites originally worked as sweeps, by the beginning of the nineteenth century not only the labor but also the contracting were performed by African Americans." Gilje and Howard go on to remark that "all that can be conclusively asserted is that before 1800 Euro-Americans identified the trade as fit only for African Americans. According to Phillips's research, this was true not only in New York but throughout the northern seaports," which would include Brown's Philadelphia. See Gilje and Rock, "'Sweep O! Sweep O!': African-American Chimney Sweeps and Citizenship in the New Nation," *William and Mary Quarterly*, 3d Ser. 51.3 (July 1994): 510–13. I am grateful to Seth Cotlar for bringing Gilje and Rock's essay to my attention.

145. See John Runcie, "'Hunting the Nigs' in Philadelphia: The Race Riot of August 1834," *Pennsylvania History* 39.2 (1972): 187–218, and 209; and David Roediger, *The Wages of Whiteness: Race and the Making of the American Working Class* (London: Verso, 1991), 106; both are quoted in Lott, *Love and Theft*, 29.

146. See Lott, *Love and Theft*, 8 and 39.

147. See Lott, *Love and Theft*, 29.

148. For the gothic knowledge that underlies the master-slave relation, see Robert H. Byer, "'The Man of the Crowd': Edgar Allan Poe In His Culture" (Ph.D. diss., Yale University, 1979), 396.

149. Fliegelman notes that "the function of speech was not so much to express feelings as to elicit particular responses. Even John Adams understood in 1759 that the point was to adapt one's voice not to the passion he felt but to 'the passion he would move.' Or to the emotion he wished to feel; for, at least in the view of painter Charles Wilson Peale, by

putting an expression on one's face one could through '*sweet contagion*' call forth the emotion to which it corresponded, thus generating natural feeling through theatrical imitation." These remarks about the way political figures in eighteenth-century America were concerned with invoking in their audiences and constituents a desired response and the citation of Peale on the connection between sympathy and contagion are highly pertinent to the problems of theatricality and sympathy I have been exploring in *Ormond*. See John Adams, *John Adams's Earliest Diary*, ed. L. H. Butterfield (Cambridge, Mass.: Harvard University Press, 1966), 74; and Charles Wilson Peale, *An Essay to Promote Domestic Happiness* (Philadelphia: 1812), 17, quoted in Fliegelman, *Declaring Independence*, 80–81.

150. See Jonas Barish, *The Antitheatrical Prejudice* (Berkeley and Los Angeles: University of California Press, 1981), 279.

151. The latter phrase is Fliegelman's. See *Declaring Independence*, 80–82.

152. See "Letter to M. D'Alembert on the Theatre," in *Politics and The Arts: "Letter To M. D'Alembert On The Theatre*," trans. Allan Bloom (1758; Ithaca: Cornell University Press, 1968), 79.

153. See Marshall, *Surprising Effects of Sympathy*, 145.

154. See Marshall, *Surprising Effects of Sympathy*, 107.

155. See Marshall, *Surprising Effects of Sympathy*, 107.

156. See Barish, *Antitheatrical Prejudice*, 277.

157. See Marshall, *Surprising Effects of Sympathy*, 133.

158. See Marshall, *Surprising Effects of Sympathy*, 109.

159. For a compelling discussion of the problem of "natural theatricality," see Fliegelman, *Declaring Independence*, 79–94.

160. For the narrative account of the antislavery emblem, see Clarkson, *History of the Rise, Progress, and Accomplishment of the Abolition of the African Slave Trade by the British Parliament*, 2 vols., (London: R. Taylor, 1808): 1:450–51, quoted in Jean Fagin Yellin, *Women and Sisters: The Antislavery Feminists in American Culture* (New Haven: Yale University Press, 1989), 6.

As late as 1800, the pins have made their way across Philadelphia's interracial community: Absalom Jones, one of the city's most prominent African American ministers and an early leader of its Free African Society, preaches in that year a Fourth of July Oration at his African Episcopal Church of St. Thomas wearing the pin on his lapel. On Jones' career, see Gary Nash, *Forging Freedom: The Formation of Philadelphia's Black Community 1720–1840* (Cambridge, Mass.: Harvard University Press, 1988), 111–19, and 126–30; for details about his Fourth of July Oration, see Sidney Kaplan, *The Black Presence in the Era of the American Revolution: 1770–1800* (New York: New York Graphic Society, 1973), 231, 235.

161. For Franklin's correspondence with Wedgwood, see Benjamin Franklin to Josiah Wedgwood, May 15, 1787, Library of Congress, Manuscripts Division, quoted in Kaplan, *The Black Presence*, 235–36.

162. Those slaves who were also hired as chimney sweeps and whose apparel was attained by scrounging the cast-off remnants of their masters' wardrobes suffered the literal and figurative onus of slavery as "human parasitism," to borrow Orlando Patterson's formulation in *Slavery and Social Death: A Comparative Study* (Cambridge, Mass.: Harvard University Press, 1982), 334–42.

In describing the garb of apprentice chimney sweeps, who were almost always children, Gilje and Rock quote Thomas Eaton's poem *Review of New York*. Eaton writes:

Next we meet a chimney sweep,
Who in the street had been asleep,

Enrob'd in rags, with sooty cap,
And issues from his mouth a clap
Of shrill alarm, which, understood,
Bespeaks a disposition good
To sweep the chimneys at a nod
To gain a crum, or shun a rod.
All cold and hungry I have seen
These helpless negroes screen
Themselves from chastisement, by oath
Denying cold and hunger both.

See Eaton, *Review of New York, or Rambles Through the City. Original Poems. Moral, Religious, Sarcastic, and Descriptive* (New York: 1813), 124, quoted in Gelje and Rock, "Sweep O!," 509.

163. Gelje and Rock describe the horrible conditions and costumes in which these urchins worked; they note that in

order to pass through the smallest openings, a sweep wore no clothing but his underwear and a stocking cap with eye slits to cover his face, however inadequately. Soot collected over the sweeps from head to toe. Eventually their bodies became calloused with scar tissue from lacerations, and their skin developed an armorlike leathery texture. Sweeps also had a tendency to develop "cancer of the scrotum" from infections caused by imbedded soot. This "sooty wart," as the "cancer" was called, led to sterility and, occasionally, death. Soot lodged under the eyelids, causing infections and leaving the telltale "red-rimmed" eye. Finally, there was enormous danger of consumption, or tuberculosis, from soot in the boys's lungs.

Citing Eaton's poem (see note above), Gelje and Rock remark that in such lines "we detect the pathos elicited by the apprentice sweep, barely earning a survival wage while striving to avoid punishment from his master's rod." See "'Sweep O!,'" 508–509.

164. The reality and limits of such brotherhood, and most specifically, its *paternalism,* obviously constitute a far more complicated story than the one I have suggested here, as not all antislavery advocates embraced their African American brethren as siblings under the skin. The colonialization movement marks only one example of the racialist attitudes held by many opponents of slavery, which include such professed antislavery figures as Harriet Beecher Stowe.

165. The full title of the pamphlet is *A Narrative Of The Proceedings Of The Black People, During The Late Awful Calamity In Philadelphia, In The Year 1793: And A Refutation Of Some Censures, Thrown upon them in some late Publications* (Philadelphia: William W. Woodward, 1794). All further references will be cited parenthetically in the text.

166. Jean Fagin Yellin devotes her entire study to exploring the origins and evolutions of the feminist antislavery emblem. See *Women and Sisters.*

167. See Marshall, *Surprising Effects of Sympathy,* 3.

168. On the gothicism of slavery's regime of surveillance see Byer, "'The Man of the Crowd'," 396; and Eric J. Sundquist, *To Wake The Nations: Race in the Making of American Literature* (Cambridge, Mass.: Harvard University Press, 1993), 54.

169. On slavery as human parasitism and ideological mystification, see Patterson, *Slavery and Social Death,* 337–338.

170. Patterson, *Slavery and Social Death,* 338.

171. See Susan L. Mizruchi's discussion of sympathetic immunity in her "Neighbors, Strangers, Corpses."

172. With the exception of scholars such as Christophersen, Carroll Smith-Rosenberg, and others currently writing on *Arthur Mervyn* (the one novel in Brown's oeuvre in which an African American presence is palpable), only Gardner notes the significance of race in *Ormond*. His observation, however, is deployed parenthetically in a paragraph listing as an instance of Brown's "long standing" "interest" in "racial cross-dressing" the villain's descent into blackface masquerade. See "Alien Nation," 446.

173. James M. Redfield discusses the significance of what he terms the "antifuneral" motif in the *Iliad*—where a hero is stripped of his armor and left to be devoured by birds and dogs. While Brown's plague is best characterized by the chaotic quality of the devastation it inflicts and thus would seem incongruent with the highly ritualized destruction that unfolds on the battlefields of the *Iliad*, it is nevertheless true that the cultural significance of "unburial" is always marked, be it the result of random freaks of nature such as contagious disease or the intentional work of human agents, antagonists at war. Redfield writes: "the dead body begins to rot. Once the *psuche* is gone, the familiar form begins to turn into something else as it blends into the flux of nature. This is the horror of dead bodies; they are interstitial things, for in death the whole person becomes a kind of excrement, the mere remains of life." He goes on to note that "the terror of conflict lies in the threat of impurity which conflict evokes. . . . The antifuneral, by which the dead are stripped and left to the scavengers, is in the *Iliad* emblematic of the impurity latent in war . . . this ultimate impurity never becomes actual in the poem; yet the threat of this impurity is the quintessential terror of the *Iliad*." Though the battlefield in *Ormond* is one of epidemic illness rather than of human strife, the issues of impurity and degradation, which point to the limits of what distinguishes culture from nature and which are raised by the scene of Whiston's death and decay, resonate powerfully with Redfield's insights about the meaning of "unburial" in Homer. See *Nature And Culture In The Iliad: The Tragedy of Hector* (Chicago: University of Chicago Press, 1975), 179, 183.

174. Jones and Allen narrate an extraordinary episode that presages in even more outrageous form the story of Whiston. They remark: "We remember an instance of cruelty, which we trust, no black man would be guilty of: two sisters[,] orderly, decent, white women were sick with the fever, one of them recovered so as to come to the door; a neighboring white man saw her, and in an angry tone asked her if her sister was dead or not? She answered no, upon which he replied, damn her, if she don't die before morning I will make her die. The poor woman[,] shocked at such an expression, from this monster of a man, made a modest reply, upon which he snatched a tub of water, and would have dashed it over her, if he had not been prevented by a black man; he then went and took a couple of fowls out of a coop, (which had been given them for nourishment) and threw them into an open alley; he had his wish, the poor woman he would make die died that night." See *A Narrative*, 9–20.

175. See Paine, *Rights of Man*, introd. Eric Foner (1791; Harmondsworth: Penguin Books, 1984), 49–50. In his discussion of the partisan debate about the uses of political propaganda in the 1790s, Fliegelman cites Paine's critique of Burke's theatrical tableaux. See *Declaring Independence*, 78.

176. See Johnson, *Equivocal Beings*, 23, 30, 23, and 46.

177. Each of Brown's cross-dressed narratives contains a female figure clothed in male garb who embodies a kind of secret signature; the transvestite character alerts the reader that the author's unconventional mode of storytelling is a self-conscious one. While *Wieland*'s hidden autograph resides in the image of Louisa Conway *mère*, fleeing Europe for America "in the disguise of a boy" (242), *Ormond*'s secret signature can be detected in another embedded story: the tale Martinette de Beauvais recounts of her days as a woman

warrior, resplendent (at least phantasmagorically) in full military drag. Brown is not the first eighteenth-century Anglo-American novelist writing in the female voice to include a figure who serves as a metacommentator on his own procedures as ventriloquist and mime. In the voice of Moll Flanders, Daniel Defoe explains that: "My governess . . . laid up a new contrivance for my going abroad, and this was to dress me up in men's clothes, and so put me into a new kind of practice. I was tall and personable, but a little too smoothed-faced for a man; however, as I seldom went abroad but in the night, it did well enough; but it was a long time before I could behave in my new clothes—I mean, as to my craft. It was impossible to be so nimble, so ready, so dexterous at these things in a dress so contrary to nature; and as I did everything clumsily, so I had neither the success nor the easiness of escape that I had before, and I resolved to leave it off." Moll in drag, complaining of the awkwardness attending such a transformation, is speaking in the name of her creator's struggles with the crossed-dressed narrative form. See Daniel Defoe, *The Fortunes and Misfortunes of the Famous Moll Flanders* (1722; Harmondsworth: Penguin Books, 1978), 208–209.

178. For the definitive contemporary biography of Sampson, see Herman Mann, *The Female Review or Memoirs of an American Young Lady* (Dedham: 1797). For a narrative account of the lecture tour Sampson undertook in the early nineteenth century, a performance promoted by biographer Mann, see Deborah Sampson Gannett, *An Address, Delivered With Applause* (1802) and *The Diary of Deborah Sampson Gannett in 1802* (Sharon: Sharon Public Library, hand-copied facsimile). It is believed that Mann composed the address for Sampson in a fascinating instance of reverse narrative cross-dressing inspired by an act of actual transvestism. See also Lucy Freeman and Alma Bond, *America's First Woman Warrior: The Courage of Deborah Sampson* (New York: Paragon House, 1992). I am grateful to Robert A. Ferguson for alerting me in the early stages of this project both to Sampson's story and to Mann's biography of the crossed-dressed patriot heroine; thanks also to Michelle Navarre Cleary for sharing bibliographical information about Sampson's lecture tour.

The notion of the female transvestite soldier rings a fascinating change on the traditional trope for *male* homosexual identity. As Christopher Craft and D. A. Miller have pointed out, the metaphor of the female soul imprisoned within an alien-seeming male body is a common literary figure for male homosexuality. See Craft's "'Kiss Me With Those Red Lips': Gender and Inversion in *Dracula*," and Miller's "*Cage Aux Folles:* Sensation and Gender in Wilkie Collins's *The Woman in White*," both in *Speaking of Gender*, ed. Elaine Showalter (New York: Routledge, 1989), 187–215; and 216–42, respectively. In Martinette's case, the fantasy is not of gender reversal, but gender suspension. It is an important distinction. Brown can hardly be said to be hostile to same sex relations—indeed, he enables his female romantic friends to retreat into the English sunset together. But his embrace of women's homosociality can best be understood as the interesting consequence or side effect of a related critique rather than as a political emphasis in its own right; Brown's charge is that fraternity in the early republic fails to provide a locus for collective cohesion because the bonds of kinship have largely lost individual and social meaning. The America of *Ormond* is, after all, one in which women are revolutionary war heroes and men are blind, impotent, and, ultimately, silenced by death. It is also a place where females who have mastered the mathematics of Newton cannot be numbered among its citizens, a place where women can kill their political enemies but cannot vote against them in public elections. Female romantic friendship provides a space for dissent from the familial metaphor conventionally used to figure the political body in the 1790s. But as an alternative social configuration, lesbianism remains a utopian prospect at best: for women in early national America have no status as political agents in the eyes of the law. See the end of this chapter for an elaboration of the argument inaugurated here.

179. See *Merriam-Webster's New Collegiate Dictionary,* 10th edition, sv "martinette."

180. On the mystifying aspects of sisterly connection, see Helena Michie, *Sororophobia: Differences Among Women in Literature and Culture* (New York: Oxford University Press, 1992).

181. Beyond sharing remarkably untraditional (because masculine) educations, these women both prove masterful at killing the men who threaten their political or personal liberty.

182. See Maxwell Whiteman, "The Yellow Fever in Philadelphia and the Protest of the Black Nurses: A Bibliographical Note," editorial frontispiece to the reprint of *A Narrative of the Proceedings of the Black People, during the Late Awful Calamity in Philadelphia, in the Year 1793* (Philadelphia: Historic Publications, n.d.).

183. *Wieland'*s Carwin obviously numbers in this company as well. See Michael Davitt Bell, "The Artist as Villain," chap. 3, in *The Development of the American Romance: The Sacrifice of Relation* (Chicago: University of Chicago Press, 1980), 45–52, and Robert A. Ferguson, *Law and Letters,* 129–149.

184. See Juliet Flower McCannell, *The Regime of the Brother: After the Patriarchy* (New York: Routledge, 1991).

185. Bruce Burgett argues for Brown's turn to a masochistic mode of male sentimentalism in writing *Clara Howard* and *Jane Talbot,* both epistolary novels published in 1801. As I hope has become clear from these final arguments, I locate that masochistic moment in his earliest gothic works—the "crossed-dressed" narratives of *Wieland* and *Ormond,* where storytelling itself is subjected to a feminizing principle. See "Masochism and Male Sentimentalism: Charles Brockden Brown's *Clara Howard,*" *Arizona Quarterly* 52.1 (spring 1996): 1–25.

Index

Italics denote pages on which illustrations appear